OBJECTIVE	
RMAN Backups	
Identify types of RMAN specific backups.	9
Use the RMAN BACKUP command to create sets.	9
Back up the control file.	9
Back up the archived redo log files.	9
Use the RMAN COPY command to create image copies.	9
User-Managed Complete Recovery	
Describe media recovery.	10
Perform recovery in Noarchivelog mode.	10
Perform complete recovery in Archivelog mode.	10
Restore datafiles to different locations.	10
Relocate and recover a tablespace by using archived redo log files.	10
Describe read-only tablespace recovery.	10
RMAN Complete Recovery	
Describe the use of RMAN for restoration and recovery.	10
Perform recovery in Noarchivelog mode.	10
Perform complete recovery in Archivelog mode.	10
Restore datafiles to different locations.	10
Relocate and recover a tablespace by using archived redo log files.	10
User-Managed Incomplete Recovery	
Describe the steps of incomplete recovery.	11
Perform an incomplete database recovery.	11
Identify the loss of current online redo log files.	11
RMAN Incomplete Recovery	
Perform an incomplete database recovery using UNTIL TIME.	11
Perform an incomplete database recovery using UNTIL SEQUENCE.	11
RMAN Maintenance	
Perform cross checking of backups and copies.	12
Update the repository when backups have been deleted.	12
Change the availability status of backups and copies.	12
Make a backup or copy exempt from the retention policy.	12
Catalog backups made with operating system commands.	12
Recovery Catalog Creation and Maintenance	
Describe the contents of the recovery catalog.	13
Create the recovery catalog.	13
Maintain the recovery catalog by using RMAN commands.	13
Use RMAN to register, resynchronize, and reset a database.	13
Query the recovery catalog to generate reports and lists.	13
Create, store, and run scripts.	13
Describe methods for backing up and recovering the recovery catalog.	13
Transporting Data Between Databases	
Describe the uses of the Export and Import utilities.	14
Describe Export and Import concepts and structures.	14
Perform simple Export and Import operations.	14
List guidelines for using Export and Import.	14
Loading Data into a Database	
Demonstrate usage of direct-load insert operations.	15
Describe the usage of SQL*Loader.	15
Perform basic SQL*Loader operations.	15
List guidelines for using SQL*Loader and direct-load insert.	15

NOTE

Exam objectives are subject to change at any time without prior notice and at Oracle's sole discretion. Please visit Oracle's Certification website (`http://www.oracle.com/education/certification/`) for the most current exam objectives listing.

SYBEX

OCP:

Oracle9*i* DBA Fundamentals II

Study Guide

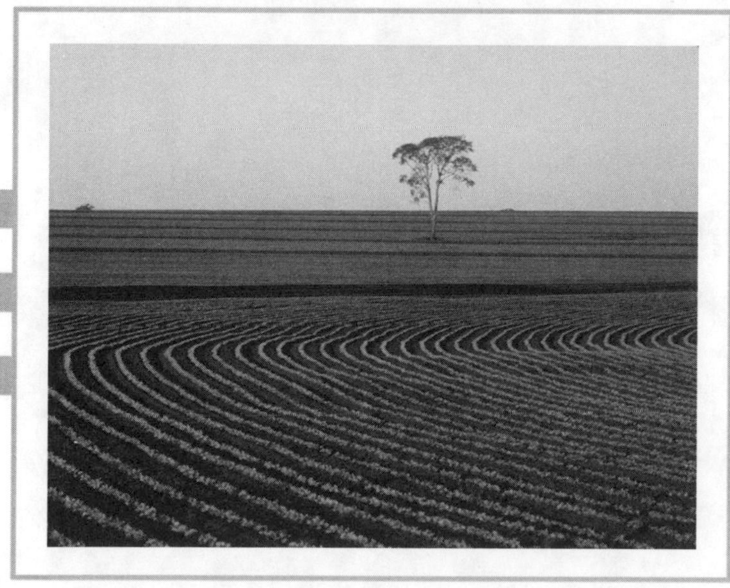

OCP:

Oracle9*i*™ DBA Fundamentals II

Study Guide

Doug Stuns

Matthew Weishan

San Francisco • London

Associate Publisher: Neil Edde
Acquisitions and Developmental Editor: Elizabeth Hurley
Editor: Rebecca Rider
Production Editor: Mae Lum
Technical Editors: John Anwanwan, Damir Bersinic
Graphic Illustrator: Tony Jonick
Electronic Publishing Specialist: Jill Niles
Proofreaders: Nanette Duffy, Emily Hsuan, David Nash, Laurie O'Connell, Nancy Riddiough
Indexer: Ann Rogers
CD Coordinator: Dan Mummert
CD Technician: Kevin Ly
Book Designer: Bill Gibson
Cover Designer: Archer Design
Cover Photographer: Photo Researchers

Library of Congress Card Number: 2002100058

ISBN: 0-7821-4064-5

Manufactured in the United States of America

10 9 8 7 6 5 4 3 2 1

To Our Valued Readers:

In a CertCities.com article dated December 15, 2001, Oracle certification was ranked #2 in a list of the "10 Hottest Certifications for 2002." This shouldn't come as a surprise, especially when you consider the fact that the OCP program nearly tripled in size (from 30,000 to 80,000) in the last year. Oracle continues to expand its dominance in the database market, and as companies begin integrating Oracle9*i* systems into their IT infrastructure, you can be assured of high demand for professionals with the Oracle Certified Associate and Oracle Certified Professional certifications.

Sybex is proud to have helped thousands of Oracle certification candidates prepare for the exams over the years, and we are excited about the opportunity to continue to provide professionals like you with the skills needed to succeed in the highly competitive IT industry.

Our authors and editors have worked hard to ensure that the Oracle9*i* Study Guide you hold in your hands is comprehensive, in-depth, and pedagogically sound. We're confident that this book will meet and exceed the demanding standards of the certification marketplace and help you, the Oracle9*i* certification candidate, succeed in your endeavors.

Good luck in pursuit of your Oracle9*i* certification!

Neil Edde
Associate Publisher—Certification
Sybex, Inc.

Software License Agreement: Terms and Conditions

The media and/or any online materials accompanying this book that are available now or in the future contain programs and/or text files (the "Software") to be used in connection with the book. SYBEX hereby grants to you a license to use the Software, subject to the terms that follow. Your purchase, acceptance, or use of the Software will constitute your acceptance of such terms.

The Software compilation is the property of SYBEX unless otherwise indicated and is protected by copyright to SYBEX or other copyright owner(s) as indicated in the media files (the "Owner(s)"). You are hereby granted a single-user license to use the Software for your personal, noncommercial use only. You may not reproduce, sell, distribute, publish, circulate, or commercially exploit the Software, or any portion thereof, without the written consent of SYBEX and the specific copyright owner(s) of any component software included on this media.

In the event that the Software or components include specific license requirements or end-user agreements, statements of condition, disclaimers, limitations or warranties ("End-User License"), those End-User Licenses supersede the terms and conditions herein as to that particular Software component. Your purchase, acceptance, or use of the Software will constitute your acceptance of such End-User Licenses.

By purchase, use or acceptance of the Software you further agree to comply with all export laws and regulations of the United States as such laws and regulations may exist from time to time.

Software Support

Components of the supplemental Software and any offers associated with them may be supported by the specific Owner(s) of that material, but they are not supported by SYBEX. Information regarding any available support may be obtained from the Owner(s) using the information provided in the appropriate read.me files or listed elsewhere on the media. Should the manufacturer(s) or other Owner(s) cease to offer support or decline to honor any offer, SYBEX bears no responsibility. This notice concerning support for the Software is provided for your information only. SYBEX is not the agent or principal of the Owner(s), and SYBEX is in no way responsible for providing any support for the Software, nor is it liable or responsible for any support provided, or not provided, by the Owner(s).

Warranty

SYBEX warrants the enclosed media to be free of physical defects for a period of ninety (90) days after purchase. The Software is not available from SYBEX in any other form or media than that enclosed herein or posted to `www.sybex.com`. If you discover a defect in the media during this warranty period, you may obtain a replacement of identical format at no charge by sending the defective media, postage prepaid, with proof of purchase to:

SYBEX Inc.
Product Support Department
1151 Marina Village Parkway
Alameda, CA 94501
Web: `http://www.sybex.com`

After the 90-day period, you can obtain replacement media of identical format by sending us the defective disk, proof of purchase, and a check or money order for $10, payable to SYBEX.

Disclaimer

SYBEX makes no warranty or representation, either expressed or implied, with respect to the Software or its contents, quality, performance, merchantability, or fitness for a particular purpose. In no event will SYBEX, its distributors, or dealers be liable to you or any other party for direct, indirect, special, incidental, consequential, or other damages arising out of the use of or inability to use the Software or its contents even if advised of the possibility of such damage. In the event that the Software includes an online update feature, SYBEX further disclaims any obligation to provide this feature for any specific duration other than the initial posting.

The exclusion of implied warranties is not permitted by some states. Therefore, the above exclusion may not apply to you. This warranty provides you with specific legal rights; there may be other rights that you may have that vary from state to state. The pricing of the book with the Software by SYBEX reflects the allocation of risk and limitations on liability contained in this agreement of Terms and Conditions.

Shareware Distribution

This Software may contain various programs that are distributed as shareware. Copyright laws apply to both shareware and ordinary commercial software, and the copyright Owner(s) retains all rights. If you try a shareware program and continue using it, you are expected to register it. Individual programs differ on details of trial periods, registration, and payment. Please observe the requirements stated in appropriate files.

Copy Protection

The Software in whole or in part may or may not be copy-protected or encrypted. However, in all cases, reselling or redistributing these files without authorization is expressly forbidden except as specifically provided for by the Owner(s) therein

To Brant and Brea
—Doug Stuns

To Rachel, Laura, Alyssa, and Karen—The real treasures of my life
—Matt Weishan

Acknowledgments

First, I want to thank the Lord, my savior, for making this all possible.

Thanks to Mae, Elizabeth, and Richard for direction and guidance throughout the writing of this book. Rebecca for your hard work, edits, and suggestions, which greatly improved this book and made my job much easier. John Anwanwan and Damir Bersinic for your technical edits and reviews, which enhanced the quality of this writing, tremendously. I want to give a belated thanks to the Hobbs family for getting me involved initially.

Finally, I want to thank my wife and family for supporting me throughout this process. Thanks for providing me the time to work on this book. I know this was a great sacrifice. I sincerely appreciate it!

—Doug Stuns

I would like to thank the entire Sybex team for another great effort. The team may have changed from the last book, but the results are as good as ever. The team of Mae Lum, Elizabeth Hurley, and Richard Mills was fantastic to work with. I would also like to extend a special thanks to Rebecca Rider for her outstanding editing job. It made my job much easier to work with this terrific group of people.

I also would like to thank Joe Johnson, once again, for giving me a chance on the original Oracle8*i* OCP series. The second time around has been just as gratifying as the first.

I would also like to thank my family for all of their love and support. Thanks for believing in me once again. With your faith and the Lord's guidance, anything is possible.

—Matt Weishan

Sybex would like to thank electronic publishing specialist Jill Niles and indexer Ann Rogers for their valuable contributions to this book.

Contents at a Glance

Contents

Introduction

There is high demand for professionals in the information technology (IT) industry, and Oracle certifications are the hottest credential in the database world. You have made the right decision to pursue certification, because being Oracle certified will give you a distinct advantage in this highly competitive market.

Many readers may already be familiar with Oracle and do not need an introduction to the Oracle database world. For those who aren't familiar with the company, Oracle, founded in 1977, sold the first commercial relational database and is now the world's leading database company and the second-largest independent software company, with revenues of more than $10 billion, serving more than 145 countries.

Oracle databases are the de facto standard for large Internet sites, and Oracle advertisers are boastful but honest when they proclaim, "The Internet Runs on Oracle." Almost all big Internet sites run Oracle databases. Oracle's penetration of the database market runs deep and is not limited to dot-com implementations. Enterprise resource planning (ERP) application suites, data warehouses, and custom applications at many companies rely on Oracle. The demand for DBA resources remains higher than others during weak economic times.

This book is intended to help you on your exciting path toward becoming an Oracle9*i* Oracle Certified Professional (OCP) and Oracle Certified Master (OCM). To get the maximum benefit from this book, you should already be knowledgeable in networking, operating systems, Oracle SQL, and DBA concepts. Using this book and a practice database, you can start learning Oracle and pass the 1Z0-032 test: Oracle9*i* Database: Fundamentals II.

Why Become an Oracle Certified Professional?

The number one reason to become an OCP is to gain more visibility and greater access to the industry's most challenging opportunities. Oracle certification is the best way to demonstrate your knowledge and skills in Oracle database systems. The certification tests are scenario-based, which is the most effective way to assess your hands-on expertise and critical problem-solving skills.

Certification is proof of your knowledge and shows that you have the skills required to support Oracle core products. The Oracle certification program can help a company identify proven performers who have demonstrated their skills and who can support the company's investment in Oracle technology. It demonstrates that you have a solid understanding of your job role and the Oracle products used in that role.

OCPs are among the best paid in the IT industry. Salary surveys consistently show the OCP certification to yield higher salaries than other certifications, including Microsoft, Novell, and Cisco.

So, whether you are beginning a career, changing careers, securing your present position, or seeking to refine and promote your position, this book is for you!

Oracle Certifications

Oracle certifications follow a track that is oriented toward a job role. There are database administration, database operator, and developer tracks. Within each track, Oracle has a three-tiered certification program:

- The first tier is the Oracle Certified Associate (OCA). OCA certification typically requires you to complete two exams, the first via the Internet and the second in a proctored environment.
- The next tier is the Oracle Certified Professional (OCP), which builds upon and requires an OCA certification. The additional requirements for OCP certification are additional proctored exams.
- The third and highest tier is the Oracle Certified Master (OCM). OCM certification builds upon and requires OCP certification. To achieve OCM certification, you must attend two advanced Oracle Education, classroom courses (from a specific list of qualifying courses) and complete a practicum exam.

The following material will address only the database administration track, because at the time of this writing, it was the only *9i* track offered by Oracle. The other tracks have 8 and *8i* certifications and will undoubtedly have *9i* certifications. See the Oracle website at `http://www.oracle.com/education/certification` for the latest information.

Oracle*9i* Certified Database Associate

The role of the database administrator (DBA) has become a key to success in today's highly complex database systems. The best DBAs work behind the scenes, but are in the spotlight when critical issues arise. They plan, create, maintain, and ensure that the database is available for the business. They are always watching the database for performance issues and to prevent unscheduled downtime. The DBA's job requires broad understanding of the architecture of Oracle database and expertise in solving problems.

The Oracle9*i* Certified Database Associate is the entry-level certification for the database administration track and is required to advance toward the more senior certification tiers. This certification requires you to pass two exams that demonstrate your knowledge of Oracle basics:

- 1Z0-007: Introduction to Oracle9*i*: SQL
- 1Z0-031: Oracle9*i* Database: Fundamentals I

The 1Z0-007 exam, Introduction to Oracle9*i*: SQL, is offered on the Internet. The 1Z0-031 exam, Oracle9*i* Database: Fundamentals I, is offered at a Sylvan Prometric facility.

Oracle9*i* Certified Professional (OCP)

The OCP tier of the database administration track challenges you to demonstrate your continuing experience and knowledge of Oracle technologies. The Oracle9*i* Certified Database Administrator certification requires achievement of the Certified Database Associate tier, as well as passing the following two exams at a Sylvan Prometric facility:

- 1Z0-032: Oracle9*i* Database: Fundamentals II
- 1Z0-033: Oracle9*i* Database: Performance Tuning

Oracle9*i* Certified Master

The Oracle9*i* Certified Master is the highest level of certification that Oracle offers. To become a certified master, you must first achieve OCP status, then complete two advanced instructor-led classes at an Oracle education facility, and finally pass a hands-on exam at Oracle Education. The classes and practicum exam are offered only at an Oracle education facility and may require travel. The advanced classes that will count toward your OCM requirement include the following:

- Oracle9*i*: Program with PL/SQL
- Oracle9*i*: Advanced PL/SQL
- Oracle9*i*: SQL Tuning Workshop

- Oracle9*i*: High Availability in an Internet Environment
- Oracle9*i*: Database: Implement Partitioning
- Oracle9*i*: Real Application Clusters Implementation
- Oracle9*i*: Data Warehouse Administration
- Oracle9*i*: Advanced Replication
- Oracle9*i*: Enterprise Manager

Passing Scores

The 1Z0-032: Oracle9*i* Database: Fundamentals II exam consists of two sections—basic and mastery. At the time this book was written, the passing score for the basic section is 71 percent, and for the mastery section it is 56 percent. Please download and read the Oracle9*i* Certification candidate guide before you take the exam. The basic section covers the fundamental concepts and the mastery section covers more difficult questions, which are mostly based on practice and experience. You must pass both sections to pass the exam. The objectives, test scoring, number of questions, and so on, are listed at `http://www.oracle.com/education/certification`.

More Information

The most current information about Oracle certification can be found at `http://www.oracle.com/education/certification`. Follow the Certification link and choose the track that you are interested in. Read the Candidate Guide for the test objectives and test contents, and keep in mind that they can change at any time without notice.

OCA/OCP Study Guides

The Oracle9*i* database administration track certification consists of four tests: two for OCA level and two more for OCP level. Sybex offers several study guides to help you achieve this certification:

- *OCA/OCP: Introduction to Oracle9i™ SQL Study Guide* (exam 1Z0-007: Introduction to Oracle9*i*: SQL)
- *OCA/OCP: Oracle9i™ DBA Database Fundamentals I Study Guide* (exam 1Z0-031: Oracle9*i* Database: Fundamentals I)

- *OCP: Oracle9i™ DBA Database Fundamentals II Study Guide* (exam 1Z0-032: Oracle9*i* Database: Fundamentals II)
- *OCP: Oracle9i™ DBA Performance Tuning* (exam 1Z0-033: Oracle9*i* Database: Performance Tuning)

Additionally, these four books are offered in a boxed set: *OCP: Oracle9i™ DBA Certification Kit.*

Skills Required for DBA Certification

To pass the certification exams, you need to master the following skills:

- Write SQL SELECT statements that display data from either single or multiple tables.
- Restrict, sort, aggregate, and manipulate data using both single and group functions.
- Create and manage tables, views, constraints, synonyms, sequences, and indexes.
- Create users and roles to control user access and maintain security.
- Understand Oracle Server architecture (database and instance).
- Understand the physical and logical storage of the database, and be able to manage space allocation and growth.
- Manage data, including its storage, loading, and reorganization.
- Manage redo logs, automatic undo, and rollback segments.
- Use globalization features to choose a database character set and National Language Support (NLS) parameters.
- Configure Oracle Net on the server side and the client side.
- Use backup and recovery options.
- Archive redo log files and hot backups.
- Perform backup and recovery operations using Recovery Manager (RMAN).
- Use data dictionary views and set database parameters.
- Configure and use Oracle Shared Server.

- Identify and tune database and SQL performance.
- Use the tuning/diagnostics tools STATSPACK, TKPROF, and EXPLAIN PLAN.
- Tune the size of data blocks, the shared pool, the buffer caches, and rollback segments.
- Diagnose contention for latches, locks, and rollback segments.

Tips for Taking the OCP Exam

Use the following tips to help you prepare for and pass each exam.

- Each OCP test contains about 55–80 questions to be completed in 90 minutes. Answer the questions you know first, so that you do not run out of time.
- Many questions on the exam have answer choices that at first glance look identical. Read the questions carefully. Do not just jump to conclusions. Make sure that you clearly understand exactly what each question asks.
- Most of the test questions are scenario-based. Some of the scenarios contain nonessential information and exhibits. You need to be able to identify what's important and what's not important.
- Do not leave any questions unanswered. There is no negative scoring. After selecting an answer, you can mark a difficult question or one that you're unsure of and come back to it later.
- When answering questions that you are not sure about, use a process of elimination to get rid of the obviously incorrect answers first. Doing this greatly improves your odds if you need to make an educated guess.
- If you're not sure of your answer, mark it for review and then look for other questions that may help you eliminate any incorrect answers. At the end of the test, you can go back and review the questions that you marked for review.

Where Do You Take the Exam?

You may take the exams at any of the more than 800 Sylvan Prometric Authorized Testing Centers around the world. For the location of a testing center near you, call 1-800-891-3926. Outside the United States and Canada, contact your local Sylvan Prometric Registration Center. Usually, the tests can be taken in any order.

To register for a proctored Oracle Certified Professional exam at a Sylvan Prometric test center:

- Determine the number of the exam you want to take.
- Register with Sylvan Prometric online at `http://www.2test.com` or in North America, by calling 1-800-891-EXAM (800-891-3926). At this point, you will be asked to pay in advance for the exam. At the time of this writing, the exams are $125 each and must be taken within one year of payment.
- When you schedule the exam, you'll get instructions regarding all appointment and cancellation procedures, the ID requirements, and information about the testing-center location.

You can schedule exams up to six weeks in advance or as soon as one working day before the day you wish to take it. If something comes up and you need to cancel or reschedule your exam appointment, contact Sylvan Prometric at least 24 hours in advance.

What Does This Book Cover?

This book covers everything you need to know to pass the Oracle9*i* Database: Fundamentals II exam. This exam is part of the Oracle9*i* Certified Database Administrator certification tier in the database administration track. It teaches you the basics of Oracle networking and backup and recovery. Each chapter begins with a list of exam objectives.

Chapter 1 Introduces the Oracle network architecture and the responsibilities of the DBA for managing the Oracle network.

Chapter 2 Discusses the setup and administration of Oracle Net on the Oracle server. It explains how to configure the Oracle Net server-side components and how to troubleshoot server-side network problems.

Chapter 3 Explains how to set up and administer Oracle Net client-side components. It demonstrates and discusses how to configure Oracle so that clients can connect to an Oracle server. It also discusses troubleshooting Oracle client-side connectivity problems.

Chapter 4 Introduces the Oracle Shared Server. It discusses when to use Shared Server and how to configure Shared Server within the Oracle environment.

Chapter 5 Introduces the backup and recovery overview. The types of failures of an Oracle database are discussed.

Chapter 6 Discusses instance and media recovery structures. Oracle processes, memory structures, and files relating to recovery are discussed. The importance of checkpointing, redo logs, and archived logs are also discussed.

Chapter 7 Explains how to configure the database for archive logging. The difference between archive logging and no archive logging is discussed.

Chapter 8 Introduces recovery manager overview and configuration. The RMAN repository, channel allocation, and RMAN configuration are discussed.

Chapter 9 Discusses user-managed and RMAN-based backup methods. Different examples are performed with each of these backup methods.

Chapter 10 Discusses user-managed and RMAN-based complete recovery methods. Different examples of complete recovery are performed.

Chapter 11 Discusses user-managed and RMAN-based incomplete recovery methods. Different examples of incomplete recovery are performed.

Chapter 12 Introduces RMAN maintenance. Maintaining the RMAN repository, retention policies, backups, and backup availability are discussed.

Chapter 13 Introduces recovery catalog creation and maintenance. This chapter describes the recovery catalog and how to create it. Performing maintenance on the recovery catalog, creating and running scripts, generating lists and reports, and backing up the recovery catalog are all discussed.

Chapter 14 Discusses transporting data between databases with the Export and Import utilities.

Chapter 15 Introduces the SQL*Loader utility and the direct-load insert operation. This chapter also discusses the use of each of these data loading methods.

Each chapter ends with review questions that are specifically designed to help you retain the knowledge presented. To really nail down your skills, read and answer each question carefully.

How to Use This Book

This book can provide a solid foundation for the serious effort of preparing for the OCP database administration exam track. To best benefit from this book, use the following study method:

1. Take the Assessment Test immediately following this introduction. (The answers are at the end of the test.) Carefully read over the explanations for any questions you get wrong, and note which chapters the material comes from. This information should help you plan your study strategy.
2. Study each chapter carefully, making sure that you fully understand the information and the test objectives listed at the beginning of each chapter. Pay extra close attention to any chapter related to questions you missed in the Assessment Test.
3. Complete all hands-on exercises in the chapter, referring to the chapter so that you understand the reason for each step you take. If you do not have an Oracle database available, be sure to study the examples carefully. Answer the Review Questions related to that chapter. (The answers appear at the end of each chapter, after the "Review Questions" section.)
4. Note the questions that confuse or trick you, and study those sections of the book again.
5. Before taking the exam, try your hand at the Bonus Exams that are included on the CD that comes with this book. The questions on these exams appear only on the CD. These will give you a complete overview of what you can expect to see on the real test.
6. Remember to use the products on the CD included with this book. The electronic flashcards and the EdgeTest exam preparation software have been specifically designed to help you study for and pass your

exam. The electronic flashcards can be used on your Windows computer or on your Palm device.

To learn all the material covered in this book, you'll need to apply yourself regularly and with discipline. Try to set aside the same time period every day to study, and select a comfortable and quiet place to do so. If you work hard, you will be surprised at how quickly you learn this material. All the best!

What's on the CD?

We have worked hard to provide some really great tools to help you with your certification process. All of the following tools should be loaded on your workstation when you're studying for the test.

The EdgeTest for Oracle Certified DBA Preparation Software

Provided by EdgeTest Learning Systems, this test-preparation software prepares you to pass the Oracle9*i* Database: Fundamentals II exam. In this test, you will find all of the questions from the book, plus two additional Bonus Exams that appear exclusively on the CD. In addition, you can take the Assessment Test, test by chapter, or take an exam randomly generated from all of the questions.

Electronic Flashcards for PC and Palm Devices

You should read the *OCP: Oracle9i Database: Fundamentals II Study Guide* carefully, particularly the Review Questions at the end of each chapter, and you should also take advantage of the Bonus Exams included on the CD. But wait, there's more! Be sure to test yourself with the flashcards included on the CD. If you can get through these questions and you understand the answers, you'll know that you're ready for the exam.

The flashcards include 150 questions specifically written to hit you hard and make sure you are ready for the exam. Between the Review Questions, the Bonus Exams, and the flashcards, you should be more than prepared for the exam.

OCP: Oracle9*i* Database: Fundamentals II Study Guide in PDF

Sybex is now offering the Oracle certification books on CD so that you can read the book on your PC or laptop. These exams appear in Adobe Acrobat format and Acrobat Reader 5 is also included on the CD so that you can view these. This will be extremely helpful to readers who fly or commute on a bus or train and don't want to carry a book, as well as to readers who find it more comfortable reading from their computer.

About the Authors

Doug Stuns, OCP, has been an Oracle DBA for more than a decade. He has worked for the Oracle Corporation in consulting and education roles for five years and is the founder and owner of SCS, Inc., an Oracle-based consulting company. To contact Doug, you can e-mail him at `stuns@scs-corp.net`.

Matthew Weishan is an OCP and Certified Technical Trainer with more than nine years of experience with Oracle databases. He is currently a Senior Specialist for EDS in Madison, Wisconsin, working as an Oracle DBA for several large clients. He also served as an Oracle DBA instructor for several years. He has over 18 years of experience in the IT industry and has worked as a senior systems analyst, lead consultant, and lead database administrator for several Fortune 500 companies. To contact Matt, you can email him at `mweishan@yahoo.com`.

Assessment Test

1. What type of incomplete recovery is based on each transaction?

   A. Time-based

   B. Change-based

   C. Cancel-based

   D. Stop-based

2. What statement best describes the recovery catalog?

   A. A mandatory feature of RMAN

   B. An optional feature of RMAN that stores metadata about the backups

   C. A mandatory feature of RMAN that stores metadata about the backups

   D. An optional feature of RMAN

3. What files can store load data when SQL*Loader is being used? (Choose all that apply.)

   A. General log files

   B. Input files

   C. Control files

   D. Discard log files

4. Which of the following are physical structures of the Oracle database? (Choose all that apply.)

   A. Control files

   B. Input files

   C. Parameter files

   D. Alert logs

5. Which of the following RMAN commands would you need to execute in order to store information in the recovery catalog and the actual data files that were backed up by OS commands?

   A. `BACKUP DATAFILE`

   B. `BACKUP`

   C. `DATAFILE COPY`

   D. `CATALOG DATAFILECOPY`

6. Which of the following is the correct way(s) to perform control file backups? (Choose all that apply.)

   A. Alter the database backup control file to TRACE.

   B. Alter the database backup control file to `'<controlfile_name>'`.

   C. Alter the system backup control file to TRACE.

   D. Alter the system backup control file to `'<controlfile_name>'`.

7. Which of these are roles of Oracle Net in the Oracle network architecture? (Choose all that apply.)

   A. Handles communications between the client and server

   B. Handles server-to-server communications

   C. Used to establish an initial connection to an Oracle server

   D. Acts as a messenger, which passes requests between clients and servers

   E. All of the above

8. What are the roles that you must grant the RMAN schema owner of the recovery catalog? (Choose all that apply.)

   A. `dba`

   B. `connect`

   C. `resource`

   D. `recovery_catalog_owner`

9. Which of the following are advantages of Shared Server? (Choose all that apply.)

    A. Fewer server processes

    B. Manages more connections with the same or less memory

    C. Better client response time

    D. All of the above

10. What type of failure requires an incomplete recovery? (Choose all that apply.)

    A. Any media failure involving the system tablespace

    B. The loss of inactive or active online redo logs

    C. The loss of an archived log since the last current backup

    D. The loss of a control file

11. Which of the following is *true* about dispatchers?

    A. They listen for client connection requests.

    B. They take the place of dedicated servers.

    C. They place client requests on a response queue.

    D. All of the above.

12. Which command-line option of the Export utility groups commands together in a common file?

    A. `config.ora`

    B. `PARFILE`

    C. `ifile`

    D. `commandfile`

13. What type of incomplete recovery requires the DBA to manually stop the recovery at a certain point?

    A. Cancel-based

    B. Time-based

    C. Change-based

    D. Sequence-based

14. What is the new parameter file that has been introduced in Oracle9*i*?

A. `spfile.ora`

B. `init.ora`

C. `config.ora`

D. `ifile.ora`

15. What utility can you use to verify corruption of both backup and online data files?

A. DBMS_REPAIR

B. DBVERIFY

C. ANALYZE

D. DB_CHECKSUM

16. When you open a database with the `ALTER DATABASE OPEN RESETLOGS`, you need to perform which command in RMAN to the incarnation of the database?

A. `REGISTER`

B. `UNREGISTER`

C. `RESET`

D. `UNSET`

17. What is the primary configuration file of the localnaming option?

A. `sqlnet.ora`

B. `tnsnames.ora`

C. `listener.ora`

D. `names.ora`

18. What is the name of the manual allocation channel method that utilizes tape?

A. `ALLOCATE CHANNEL C1 TYPE 'SBT_TAPE'`

B. `ALLOCATE CHANNEL C1 TYPE DLT_TAPE`

C. `CONFIGURE DEFAULT DEVICE TYPE SBT_TAPE`

D. `CONFIGURE DEFAULT DEVICE TYPE TAPE`

19. What prerequisites are required to implement direct-load insert? (Choose all that apply.)

A. Parallel DML must be enabled.

B. Initialization parameters must be configured for parallel query.

C. The SQL*Loader utility must be configured for parallel processing.

D. There must be hints in DML statements.

E. Multiple SQL*Loader control files and data files must be present.

20. What does Dynamic Registration do?

A. Allows a listener to automatically register with an Oracle server

B. Allows an Oracle server to automatically register with a listener

C. Allows clients to automatically register with an Oracle listener

D. None of the above

21. An open backup can be performed when which of the following is true about the database? (Choose all that apply.)

A. It is in `NOARCHIVELOG` mode.

B. It is in `ARCHIVELOG` mode.

C. When tablespaces are placed in `BACKUP` mode with the `ALTER TABLESPACE` *<tablespace_name>* `BEGIN BACKUP` command.

D. The database is shut down.

22. Which of the following backup and recovery parameters utilize their operations within the `LARGE_POOL` memory of the SGA? (Choose all that apply.)

A. `DBWR_IO_SLAVES`

B. `ASYNC_IO_SLAVES`

C. `BACKUP_TAPE_IO_SLAVES`

D. `SYNCH_IO_SLAVES`

23. Which statement best describes incomplete recovery?

A. No data whatsoever is lost.

B. Data is lost after the point of failure.

C. Some data is lost because the recovery is prior to the point failure.

D. Some data is lost because the data file recovery is incomplete.

24. Which of the following best describes network access control?

A. It allows clients and servers using different protocols to communicate.

B. It sets up rules to allow or disallow connections to Oracle servers.

C. It funnels client connections into a single outgoing connection to the Oracle server.

D. None of the above.

25. Resynching the recovery catalog should be performed when you do what to the target database?

A. Undo a database resynch.

B. Remove a database reset.

C. Undo the most recent database resynch only.

D. Make a physical change to the target database.

26. Which commands move data files in the RMAN recovery process? (Choose all that apply.)

A. `SET NEWFILE`

B. `SET RENAME`

C. `SET NEWNAME`

D. `SWITCH`

27. The main difference between logging and tracing is

A. Tracing cannot be disabled.

B. Logging cannot be disabled.

C. Logging records only significant events.

D. Tracing records only significant events.

28. Which of the following parameters ensures the number of successful archive destinations before the redo information can be written over?

A. LOG_ARCHIVE_SUCCESS

B. LOG_ARCHIVE_MIN_SUCCEED_DEST

C. LOG_MIN_SUCCESS

D. LOG_ARCHIVE_SUCCEED

29. What is the location of the trace file generated when the Oracle PMON process encounters an error?

A. USER_DUMP_DEST

B. BACKGROUND_DUMP_DEST

C. CORE_DUMP_DEST

D. ARCH_DUMP_DEST

30. Which of the following parameters is used to improve the performance of instance recovery operations?

A. FAST_START_MTTR_TARGET

B. FAST_START

C. CHECKPOINT_INTERVAL

D. CHECKPOINT

31. What utility can be used to check to see if a client can see an Oracle listener?

A. netstat

B. namesctl

C. tnsping

D. lsnrctl

E. None of the above

32. Which of the following commands generate reports from the recovery catalog or target database control file? (Choose all that apply.)

    A. REPORT

    B. LIST

    C. SELECT

    D. PUTLINE

33. Which of the following Oracle processes is not mandatory at startup?

    A. SMON

    B. PMON

    C. DBWR

    D. ARCH

34. Which of the following is a major difference between the RESTORE command in earlier versions of RMAN and in Oracle9*i* RMAN?

    A. Nothing has changed.

    B. The decision about whether files need to be restored or not.

    C. Only backup sets are restored.

    D. Only image copies are restored.

35. Which of the following is *true* about shared servers?

    A. They talk to dispatchers.

    B. They execute client requests.

    C. They talk directly to the listener.

    D. They talk directly to a client process.

36. Which `init.ora` parameter is responsible for setting multiple remote archive locations?

    A. LOG_ARCHIVE_DUPLEX_DEST

    B. LOG_ARCHIVE_DEST_*n*

    C. LOG_DEST_ARCHIVE_*n*

    D. LOG_ARCHIVE_DEST_DUPLEX

37. Which of these is *not* a layer of the Oracle Net Stack?
    - **A.** Two-Task Common
    - **B.** Oracle Net Foundation
    - **C.** Oracle Call Interface
    - **D.** Application
    - **E.** All of these are layers in the Oracle Net Stack

38. What special activity must be performed to execute a `CROSSCHECK` command?
    - **A.** `ALLOCATE CHANNEL`
    - **B.** `ALLOCATE CHANNEL FOR MAINTENANCE TYPE DISK`
    - **C.** `AUTOMATIC CHANNEL ALLOCATION`
    - **D.** `ALLOCATE CHANNEL FOR UPGRADE TYPE DISK`

39. Which of these is *not* a way to resolve a net service name?
    - **A.** Localnaming
    - **B.** Hostnaming
    - **C.** Oracle Internet Directory
    - **D.** Internal Naming

40. What is the correct command syntax you need to use to execute a script called `complete_bac` within the recovery catalog?
    - **A.** `start {execute script complete_bac;}`
    - **B.** `RUN { EXECUTE SCRIPT complete_bac; }`
    - **C.** `execute script complete_bac;`
    - **D.** `run execute script complete_bac;`

41. Which type of read-only tablespace recovery causes restoration and recovery of the tablespace and associated data files? (Choose all that apply.)

    A. Read-only backup and read-only recovery

    B. Read-only backup and read-write recovery

    C. Read-write backup and read-only recovery with backup taken immediately after it was made read only

    D. Read-write backup and read-only recovery

42. What new Oracle9*i* feature allows you to query old data even if the original data has been deleted?

    A. Flashback Query

    B. Parallel query

    C. Fast recovery

    D. Undo query

43. Third-party tape hardware vendors require what aspect of RMAN to function properly?

    A. Recovery catalog

    B. Media management library

    C. RMAN in GUI through Enterprise Manager

    D. RMAN in command line mode

44. What are the two different technical methods of exporting data? (Choose all that apply.)

    A. Conventional

    B. User

    C. Full

    D. Direct export

45. A client is unable to connect to the PROD Oracle Server. Which of the following client-side checks could you NOT perform from the client workstation to troubleshoot the problem?

    A. Check the NAMES.DIRECTORY_PATH in the sqlnet.ora file on the client.

    B. Perform tnsping PROD from the client.

    C. Perform lsnrctl services from the client.

    D. Check the TNS_ADMIN Registry setting on the client.

46. Which command is responsible for allowing you to move data files to a new location?

    A. ALTER DATABASE MOVE

    B. ALTER DATABASE RENAME

    C. ALTER SYSTEM MOVE

    D. ALTER SYSTEM RENAME

47. Which of the following best describes the function of the Oracle Net Manager?

    A. It is a graphical tool used to configure critical Oracle network files.

    B. It is a tool used to configure the Oracle protocols.

    C. It is a graphical tool used to monitor Oracle connections.

    D. It is a tool used to troubleshoot Oracle connection problems.

48. What status determines that the tape is not available in the CROSSCHECK comparison?

    A. NOT AVAILABLE

    B. UNAVAILABLE

    C. EXPIRED

    D. INVALID

49. What configuration file controls the listener?

A. `tnsnames.ora`

B. `listener.ora`

C. `sqlnet.ora`

D. `names.ora`

50. The RMAN repository best defines what? (Choose all that apply.)

A. Recovery catalog

B. Control file

C. Target database

D. ATL database

51. Process failures and instance failures are both what types of failure?

A. Media failure

B. User failure

C. Non-media failure

D. Statement failure

52. Which `init.ora` parameter configures the database for automatic archiving?

A. `LOG_ARCHIVE_START=TRUE`

B. `LOG_START_ARCHIVE=TRUE`

C. `LOG_AUTO_ARCHIVE=TRUE`

D. `LOG_ARCHIVE_AUTO=TRUE`

53. Which command-line utility is used to start and stop the listener?

A. `listener`

B. `lsnrctl`

C. `listen`

D. `listen_ctl`

54. User-managed backup and recovery best defines which statement?

    A. Custom backup and recovery performed with OS commands and database commands

    B. Non-automated RMAN-based backups

    C. A new type of backup that uses RMAN but is performed by a user

    D. Automated RMAN-based backup

55. What Oracle background process has the responsibility of performing the roll forward in instance recovery?

    A. PMON

    B. SMON

    C. RECO

    D. DBWR

56. Which of the following commands would you use to make a backup set unavailable?

    A. `CHANGE`

    B. `MAKE`

    C. `FORCE`

    D. `EXPIRE`

57. What are some of the issues of network complexity that the database administrator should consider? (Choose all that apply.)

    A. How much time it will take to configure a client

    B. What type of work clients will be performing

    C. What type of protocols are being used

    D. The size and number of transactions that will be done

    E. All of the above

58. Complete recovery is best defined by which of the following statements?

    A. Most transactions are recovered.

    B. All transactions are recovered except the last archived log.

    C. All committed transactions are recovered.

    D. There is no data lost whatsoever.

59. What are the different technical methods of loading data with the SQL*Loader utility? (Choose all that apply.)

    A. Direct-path load

    B. Conventional load

    C. Default-path load

    D. External-path load

60. What are the three primary network configurations?

    A. N-tier architecture

    B. Single-tier architecture

    C. Multi-tier architecture

    D. Two-tier architecture

61. Which of the following recoveries can be performed when the database is in `ARCHIVELOG` mode?

    A. Only incomplete recovery

    B. Only complete recovery

    C. Only partial recovery

    D. Complete recovery and incomplete recovery

62. What is the primary purpose of using checkpoints?

    A. To decrease free memory buffers in the SGA

    B. To write non-modified database buffers to the database files and to synchronize the physical structures of the database accordingly

    C. To record modified database buffers that are written to the database files and to synchronize the physical structures of the database accordingly

    D. To increase free memory buffers in the SGA

63. What command would you use to retain a backup past the retention date?

A. `HOLD`

B. `RETAIN`

C. `KEEP`

D. `STORE`

64. Which view can be used to identify clean-up issues after a failed hot or online backup?

A. `V$BACKUP`

B. `ALL_BACKUP`

C. `USER_BACKUP`

D. `DBA_BACKUP`

65. How does Oracle Shared Server differ from a dedicated server? (Choose all that apply.)

A. Clients use dispatchers instead of dedicated connections.

B. The System Global Area contains request and response queues.

C. Shared server processes execute client requests.

D. All of the above.

66. What is the disadvantage of the hostnaming option?

A. It cannot use bequeath connections.

B. It cannot use Oracle Shared Server connections.

C. It cannot use client load balancing.

D. All of the above.

67. Which of the following options is the RMAN BACKUP command capable of performing? (Choose all that apply.)

 A. Incremental backup

 B. Full backup

 C. Image copy

 D. Current control file backup

 E. Backup set creation

68. What does IIOP stand for?

 A. Internet Interactive Objects Protocol

 B. Internet Instance Objects Protocol

 C. Internet Inter-Orb Protocol

 D. Internet Inter-Objects Protocol

 E. None of the above

69. What type of failure would require the DBA to issue the RECOVER DATABASE command?

 A. User process

 B. Media failure

 C. Instance failure

 D. Statement failure

70. What mode must that database be in to run the ALTER TABLESPACE <*tablespace_name*> BEGIN BACKUP command?

 A. NOARCHIVELOG

 B. `startup nomount`

 C. `startup mount`

 D. ARCHIVELOG

Answers to Assessment Test

1. B. Change-based recovery is based upon a unique SCN number that each transaction uniquely contains. See Chapter 11 for more information.

2. B. The recovery catalog is an optional feature of RMAN. Though Oracle recommends that you use it, it isn't required. One major benefit of the recovery catalog is that it stores metadata about backups in a database that can be reported or queried. See Chapter 8 for more information.

3. C. The data file or control file both can be used to store load data. The control file should only store small data loads for one-time use or test purposes. See Chapter 15 for more information.

4. A, C. Control files and parameter files make up two of the physical structures of the Oracle database. Data files and redo logs make up the other physical structures. See Chapter 6 for more information.

5. D. The command `CATALOG DATAFILECOPY` backs up data files that were copied or backed up by OS commands in user-managed backups. See Chapter 12 for more information.

6. A, B. The control file can be backed up in two ways: in ASCII format, it can be backed up to a `TRACE` file, or in binary format, it can be backed up to a new location. The `ALTER DATABASE BACKUP CONTROLFILE TO TRACE` and `ALTER DATABASE BACKUP CONTROLFILE TO '<controlfile_name>'` commands perform backups of the control file to ASCII format and to binary format. See Chapter 9 for more information.

7. E. Oracle Net is responsible for handling client-to-server and server-to-server communications in an Oracle environment. It manages the flow of information in the Oracle network infrastructure. Oracle Net is used to establish the initial connection to the Oracle server and then it acts as the messenger, which passes requests from the client back to the server or between two Oracle servers. See Chapter 1 for more information.

8. B, C, D. The roles that are required for the RMAN schema that owns the recovery catalog are `connect`, `resource`, and `recovery_catalog_owner`. See Chapter 13 for more information.

9. A, B. Oracle Shared Server allows Oracle servers to manage a greater number of connections utilizing the same amount or less memory and process resources. If an Oracle server is constrained by these resources, Oracle Shared Server can be an alternative configuration that can provide relief. See Chapter 4 for more information.

10. B, C. The loss of inactive or active online redo logs will require an incomplete recovery because the backup will not have all the required logs to apply to the database. The loss of an archived log since the last current backup will also not allow a complete recovery for the same reason as a missing redo log. See Chapter 11 for more information.

11. B. Dispatchers take the place of the dedicated server processes. The dispatchers are responsible for responding to client requests by placing the requests on a request queue (not a response queue) in the SGA; they also retrieve completed requests that were placed on a response queue by the shared server and pass them back to the client. See Chapter 4 for more information.

12. B. The `PARFILE` command option allows you to group export commands together in a file so that you don't have to interactively respond to the prompts when you are running the export. This also allows you to script exports more efficiently. See Chapter 14 for more information.

13. A. Cancel-based recovery requires the DBA to manually cancel the recovery process at the command line. See Chapter 11 for more information.

14. A. The `spfile.ora` is new for Oracle9*i*. This is the binary initialization file that is the default when Oracle is started. This file contains persistent parameters. The `init.ora` file is searched only if there isn't a `spfile.ora` initialization file. See Chapter 6 for more information.

15. B. The DBVERIFY utility can verify both online data files and copies of online data files. See Chapter 9 for more information.

16. C. The RESET command must be used on the incarnation of the database within the recovery catalog if the target database has been opened with ALTER DATABASE OPEN RESETLOGS. See Chapter 13 for more information.

17. B. The main characteristic of the localnaming method is that it uses the tnsnames.ora file to resolve service names. In fact, this method is sometimes called the tnsnames.ora method. The file contains information about the service name and connect descriptors for each service name that a client can contact. See Chapter 3 for more information.

18. A. CONFIGURE DEFAULT DEVICE settings configure the allocation channel automatically. ALLOCATE CHANNEL <*channel_name*> TYPE methods are used to manually configure channels. The type 'SBT_TAPE' configures the manual channel for tape. See Chapter 8 for more information.

19. A, B, D. The database must be configured for parallel query or it must have the appropriate initialization parameters, such as PARALLEL_MIN_SERVERS and PARALLEL_MAX_SERVERS, set up. The session must be enabled to run parallel DML. And the appropriate hints must be entered in the DML statements to allow direct-load insert. See Chapter 15 for more information.

20. B. Dynamic Registration allows an Oracle server to automatically register with a listener. This reduces the amount of maintenance work the DBA has to do to maintain the listener.ora file in a localnaming environment. See Chapter 2 for more information.

21. B, C. An open backup is also called a hot backup and it can be performed when the database is in ARCHIVELOG mode by executing the ALTER TABLESPACE <*tablespace_name*> BEGIN BACKUP command. See Chapter 9 for more information.

22. A, C. The DBWR_IO_SLAVES and BACKUP_TAPE_IO_SLAVES are initialization parameters that can improve the performance of backup and recovery operations. These parameters use the LARGE_POOL memory to perform their operations. See Chapter 6 for more information.

23. C. The statement that accurately describes incomplete recovery is "Some data is lost because the recovery is prior to the point of failure." See Chapter 11 for more information.

24. B. Client access control is a feature of Connection Manager that makes Connection Manager function in a manner similar to that of a firewall. Connections can be accepted or rejected on the basis of the client location, the destination server, and the Oracle service that the client is attempting to connect to. This gives the DBA flexibility they need to configure access control to the Oracle environment. See Chapter 1 for more information.

25. D. The `resynch` command should be used when you make physical changes to the target database, such as adding new data files or control files. See Chapter 13 for more information.

26. C, D. The `SET NEWNAME` and `SWITCH` commands work together to restore RMAN backups to new locations. See Chapter 10 for more information.

27. C. Logging records significant events, such as starting and stopping the listener, along with certain kinds of network errors. Tracing records all events that occur, even when an error does not happen. The trace file provides a great deal of information that logs do not. See Chapter 2 for more information.

28. B. The `LOG_ARCHIVE_MIN_SUCCEED_DEST` parameter determines the number of successful archive destinations required before the redo logs can be overwritten. See Chapter 7 for more information.

29. B. The Oracle PMON process is a background process. All trace files generated from the background process go into the `BACKGROUND_DUMP_DEST` location. See Chapter 12 for more information.

30. A. The `FAST_START_MTTR_TARGET` parameter determines the number of seconds that instance recovery will require. This parameter is an integer value between 0 and 3600. See Chapter 6 for more information.

31. C. The `tnsping` utility can be used to check to see if a client can contact a listener. The command format is `tnsping` *`<databasename>`* *`<number of tries>`*. For example, `tnsping DBA 3` would attempt to contact the DBA database three times. This utility also provides information on how long it takes to contact the listener. See Chapter 3 for more information.

32. A, B. The `REPORT` and `LIST` commands generate report outputs in the RMAN utility. See Chapter 13 for more information.

33. D. The ARCH or ARCn process is not a mandatory process. Archive logging can be enabled and disabled. See Chapter 6 for more information.

34. B. In Oracle9*i*, the `RESTORE` command now makes the decision of whether or not files need to be restored. In earlier versions of RMAN, files were restored upon request even if it was unnecessary. See Chapter 10 for more information.

35. B. The shared server processes are responsible for executing the client requests. They retrieve the requests from a request queue and place the completed request in the appropriate dispatcher response queue. See Chapter 4 for more information.

36. B. `LOG_ARCHIVE_DEST_`*`n`* (*n* being integer value) is responsible for multiple remote archive locations. `LOG_ARCHIVE_DUPLEX_DEST` is also capable of multiple destinations but not ones that are remote. See Chapter 7 for more information.

37. E. All of these are part of the Oracle Net Stack. The stack consists of Application, OCI, Two-Task Common, Oracle Net Foundation, Oracle Protocol Adapters, and Network Protocol. See Chapter 1 for more information.

38. B. The `CROSSCHECK` command requires the use of the `ALLOCATE CHANNEL FOR MAINTENANCE TYPE DISK` or `SBT_TAPE` to perform comparison activities on the disk/tape media and the recovery catalog contents. See Chapter 12 for more information.

39. D. Internal Naming is not one of the methods used to resolve a net service name, but localnaming, hostnaming, and Oracle Internet Directory are. See Chapter 3 for more information.

40. B. The correct syntax to execute the script is `RUN { EXECUTE SCRIPT <script_name>; }`. For more information, see Chapter 13.

41. B, D. Choice B, read-only backup and read-write recovery, will require the restoration and recovery of the data files because changes have been made to the database since the backup. Choice D will also require restoration of the data file and recovery up to the point when the tablespace was made read-only. In choice A, no changes are made because the tablespace is read-only throughout. Choice C doesn't require restoration and recovery because the backup of the database was taken immediately after the tablespace was made read-only. See Chapter 10 for more information.

42. A. Flashback Query allows you to query old deleted data by rebuilding the necessary data elements in the undo tablespaces. See Chapter 5 for more information.

43. B. The media management library (MML), or Media Management Layer, is a third-party vendor library, which is linked in with the Oracle kernel so that the server session generated by RMAN interfaces with the third-party vendor's hardware. See Chapter 8 for more information.

44. A, D. The two methods of exporting data are conventional and direct export. Conventional is the default method, which uses the standard SQL command processing, and direct export bypasses certain aspects of the SQL evaluation layer to improve performance. See Chapter 14 for more information.

45. C. The listener would not be running on the client. This would be a server-side check that would be performed. See Chapter 2 for more information.

46. B. The `ALTER DATABASE RENAME '<datafile_name_and_location>' to '<new_datafile_name_and_location>'` is the command that allows you to move a data file to a new location. Remember that OS commands, such as `cp` in Unix, are necessary to copy the file to the new location. The `ALTER DATABASE RENAME` command just updates the control file and data dictionary. See Chapter 10 for more information.

47. A. The Oracle Net Manager is a graphical tool that provides a way to configure most of the critical network files for the Oracle server. See Chapter 2 for more information.

48. C. The backup sets that are not on the media disk/tape but are in the recovery catalog return a status of `EXPIRED`. See Chapter 12 for more information.

49. B. The `listener.ora` file contains the configuration information for the listener. This file contains information about the listening locations, the service names that the listener is listening for, and a section for optional listener parameters, such as logging and tracing parameters. There should be only one `listener.ora` file on a machine. If multiple listeners are used, each listener should have its own entry in the `listener.ora` file. See Chapter 2 for more information.

50. A, B. The RMAN repository is the control file that stores the backup information if the recovery catalog is not used. The recovery catalog is a database that stores the RMAN repository information, otherwise the RMAN repository is the target database's control file. See Chapter 8 for more information.

51. C. Process failures and instance failures are both types of non-media failure. These types of failure are usually less critical. See Chapter 5 for more information.

52. A. The correct parameter is `LOG_ARCHIVE_START=TRUE`. See Chapter 7 for more information.

53. B. The `lsnrctl` command-line utility is used to start and stop the listener. You can also use this utility to get information about the status of the listener and make modifications to the `listener.ora` file. See Chapter 2 for more information.

54. A. User-managed backup is the term used to describe the standard backups that have been used from the inception of Oracle. These backups are usually custom written through the use of OS and database commands. See Chapter 9 for more information.

55. B. The system monitor (SMON) process is responsible for applying all of the committed or uncommitted changes in the online redo logs. See Chapter 6 for more information.

56. A. The `CHANGE` command makes the backup set either available or unavailable in the recovery catalog. See Chapter 12 for more information.

57. B, C, D. The DBA needs to consider such items as the number of clients the network will need to support, the type of work the clients will be doing, the locations of the clients in the network, and the size of transactions that will be done in the network. See Chapter 1 for more information.

58. D. Complete recovery means that all transactions are recovered. No data is lost and none must be reentered when the database is recovered. See Chapter 10 for more information.

59. A, B, D. The conventional load is the default load that performs normal SQL command processing. The direct-path load performs an expedited processing that bypasses the buffer and writes directly to data files. The external-path load is a load used for processing external files. See Chapter 15 for more information.

60. A, B, D. The three primary network configurations are single-tier, two-tier, and n-tier architecture. Single-tier was the predominant architecture for many years when the mainframe dominated the corporate environment. Two-tier architecture came into vogue with the introduction of the PC and has been a dominant architecture ever since. With the inception of the Internet, more organizations are turning towards n-tier architecture as a means to leverage many computers and enhance flexibility and performance of their applications. See Chapter 1 for more information.

61. D. When the database is in `ARCHIVELOG` mode, both complete and incomplete recovery can be performed. See Chapter 7 for more information.

62. C. The main purpose of the database checkpoint is to record that the modified buffers have been written to the data files and to establish data consistency, which enables faster recovery in the event of a failure. See Chapter 6 for more information.

63. C. The KEEP command causes a backup to be kept past the retention setting in the database. See Chapter 12 for more information.

64. A. The V$BACKUP view can be used to identify whether a database is actively being backed up or not. See Chapter 9 for more information.

65. D. Oracle Shared Server uses a shared model. Clients share processes called dispatchers that handle their requests. Clients also share processes called shared servers that execute their requests. The sharing is done through modifications to the SGA. See Chapter 4 for more information.

66. C. The disadvantage is that certain functionality, such as client load balancing and failover, is not available when you use the hostnaming method. See Chapter 3 for more information.

67. A, B, D, E. The RMAN BACKUP command is capable of performing all of the options with the exception of creating image copies. Image copies are created by the RMAN COPY command. See Chapter 9 for more information.

68. C. The Internet Inter-Orb Protocol is supported by Oracle Net to allow for support of Enterprise JavaBeans and CORBA. See Chapter 2 for more information.

69. B. A media failure would most likely cause the DBA to get actively involved in the recovery of the database by entering recovery commands if this was a user-managed recovery. The other failures mentioned are usually handled by Oracle automatically. See Chapter 5 for more information.

70. D. The database must be in ARCHIVELOG mode so that the tablespaces can be backed up online. See Chapter 7 for more information.

Introduction to Network Administration

ORACLE9*i*: DBA FUNDAMENTALS II EXAM OBJECTIVES COVERED IN THIS CHAPTER:

- ✓ **Explain solutions included with Oracle9*i* for managing complex networks.**
- ✓ **Describe Oracle networking add-on solutions.**
- ✓ **Explain the key components of the Oracle Net layered architecture.**
- ✓ **Explain Oracle Net Services role in client server connections.**
- ✓ **Describe how web client connections are established through Oracle networking products.**

Exam objectives are subject to change at any time without prior notice and at Oracle's sole discretion. Please visit Oracle's Certification website (`http://www.oracle.com/education/certification/`) for the most current exam objectives listing.

Networks have evolved from simple terminal-based systems to complex multitiered systems. Modern networks can be comprised of many computers on multiple operating systems using a wide variety of protocols and communicating across wide geographic areas. One need look no further than the explosion of the Internet to see how networking has matured and what a profound impact networks are having on the way we work and communicate with one another.

While networks have become increasingly complex, they also have become easier to use and manage. For instance, we all take advantage of the Internet without knowing or caring about the components that make this communication possible because the complexity of this huge network is completely hidden from us.

The experienced Oracle database administrator has seen this maturation process in the Oracle network architecture as well. From the first version of SQL*Net to the latest releases of Oracle Net, Oracle has evolved its network strategy and infrastructure to meet the demands of the rapidly changing landscape of network communications.

This chapter highlights the areas that database administrators (DBAs) need to consider when implementing an Oracle network strategy. It also looks at the responsibilities the database administrator has when managing an Oracle network. The chapter then explores the most common types of network configurations and introduces the features of Oracle Net—the connectivity management software that is the backbone of the Oracle network architecture. It will also explore the Oracle network architecture and summarize the Oracle network infrastructure.

Network Design Considerations

There are many factors involved in making network design decisions. First and foremost is the design of the Oracle network architecture itself. It is flexible and configurable, and it has the scalability to accommodate a range of network sizes. Also, when you are working with an Oracle network, there are a variety of network configurations to choose from. The sections that follow summarize the areas that the DBA needs to consider when designing the Oracle network infrastructure.

Network Complexity Issues

The complexity of the network plays an important role in many of your network design decisions. Consider the following questions to determine network complexity:

- How many clients will the network need to support?
- What type of work will the clients be doing?
- What are the locations of the clients? In complex networks, clients may be geographically dispersed over a wide area.
- What types of clients are going to be supported? Will these be PC-based clients or terminal-based clients? Will these be thin clients that will do little processing or fat clients that will do the majority of the application processing?
- What is the projected growth of the network?
- Where will the processing take place? Will there be any middle-tier servers involved, such as an application server or transaction server?
- What types of network protocols will be used to communicate between the clients and servers?
- Will Oracle servers have to communicate with other Oracle servers in the enterprise?
- Will the network involve multiple operating systems?
- Are there any special networking requirements for the applications that will be used? This is especially important to consider when you are dealing with third-party applications.

Network Security Issues

Network security has become even more critical as companies expose their systems to larger and larger numbers of users through internets and intranets. Consider the following questions to determine the security of a network:

- Does the organization have any special requirements for secure network connections? What kinds of information will be sent across the Oracle network?
- Can you ensure secure connections across a network without risk of information tampering? This may involve sending the data in a format that makes it tamperproof and also ensures that the data cannot be captured and read by parties other than the client and the intended Oracle server.
- Is there a need to centralize the authorizations an individual has to each of the Oracle servers? In large organizations with many Oracle services, this can be a management and administration issue.

Interfacing Existing Systems with New Systems

The following issues should be considered when existing computer systems must communicate with Oracle server networks:

- Does the application that needs to perform the communication require a seamless, real-time interface?
- Does the existing system use a non-Oracle database such as DB2 or Sybase?
- Will information be transferred from the existing system to the Oracle server on a periodic basis? If so, what is the frequency and what transport mechanisms should be used? Will the Oracle server need to send information back to the existing system?
- Do applications need to gather data from multiple sources, including Oracle and non-Oracle databases, simultaneously?
- What are the applications involved that require this interface?
- Will these network requirements necessitate design changes to existing systems?

Network Responsibilities for the DBA

The database administrator has many design issues to consider and plays an important role when implementing a network of Oracle servers in the enterprise. Here are some of the key responsibilities of the DBA in the Oracle network implementation process:

- Understand the network configuration options available and know which options should be used based on the requirements of the organization.
- Understand the underlying network architecture of the organization in order to make informed design decisions.
- Work closely with the network engineers to ensure consistent and reliable connections to the Oracle servers.
- Understand the tools available for configuring and managing the network.
- Troubleshoot connection problems on the client, middle tier, and server.
- Ensure secure connections and use the available network configurations, when necessary, to attain higher degrees of security for sensitive data transmissions.
- Stay abreast of trends in the industry and changes to the Oracle architecture that may have an impact on network design decisions.

Network Configurations

There are three basic types of network configurations to select from when you are designing an Oracle infrastructure. The simplest type is the single-tier architecture. This has been around for years and is characterized by the use of terminals for serial connections to the Oracle server. The other types of network configurations are the two-tier, or client/server, architecture and the most recently introduced n-tier architecture. Let's take a look at each of these configuration alternatives.

Single-Tier Architecture

Single-tier architecture was the standard for many years before the birth of the PC. Applications utilizing single-tier architecture are sometimes referred to as *green-screen applications* because most of the terminals using them, such as the IBM 3270 terminal, have green screens. Single-tier architecture is commonly associated with mainframe-type applications.

This architecture is still in use today for many mission-critical applications, such as Order Processing and Fulfillment and Inventory Control, because it is the simplest architecture to configure and administer. Because the terminals are directly connected to the host computer, the complexities of network protocols and multiple operating systems don't exist.

When a single-tier architecture is being used, users interact with the database using terminals. These terminals are non-graphical, character-based devices. Figure 1.1 shows an example of the single-tier architecture. In this type of architecture, client terminals are directly connected to larger server systems such as mainframes. All of the intelligence exists on the mainframe, and all processing takes place there. Simple serial connections also exist on the mainframe. Although no complex network architecture is necessary, a single-tier architecture is somewhat limiting in terms of scalability and flexibility. Because all of the processing must take place on the server, the server can become the bottleneck to increasing performance.

FIGURE 1.1 Single-tier architecture

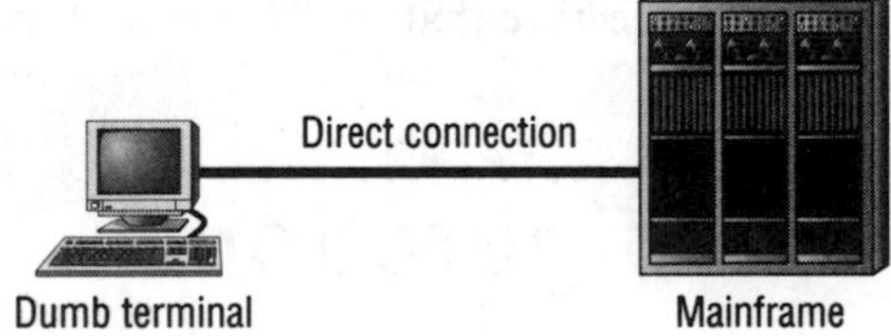

Two-Tier Architecture

Two-tier architecture gained popularity with the introduction of the PC and is commonly referred to as client/server computing. In a two-tier environment, clients connect to servers over a network using a network protocol, which is the agreed-upon method for the client to communicate with the server. TCP/IP is a very popular network protocol and has become the de facto standard of network computing. Whether TCP/IP or some other network protocol is chosen, both the client and the server must be able to understand the chosen protocol. Figure 1.2 shows an example of a two-tier architecture.

FIGURE 1.2 Two-tier architecture

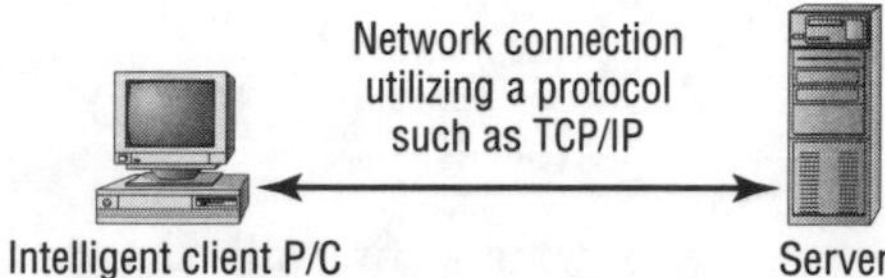

This architecture has definite benefits over single-tier architecture. First of all, client/server computing introduces the graphical user interface; this interface is easier to understand and learn, and it offers more flexibility than the traditional character-based interfaces of the single-tier architecture. Also, two-tier architecture allows the client computer to share the application processing load. To a certain degree, this reduces the processing requirements of the server.

The two-tier architecture does have some faults, even though at one time, it was thought to be the panacea of all networking architectures. Unfortunately, the main problem, that of scalability, persists. Notice that the term client/server computing contains a slash (/). The slash represents the invisible component of the two-tier architecture and the one that is often overlooked: the network!

When prototyping projects, many developers fail to consider the network component and soon find out that what worked well in a small environment may not scale effectively to larger, more complex systems. There was a great deal of redundancy in the two-tier architecture model because application software was required on every desktop. As a result of this scenario, many companies end up with bloated PCs and large servers that still do not provide adequate performance. What is needed is a more scalable model for network communications. That is what n-tier architecture provides.

N-Tier Architecture

N-tier architecture is the next logical step after two-tier architecture. Instead of dividing application processing work between a client and a server, you divide the work up among three or more machines. The n-tier architecture introduces *middleware* components, one or more computers that are situated between the client and the Oracle server, which can be used for a variety of tasks. Some of those tasks include the following:

- Moving data between machines that work with different network protocols.
- Serving as firewalls that can control client access to the servers.
- Offloading processing of the business logic from the clients and servers to the middle tier.
- Executing transactions and monitoring activity between clients and servers to balance the load among multiple servers.
- Acting as a gateway to bridge existing systems to new systems.

The Internet provides the ultimate n-tier architecture with the user's browser providing a consistent presentation interface. This common interface means less training of staff and also increases the potential reuse of client-side application components.

N-tier architecture makes it possible to take advantage of technologies such as networked computers. Such computers can make for economical, low-maintenance alternatives to the personal computer. Because much of the application processing can be done by application servers, the client computing requirements for these networked computers are greatly reduced. In addition, the processing of transactions can also be offloaded to transaction servers, which reduces the burden on the database servers.

The n-tier model is very scalable and divides the tasks of presentation, business logic and routing, and database processing among many machines, which means that this model accommodates large applications. In addition, the reduction of processing load on the database servers means that the servers can do more work with the same amount of resources. Also, the transaction servers can balance the flow of network transactions intelligently, and application servers can reduce the processing and memory requirements of the client (see Figure 1.3).

FIGURE 1.3 N-tier architecture

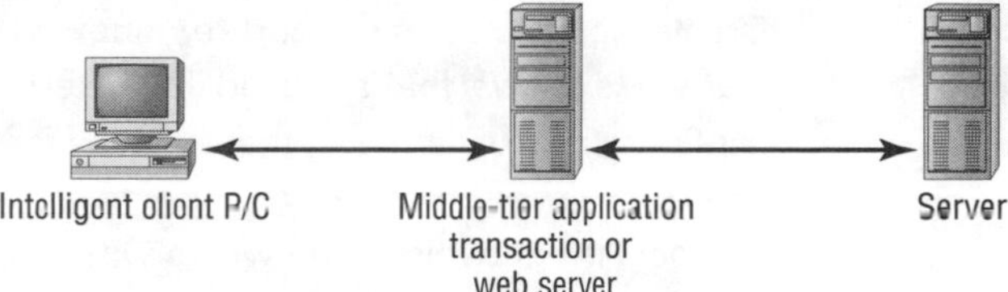

Overview of Oracle Net Features

Oracle Net is the glue that bonds the Oracle network together. It is responsible for handling client-to-server and server-to-server communications, and it can be configured on the client, the middle-tier application, web servers, and the Oracle server.

Oracle Net also manages the flow of information in the Oracle network infrastructure. First, it is used to establish the initial connection to the Oracle server, and then it acts as the messenger, passing requests from the client back to the server or passing them between two Oracle servers. Basically, Oracle Net handles all negotiations between the client and server during the client connection. In the section entitled "The Oracle Net Stack Architecture" later in this chapter, we discuss the architectural design of Oracle Net.

In addition to functioning as an information manager, Oracle Net supports the use of middleware products such as Oracle9*i* Application Server (Oracle9*i*AS) and Oracle Connection Manager. These products allow n-tier architectures to be used in the enterprise, which increases the flexibility and performance of application designs.

To learn more about these products and some of the features of Oracle Net, read the following sections, which mirror the five categories of networking solutions that Oracle Net provides: Connectivity, Directory Services, Scalability, Security, and Accessibility.

Connectivity: Multi-Protocol Support

Oracle Net supports a wide range of industry-standard protocols including TCP/IP, IBM LU6.2, Named Pipes, and DECnet. (Unlike its predecessor Net8, Oracle Net no longer supports the Novell IPX/SPX protocol.) This support is handled transparently and allows Oracle Net to establish connectivity to a wide range of computers and a wide range of operating environments.

Oracle Net now adds support for a new protocol designed for *System Area Networks (SANs)* that are used in clustered environments. (SANs are special configurations of hardware that are used for situations in which multiple servers need high-speed communications between them.) The new *Virtual Interface (VI) protocol* is lightweight and works with a specific hardware configuration to relieve network activity responsibility from the CPUs and place it on special network adapters. See the Oracle9*i* Net Services Administrator's Guide (Part No. A90154-01) for details on the use, configuration, and restrictions on the VI protocol. This guide may be obtained from the Oracle Technology Network website at `technet.oracle.com`. At this website, you will find all of the Oracle9*i* documentation in either Adobe Acrobat format or HTML format.

Connectivity: Multiple Operating Systems

Oracle Net can operate on many different operating system platforms, from Windows NT/2000, to all variants of Unix, to large mainframe-based operating systems. This range allows users to bridge existing systems to other Unix or PC-based systems, which increases the data access flexibility of the organization without making wholesale changes to the existing systems.

Connectivity: Java and Internet

With the introduction of Oracle8*i*, Oracle enabled connectivity to Oracle servers from applications using Java components such as Enterprise JavaBeans and Common Object Request Broker Architecture (CORBA), which is a standard for defining object interaction across a network. Oracle Net continues this trend by supporting standard connectivity solutions such as the Internet Inter-ORB Protocol (IIOP) and the General Inter-ORB Protocol (GIOP). These features allow clients to connect to applications interfacing with an Oracle database via a web browser. By utilizing features such as Secured Sockets Layer (SSL), client connections can obtain a greater degree of security across the Internet.

Directory Services: Directory Naming

Directory Naming allows for network names to be resolved through a centralized naming repository. The central repository takes the form of a Lightweight Directory Access Protocol (LDAP)–compliant server. LDAP is a protocol and language that defines a standard method of storage, identification, and retrieval of services. It provides a simplified way to manage directories of information, whether this information is about users in an organization or Oracle instances connected to a network. The LDAP server allows for a standard form of managing and resolving names in an Oracle environment. The quality of these services excels because LDAP provides a single industry standard interface to a directory service such as Oracle Internet Directory (OID). By utilizing Oracle Internet Directory, you ensure security and reliability of the directory information because information is stored in the Oracle database.

As of Oracle9*i*, Directory Naming has become the preferred method of centralized naming within an Oracle environment, replacing the Oracle Names Server. The Oracle Names Server can still be utilized in Oracle8*i* and earlier versions, however. The Oracle Names Server can also still be configured as a proxy to an LDAP-compliant Names Directory Service to ease the migration from Oracle Names to Directory Naming.

Directory Services: Oracle Internet Directory

The Oracle Internet Directory (OID) is an LDAP 3–compliant directory service, which provides the repository and infrastructure needed to enable a centralized naming solution using Directory Naming. OID can be used with both Oracle8*i* and 9*i* databases. In Oracle9*i*, the OID runs as an application. The OID service can be run on a remote server and it can communicate with the Oracle server using Oracle Net. The OID is a scalable architecture, and it provides mechanisms for replicating service information among other Oracle servers.

OID also provides security in a number of ways. First of all, it can be integrated into a Secure Sockets Layer (SSL) environment to ensure user authentication. Also, an administrator can maintain policies that grant or deny access to services. These policies are defined for entities within the Oracle Internet Directory tree structure.

Scalability: Oracle Shared Server

Oracle Shared Server (formerly known as Multithreaded Server) is an optional configuration of the Oracle server that allows support for a larger number of concurrent connections without increasing physical resource requirements. This is accomplished by sharing resources among groups of users.

Scalability: Connection Manager

Oracle Connection Manager is a middleware solution that provides three additional scalability features:

Multiplexing Connection Manager can group together many client connections and send them as a single multiplexed network connection to the Oracle server. This reduces the total number of network connections the server has to manage.

Network access Connection Manager can be configured with rules that restrict access by IP address. This rules-based configuration can be set up to accept or reject client connection requests. Also, connections can be restricted by point of origin, destination server, or Oracle server.

Cross-protocol connectivity This feature allows clients and servers that use different network protocols to communicate. Connection Manager acts as a translator, providing two-way protocol conversion.

Oracle Connection Manager is controlled by a set of background processes that manage the communications between clients and servers. This option is not configured using the graphical Oracle Net Manager tool. Figure 1.4 provides an overview of the Connection Manager architecture.

FIGURE 1.4 Connection Manager architecture

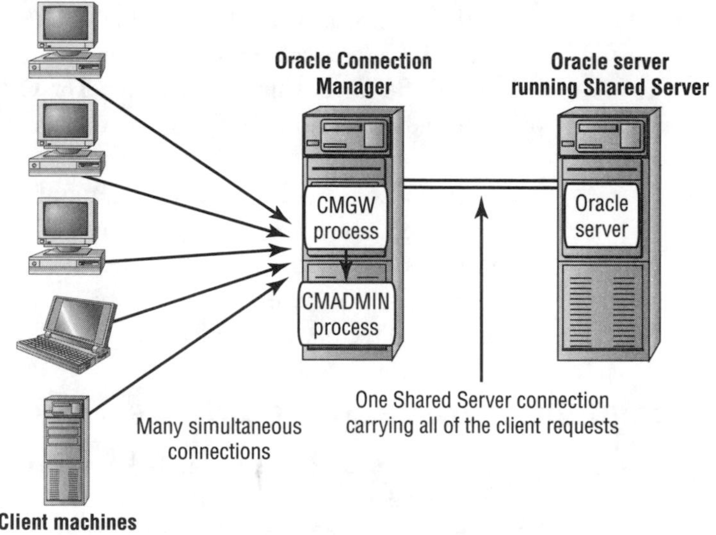

Security: Advanced Security

The threat of data tampering is becoming an issue of increasing concern to many organizations as network systems continue to grow in number and complexity and as users gain increasing access to systems. Sensitive business transactions are being conducted with greater frequency and, in many cases, are not protected from unauthorized tampering or message interception.

Oracle Advanced Security, formerly known as the Advanced Security Option and the Advanced Networking Option, not only provides the tools necessary to ensure secure transmissions of sensitive information, but it also provides mechanisms to confidently identify and authenticate users in the Oracle enterprise.

When configured on the client and the Oracle server, Oracle Advanced Security supports secured data transactions by encrypting and optionally checksumming the transmission of information that is sent in a transaction. Oracle supports encryption and checksumming by taking advantage of industry-standard algorithms, such as RSA RC4, Standard DES and Triple DES, and MD5 checksumming. These security features ensure that data transmitted from the client has not been altered during transmission to the Oracle server.

Oracle Advanced Security also gives the database administrator the ability to authenticate users connecting to the Oracle servers. In fact, there are a number of authentication features for ensuring that users are really who they claim to be. These are offered in the form of token cards, which use a physical card and a user identifying PIN number to gain access to the system; the biometrics option, which uses fingerprint technology to authenticate user connection requests; Public Key; and certificate-based authentication.

Another feature of Oracle Advanced Security is the ability to have a single sign-on mechanism for clients. Single sign-on is accomplished with a centralized security server that allows the user to connect to any of the Oracle services in the enterprise using a single user ID and password. Oracle leverages the industry-standard features of Kerberos to enable these capabilities. (Kerberos is an authentication mechanism based on the sharing of secrets between two systems.) This greatly simplifies the privilege matrix that administrators must manage when they are dealing with large numbers of users and systems.

Security: Firewall Support

Firewalls have become an important security mechanism in corporate networks. *Firewalls* are generally a combination of hardware and software that are used to control network traffic and prevent intruders from compromising corporate network security. Firewalls fall into two broad categories:

IP-filtering firewalls *IP-filtering firewalls* monitor the network packet traffic on IP networks and filter out packets that either originated or did not originate from specific groups of machines. The information contained in the IP packet header is interrogated to obtain this information. Vendors of this type of firewall include Network Associates and Axent Communications.

Proxy-based firewalls *Proxy-based firewalls* prevent information from outside the firewall from flowing directly into the corporate network. Instead, the firewall acts as a gatekeeper, inspecting packets and sending only the appropriate information through to the corporate network. This prevents any direct communication between clients outside the firewall and applications inside the firewall. Check Point Software Technologies and Cisco are examples of vendors that market proxy-based firewalls.

Oracle works closely with the vendors of both types of product to ensure support of database traffic through these types of mechanism. Oracle supplies the Oracle Net Application Proxy Kit to the vendors of firewalls. This product can be incorporated into the firewall architecture to allow database packets to pass through the firewall and still maintain a high degree of security.

Real World Scenario

Know Thy Firewall

It is important to understand your network infrastructure, the network routes you are using to obtain database connections, and the type of firewall products you are using. I have had more than one situation in which firewalls have caused connectivity issues between a client and an Oracle server.

For instance, I remember what happened after a small patch was applied to a firewall when I was working as a DBA for one of my former employers. In this case, employees started experiencing intermittent disconnects from the Oracle database. It took many days of investigation and network tracing before we pinned down the exact problem. When we did, we contacted the firewall vendor and they sent us a new patch to apply that corrected the problem.

More recently, when I was working as a DBA for a large corporate client, the development staff started experiencing a similar problem. It turns out that the networking routes for the development staff had been modified to have connections routed through a new firewall. This firewall was configured to have a connection timeout after 20 minutes of inactivity, which was too short an amount of time for this department. As a result, we increased the timeout parameter to accommodate the development staff's needs.

These are examples of the types of network changes that a DBA needs to be aware of to avoid unnecessary downtime and to avoid wasting staff time and resources.

Accessibility: Heterogeneous Services

Heterogeneous Services provide the ability to communicate with non-Oracle databases and services. These services allow organizations to leverage and interact with their existing data stores without having to necessarily move the data to an Oracle server.

The suite of *Heterogeneous Services* is comprised of the *Oracle Transparent Gateway* and *Generic Connectivity*. These products allow Oracle to communicate with non-Oracle data sources in a seamless configuration. Heterogeneous Services also integrate existing systems with the Oracle environment, which allows you to leverage your investment in those systems. These services also allow for two-way communication and replication from Oracle data sources to non-Oracle data sources.

Transparent Gateway The Transparent Gateway product seamlessly extends the reach of Oracle to non-Oracle data stores, which allows you to treat non-Oracle data sources as if they were part of the Oracle environment. In fact, the user is not even aware that the data being accessed is coming from a non-Oracle source. This can significantly reduce the time and investment necessary to transition from existing systems to the Oracle environment. Transparent Gateway fully supports SQL and the Oracle transaction control features, and it currently supports access to more than 30 non-Oracle data sources.

Generic Connectivity Generic Connectivity provides a set of agents, which contain basic connectivity capabilities. It also provides a foundation so that you can custom build connectivity solutions using standard

OLE DB, Microsoft's interface to data access. OLE DB requires an Open Database Connectivity (ODBC) driver to interface to the agents. You can also use ODBC as a stand-alone connection solution. For example, with the proper Oracle ODBC driver, you can access an Oracle database from programs such as Microsoft Excel. (These drivers can be obtained from Oracle or third-party vendors.) Because these drivers are generic in nature, they do not provide as robust an interface to external services as does the Transparent Gateway.

Accessibility: External Procedures

In some development efforts, it may be necessary to interface with procedures that reside outside of the database. These procedures are typically written in a third-generation language, such as C. Oracle Net provides the ability to invoke such external procedures from Oracle PL/SQL callouts. When a call is made, a process will be started that acts as an interface between Oracle and the external procedure. This callout process defaults to the name *extproc*. The listener is then responsible for supplying information, such as a library or procedure name and any parameters, to the called procedure. These programs are then loaded and executed under the control of the extproc process.

The Oracle Net Stack Architecture

The Oracle Net software is comprised of a series of programs that form a type of stack architecture. Each of these programs is responsible for handling various aspects of network communications, and each functions as a layer of the stack. This section discusses the architecture of the Oracle Net stack and defines the responsibilities of each portion. To successfully complete the OCP exam, you need to understand the structure and responsibilities of the Oracle Net stack. The structure and function of the Oracle Net stack is based on the Open Systems Interconnection (OSI) model.

The OSI Model

The *Open Systems Interconnection (OSI)* model is a widely accepted model that defines how data communications are carried out across a network.

There are seven layers in the OSI model, and each layer is responsible for some aspect of network communication. The upper layers of the model handle responsibilities such as communicating with the application and presenting data. The lower layers are responsible for transporting data across the network. The upper layers pass information, such as the destination of the data and how the data should be handled, to the lower layers. The lower layers communicate status information back to the upper layers. Table 1.1 shows the layers of the OSI model and the responsibilities each has in order for communications across a network to be executed. As you can see from this table, this layered approach allows for a separation of responsibilities. It also allows for the separation of the logical aspects of network communications, such as presentation and data management, from the physical aspects of communications, such as the physical transmission of bits across a network.

TABLE 1.1 The Layers of the OSI Model

OSI Model Layer	Responsibilities
Application Layer	Interacts with the application. Accepts commands and returns data.
Presentation Layer	Settles data differences between client and server. Also responsible for data format.
Session Layer	Manages network traffic flow. Determines whether data is being sent or received.
Transport Layer	Handles interaction of the network processes on the source and destination. Error correction and detection occurs here.
Network Layer	Delivers data between nodes.
Data Link Layer	Maintains connection reliability and retransmission functionality.
Physical Layer	Transmits electrical signals across the network.

The Oracle Communications Stack

The OSI model is the foundation of the Oracle communications stack architecture. Each of the layers of the Oracle communications stack has characteristics and responsibilities that are patterned after the OSI model. Oracle interacts with the underlying network at the very highest levels of the OSI model. In essence, it is positioned above the underlying network infrastructure and communicates with the underlying network.

Oracle uses Oracle Net on the client and server to facilitate communications. The communications stack functions as a conduit to share and manage data between the client and server. The layers of Oracle communications stack are as follows:

- The application (client) layer
- The Oracle Call Interface (OCI) layer (client) or Oracle Program Interface (OPI) layer (server)
- The Two-Task Common (TTC) layer
- The Oracle Net Foundation layer
- The Oracle Protocol Adapters (OPA) layer
- The Network Specific Protocols layer
- The Network Program Interface (NPI for server-to-server communications only) layer

Figure 1.5 depicts the relationship of each of the layers of the stack on both the client and the server. The client process makes network calls that traverse down the Oracle Net client layers to the network protocol. The server receives the network request, processes it, and returns the results to the client.

The Application Layer (Client)

The *application layer* of the Oracle communications stack provides the same functionality as the Application Layer of the OSI model. This layer is responsible for interacting with the user, which involves providing the interface components, screen, and data control elements. Interfaces such as forms or menus are examples of the application layer. This layer communicates with the Oracle Call Interface (OCI) layer.

FIGURE 1.5 Oracle Net stack architecture

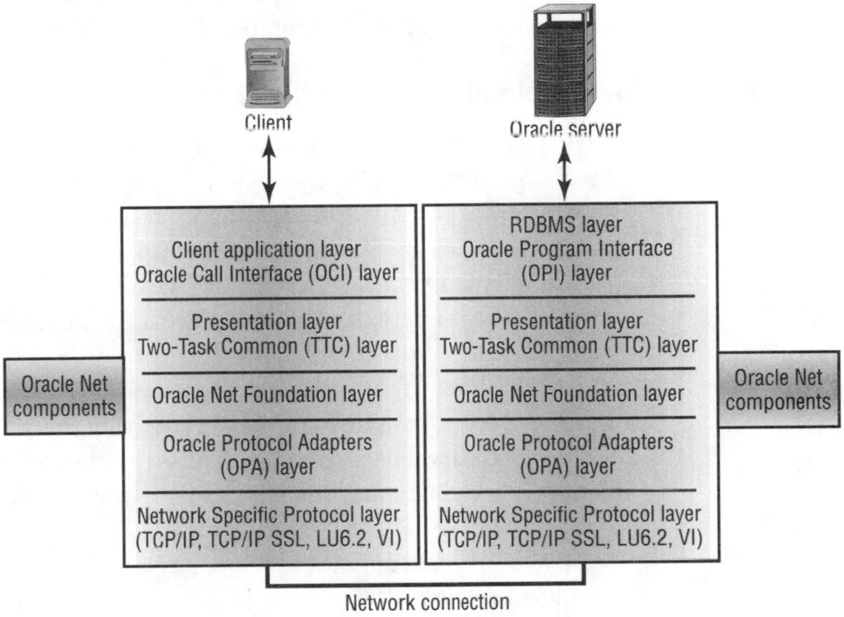

The Oracle Call Interface (OCI) Layer (Client)

The *Oracle Call Interface (OCI) layer* is responsible for all of the SQL processing that occurs between a client and the Oracle server. The OCI layer exists on the client only. There is an analogous server component called the *Oracle Program Interface (OPI) layer* on the server. The OCI layer is responsible for opening and closing cursors, binding variables in the server's shared memory space, and fetching rows. Because the OCI is an open architecture, third-party products can write applications that interface directly with this layer of the communications stack. The OCI layer passes information directly to the Two-Task Common (TTC) layer.

The Two-Task Common (TTC) Layer

The *Two-Task Common (TTC) layer* is responsible for negotiating any datatype or character set differences between the client and the server. The Two-Task Common layer acts as a translator, converting values from one character set to another. The TTC will determine if any datatype differences are present when the connection is established. The TTC layer passes information to the Oracle Net Foundation layer. This layer shares some of the characteristics of the Presentation Layer from the OSI model.

The Oracle Net Foundation Layer

The *Oracle Net Foundation layer* (formerly known as the Transparent Network Substrate or TNS layer) is an integral component of the Oracle communications stack architecture, and it is analogous to the Session Layer in the OSI model. It is based on the Transparent Network Substrate (TNS), which allows Oracle Net to be a very flexible architecture, interfacing with a wide variety of network protocols. The TNS interface shields both the client and server from the complexities of network communications.

At this layer of the communications stack, Oracle Net interfaces with the other layers of the stack and their underlying protocols. It is this layer that provides the level of abstraction necessary to make Oracle Net a flexible and adaptable architecture, and it is this layer that compensates for differences in connectivity issues between machines and underlying protocols. This layer also handles interrupt messages and passes information directly to the Oracle Protocol Adapters (OPA) layer. The Oracle Net Foundation layer has several sublayers:

Network interface (NI) sublayer The network interface sublayer provides a common interface on which the clients and servers can process functions. This layer of the stack is also responsible for handling any break requests.

Network routing (NR) sublayer This is where Oracle Net keeps its network roadmap of how to get from the source or client to the destination or server.

Network naming (NN) sublayer This layer takes network alias information and changes it into Oracle Net destination address information.

Network authentication (NA) sublayer This layer is responsible for any negotiations necessary for authenticating connections.

Network session (NS) sublayer The network session layer handles the bulk of activity in an Oracle network connection. This layer is responsible for such things as negotiating the initial connection request from the client. It is also responsible for managing the Oracle Net buffer contents and passing the buffer information between the client and the server. It also handles special features of connection management, such as buffer pooling and multiplexing, if these options are used.

The Oracle Protocol Adapters (OPA) Layer

The *Oracle Protocol Adapters (OPA) layer* interfaces with the underlying network. This becomes the entry point into the underlying network. This layer maps the Oracle Net Foundation layer functions to the analogous functions in the underlying protocol. There are different adapters for each protocol supported. This layer, in conjunction with the Network Specific Protocol layer, is analogous to the Network Layer in the OSI model.

The Network Specific Protocol Layer

This is the actual transport layer that carries the information from the client to the server. Some of the protocols supported by Oracle Net include TCP/IP, and DECnet. These protocols are not supplied with the Oracle software and must be in place to facilitate network communications.

The Oracle Program Interface (OPI) Layer (Server Only)

For every request made from the client, the Oracle Program Interface layer is responsible for sending the appropriate response. So when clients issue SQL statements requesting data from the database, the OPI interface fulfills that request. In server-to-server communication, the Network Program Interface (NPI) is used instead of the OPI.

The Network Program Interface (NPI) Layer (Server Only)

The *Network Program Interface (NPI)* layer is found only on the Oracle server. It is analogous to the OCI on the client. This layer is responsible for server-to-server communications, whereas the OPI is used in client-server communications and is used in distributed environments where databases communicate with each other across database links. This layer is analogous to the Presentation Layer of the OSI model, but from the server perspective.

Oracle Net and Java Support

To provide the ability to interface with Java code that can be written and deployed inside the Oracle server environment, Oracle Net supports the General Inter-ORB Protocol (GIOP). This protocol allows Object Request

Brokers to talk to one another over the Internet. An *Object Request Broker* is a piece of software that handles the routing of object requests in a distributed network. The Internet Inter-ORB Protocol (IIOP) is a flavor of GIOP running under TCP/IP that supports the Secured Sockets Layer (SSL) for making secured network connections across the Internet. This type of connectivity would be used if an application were accessing Java procedures that were written and stored in the Oracle database. In this case, the Oracle9*i* Java Virtual Machine (JVM) would be running on the Oracle server, providing the Object Request Broker functionality.

The only portion of Oracle Net that is required is the Oracle Net Foundation layer. This streamlined communications stack allows for more efficient connectivity of Oracle servers when server-side Java procedures are being used. Figure 1.6 shows how the modifications streamline the Oracle communications stack.

FIGURE 1.6 IIOP stack communications

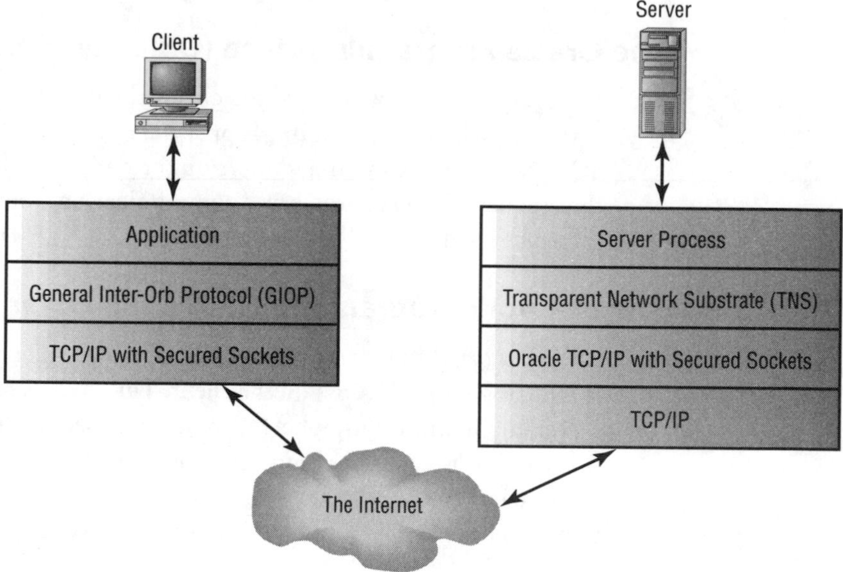

Oracle Net also provides robust connectivity for web-based applications. Connections to the Oracle server are available directly through Java applications, Java applets, or via an application server such as Oracle9*i*AS.

Internet Connectivity with Oracle Net

Connections initiated to an Oracle server via a web browser are much like client-server applications. The main difference is that the application server acts as the client, providing communications to and from the Oracle server. If a Java application resides on the web server, the *Java Database Connectivity (JDBC)* OCI driver is used to initiate communications to the Oracle server. (JDBC is an interface that allows Java programs to interact with data stored in tabular form, such as in an Oracle database.) If the connection is made via a Java applet, then the JDBC Thin Driver is used. The JDBC Thin Driver does not require Oracle client software to be installed, hence the term "thin driver." This driver provides the connectivity from the applet to the Oracle server.

Typically in this environment, an HTTP request is initiated at the client and sent to the application server. The application server forwards the request to the appropriate database service for processing. Oracle Net serves as the mechanism for communication between the application server and the database. HTTP is used to send the request to the application server and to receive the response from the application server. Figure 1.7 shows an example of web connections when using a Java application.

FIGURE 1.7 Web connectivity via a Java application

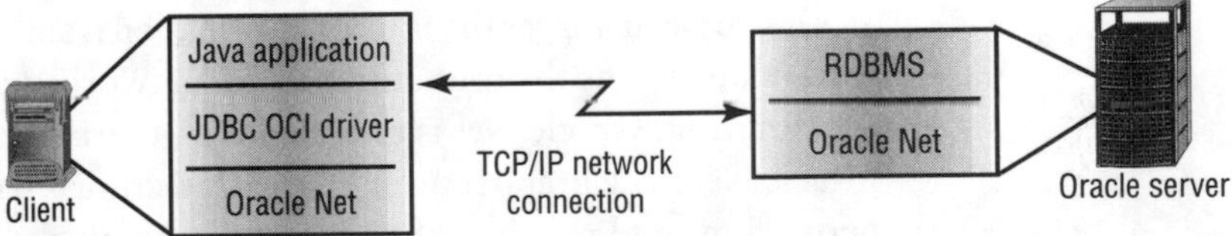

Web Connections with No Application Server

A database can be configured to accept requests directly from a web environment without a middle-tier application server. This is because HTTP and IIOP can be configured on the Oracle server to accommodate these types of connections. Oracle supports the development and deployment of common Java objects, such as Enterprise JavaBeans (EJB), within the Oracle server itself. A client can make a request to the Oracle database and interface with these components directly. Oracle Net must be configured on the server to accept and process these types of requests. What makes this solution attractive is that no software needs to be deployed to the client; all the client needs is a web browser to interact with the database.

Summary

There are several key components that are necessary to understand in order to succeed when you are networking in an Oracle environment. The main responsibilities of the network administrator include determining the applications and type of connections that will be supported, the number of users and the locations from which they will be accessing the network, and the security issues involved in protecting sensitive information, such as single sign-on and data encryption.

In addition to being aware of their own responsibilities, the DBA needs to choose from the three basic types of network configurations when setting up their Oracle network: single-tier architecture, two-tier architecture, and n-tier architecture. Because systems have evolved from the simpler single-tier architecture to the more complex n-tier architecture, which can include connections through middle-tier servers and the Internet, database administrators will most likely find themselves choosing between the two architectures that Oracle Net is an integral part of: two-tier or n-tier architectures.

Oracle Net manages the flow of information from client computers to Oracle servers and forms the foundation of all networked computing in the Oracle environment. Oracle Net is comprised of a series of layers that make up the Oracle Net stack architecture. This architecture is based on the OSI model of networking and provides the basic building blocks of network interaction. Each layer in the Oracle Net stack is responsible for one or more networking tasks. Requests and responses are sent up and down the stack, which exists on both the client and the server.

In addition to the main network architecture that supports connections to an Oracle server, Oracle Net provides services that can be divided into five main categories: Connectivity, Directory Services, Scalability, Security, and Accessibility. Connectivity solutions include support for multiple protocols, multiple operating systems, and Java and Internet. Directory Services provide an infrastructure to resolve Oracle service names through a centralized naming repository. Scalability solutions include Connection Manager and Oracle Shared Server. Security options include Oracle Advanced Security, which provides an additional layer of security options and robust support for many varieties of firewalls. Accessibility support includes Heterogeneous Services and support for calling external procedures. Oracle Net also provides connectivity to Java stored procedures: the HTTP and IIOP protocols.

This chapter provides the foundation of knowledge that you will need to understand when you are designing an Oracle network infrastructure. The decisions you make about the network design have ramifications in terms of the scalability, security, and flexibility of your Oracle environment. When you understand the underlying network architecture and the network options available to you, you will be able to make informed choices when you are designing your Oracle network.

Exam Essentials

Know the database administrator's responsibilities and how they relate to network administration. You should be able to list the responsibilities of the database administrator with respect to network administration. Can you define the basic network configuration choices and summarize the strengths and weaknesses of these options?

Understand what Oracle Net is and the functionality it provides. You should be able to define the five categories of functionality that Oracle Net provides and what functionality falls into each category. You should also understand what functionality the Oracle Shared Server and Oracle Connection Manager options provide. In addition, you should be able to define Oracle Advanced Security and know when to use it.

Be able to define the uses of the Heterogeneous Services and the situations in which these options are useful. Heterogeneous Services provide the ability to communicate with non-Oracle databases and services. These services allow organizations to leverage and interact with their existing data stores without having to necessarily move the data to an Oracle server.

Be able to define the Oracle Net stack architecture. The Oracle Net architecture is based on the OSI model of network computing. This model divides the responsibility of conducting network transactions among various layers. You should know the names and definitions of the various layers of the Oracle Net stack.

Understand Oracle Net support for Java stored on the Oracle server. Oracle supports Java stored on the server by supporting GIOP, which allows Object Request Brokers to talk to one another over the Internet. The Oracle9*i* JVM provides the Object Request Broker functionality on the Oracle server.

Be familiar with Oracle's Internet connection options. You should have a basic understanding of the connection options Oracle provides from the Internet. This includes connections made via an application server and connections made directly to the Oracle server from a web browser.

Key Terms

Before you take the exam, be certain you are familiar with the following terms:

application layer
extproc
firewall
Generic Connectivity
Heterogeneous Services
IP-filtering firewall
Java Database Connectivity (JDBC)
middleware
Network Program Interface (NPI)
n-tier architecture
Object Request Broker
Open Systems Interconnection (OSI)
Oracle Advanced Security
Oracle Call Interface (OCI) layer
Oracle Connection Manager
Oracle Net Foundation layer
Oracle Program Interface (OPI) layer
Oracle Protocol Adapters (OPA) layer
Oracle Shared Server
Oracle Transparent Gateway
proxy-based firewall
single-tier architecture
System Area Network (SAN)
Two-Task Common (TTC) layer
two-tier architecture
Virtual Interface (VI) protocol

Review Questions

1. All of the following are examples of networking architectures *except*:

   A. Client/server

   B. N-tier

   C. Single-tier

   D. Two-tier

   E. All of the above are examples of network architectures.

2. You manage one non-Oracle database and several Oracle databases. An application needs to access the non-Oracle databases as if it were part of the Oracle databases. What tool will solve this business problem? Choose the best answer.

   A. Oracle Advanced Security

   B. Oracle Connection Manager

   C. Heterogeneous Services

   D. Oracle Net

   E. None of the above

3. Which of the following is *true* about Oracle Net?

   A. It is not an option included in the Oracle Enterprise installation.

   B. It only works on TCP/IP platforms.

   C. It has an open API.

   D. It is never installed directly on a client workstation.

4. A DBA wants to centrally administer all of the Oracle network services in a large Oracle9*i* installation with many network services. Which facility would best provide this functionality at minimal cost?

   A. Advanced Security

   B. Heterogeneous Services

   C. Oracle Shared Server

   D. Oracle Internet Directory

5. What are TCP/IP, DECnet, and LU6.2 all examples of?

   A. Computer programming languages

   B. Oracle Net connection tools

   C. Networking protocols

   D. Network programming languages

6. Which feature of Oracle Net best describes this statement: "Oracle Net supports TCP/IP and LU6.2."?

   A. GUI tools integration

   B. Robust tracing and diagnostic tools

   C. Zero configuration on the client

   D. Network transport protocol support

7. What is a solution that Oracle9*i* employs with Oracle Net that allows connectivity of Java Components such as Enterprise JavaBeans?

   A. LU6.2

   B. IPA

   C. GIOP

   D. Oracle Internet Directory

8. What is the standard that the Oracle Net communications stack is based on?

   A. OCI

   B. NPI

   C. OSI

   D. API

9. "Responsible for moving bits across the wire" describes which of the following OSI layers?

   A. Application Layer

   B. Physical Layer

   C. Data Link Layer

   D. Network Layer

10. What is the default name of the process that is used to make external calls via Oracle Net?

    A. externalproc

    B. external

    C. extproc

    D. procext

11. IIOP is an example of which of the following?

    A. Tools to use for Oracle Net

    B. Oracle network integration utilities

    C. Internet network protocol

    D. Portions of the Oracle Net stack

12. Connection Manager provides which of the following?

    A. Multiplexing

    B. Cross protocol connectivity

    C. Network access control

    D. All of the above

13. Which of the following is true about the OCI layer?

    A. It displays the graphical interface.

    B. Its datatype conversions are handled.

    C. It interfaces directly with the protocol adapters.

    D. It interfaces directly with the TTC layer.

    E. None of the above.

14. To which of the choices below does the following statement apply? "Prevents direct communication between a client and applications inside the corporate network."

    A. Proxy-based firewalls

    B. Filter-based firewalls

    C. Both types of firewalls

    D. Neither type of firewall

15. When a connection is made via a Java applet, what type of driver is utilized?

    A. JDBC OCI driver

    B. JDBC Thin Driver

    C. ODBC driver

    D. OCI driver

16. A client workstation connects to a transaction server, which passes on requests to the Oracle database. This is a description of which of the following?

    A. Single-tier architecture

    B. Client/server architecture

    C. N-tier architecture

    D. None of the above

17. Which Oracle Net networking product can be best described as middleware?

A. Oracle Internet Directory

B. Oracle Connection Manager

C. Oracle Advanced Networking

D. Oracle Shared Server

18. Which of the following are characteristics of complex networks?

A. Multiple protocols

B. Diverse geographic locations

C. Multiple operating systems

D. Multiple hardware platforms

E. All of the above

19. What is the preferred method of centralized naming in an Oracle9*i* environment?

A. Oracle Names Server

B. Oracle Connection Manager

C. Oracle Shared Server

D. Directory Naming with Oracle Internet Directory

20. Which of the following is an example of the ability to group connections together?

A. Protocol Interchange

B. Network Access Control

C. Multiplexing

D. Data Integrity checking

E. None of the above

Answers to Review Questions

1. E. All of these are examples of network connectivity configurations. Networking can be as simple as a dumb terminal connected directly to a server via a serial connection. It can also be as complex as an n-tier architecture that may involve clients, middleware, the Internet, and database servers.

2. C. Oracle Advanced Security would not solve this application problem because it addresses security and not accessibility to non-Oracle databases. Oracle Net would be part of the solution, but another Oracle Network component is necessary. Connection Manager would also not be able to accommodate this requirement on its own. Heterogeneous Services is the correct answer because these services provide cross-platform connectivity to non-Oracle databases.

3. C. Oracle Net is included in the Oracle Enterprise installation and works with a variety of protocols. It also has a client and a server component. The only statement that is true about Oracle Net is that it has an open Applications Program Interface (API), which means that third-party software can write to these specifications to interact directly with Oracle Net.

4. D. Advanced Security, Heterogeneous Services, and Oracle Shared Server would not provide a solution to this business need because none of these address the issue of centrally managing network services. The best solution to the problem is the Oracle Internet Directory because it would facilitate centralized naming.

5. C. TCP/IP, DECnet, and LU6.2 are all examples of network protocols.

6. D. Oracle Net allows for support of multiple protocols. TCP/IP and LU6.2 are two examples of the protocols that Oracle Net supports.

7. C. The General Inter-ORB Protocol is a protocol that supports connectivity of Java components.

8. C. The Oracle Net communications stack is based on the Open Systems Interconnection (OSI) model. NPI and OCI are parts of the Oracle Net stack and API stands for Applications Program Interface.

9. B. The Physical Layer is responsible for sending the actual data bits across the network. The other layers are all above this base layer.

10. C. The default name of the external procedure process is extproc. `lsnrctl` is a utility used to manage the listener service. External and procext are not valid responses.

11. C. IIOP is an example of an Internet network protocol.

12. D. Connection Manager is a middleware solution that provides for multiplexing of connections, cross protocol connectivity, and network access control. All of the answers describe Connection Manager.

13. D. The OCI layer is below the application layer and above the TTC layer. The call interface handles such things as cursor management and SQL execution. This information is passed on to the Two-Task Common layer.

14. A. Proxy-based firewalls prevent any direct contact between a client and applications inside a corporate firewall. Filter-based firewalls inspect the packet headers but pass the packet on without modification to the destination application. Proxy-based firewalls act more as a relay between external clients and internal applications.

15. B. The JDBC Thin Driver would be utilized if a Java applet is used to communicate with an Oracle database through an application server.

16. C. When you introduce middle tiers into the processing of a transaction, this is known as n-tier architecture.

17. B. The Connection Manager is a middle-tier option that provides multi-protocol interchange, connection concentration, and client access control.

18. E. All of these are characteristics of complex networks.

19. D. Oracle Internet Directory and Directory Naming are displacing the Oracle Names Server as the preferred method of centralized naming.

20. C. Multiplexing is a characteristic of the Oracle Connection Manager that allows several incoming requests to be handled and transmitted simultaneously over a single outgoing connection. This is a scalability feature provided by Connection Manager.

Configuring Oracle Net on the Server

ORACLE9*i*: DBA FUNDAMENTALS II EXAM OBJECTIVES COVERED IN THIS CHAPTER:

- ✓ Identify how the listener responds to incoming connections.
- ✓ Configure the listener using Oracle Net Manager.
- ✓ Control the listener using the Listener Control Utility (lsnrctl).
- ✓ Describe Dynamic Service Registration.
- ✓ Configure the listener for IIOP and HTTP connections.

Exam objectives are subject to change at any time without prior notice and at Oracle's sole discretion. Please visit Oracle's Certification website (`http://www.oracle.com/education/certification/`) for the most current exam objectives listing.

The DBA must configure Oracle Net on the server in order for client connections to be established. This chapter will focus on how to configure the basic network elements of the Oracle server.

First, we'll discuss ways to manage and configure the main Oracle server network components and the listener process, as well as how to use the Oracle Net Manager and the `lsnrctl` command line utility. We'll also discuss the Dynamic Registration feature, which allows instances to automatically register with listeners on an Oracle server. We will also look at how to configure the listener so that it can connect clients to an Oracle server over the Internet using IIOP and HTTP connections. Finally, we will explore ways to troubleshoot server-side connectivity problems.

This chapter describes the first steps you need to take when you are configuring the Oracle Net environment. Once Oracle Net is properly configured on the database server, clients will be able to connect to the Oracle database without being directly connected to the server where the Oracle database is located. Without this configuration, this type of connectivity cannot be accomplished.

The Oracle Listener

The Oracle *listener* is the main server-side Oracle networking component that allows connections to be established between client computers and an Oracle database. You can think of the listener as a big ear that listens for connection requests to Oracle services.

The type of Oracle service being requested is part of the connection descriptor information supplied by the process requesting a connection, and the service name resolves to an Oracle database. The listener can listen for any number of databases configured on the server, and it is able to listen for requests being transported on a variety of protocols, such as TCP/IP, DECnet, and LU6.2. A client connection can be initiated from the same machine the listener resides on, or it may come from some remote location.

The listener is configured using a centralized file called *listener.ora*. Though there is only one `listener.ora` file configured per machine, there may be numerous listeners on a server, and it is this file that contains all of the configuration information for every listener configured on the server. If there are multiple listeners configured on a single server, they are usually there to balance connection requests and minimize the burden of connections on a single listener.

The content and structure of the `listener.ora` file will be discussed later in this chapter.

Every listener is a named process that is running on the server. The default name of the Oracle listener is `LISTENER` and it is typically created when you install Oracle. If you configure multiple listeners, each one would have a unique name. Below is an example of the default configuration of the `listener.ora` file.

```
# LISTENER.ORA Network Configuration File:
D:\oracle\ora90\network\admin\listener.ora
# Generated by Oracle configuration tools.

LISTENER =
  (DESCRIPTION_LIST =
    (DESCRIPTION =
      (ADDRESS_LIST =
        (ADDRESS = (PROTOCOL = TCP)(HOST = mjworn)
          (PORT = 1521)))
      (ADDRESS_LIST =
        (ADDRESS = (PROTOCOL = IPC)(KEY = EXTPROC0))
      )
    )
  )

SID_LIST_LISTENER =
  (SID_LIST =
```

```
        (SID_DESC =
          (SID_NAME = PLSExtProc)
          (ORACLE_HOME = D:\oracle\ora90)
          (PROGRAM = extproc)
        )
        (SID_DESC =
          (GLOBAL_DBNAME = ORCL)
          (ORACLE_HOME = D:\oracle\ora90)
          (SID_NAME = ORCL)
        )
      )
```

How Do Listeners Respond to Connection Requests?

There are several ways a listener can respond to a client request for a connection. The response is dependent upon several factors, such as how the server-side network components are configured and what type of connection the client is requesting. The listener will then respond to the connection request in one of two ways.

The listener can spawn a new process and pass control of the client session to the process. In a *dedicated server* environment, every client connection is serviced by its own server-side process. Server-side processes are not shared among clients. Depending on the capabilities of the operating system, two types of dedicated server connections are possible: *bequeath connections* and *redirect connections*. Each results in a separate process that handles client processing, but the mechanics of the actual connection initiation process are different.

As of Oracle9*i*, prespawned dedicated processes are no longer supported.

Bequeath Connections

Bequeath connections are possible when the underlying operating system, such as Unix, supports the inheritance of network endpoints. What this means is that the operating system has the ability to spawn a new process and pass information to this process; this allows the operating system server process to initiate a conversation with the client immediately.

Another name for bequeath connections is direct hand-off connections.

The following steps, which show the connection process for the bequeath connections, are exhibited in Figure 2.1:

1. The client contacts the Oracle server after resolving the service name.
2. The server spawns a dedicated process and bequeaths control of the connection to the process. The new process inherits all control information of the spawned process, including the TCP/IP socket information from the server that spawned the process.
3. The server process notifies the client to start sending information to it by sending a RESEND packet to the client.
4. The client sends a CONNECT packet to the newly established server process.
5. The server responds back with an ACCEPT packet and now manages the client requests.

FIGURE 2.1 Bequeath connection process

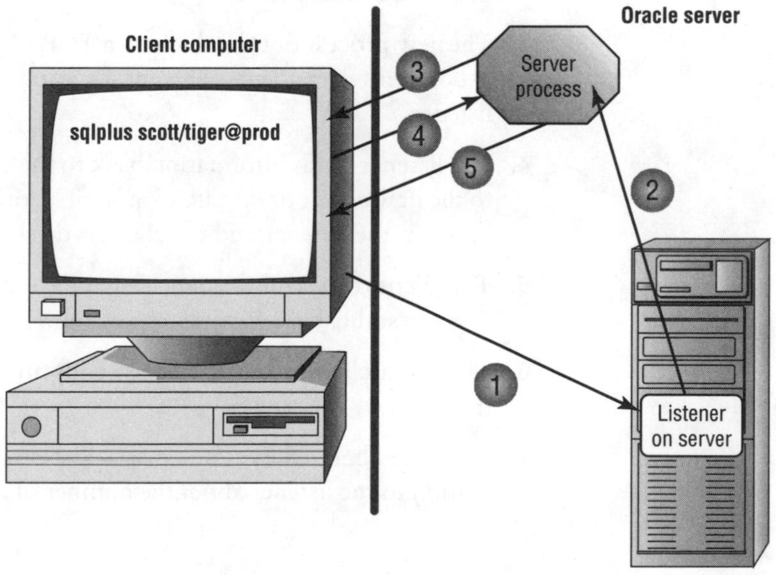

In order to have bequeathed sessions supported on Windows NT/2000, the Registry setting `USE_SHARED_SOCKET` needs to be set. This setting can be set in `HKEY_LOCAL_MACHINE` ➤ `SOFTWARE` ➤ `ORACLE` ➤ `HOME`*X* where *X* is equal to the `HOME` that you are using, such as `HOME0`. By default, this Registry setting is not initialized and therefore Windows NT/2000 will use a redirect type connection to establish communication when dedicated clients connections are used.

Redirect Connections

The listener can also redirect the user to a server process or a dispatcher process. This type of connection can occur when the operating system does not directly support bequeath connections or the listener is not on the same physical machine as the Oracle server.

The following steps are illustrated in Figure 2.2:

1. The client contacts the Oracle server after resolving the service name.
2. The listener spawns a new process or dispatcher in the case of Oracle Shared Server. In the case of Oracle Shared Servers, if there is remaining capacity on existing shared servers, then a dispatcher process will not need to be spawned.
3. The new process or thread selects a TCP/IP port to use to control interaction with user clients. This information is then passed back to the listener.
4. The listener sends information back to the client, redirecting the client to the new server or dispatcher port. The original network connection between the listener and the client is disconnected.
5. The client then sends a connect signal to the server or dispatcher process to establish a network connection.
6. The dispatcher or server process sends an acknowledgement back to the client.
7. If Oracle Shared Server processes are being used, PMON sends information to the listener about the number of connections being serviced

by the dispatchers. The listener uses this information to maintain consistent loads between the dispatchers.

FIGURE 2.2 Redirect connection process

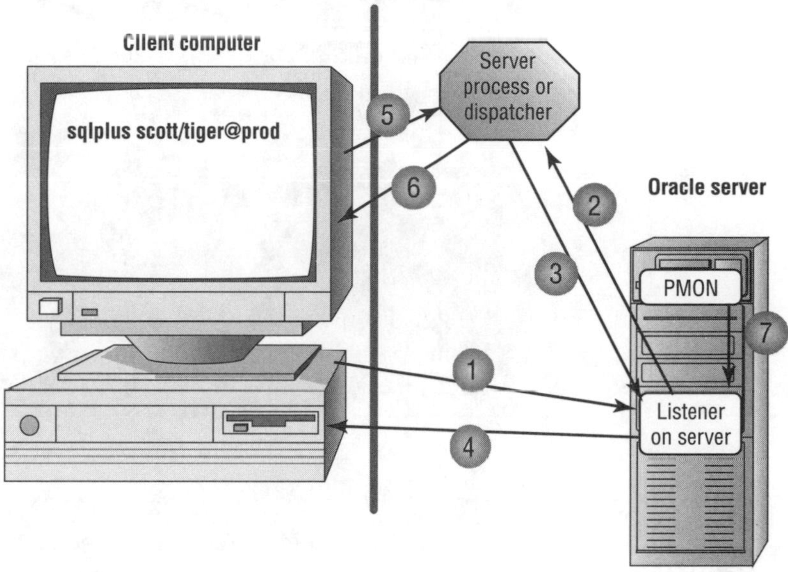

Managing Oracle Listeners

There are a number of ways in which a DBA can configure the server-side listener files. As part of the initial Oracle installation process, the installer will prompt the DBA to create a default listener. If the DBA does not want to supply one in this manner, they can also use the Oracle Net Configuration Assistant to configure a listener. If this method is chosen, the installer uses the set of screens that are a part of this assistant to do the initial listener configuration. Figure 2.3 shows an example of the opening screen for the Oracle Net Configuration Assistant.

FIGURE 2.3 Oracle Net Configuration Assistant opening screen

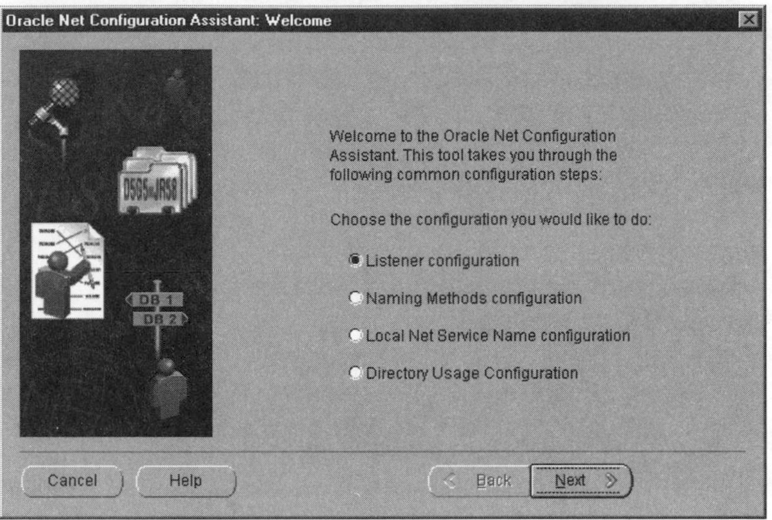

The Oracle Net Configuration Assistant is meant to be an easy, wizard-based tool that you can use to conduct a basic setup for both client- and server-side network products.

Static service registration occurs when entries are added to the `listener.ora` file manually by using the Oracle Net Assistant. It is static because you are adding this information manually. Static service registration is necessary if you will be connecting to pre-Oracle8*i* instances using Oracle Enterprise Manager or you will be connecting to external services.

There is another method of managing listeners that does not require the manual updating of service information in the `listener.ora` file. This is called *dynamic service registration*. Dynamic service registration is a feature that allows an Oracle instance to automatically register itself with an Oracle listener. The benefit of this feature is that it does not require the DBA to perform any updates of server-side network files when new Oracle instances are created. Dynamic service registration will be covered in more detail in the section entitled "Dynamic Registration of Services" later in this chapter.

If you are using Oracle9*i*, you must configure an Oracle9*i* listener to connect to the Oracle server. Oracle9*i* listeners are backward compatible and can listen for connection requests to earlier Oracle database versions.

If you want to be able to set up more than just basic configurations of Oracle network files, you will have to use the Oracle Net Manager. In the next few sections, you will learn how to use the Oracle Net Manager to configure the server-side network files.

Using Oracle Net Manager

Oracle Net Manager is a tool you can use to create and manage most client- and server-side configuration files. The Oracle Net Manager has evolved from the Oracle7 tool, Network Manager, to the latest Oracle9*i* version. Throughout this evolution, Oracle has continued to enhance the functionality and usability of the tool.

We strongly recommend using the Oracle Net Manager to create and manage all of your network files. This is because these files need to be in a specific format, and the Oracle Net Manager ensures that the files are created in that format. If the files are not in the correct format, you may have problems with your network connections. Something as subtle as an extra space or tab can cause problems with network connections, so if you were used to cutting and pasting old entries to create new entries in these files, it is better now to use Oracle Net Manager to create new entries.

If you are using a Windows NT/2000 environment, you can start the Oracle Net Manager by choosing Start ➢ Programs ➢ *Your Oracle9*i *Programs choice* ➢ Configuration and Migration Tools ➢ Oracle Net Manager. In a Unix environment, you can start it by running `./netmgr` from your `$ORACLE_HOME/bin` directory.

Figure 2.4 shows an example of the Oracle Net Manager opening page.

FIGURE 2.4 Opening screen for Oracle Net Manager

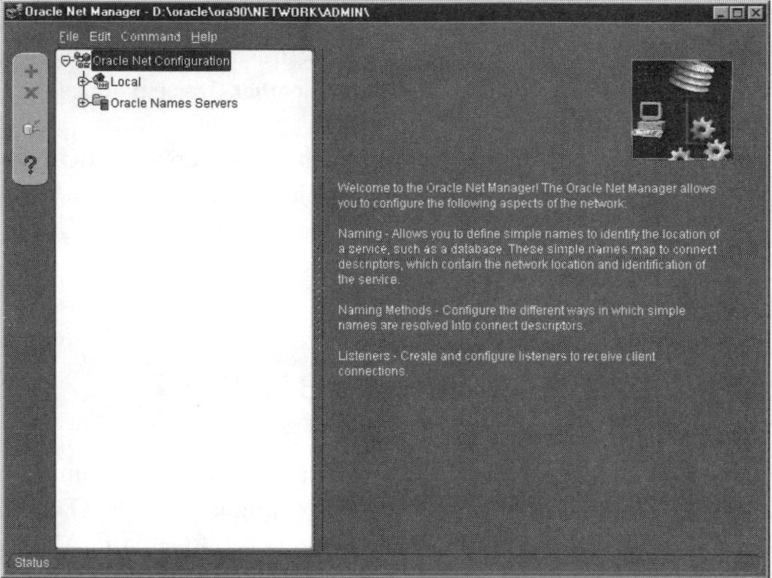

Configuring Listener Services Using the Oracle Net Manager

You will want to use the Oracle Net Manager to configure the listener. As stated in Chapter 1, "Introduction to Network Administration," the Oracle Net Manager provides an easy-to-use graphical interface for configuring most of the network files you will be using. By using Oracle Net Manager, you can ensure that the files are created in a consistent format, which will reduce the potential for connection problems.

When you first start the Oracle Net Manager, the opening screen displays a list of icons down the right-hand side of the screen under the Network folder. The choices under the Local folder relate to different network configuration files. Here are the different network file choices and what each configures.

Icon	File Configured
Profile	`sqlnet.ora`
Service Naming	`tnsnames.ora`
Listeners	`listener.ora`
Oracle Names Servers	`names.ora`

As stated in the previous chapter, Oracle Names Server is being replaced by the Oracle Internet Directory as the preferred method for centralized Oracle service names resolution. However, Oracle Names Server can still be configured from Oracle Net Manager and is supported under Oracle9*i*. However, no revisions are being done to the product, and future releases of Oracle may not support Names Server.

Creating the Listener

Earlier, we said that by default, Oracle will create a listener called `LISTENER` when it is initially installed. The default settings that Oracle uses for the `listener.ora` file are shown here.

Section of the File	Setting
Listener Name	`LISTENER`
Port	`1521`
Protocols	`TCP/IP and IPC`
Host Name	`Default Host Name`
SID Name	`Default Instance`

You can use Oracle Net Manager to create a non-default listener or change the definition of existing listeners. The Oracle Net Manager has a wizard interface for creating most of the basic network elements, such as the `listener.ora` and `tnsnames.ora` files.

Follow these steps to create the listener:

1. Click the plus (+) sign next to the Local icon.
2. Click the Listeners folder.
3. Click the plus sign icon or select Create from the Edit menu.
4. The Choose Listener Name dialog box appears. If this is the first listener being created, the Oracle Net Manager defaults to `LISTENER` if no listener is configured or to `LISTENER1` if a default listener is already

created. Click OK if this is correct or enter a new name. Here is an example of the Choose Listener Name screen.

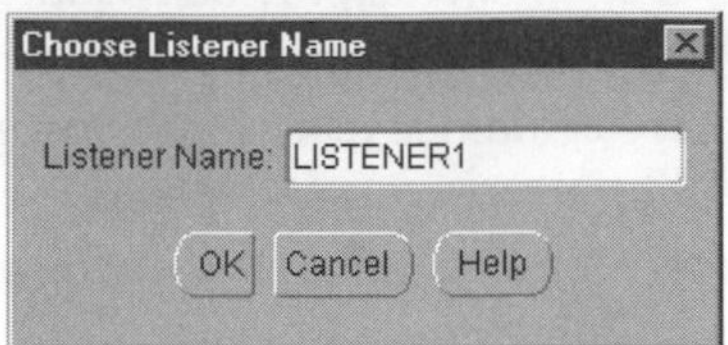

5. After you have chosen a name for the listener, you can configure the listening locations; to do this, click the Listening Locations drop-down list box and make your selection. Then click the Add Address button at the bottom of the screen as shown in Figure 2.5.

FIGURE 2.5 Listener Locations screen from Oracle Net Manager

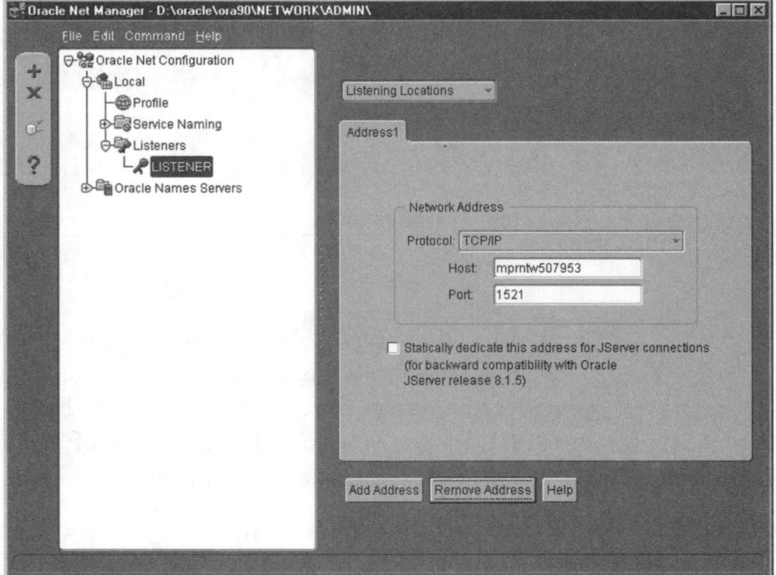

6. A new screen appears on the right side of Oracle Net Manager. Depending on your protocol, the prompts will be somewhat different. By default, TCP/IP information is displayed. If you are using TCP/IP, the Host and Port fields are filled in for you. The *host* is the name of the machine in which the listener is running, and the *port* is the listening location for TCP/IP connections. The default value for the port is 1521.

7. Save your information by selecting File ➤ Save Network Configuration. After saving your information, look in the directory where it was saved.

You always know where the files are stored by looking at the top banner of the Oracle Net Manager screen.

The Oracle Net Manager actually creates three files in this process: `listener.ora`, `tnsnames.ora`, and `sqlnet.ora`. The `tnsnames.ora` does not contain any information. The `sqlnet.ora` file may contain a few entries at this point, but these can be ignored for right now. The `listener.ora` file will contain information as shown in the code listed below. We will discuss the structure and content of the `listener.ora` file later on in the chapter.

```
# LISTENER.ORA Network Configuration File:
D:\oracle\ora90\network\admin\listener.ora
# Generated by Oracle configuration tools.

LISTENER1 =
  (DESCRIPTION_LIST =
    (DESCRIPTION =
      (ADDRESS_LIST =
        (ADDRESS = (PROTOCOL = TCP)(HOST = mjworn)
          (PORT = 1521)))
    )
  )
```

Adding Service Name Information to the Listener

After the listener has been created with the name, protocol, and listening location information, you define the network services that the listener is responsible for connecting users to. There is no limit to the number of network service names for which a listener can listen.

The steps to add the service name information are as follows:

1. Select the listener to configure by clicking the Listeners icon and highlighting the name of the listener you wish to configure.
2. After selecting the listener, choose Database Services from the drop-down list box at the top right of the screen.

3. Click the Add Database button at the bottom of the screen.
4. Enter values in the prompts for Global Database Name, Oracle Home Directory, and SID. The entries for SID and the global database name are the same if you are using a flat naming convention (see Figure 2.6).

FIGURE 2.6 Add Service screen from Oracle Net Manager

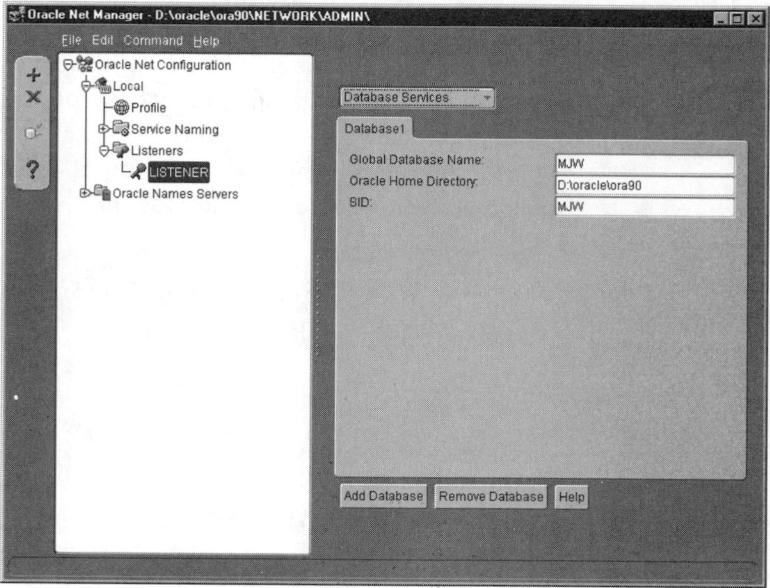

5. Choose File ➤ Save to save your configuration. Here is an example of the completed `listener.ora` file:

```
# LISTENER.ORA Network Configuration File:
D:\oracle\ora90\network\admin\listener.ora
# Generated by Oracle configuration tools.

LISTENER =
  (DESCRIPTION_LIST =
    (DESCRIPTION =
      (ADDRESS_LIST =
        (ADDRESS = (PROTOCOL = TCP)
          (HOST = mprntw507953)(PORT = 1521)))
```

```
        (ADDRESS_LIST =
          (ADDRESS = (PROTOCOL = IPC)(KEY = EXTPROC0))
        )
      )
    )

SID_LIST_LISTENER =
  (SID_LIST =
    (SID_DESC =
      (SID_NAME = PLSExtProc)
      (ORACLE_HOME = D:\oracle\ora90)
      (PROGRAM = extproc)
    )
    (SID_DESC =
      (GLOBAL_DBNAME = MJW)
      (ORACLE_HOME = D:\oracle\ora90)
      (SID_NAME = MJW)
    )
  )
```

Table 2.1 describes each of the `listener.ora` parameters for the Listening Location section of the `listener.ora` file.

TABLE 2.1 Parameters for the Listening Location Section of `listener.ora`

Parameter	Description
LISTENER	Indicates the starting point of a listener definition. This is actually the name of the listener being defined. The default name is LISTENER.
DESCRIPTION	Describes each of the listening locations.
ADDRESS_LIST	Contains address information about the locations where the listener is listening.
PROTOCOL	Designates the protocol for this listening location.
HOST	Houses the name of the machine the listener resides on.

TABLE 2.1 Parameters for the Listening Location Section of `listener.ora` *(continued)*

Parameter	Description
PORT	Contains the address the listener is listening on.
SID_LIST_LISTENER	Defines the list of Oracle services that the listener is configured to listen for.
SID_DESC	Describes each Oracle SID.
GLOBAL_DBNAME	Identifies the global database name. This entry should match the SERVICE_NAMES entry in the init.ora file for the Oracle service.
ORACLE_HOME	Shows the location of the Oracle Executables on the server.
SID_NAME	Contains the name of the Oracle SID for the Oracle Instance.

Adding Additional Listeners

To add more listeners, follow the steps outlined above. Listeners must have unique names and listen on separate ports, so give the listener a new name and assign it to a different port (1522, for example). You also must assign service names to the listener.

Optional *listener.ora* Parameters

You can set optional parameters that add functionality to the listener. Optional parameters are added by choosing the General Parameters drop-down list box at the top right of the screen. Table 2.2 describes these parameters and where they can be found in the Oracle Net Manager.

As you will see, some parameters cannot be added directly from the Oracle Net Manager and have to be added manually. These optional parameters also have the listener name appended to them so that you can tell which listener definition they belong to. For example, if the parameter STARTUP_WAIT_TIME is set for the default listener, the parameter created is START_WAIT_TIME_LISTENER.

TABLE 2.2 Optional listener.ora Parameter Definitions

Oracle Net Manager Prompt	listener.ora Parameter	Description
Startup Wait Time	STARTUP_WAIT_TIME	Defines how long a listener will wait before it responds to a STATUS command in the lsnrctl command line utility.
Unavailable from Net Manager	CONNECT_TIMEOUT	Defines how long a listener will wait for a valid response from a client once a session is initiated. The default is 10 seconds.
Unavailable from Net Manager	SAVE_CONFIG_ON_STOP	Specifies whether modifications made during an lsnrctl session should be saved when exiting.
Log File	LOG_FILE–Will not be in listener.ora file if default setting is used. By default, listener logging is enabled with the log created in the default location.	Specifies where a listener will write log information. This is ON by default and defaults to %ORACLE_HOME%\network\log\listener.log.
Trace Level	TRACE_LEVEL–Not present if tracing is disabled. Default is OFF.	Sets the level of detail if listener connections are being traced. Valid values include Off, User, Support, Admin.
Trace File	TRACE_FILE	Specifies the location of listener trace information. Defaults to %ORACLE_HOME\network\trace\listener.trc.

TABLE 2.2 Optional `listener.ora` Parameter Definitions *(continued)*

Oracle Net Manager Prompt	`listener.ora` Parameter	Description
Require a Password for listener operations	`PASSWORDS`	Specifies password required to perform administrative tasks in the `lsnrctl` command line utility.

Managing the Listener Using *lsnrctl*

Once you have created and saved the listener definition, you need to start the listener. The listener must be started before clients can connect to it and request database connections. The listener cannot be started or stopped from the Oracle Net Manager.

The listener is started using the command line tool *lsnrctl*. Other Oracle network components, such as Connection Manager, have command line tools that are used to stop and start the associated processes.

On Windows NT/2000, the listener runs as a service. Services are programs that run in the background on Windows NT/2000. You can start the listener from the Windows NT/2000 Services panel. Choose Start ➢ Settings ➢ Control Panel ➢ Services. Then select the name of the listener service from the list of services. If your `%ORACLE_HOME%` directory was `ORANT`, and the name of your listener was `Listener`, you would look for a name such as `OracleOraHome90TNSListener`. Select the listener name and choose Start.

The `lsnrctl` Utility

The `lsnrctl` utility is located in the `%ORACLE_HOME%\bin` directory on Windows NT/2000 and in `$ORACLE_HOME/bin` on Unix systems. Windows NT/2000 users familiar with earlier releases of Oracle will notice that utility names no longer have version extensions. For example, in Oracle8, the tool was called `lsnrctl80`. All of the tools now have a consistent name across platforms—the version extensions have been dropped to comply with this.

Type **lsnrctl** at the command line. The code below shows what a resulting login screen looks like:

```
C:\>lsnrctl

LSNRCTL for 32-bit Windows: Version 9.0.1.1.1 - Production
on 08-OCT-2001 20:30:
02

Copyright (c) 1991, 2001, Oracle Corporation.  All rights
reserved.

Welcome to LSNRCTL, type "help" for information.

LSNRCTL>
```

Starting the Listener

The listener has commands to perform various functions. You can type **help** at the LSNRCTL> prompt to get a list of these commands. To start the default listener named LISTENER, type **start** at the prompt. If you want to start a different listener, you would have to type in that listener name after `start`. For example, typing **start listener1** would start the LISTENER1 listener. The following code shows the results of starting the default listener:

```
C:\>lsnrctl start

LSNRCTL for 32-bit Windows: Version 9.0.1.1.1 - Production
on 08-OCT-2001 20:32:09
Copyright (c) 1991, 2001, Oracle Corporation.  All rights
reserved.
Starting tnslsnr: please wait...
TNSLSNR for 32-bit Windows: Version 9.0.1.1.1 - Production
System parameter file is
D:\oracle\ora90\network\admin\listener.ora
Log messages written to
D:\oracle\ora90\network\log\listener.log
Listening on:
(DESCRIPTION=(ADDRESS=(PROTOCOL=tcp)(HOST=mprntw507953.cmg
.com)(PORT=1521)))
```

```
Listening on:
(DESCRIPTION=(ADDRESS=(PROTOCOL=ipc)(PIPENAME=\\.\pipe\EXT
PROC0ipc)))
Connecting to
(DESCRIPTION=(ADDRESS=(PROTOCOL=TCP)(HOST=mprntw507953)
(PORT=1521)))
STATUS of the LISTENER
------------------------
Alias                      LISTENER
Version                    TNSLSNR for 32-bit Windows:
                           Version 9.0.1.1.1 - Production
Start Date                 08-OCT-2001 20:32:11
Uptime                     0 days 0 hr. 0 min. 2 sec
Trace Level                off
Security                   OFF
SNMP                       OFF
Listener Parameter File
D:\oracle\ora90\network\admin\listener.ora
Listener Log File
D:\oracle\ora90\network\log\listener.log
Listening Endpoints Summary...
(DESCRIPTION=(ADDRESS=(PROTOCOL=tcp)(HOST=mprntw507953.cmg
.com)(PORT=1521)))
(DESCRIPTION=(ADDRESS=(PROTOCOL=ipc)(PIPENAME=\\.\pipe\EXT
PROC0ipc)))
Services Summary...
Service "MJW" has 1 instance(s).
  Instance "MJW", status UNKNOWN, has 1 handler(s) for
this service...
Service "PLSExtProc" has 1 instance(s).
  Instance "PLSExtProc", status UNKNOWN, has 1 handler(s)
for this service...
The command completed successfully
```

This listing shows a summary of information presented; it includes information such as the services the listener is listening for, the log locations, and whether tracing is enabled for the listener.

Reloading the Listener

If the listener is running and modifications are made to the `listener.ora` file either manually or with Oracle Net Manager, the listener has to be reloaded to refresh the listener with the most current information. The `reload` command will reread the `listener.ora` file for the new definitions. As you can see, it is not necessary to stop and start the listener to reload it. Though stopping and restarting the listener can also accomplish a reload, using the `reload` command is better because the listener is not actually stopped, which makes this process more efficient. The following code shows an example of the `reload` command:

Reloading the listener has no effect on clients connected to the Oracle server.

```
C:\>lsnrctl reload

LSNRCTL for 32-bit Windows: Version 9.0.1.1.1 - Production
on 08-OCT-2001 20:34:26
Copyright (c) 1991, 2001, Oracle Corporation.  All rights
reserved.
Connecting to
(DESCRIPTION=(ADDRESS=(PROTOCOL=TCP)(HOST=mprntw507953)
(PORT=1521)))
The command completed successfully
```

Showing the Status of the Listener

You can display the status of the listener by using the `status` command. The `status` command shows whether the listener is active, the locations of the logs and trace files, how long the listener has been running, and the services for the listener. This is a quick way to verify that the listener is up and running with no problems. The code below shows the result of the `lsnrctl status` command.

```
C:\>lsnrctl status
LSNRCTL for 32-bit Windows: Version 9.0.1.1.1 - Production
on 08-OCT-2001 20:36:14
Copyright (c) 1991, 2001, Oracle Corporation.  All rights
reserved.
```

```
Connecting to
(DESCRIPTION=(ADDRESS=(PROTOCOL=TCP)(HOST=mprntw507953)
(PORT=1521)))
STATUS of the LISTENER
------------------------
Alias                     LISTENER
Version                   TNSLSNR for 32-bit Windows:
                          Version 9.0.1.1.1 - Production
Start Date                08-OCT-2001 20:32:11
Uptime                    0 days 0 hr. 4 min. 4 sec
Trace Level               off
Security                  OFF
SNMP                      OFF
Listener Parameter File
D:\oracle\ora90\network\admin\listener.ora
Listener Log File
D:\oracle\ora90\network\log\listener.log
Listening Endpoints Summary...

(DESCRIPTION=(ADDRESS=(PROTOCOL=tcp)(HOST=mprntw507953.cmg
.com)(PORT=1521)))
(DESCRIPTION=(ADDRESS=(PROTOCOL=ipc)(PIPENAME=\\.\pipe\EXT
PROC0ipc)))
(DESCRIPTION=(ADDRESS=(PROTOCOL=tcps)(HOST=127.0.0.1)(PORT
=2482))(PRESENTATION=GIOP)(SESSION=RAW))
(DESCRIPTION=(ADDRESS=(PROTOCOL=tcp)(HOST=127.0.0.1)(PORT=
2481))(PRESENTATION=GIOP)(SESSION=RAW))
(DESCRIPTION=(ADDRESS=(PROTOCOL=tcps)(HOST=127.0.0.1)(PORT
=9090))(PRESENTATION=http://admin)(SESSION=RAW))
(DESCRIPTION=(ADDRESS=(PROTOCOL=tcp)(HOST=127.0.0.1)(PORT=
8080))(PRESENTATION=http://admin)(SESSION=RAW))
Services Summary...
Service "MJW" has 2 instance(s).
  Instance "MJW", status UNKNOWN, has 1 handler(s) for
this service...
  Instance "MJW", status READY, has 3 handler(s) for this
service...
Service "PLSExtProc" has 1 instance(s).
```

```
  Instance "PLSExtProc", status UNKNOWN, has 1 handler(s)
for this service...
The command completed successfully
```

Listing the Services for the Listener

The `lsnrctl services` command displays information about the services, such as whether or not the services have any dedicated prespawned server processes or dispatched processes associated with them, and how many connections have been accepted and rejected per service. Use this method to check if a listener is listening for a particular service. The following code shows an example of running the `services` command:

```
C:\>lsnrctl services

LSNRCTL for 32-bit Windows: Version 9.0.1.1.1 - Production
on 08-OCT-2001 20:39:14

Copyright (c) 1991, 2001, Oracle Corporation.  All rights
reserved.

Connecting to
(DESCRIPTION=(ADDRESS=(PROTOCOL=TCP)(HOST=mprntw507953)
(PORT=1521)))
Services Summary...
Service "MJW" has 2 instance(s).
  Instance "MJW", status UNKNOWN, has 1 handler(s) for
this service...
    Handler(s):
      "DEDICATED" established:0 refused:0
         LOCAL SERVER
  Instance "MJW", status READY, has 3 handler(s) for this
service...
    Handler(s):
      "D001" established:0 refused:0 current:0 max:1002
state:ready
         DISPATCHER <machine: MPRNTW507953, pid: 373>

(ADDRESS=(PROTOCOL=tcp)(HOST=mprntw507953.cmg.com)
  (PORT=1038))
```

```
      "D000" established:0 refused:0 current:0 max:1002
state:ready
         DISPATCHER <machine: MPRNTW507953, pid: 370>

(ADDRESS=(PROTOCOL=tcp)(HOST=mprntw507953.cmg.com)
  (PORT=1036))
      "DEDICATED" established:0 refused:0 state:ready
         LOCAL SERVER
Service "PLSExtProc" has 1 instance(s).
  Instance "PLSExtProc", status UNKNOWN, has 1 handler(s)
for this service...
    Handler(s):
      "DEDICATED" established:0 refused:0
         LOCAL SERVER
The command completed successfully
```

Other Commands in *lsnrctl*

There are other commands that can be run in `lsnrctl`. Table 2.3 shows a summary of the other commands. Type the command at the `lsnrctl` prompt to execute it.

TABLE 2.3 Summary of the `lsnrctl` Commands

Command	Definition
`change_password`	Allows a user to change the password needed to stop the listener.
`exit`	Exits the `lsnrctl` utility.
`quit`	Performs the same function as EXIT.
`reload`	Rereads the `listener.ora` file without stopping the listener. Used to refresh the listener if changes are made to the file.
`save_config`	Makes a copy of the `listener.ora` file called `listener.bak` when changes are made to the `listener.ora` file from `lsnrctl`.

TABLE 2.3 Summary of the `lsnrctl` Commands *(continued)*

Command	Definition
`services`	Lists a summary of services and details information on the number of connections established and the number of connections refused for each protocol service handler.
`start listener`	Starts the named listener.
`status listener`	Shows the status of the named listener.
`stop listener`	Stops the named listener.
`trace`	Turns on tracing for the listener.
`version`	Displays the version of the Oracle Net software and protocol adapters.

set Commands in *lsnrctl*

The `lsnrctl` utility also has commands called `set` commands. These commands are issued by typing **`set`** ***<commandname>*** at the LSNRCTL> prompt. The `set` commands are used to make modifications to the `listener.ora` file, such as setting up logging and tracing. Most of these parameters can be set using the Oracle Net Manager. To display the current setting of a parameter, use the `show` command. `show` is used to display the current settings of the parameters set using the `set` command. Table 2.4 shows a summary of the `lsnrctl` `set` commands. If you just type in **`set`** or **`show`**, you will see a listing of all of the commands.

TABLE 2.4 Summary of the `lsnrctl` `set` Commands

set Command	Description
`current_listener`	Sets the listener to make modifications to or shows the name of the current listener.
`displaymode`	Sets display for the `lsnrctl` utility to RAW, COMPACT, NORMAL, or VERBOSE.

TABLE 2.4 Summary of the lsnrctl set Commands *(continued)*

set Command	Description
log_status	Shows whether logging is on or off for the listener.
log_file	Shows the name of listener log file.
log_directory	Shows the log directory location.
rawmode	Shows more detail on STATUS and SERVICES when set to ON. Values: ON or OFF.
startup_waittime	Sets the length of time a listener will wait to respond to a status command in the lsnrctl command line utility.
spawn	Starts external services that the listener is listening for and that are running on the server.
save_config_on_stop	Saves changes to the listener.ora file when exiting lsnrctl.
trc_level	Sets the trace level to OFF, USER, ADMIN, SUPPORT.
trc_file	Sets the name of the listener trace file.
trc_directory	Sets the name of the listener trace directory.

Stopping the Listener

In order to stop the listener, you must issue the *lsnrctl stop* command. This command will stop the default listener. To stop a non-default listener, include the name of the listener. For example, to stop the LISTENER1, type **lsnrctl stop listener1**. If you are in the lsnrctl> facility, you will stop whatever listener is the current listener defined by the current_listener setting. To see what the current listener is set to, use the show command. The default value is LISTENER.

Stopping the listener does not affect clients connected to the database. It only means that no new connections can use this listener until the listener is restarted. The following code shows what the stop command looks like:

```
C:\>lsnrctl stop
```

```
LSNRCTL for 32-bit Windows: Version 9.0.1.1.1 - Production
on 08-OCT-2001 20:43:52
Copyright (c) 1991, 2001, Oracle Corporation.  All rights
reserved.
Connecting to
(DESCRIPTION=(ADDRESS=(PROTOCOL=TCP)(HOST=mprntw507953)
(PORT=1521)))
The command completed successfully
```

Dynamic Registration of Services

Oracle9*i* databases have the ability to automatically register their presence with an existing listener. The instance will register with the listener defined on the local machine. Dynamic service registration allows you to take advantage of other features, such as load balancing and automatic failover. The PMON process is responsible for registering this information with the listener.

When dynamic service registration is used, you will not see the service listed in the `listener.ora` file. To see the service listed, you should run the `lsnrctl services` command. Be aware that if the listener is started after the Oracle instance, there may be a time lag before the instance actually registers information with the listener.

In order for an instance to automatically register with a listener, the listener must be configured as a default listener, or you must specify the `init.ora` parameter `LOCAL_LISTENER`. The `LOCAL_LISTENER` parameter defines the location of the listener with which you want the Oracle server to register. A default listener definition is show below:

```
Listener Name = LISTENER
Port = 1521
Protocol = TCP/IP
```

And here is an example of the `LOCAL_LISTENER` parameter being used to register the Oracle server with a non-default listener:

```
local_listener="(ADDRESS_LIST = (Address =
(Protocol = TCP) (Host=weishan) (Port=1522)))
```

In the example above, the Oracle server will register with the listener listening on Port 1522 using TCP/IP. This is a non-default port location, so you must use the `LOCAL_LISTENER` parameter in order for the registration to take place.

Two other init.ora parameters need to be configured to allow an instance to register information with the listener. There are two parameters used to allow automatic registration, INSTANCE_NAME and SERVICE_NAMES.

The INSTANCE_NAME parameter is set to the name of the Oracle instance you would like to register with the listener. The SERVICE_NAMES parameter is a combination of the instance name and the domain name. The domain name is set to the value of the DB_DOMAIN initialization parameter. For example, if your DB_DOMAIN is set to GR.COM and your Oracle instance was DBA, the parameters would be set as follows:

```
Instance_name = DBA
Service_names = DBA.GR.COM
```

If you are not using domain names, the INSTANCE_NAME and SERVICE_NAMES parameters should be set to the same values.

Configure the Listener for Oracle9*i* JVM

You can configure the Oracle Net services to respond to requests to the Oracle9*i* Java Virtual Machine (JVM) over TCP/IP or TCP/IP with Secure Sockets Layer (SSL). The Java Virtual Machine runs within the Oracle server. Client processes can interact with processes that run within the JVM directly over HTTP or Internet Inter-ORB Protocol (IIOP).

If you are using pre-Oracle 8.1 instances with these options, the listener addresses must be configured manually as outlined below. If you are using Oracle9*i* databases and listeners, dynamic registration would take care of registering these services with the listener.

The steps to add the service name information are as follows:

1. Start the Oracle Net Manager.
2. Choose Local and Listener.
3. Select a listener and then choose Listening Locations from the drop-down choices on the right-hand panel.
4. Choose Add Address.
5. Select TCP/IP or TCP/IP With SSL.
6. Enter a hostname in the database host field.

7. Enter port 2481 for the TCP/IP protocol or 2482 for TCP/IP with SSL protocol.
8. Select Statically Dedicate This Address For Jserver Connections.
9. Select File and Save Configuration.

Here is an example of the entry made in the `listener.ora` file that contains the configuration information to connect to an Oracle server over TCP/IP with SSL using IIOP or HTTP:

```
# LISTENER.ORA Network Configuration File:
D:\oracle\ora90\NETWORK\ADMIN\listener.ora
# Generated by Oracle configuration tools.

LISTENER =
  (DESCRIPTION_LIST =
    (DESCRIPTION =
      (ADDRESS = (PROTOCOL = TCP)(HOST =
mprntw507953)(PORT = 1521)))
    (DESCRIPTION =
      (ADDRESS = (PROTOCOL = TCPS)(HOST =
mprntw507953)(PORT = 2482))
      (PROTOCOL_STACK =
        (PRESENTATION = GIOP)
        (SESSION = RAW)
      )
    )
  )
```

Troubleshooting Server-Side Connection Problems

Even if it seems that you have configured Oracle server-side components correctly, network errors may still occur that need to be addressed. There are any number of reasons for a network problem:

- The client, middle tier, or Oracle server may not be configured properly.
- The client may not be able to resolve the net service name.

- The underlying network protocol may not be active on the server; for example, the TCP/IP process on the server may not be running.
- The user may enter an incorrect net service name, user ID, or password.

These types of errors can be diagnosed and corrected easily. In the section entitled "Server-Side Computer and Database Checks," you will see how to diagnose and correct connection problems originating from the Oracle server. In the next chapter, we will discuss troubleshooting problems with client-side network configuration.

When a client has a connection problem that is up to you to fix, it is helpful to first gather information about the situation. Make sure you record the following information:

- The Oracle error received.
- The location of the client. Is the client connecting from a remote location, or is the client connected directly to the server?
- The name of the Oracle server to which the client is attempting to connect.
- Check if other clients are having connection problems. If other clients are experiencing problems, are these clients in the same general location?
- Ask the user what is failing. Is it the application being used or the connection?

We will now look at the particular network areas to check and the methods used to further diagnose connection problems from the Oracle server. We will also look at the Oracle error codes that will help identify and correct the problems.

Server-Side Computer and Database Checks

There are several server-side checks that can be performed if a connection problem occurs. Before running such checks, make sure the machine is running, that the Oracle server is available, and that the listener is active. Here is a summary of checks to perform on the server.

Check Server Machine

Make sure the server machine is active and available for connections. On some systems, it is possible to start a system in a restricted mode that allows only supervisors or administrators to log in to the computer. Make sure that the computer is open and available to all users.

On a TCP/IP network, you can use the ping utility to test for connectivity to the server. Here is an example of using ping to test a network connection to a machine called `matt`:

```
C:\users\default>ping matt

Pinging cupira03.cmg.com [10.69.30.113] with 32 bytes of
data:

Reply from 10.69.30.113: bytes=32 time=10ms TTL=248
Reply from 10.69.30.113: bytes=32 time=10ms TTL=248
Reply from 10.69.30.113: bytes=32 time<10ms TTL=248
Reply from 10.69.30.113: bytes=32 time=10ms TTL=248
```

The reply indicates that the machine can be seen on the network.

Check Database

Make sure the database is running. Connect to the Oracle server and log in to the database using a tool like SQL*Plus. You should first attempt to do a local connection, which does not use the Oracle listener.

To connect to the Oracle server using a local connection, set your `ORACLE_SID` environmental variable to the name of the Oracle instance you want to connect to. Then, attempt to connect to SQL*Plus. The following example is a connection sequence on Windows NT/2000 that fails because the database is not running. For example, if the database you are attempting to connect to were named `MJW`, the following code example could be used in a Windows NT/2000 environment for your test:

```
D:\>set ORACLE_SID=MJW
D:\>sqlplus system/manager

SQL*Plus: Release 9.0.1.0.0 - Production on Mon Oct 15
11:32:05 2001

(c) Copyright 2000 Oracle Corporation.  All rights
reserved.

ERROR:
ORA-01034: ORACLE not available
```

```
ORA-27101: shared memory realm does not exist


Enter user-name:
```

An ORA-01034 error means the Oracle instance is not running. You need to start up the Oracle instance. The ORA-27101 error means that there is currently no instance available to connect to for the specified ORACLE_SID.

Verify That Database Is Open to All Users

A database can be opened in restricted mode. This means that only users with restricted mode access can use the system. This is not a networking problem, but it will lead to clients being unable to connect to the Oracle server.

```
D:\>sqlplus scott/tiger@MJW

SQL*Plus: Release 9.0.1.0.0 - Production on Mon Oct 15
11:37:25 2001

(c) Copyright 2000 Oracle Corporation.  All rights
reserved.

ERROR:
ORA-01035: ORACLE only available to users with RESTRICTED
SESSION privilege


Enter user-name:
```

Check User Privileges

Make sure the user attempting to establish the connection has been granted the CREATE SESSION privilege to the database. This privilege is needed for a user to connect to the Oracle server. If the client does not have this privilege, you must grant it to the user. To do so, follow this example:

```
D:\oracle\ora90\BIN>sqlplus matt/matt
SQL*Plus: Release 9.0.1.0.1 - Production on Mon Oct 15
14:04:51 2001
```

```
(c) Copyright 2001 Oracle Corporation.  All rights
reserved.
ERROR:
ORA-01045: user MATT lacks CREATE SESSION privilege; logon
denied
```

Here is an example of how a DBA would grant the CREATE SESSION privilege to a user:

```
SQL> grant create session to matt;
Grant succeeded
SQL>
```

Server-Side Checks Network Checks

After you validate that the server where the database is located is up and available and you verify that the user has proper privileges, you should begin checking for any underlying network problems on the server.

Check Listener

Make sure the listener is running on the Oracle server. Make sure you check the services for all of the listeners on the Oracle server; you can use the `lsnrctl status` command to do this. The following command shows the status of the default listener named `LISTENER`:

```
D:\>lsnrctl status

LSNRCTL for 32-bit Windows: Version 9.0.1.1.1 - Production
on 03-JAN-2002 10:56:04

Copyright (c) 1991, 2001, Oracle Corporation.  All rights
reserved.

Connecting to
(DESCRIPTION=(ADDRESS=(PROTOCOL=TCP)(HOST=mprntw507953)
   (PORT=1521)))
```

```
STATUS of the LISTENER
------------------------
Alias                     LISTENER
Version                   TNSLSNR for 32-bit Windows:
                          Version 9.0.1.1.1 - Production
Start Date                03-JAN-2002 08:38:30
Uptime                    0 days 2 hr. 17 min. 34 sec
Trace Level               off
Security                  OFF
SNMP                      OFF
Listener Parameter File
D:\oracle\ora90\network\admin\listener.ora
Listener Log File
D:\oracle\ora90\network\log\listener.log
Listening Endpoints Summary...
 (DESCRIPTION=(ADDRESS=(PROTOCOL=tcp)(HOST=10.72.127.148)
   (PORT=2481))(PRESENTATION=GIOP)(SESSION=RAW))

(DESCRIPTION=(ADDRESS=(PROTOCOL=tcps)(HOST=10.72.127.148)
  (PORT=2482))(PRESENTATION=GIOP)(SESSION=RAW))
Services Summary...
Service "MJW" has 1 instance(s).
Instance "MJW", status READY, has 3 handler(s) for this
service...
Service "PLSExtProc" has 1 instance(s).
  Instance "PLSExtProc", status UNKNOWN, has 1 handler(s)
for this service...
The command completed successfully
```

Also check the services for which the listener is listening. You must see the service to which the client is attempting to connect. If the service is not listed, the client may be entering the wrong service, or the listener may not be configured to listen for this service.

Check *GLOBAL_DBNAME*

If the client is using the hostnaming method, make sure the `GLOBAL_DBNAME` parameter is set to the name of the host machine. You can find this parameter in the service definition of the `listener.ora` file. Verify the setting by reviewing the `listener.ora` configuration.

Check Listener Protocols

Check the protocols the listener is configured for. This is displayed by the `lsnrctl` services command. Make sure the protocol of the service matches the protocol the client is using when requesting a connection. If the client is requesting to connect with a protocol the listener is not listening for, the user will receive an ORA-12541 "No Listener" error.

Check Server Protocols

Make sure the underlying network protocol on the server is active. For systems that run TCP/IP, you can attempt to use the `ping` command to ping the server. This will verify that the TCP/IP daemon process is active on the server. There are other ways to check this, such as verifying the services on Windows NT/2000 or with the `ps` command on Unix. An example of the `ping` command can be found in the next chapter.

Check Server Protocol Adapters

Make sure the appropriate protocol adapters have been installed on the server. On most platforms, you can invoke the Oracle Universal Installer program and check the list of installed protocols. On Unix platforms, you can use the adapter utility to make sure the appropriate adapters have been linked to Oracle. An example of how to run this utility is provided below. This utility is located in the `$ORACLE_HOME/bin` directory.

```
[root@localhost] ./adapters oracle

Net protocol adapters linked with oracle are:

    BEQ
    IPC
    TCP/IP
    RAW

Net Naming Adapters linked with oracle are:

    Oracle TNS Naming Adapter
    Oracle Naming Adapter
```

```
Advanced Networking Option/Network Security products
 linked with oracle are:

   Oracle Security server Authentication Adapter
```

If the required protocol adapter is not listed, you have to install the adapter. This can be done by using the Oracle Installer, installing the Oracle Net Server software, and choosing the appropriate adapters during the installation process.

Check for Connection Timeouts

If the client is receiving an ORA-12535 or an ORA-12547 error, the client is timing out before a valid connection is established. This can occur if you have a slow network connection. You can attempt to solve this problem by increasing the time that the listener will wait for a valid response from the client; simply set the `CONNECT_TIMEOUT` parameter to a higher number. This is the number of seconds the listener waits for a valid response from the client when establishing a connection.

Oracle Net Logging and Tracing on the Server

If a network problem persists, you can use logging and tracing to help resolve it. Oracle generates information into log files and trace files that can assist you in tracking down network connection problems. You can use logging to find out general information about the success or failure of certain components of the Oracle Network. Tracing can be used to get in-depth information about specific network connections.

By default, Oracle produces logs for clients and the Oracle listener. Client logging cannot be disabled.

Logging records significant events, such as starting and stopping the listener, along with certain kinds of network errors. Errors are generated in the log in the form of an error stack. The listener log records information such as the version number, connection attempts, and the protocols it is listening for. Logging can be enabled at the client, middle tier, and server locations.

Tracing, which you can also enable at the client, middle-tier, or server location, records all events that occur on a network, even when an error does not happen. The trace file provides a great deal of information that logs do not, such as the number of network round trips made during network connection or the number of packets sent and received during a network connection. Tracing enables you to collect a thorough listing of the actual sequence of the statements as a network connection is being processed. This gives you a much more detailed picture of what is occurring with connections the listener is processing.

Real World Scenario

Use Tracing Sparingly

Tracing should be used only as a last resort if you are having connectivity problems between the client and server. You should complete all of the server-side checks described above before you resort to tracing. This is because the tracing process generates a significant amount of overhead and, depending on the trace level set, it can create some very large files. This activity will impede system I/O performance because of all of the information that is written to the logs, and if left unchecked, it could fill up your disk or filesystem.

I was once involved with a large project that was using JDBC to connect to the Oracle server. We were having difficulty with connections being periodically dropped between the JDBC client and the Oracle server. Tracing was enabled to try to assist in figuring out what the problem was. We did eventually correct the problem (it was a problem with how our DNS Names server was configured), but the tracing was left on inadvertently. When the system eventually went into production, the trace files grew so large that they filled up the disk where tracing was being collected. To prevent this from happening, it is important to periodically ensure that the trace parameters are not turned on, and if they are, they should be turned off.

Use the Oracle Net Manager to enable most logging and tracing parameters. Many of the logging and tracing parameters are found in the `sqlnet.ora` file. Let's take a look at how to enable logging and tracing for the various components in an Oracle Network.

Server Logging

By default, the listener is configured to enable the generation of a log file. The log file records information about listener startup and shutdown, successful and unsuccessful connection attempts, and certain types of network errors. By default, the listener log location is `$ORACLE_HOME/network/log` on Unix and `%ORACLE_HOME%\network\log` on Windows NT/2000. The default name of the file is `listener.log`.

The format of the information in the `listener.log` file is a fixed-length, delimited format with each field separated by an asterisk. If you want to do further analysis of the information in the log, the data in the log can be loaded into an Oracle table using a tool like SQL*Loader. Notice in the sample listing below that the file contains information about connection attempts, the name of the program executing the request, and the name of the client attempting to connect. The last field will contain a zero if a request was successfully completed.

```
TNSLSNR for 32-bit Windows: Version 9.0.1.1.1 - Production
on 02-OCT-2001 09:52:02

Copyright (c) 1991, 2001, Oracle Corporation.  All rights
reserved.

System parameter file is
D:\oracle\ora90\network\admin\listener.ora
Log messages written to
D:\oracle\ora90\network\log\listener.log
Trace information written to
D:\oracle\ora90\network\trace\listener.trc
Trace level is currently 0

Started with pid=260
Listening on:
(DESCRIPTION=(ADDRESS=(PROTOCOL=tcp)(HOST=mprntw507953.cmg
.com)(PORT=1521)))
Listening on:
(DESCRIPTION=(ADDRESS=(PROTOCOL=ipc)(PIPENAME=\\.\pipe\EXT
PROC0ipc)))

TIMESTAMP * CONNECT DATA [* PROTOCOL INFO] * EVENT [* SID]
* RETURN CODE
```

```
02-OCT-2001 09:52:07 * (CONNECT_
DATA=(CID=(PROGRAM=)(HOST=)(USER=CBIWEIS))(COMMAND=status)
(ARGUMENTS=64)(SERVICE=LISTENER)(VERSION=150999297)) *
status * 0
02-OCT-2001 10:15:54 * service_register * MJW * 0
02-OCT-2001 10:16:02 * service_update * MJW * 0
02-OCT-2001 10:16:03 * service_update * MJW * 0
```

Server Tracing

As mentioned earlier, tracing gathers information about the flow of traffic across a network connection. Data is transmitted back and forth in the form of packets. A packet contains sender information, receiver information, and data. Even a single network request may generate a large amount of packets.

In the trace file, each line of the file starts with the name of the procedure executed in one of the Oracle Net layers followed by a set of hexadecimal numbers. The hexadecimal numbers are the actual data transmitted. If you are not encrypting the data, sometimes you will see the actual data after the hexadecimal numbers.

Each of the Oracle Net procedures is responsible for a different action. Each packet has a different code type depending on the action being taken. All of the packet types start with NSP. Here is a summary of the common packet types.

Packet Keyword	Packet Type
NSPTAC	Accept
NSPTRF	Refuse
NSPTRS	Resend
NSPDA	Data
NSPCNL	Control
NSPTMK	Marker

If you are doing server-to-server communications and have a `sqlnet.ora` file on the server, you can enter information in the Server Information section of the Oracle Net Manager tracing screen. This provides tracing information for server-to-server communications.

There are also several numeric codes that are used to help diagnose and troubleshoot problems with Oracle Net connections. These codes can be found in the trace files. Here is an example of a line from the trace file that contains a code value:

```
nspsend: plen=12, type=4
```

Here is a summary of the numeric codes that you could encounter in a trace file.

Code	Packet Type
1	Connect packet
2	Accept packet
3	Acknowledge packet
4	Refuse packet
5	Redirect packet
6	Data packet
7	Null packet, empty data
9	Abort packet
11	Resend packet
12	Marker packet
13	Attention packet
14	Control information packet

Enabling Server Tracing

You can enable server tracing from the same Oracle Net Manager screens shown earlier. Simply choose the Tracing Enabled radio button. The default filename and location is `ORACLE_HOME/network/trace/listener.trc` in Unix and `ORACLE_HOME\network\trace\listener.trc` on Windows NT/2000. You can set the trace level to `OFF`, `USER`, `ADMIN`, or `SUPPORT`. The `USER` level will detect specific user errors. The `ADMIN` level contains all of the user-level information along with installation-specific errors. `SUPPORT` is the highest level and can be used to produce information that may be beneficial to Oracle

Support personnel. This level also can produce very large trace files. The following listing shows an example of a listener trace file:

```
nsglhfre: entry
nsglhrem: entry
nsglhrem: entry
nsglhfre: Deallocating cxd 0x4364d0.
nsglhfre: exit
nsglma: Reporting the following error stack:
TNS-01150: The address of the specified listener name is
incorrect
 TNS-01153: Failed to process string:
(DESCRIPTION=(ADDRESS=(PROTOCOL=TC)(HOST=mprntw507953)
   (PORT=1521)))
nsrefuse: entry
nsdo: entry
nsdo: cid=0, opcode=67, *bl=437, *what=10, uflgs=0x0,
cflgs=0x3
nsdo: rank=64, nsctxrnk=0
nsdo: nsctx: state=2, flg=0x4204, mvd=0
nsdo: gtn=152, gtc=152, ptn=10, ptc=2019
nscon: entry
nscon: sending NSPTRF packet
nspsend: entry
nspsend: plen=12, type=4
ntpwr: entry
ntpwr: exit
```

You can tell what section of the Oracle Net stack the trace file is in by looking at the first two characters of the program names in the trace file. In the example above, `nscon` refers to the network session (NS) sublayer of the Oracle Net Foundation Layer. A message is being sent back to the client in the form of an NSPTRF packet. This is a *refuse packet*, which means that the requested action is being denied.

You see the Oracle error number embedded in the error message. In this example, a TNS-01153 error was generated. This error means that the listener failed to start. It also shows the line of information that the listener is failing on. This error could be the result of a problem with another process listening on the same location or a syntax problem in the `listener.ora` file. Basically, this error states that a syntax error has occurred, because the protocol was specified as TC and not TCP. In addition to this error, there are some more recent ones. The most recent errors are located at the bottom of the file.

The next example shows a section of the `listener.ora` file with the logging and tracing parameters enabled:

```
# D:\ORACLE\ORA90\NETWORK\ADMIN\LISTENER.ORA Configuration
# File:D:\Oracle\Ora90\NETWORK\ADMIN\listener.ora
# Generated by Oracle Oracle Net Manager

TRACE_LEVEL_LISTENER = ADMIN
TRACE_FILE_LISTENER = LISTENER.trc
TRACE_DIRECTORY_LISTENER = D:\Oracle\Ora8\network\trace
LOG_DIRECTORY_LISTENER = D:\Oracle\Ora8\network\log
LOG_FILE_LISTENER = LISTENER.log
```

Table 2.5 contains a summary of the meaning of each of these parameters.

TABLE 2.5 `listener.ora` Log and Trace Parameters

Parameter	Definition
TRACE_LEVEL_LISTENER	This parameter turns tracing on and off. The levels are OFF, USER, ADMIN, and SUPPORT. SUPPORT generates the greatest amount of data.
TRACE_FILE_LISTENER	The name of the trace file.
TRACE_DIRECTORY_LISTENER	The directory where trace files are written.
LOG_DIRECTORY_LISTENER	The directory where log files are written.
LOG_FILE_LISTENER	The name of the listener log file.

Summary

The listener is the main server-side component in the Oracle Net environment. Listener configuration information is stored in the `listener.ora` file, and the listener is managed using the `lsnrctl` command line utility. You configure the listener by using the Oracle Net Manager. The Oracle Net Manager provides a graphical interface for creating most of the Oracle Net files you will use for Oracle including the `listener.ora` file. If multiple listeners are configured, each one will have a separate entry in the `listener.ora` file.

Depending on the capabilities of the operating system, two types of dedicated server connections are possible: bequeath and redirect connections. Bequeath connections are possible if the operating system supports a direct handoff of connection information from one process to another. Redirect sessions are used when the operating system does not support this type of interprocess communication. It requires extra communication between the listener process, the server process, and the client process.

Oracle9*i* provides a feature called Dynamic Registration of Services. This feature allows an Oracle instance to automatically register itself with a listener. The listener must be configured with TCP/IP and listen on Port 1521, or you must specify the parameter `LOCAL_LISTENER` in the `init.ora` file. You have to set the parameters `INSTANCE_NAME` and `SERVICE_NAMES` in the `init.ora` file for the Oracle instance to enable Dynamic Registration.

You can configure logging and tracing on the Oracle Server using Oracle Net Manager. Logging records significant events, such as starting and stopping the listener, along with certain kinds of network errors. Errors are generated in the log in the form of an error stack. Tracing records all events that occur even when an error does not happen. The trace file provides a great deal of information that logs do not. Tracing uses much more space than logging and can also have an impact on system performance. Enable tracing only if other methods of troubleshooting fail to resolve the problem.

Configuring the Oracle server correctly is the first step to successfully implementing Oracle in a network environment. If you do not have the Oracle server network components configured correctly, you will be unable to provide connection support to clients in the Oracle environment. The server network components should be configured and tested prior to moving on to configuring the Oracle clients as described in Chapter 3.

Exam Essentials

Be able to define the main responsibilities of the Oracle listener. To fully understand the function of the Oracle listener, you should understand how the listener responds to client connection requests. In addition, you should know the difference between bequeath connections and redirect connections, and you should know under what circumstances the listener will use each. Also, you should be able to outline the steps involved in using each of these connection types.

Be able to define what the `listener.ora` file is and the ways in which the file is created. To understand the purpose of this file, you should know its default contents and know how to make changes to it using the Oracle Net Manager tool. In addition, you should be able to define the different sections of the file and know the definitions of the optional parameters it contains. You should also understand the structure of the `listener.ora` file when one or more listeners are configured.

Understand how to use the `lsnrctl` command line utility. In order to start up and shut down the listener, you should know how to use the `lsnrctl` command line utility. You will also need to be able to explain the command line options for the `lsnrctl` utility, such as `services`, `status`, and `reload`. When using this utility, you should also know the different options available to you and you should be able to define the various `set` commands.

Understand the concepts of static and dynamic service registration. Be able to define the difference between static service registration and dynamic service registration and know what the advantages are of using dynamic service registration over static service registration. Also, be aware of the situations in which you have to use static service registration. And lastly, be familiar with the `init.ora` parameters that you will need to set in order to enable dynamic service registration.

Understand the basics of Oracle and Java connectivity. You should know the basics of configuring Oracle to enable connections to the Oracle9*i* JVM using IIOP and HTTP.

Be able to diagnose and correct network connectivity problems. You should know the types of server-side errors that can occur and how to diagnose and correct these problems. You should be able to define the difference between logging and tracing and know how to use the types of packet information that you may find in a trace file.

Key Terms

Before you take the exam, be certain you are familiar with the following terms:

bequeath connection	`lsnrctl`
dedicated server	`lsnrctl stop`
dynamic service registration	port
host	redirect connection
listener	refuse packet
`listener.ora`	static service registration
logging	tracing

Review Questions

1. Which file must be present on the Oracle server to start the Oracle listener?

   A. `listener.ora`

   B. `lsnrctl.ora`

   C. `sqlnet.ora`

   D. `tnsnames.ora`

2. What are the possible ways in which the listener may connect a user to an Oracle9*i* instance? (Choose all that apply.)

   A. Prespawned connection

   B. Redirect connection

   C. Bequeath connection

   D. Multipass connection

3. What is the default name of the Oracle listener?

   A. `lsnrctl`

   B. `Listen`

   C. `sqlnet`

   D. `tnslistener`

   E. None of the above

4. What is the maximum number of databases a listener processes?

   A. 1 database

   B. 2 databases

   C. 10 databases

   D. 25 databases

   E. None of the above

5. What is the maximum number of `listener.ora` files that should exist on a server?

   A. One

   B. Two

   C. Four

   D. Eight

   E. None of the above

6. Which of the following does this phrase characterize? "…records all events that occur on a network, even when an error does not happen."

   A. Oracle Net Manager

   B. Network tracing

   C. Network logging

   D. None of the above

7. When automatic registration of services is used, you will not see the service listed in which of the following files?

   A. `sqlnet.ora`

   B. `tnsnames.ora`

   C. `listener.ora`

   D. None of the above

8. Which of the following are *not* default `listener.ora` settings? (Choose all that apply.)

   A. `Listener name = LISTENER`

   B. `Port = 1521`

   C. `Protocol = IPX`

   D. `Protocol = TCP/IP`

   E. `Listener name = lsnrctl`

9. Which of the following is the command-line interface used to administer the listener?

   A. `LISTENER`

   B. `lismgr`

   C. `TCPCTL`

   D. `lsnrctl`

   E. None of the above

10. Which Oracle Net Manager icon should you choose to manage listeners?

    A. Services

    B. Listener Names

    C. Profile

    D. Listeners

    E. None of the above

11. Which parameter sets the number of seconds a server process waits to get a valid client request?

    A. `connect_waittime_`*`listener_name`*

    B. `connect_wait_`*`listener_name`*

    C. `timeout_`*`listener_name`*

    D. `connect_timeout_`*`listener_name`*

12. Which of the following is the trace level that will produce the largest amount of information?

    A. `ADMIN`

    B. `USER`

    C. `ALL`

    D. `SUPPORT`

    E. None of the above

13. What is the maximum number of listeners that can be configured for a server?

    A. One

    B. Two

    C. Four

    D. Eight

    E. None of the above

14. There is a listener called `LISTENER`. Which of the following is the correct way to start this listener?

    A. `lsnrctl startup listener`

    B. `lsnrctl start`

    C. `listener start`

    D. `listener start listener`

15. There is a listener called `listenerA`. Which of the following is the correct command to start this listener?

    A. `lsnrctl startup listenerA`

    B. `lsnrctl start`

    C. `listener start`

    D. `listener startup`

    E. `lsnrctl start listenerA`

16. Modifications have been made to the `listener.ora` file from Oracle Net Manager. When will these modifications take effect?

    A. Immediately

    B. After exiting the Oracle Net Manager

    C. Upon saving the `listener.ora` file

    D. After executing `lsnrctl refresh`

    E. None of the above

17. There is a listener called `listener1` that you want to edit using the `lsnrctl` utility. What command would you use to target the listener as the current listener for editing?

A. `set current_listener listener1`

B. `accept current_listener listener1`

C. `reload listener listener1`

D. `refresh listener listener1`

18. Modifications have been made using the `lsnrctl` facility. What must be set to `ON` in order to make the changes permanent?

A. `save_configuration`

B. `save_listener.ora`

C. `save_config_on_stop`

D. `configuration_save`

19. The administrator or DBA wants to make a backup of the listener file after making changes using `lsnrctl`. Which command must be implemented to make this backup from the `lsnrctl` facility?

A. `create_backup`

B. `save_config_on_stop`

C. `save_config`

D. `save_backup`

20. What is the port number to use when you are configuring the listener for Oracle9*i* JVM on TCP/IP with SSL?

A. 1521

B. 2482

C. 2481

D. 1526

E. None of the above

Answers to Review Questions

1. A. The listener is the process that manages incoming connection requests. The `listener.ora` file is used to configure the listener. The `sqlnet.ora` file is an optional client- and server-side file. The `tnsnames.ora` file is used for doing local naming resolution. There is no such file as `lsnrctl.ora`.

2. B, C. The listener can handle a connection request in one of two ways: it can spawn a process and bequeath (pass) control to that process, or it can redirect the process to a dedicated process or dispatcher when using Oracle Shared Server.

3. E. When creating a listener with the Oracle Net Manager, the Assistant recommends `LISTENER` as the default name. When you are starting and stopping the listener via the command line tool, the tool assumes the name of the listener is `LISTENER` if no listener name is supplied.

4. E. There is no physical limit to the number of services a listener can listen for.

5. A. Although a listener can listen for an unlimited number of services, only one `listener.ora` file is used. If multiple listeners are configured, there will still be only one listener.

6. B. Network tracing is what records all events on the network even if there is no error involved. Tracing should be used sparingly and only as a last resort in the case of network problems. Logging will log only significant events such as listener startup and connection requests.

7. C. When services are dynamically registered with the listener, their information is not present in the `listener.ora` file.

8. C, E. A default listener has a name of `LISTENER` and listens on Port 1521 for TCP/IP connections.

9. D. `LISTENER` is the default name of the Oracle listener. There is no such utility as `lismgr`. TCPCTL was actually an old utility used to start and stop the SQL*NET version 1 listener. The `lsnrctl` command is used to manage the listener.

10. D. Become familiar with the Oracle Net Manager interface. Listeners is the correct choice. Profile is used for `sqlnet.ora` administration. The other choices are not valid menu options.

11. D. When a user makes a connection request, the listener passes control to some server process or dispatcher. Once the user is attached to this process, all negotiations and interaction with the database pass through this process. If the user supplies an invalid user ID or password, the process waits for a period of time for a valid response. If the user does not contact the server process with a valid response in the allotted time, the server process terminates, and the user must contact the listener so that the listener can again spawn a process or redirect the client to an existing dispatcher. This period of time that the process waits is specified by the `connect_timeout_`*`listener_name`* parameter. This parameter is specified in seconds.

12. D. The highest level of tracing available is the `SUPPORT` level. This is the level that would be used to trace packet traffic information.

13. E. There is no maximum number of listeners that can be configured per server.

14. B. The default listener name is `LISTENER`. Since this is the default, simply enter `lsnrctl start`. The name `LISTENER` is assumed to be the listener to start in this case.

15. E. Oracle expects the listener to be called `LISTENER` by default. The name of the facility to start the listener is `lsnrctl`. Using `lsnrctl start` will start the default listener. To start a listener with another name, enter **`lsnrctl start`** ***`listener_name`***.

16. E. Anytime modifications are made to the listener file using the Oracle Net Manager, either manually or by using `lsnrctl`, the listener must be reloaded for the modifications to take effect. To perform this reload, get to a command line and enter **`lsnrctl reload`**. You could also stop and start the listener, which will have the same effect. Since `lsnrctl reload` is not one of the choices, none of the above is the correct answer.

17. A. If you want to administer any listener besides the default listener when using `lsnrctl`, you must target that listener. `set` commands are used to change `lsnrctl` session settings. So, `set current_listener listener1` would be the correct command.

18. C. Changes made to the `listener.ora` file in the `lsnrctl` facility can be made permanent. To make changes permanent, set the `save_config_on_stop` option to `ON`.

19. C. The DBA can make a backup of the existing `listener.ora` file after making modifications to it using `lsnrctl`. The backup will be named `listener.bak`. This is done with the `save_config` option.

20. B. Port 2482 is the port to use when you want to configure Oracle Net for HTTP and IIOP connections over TCP/IP with SSL. Port 2481 is used when TCP/IP is used for HTTP and IIOP connections.

Configuring Oracle Net for the Client

ORACLE9*i*: DBA FUNDAMENTALS II EXAM OBJECTIVES COVERED IN THIS CHAPTER:

✓ Describe the difference between host naming and local service name resolution.

✓ Use Oracle Net Configuration Assistant to configure: Host Naming, Local naming method, Net service names.

✓ Perform simple connection troubleshooting.

Exam objectives are subject to change at any time without prior notice and at Oracle's sole discretion. Please visit Oracle's Certification website (`http://www.oracle.com/education/certification/`) for the most current exam objectives listing.

Once the Oracle server is properly configured, you can focus on getting the clients configured to allow for connectivity to the Oracle server. This chapter details the basic network elements of Oracle client configuration. It discusses the different types of service name models you can choose from when creating net service names. In addition, it details available service resolution configurations and how to configure hostnaming and localnaming using the Oracle Net Manager. It also discusses the types of client-side failures that can happen and how to troubleshoot client-side connection problems.

It is important to understand how to configure the Oracle clients for connectivity to the Oracle servers. Without proper knowledge of how to configure the client, you are limited in your connection choices to the server. The DBA must understand the network needs of the organization and the type of connectivity that is required, client/server connections versus 3-tier connectivity, for example, in order to make the appropriate choices about client-side configuration. This chapter should help clarify the client-side connectivity options available to you and how to troubleshoot client connection problems.

Client-Side Names Resolution Options

When a client needs to connect to an Oracle server, the client must supply three pieces of information: their user ID, password, and net service name. The net service name provides the necessary information, in the form of a connect descriptor, to locate an Oracle service in a network.

This connect descriptor describes the path to the Oracle server and its service name, which is an alias for an Oracle database. This information is kept in different locations depending on the names resolution method that you choose. The three methods of net service name resolution are hostnaming, localnaming, and the Oracle Internet Directory. Normally, you will choose just one of these methods, but you can use any combination.

The Oracle Names Server is still available in Oracle9*i*, although no further development is being done for the Oracle Names Server. The Oracle Names Server is being replaced by the Oracle Internet Directory as the preferred names resolution method for large Oracle networks.

Choosing hostnaming is advantageous when you want to reduce the amount of configuration work necessary. However, there are a few prerequisites that you must consider before you use this option; we will talk about these and discuss configuring this method for use shortly. This option is typically used in small networks that have few Oracle servers to maintain.

Localnaming is the most popular names resolution method used. This method involves configuring the `tnsnames.ora` file, which contains the connect descriptor information to resolve the net service names. You will see how to configure localnaming after the discussion of hostnaming that follows.

Oracle Internet Directory is advantageous when you are dealing with complex networks that have many Oracle servers. When the DBA chooses this method, they will be able to configure and manage net service names and connect descriptor information in a central location. It is important to understand that Oracle Internet Directory is available, but in-depth knowledge of this option is not necessary for success on the OCP exam.

The Hostnaming Method

In small networks with few Oracle servers to manage, you can take advantage of the *hostnaming method*. Hostnaming saves you from having to do configuration work on the clients, although it does have limitations. There are four prerequisites to using hostnaming:

- You must use TCP/IP as your network protocol.
- You must not use any advanced networking features, such as Oracle Connection Manager.
- You must have an external naming service, such as DNS, or have a `HOSTS` file available to the client.
- The listener must be set up with the `GLOBAL_DBNAME` parameter equal to the name of the machine.

Configuring the Hostnaming Method

By default, Oracle will only attempt to use the hostnaming method from the client after it attempts connections using localnaming. If you want to override this default search path for resolving names, set the *NAMES.DIRECTORY_PATH* parameter in the `sqlnet.ora` file on the client so that it searches for hostnaming only. You can configure this parameter using the Oracle Net Manager (see Figure 3.1).

To configure the parameter using Oracle Net Manager, choose Profile from the Local tab and select Naming from the drop-down list at the top of the screen. This brings up a list of naming methods that are available. The Selected Methods list displays the naming methods being used and the order in which the methods are used to resolve service names. The Available Methods list displays the methods that have not been included in the selected methods.

To change the list of available methods, use your mouse to highlight a method name and click the arrow key (>) to include it in the list of selected methods. You can remove a name by selecting it in the list of selected methods and clicking the other arrow key (<). You can also use the Demote and Promote buttons to change the order of the list. Select a name from the Selected Methods list and click the Demote button to move the name down the list or click the Promote button to move the name up the list. Make sure that HOSTNAME shows up in the Selected Methods column.

FIGURE 3.1 Oracle Net Manager `sqlnet.ora` Profile screen

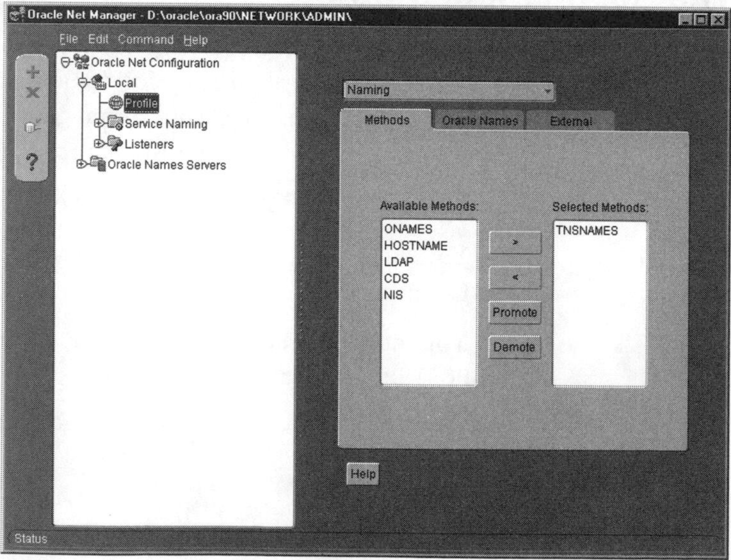

Once you save the configuration, Oracle will update the `sqlnet.ora` file with the changes that you have made. The following is an example of the `sqlnet.ora` file.

```
# SQLNET.ORA Network Configuration File:
D:\oracle\ora90\network\admin\sqlnet.ora
# Generated by Oracle configuration tools.

NAMES.DEFAULT_DOMAIN = cmg.com
NAMES.DIRECTORY_PATH= (HOSTNAME)
```

The hostnaming method does not require any client-side configuration files. As long as the client has the TCP/IP adapter installed and the Oracle client Net Services, the client can use the hostnaming method. You can check TCP/IP connectivity from the client using the TCP/IP utility ping. *Ping* attempts to contact the server by sending a small request packet. The server will respond in kind with an acknowledgment. The following code shows an example of how ping works and how fast the round trip takes from client to server and back:

```
C:\>ping mil02ora

Pinging mil02ora [10.1.5.210] with 32 bytes of data:

Reply from 10.1.5.210: bytes=32 time<10ms TTL=128
Reply from 10.1.5.210: bytes=32 time<10ms TTL=128
Reply from 10.1.5.210: bytes=32 time<10ms TTL=128
Reply from 10.1.5.210: bytes=32 time<10ms TTL=128
```

The server must be configured with a listener running TCP/IP. The listener must be listening on the default port of 1521. If the instance has not been dynamically registered with the listener, you must configure the listener with the `GLOBAL_DBNAME` parameter (Chapter 2, "Configuring Oracle Net on the Server," explains how to configure the listener.) The code listed below shows what the `listener.ora` file looks like when it is configured with this parameter. In this example, the hostname is `GR99c0073`. This is the name of the physical machine on which the listener process is running.

```
# C:\V9i\NETWORK\ADMIN\LISTENER.ORA Configuration
# File:C:\v9i\NETWORK\ADMIN\listener.ora
# Generated by Oracle Oracle Net Manager

LISTENER =
  (DESCRIPTION =
```

```
      (ADDRESS = (PROTOCOL = TCP)(HOST = gr99c0073)
      (PORT = 1521))
      (PROTOCOL_STACK =
        (PRESENTATION = TTC)
        (SESSION = NS)
      )
    )

  SID_LIST_LISTENER =
    (SID_LIST =
      (SID_DESC =
        (GLOBAL_DBNAME = GR99c0073) - machine listener is on
        (ORACLE_HOME = c:\v9i)
        (SID_NAME = DBA)
      )
    )
```

Figure 3.2 shows the Oracle Net Manager Database Services screen. Each database that the listener will be serving will be created as a separate entry. Provide the global database name, Oracle Home directory, and Oracle SID information. This completes the configuration work for the database portion of listener configuration.

FIGURE 3.2 Oracle Net Manager `listener.ora` setup for hostnaming

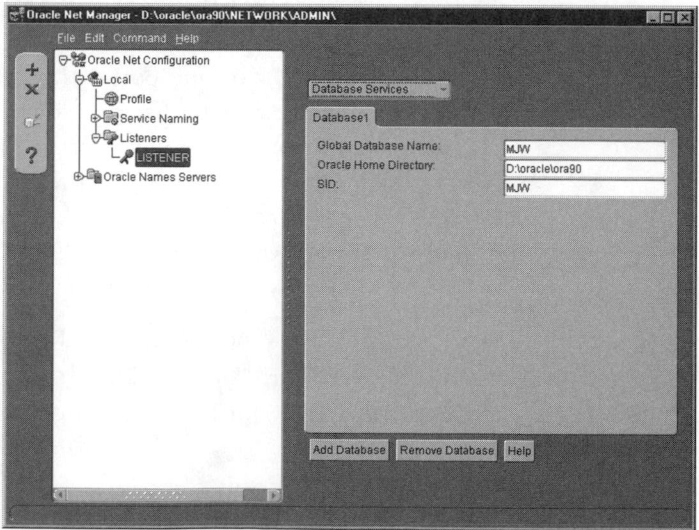

Connection Process when Using Hostnaming

When hostnaming is being used, the client must supply a user ID and password along with the name of the machine they want to connect to. For example, if the user Matt with password of *casey* wants to connect to a database residing on machine GR99c0073, he would enter **Sqlplus matt/casey@gr99c0073.**

The hostname would be resolved by either a HOSTS file or by an external naming environment, such as DNS. External naming methods, such as DNS, are preferred over a HOSTS file because they facilitate centralized management of hostnames. The following code contains an example of a HOSTS file from a Windows NT/2000 environment. The default location for the HOSTS file on a Unix system is in the /etc directory. On Windows NT 2000, the default location is c:\winnt\system32\drivers\etc. Once the hostname is resolved, the connection is made to the machine.

```
Copyright (c) 1993-1995 Microsoft Corp.
#
# This is a sample HOSTS file used by Microsoft
# TCP/IP for Windows NT.
#
# This file contains the mappings of IP addresses
# to hostnames. Each
# entry should be kept on an individual line.
# The IP address should
# be placed in the first column followed
# by the corresponding hostname.
# The IP address and the hostname should be separated
# by at least one
# space.
#
# Additionally, comments (such as these) may be
# inserted on individual
# lines or following the machine name denoted
# by a '#' symbol.
#
# For example:
#
#  102.54.94.97     rhino.acme.com   # source server
#   38.25.63.10     x.acme.com       # x client host
```

```
127.0.0.1         localhost
10.2.0.91         gr99c0073 # Oracle Database Server
```

The listener receives the request and looks for a matching GLOBAL_DBNAME. If it is found, the connection is established as a dedicated, or dispatched, connection depending on the configuration of the Oracle server. Figure 3.3 illustrates the following hostnaming connection process.

1. The client contacts the DNS server or local HOSTS file.
2. The client contacts the Oracle server.
3. The server spawns a dedicated process and redirects the connection to the newly spawned process or redirects the connection to a dispatched process when you are using the Oracle Shared Server.
4. The server passes connection information back to the client.
5. The client is now in direct contact with the server process or dispatcher.

FIGURE 3.3 Hostnaming connection summary

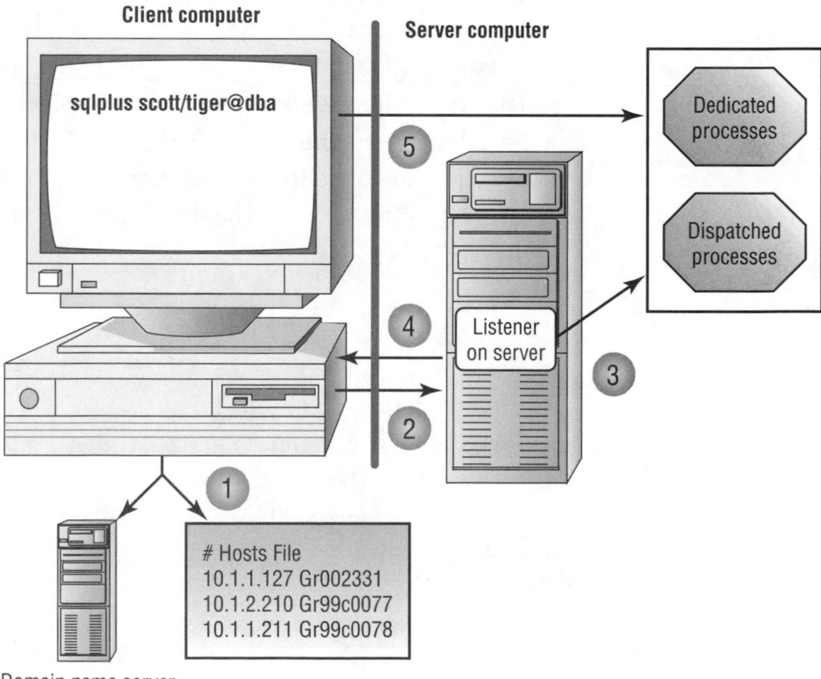

Configuring Multiple Services on the Same Host Using Hostnaming

If you have multiple Oracle servers on the same machine, it is possible to continue using the hostnaming method. To do so, you must have separate hostname address entries in your HOSTS file or in your external naming service for each of the separate Oracle services. For example, if we had two Oracle services, one called DBA and one called PROD, on a machine with an IP address of 10.2.0.91, you could configure your HOSTS name with following entry:

```
10.2.0.91       DBA  # Alias for MACH1 server for DBA  DBA
10.2.0.91       PROD # Alias for MACH1 server for PROD  PROD
```

Notice that each of these names resolve to the same IP address. You also need to configure your listener with two entries, one for DBA and one for PROD, both with the GLOBAL_DBNAME parameter set to DBA and PROD respectively. (If you were using the hierarchical naming model with domain names, include the domain name on the GLOBAL_DBNAME parameter.)

The Localnaming Method

The *localnaming method* is probably the most widely used and well-known method of resolving net service names. Most users know this method as the tnsnames.ora method because it uses the tnsnames.ora file.

To use the localnaming method, you must configure the *tnsnames.ora* file, which can be in any location, as long as the client can get to it. The default location for the tnsnames.ora file and the sqlnet.ora file is %ORACLE_HOME%\network\admin on Windows NT/2000, and $ORACLE_HOME/network/admin on Unix systems. If you want to change the location of this file, set the environmental variable *TNS_ADMIN*. In Unix-based systems, TNS_ADMIN can be exported to the user's shell environment or be set in the user's profile. In Windows NT/2000, this setting is placed in the Registry. The Windows NT/2000 Registry key that stores the TNS_ADMIN may vary depending on your particular setup. Generally, it can be found somewhere under the Hkey_local_machine/software/oracle Registry key, but it may be at a lower level depending on your configuration.

Most installations probably keep the files in these default locations on the client and server. Some users create shared disks and place the tnsnames.ora and sqlnet.ora files in this shared location to take a centralized approach to managing these files. If server-to-server communication is necessary, these files need to be on the server. The default location on the server is the same as the default location on the client.

Configuring the Localnaming Method Using Oracle Net Manager

The localnaming method is configured using the Oracle Net Manager. To start this configuration, open the Oracle Net Manager and click the Service Naming selection under the Local tab. Click the plus sign on the left side of the screen or choose Create from the Edit menu (see Figure 3.4).

FIGURE 3.4 Oracle Net Manager title screen with Service Naming option chosen

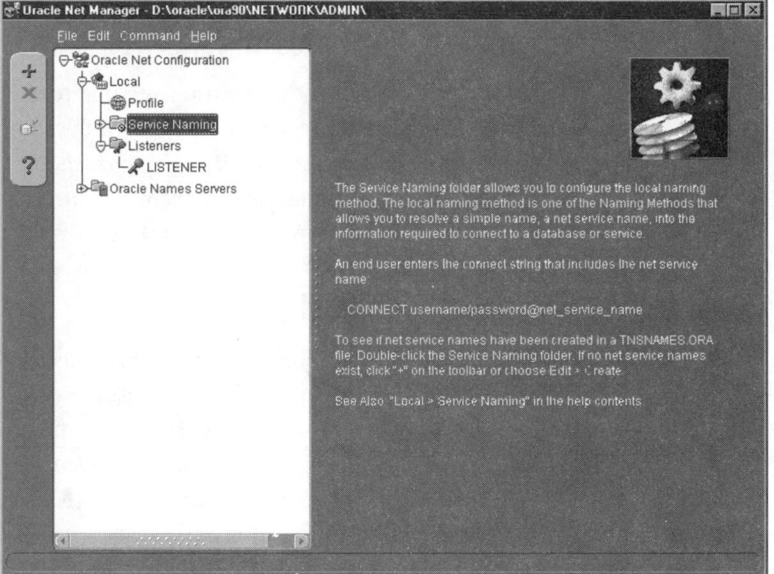

The Oracle Net Manager will present you with the Net Service Name wizard, which will guide you through the process of creating the net service names definition.

Choose a Net Service Name

When you configure a client to use the localnaming method, first you must choose a *net service name*. This is the name users enter when they are referring to the location they want to connect to. The name you supply here should not include the domain portion if you are using the hierarchical naming mode. Click the Next button to continue. Figure 3.5 shows an example of choosing the net service name.

FIGURE 3.5 Choosing a net service name

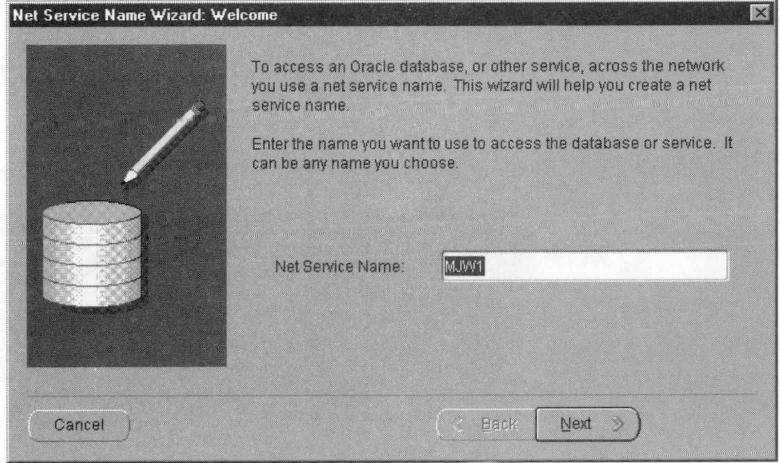

Choose a Network Protocol

The next step is to enter the type of protocol the client should use when they connect to the server for this net service name. By default, TCP/IP is chosen. The list of protocols will vary depending on your platform. Click the Next button to continue (see Figure 3.6).

FIGURE 3.6 Oracle Net Manager Network Protocol screen

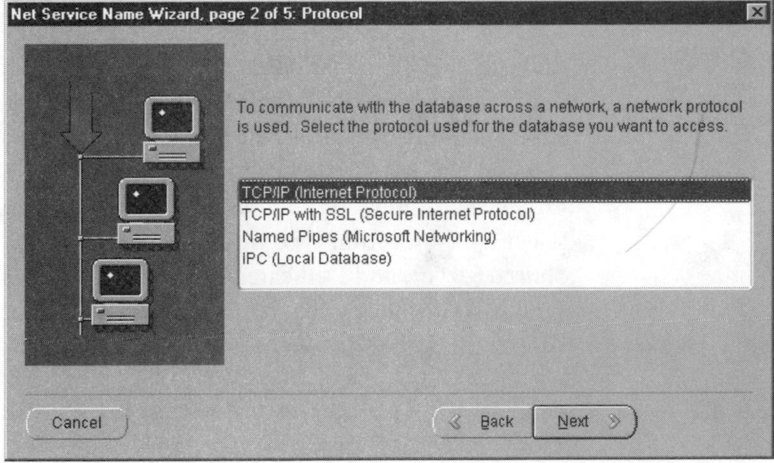

Choose the Hostname and the Port

This step will vary depending on the protocol you chose in the previous step. If TCP/IP was chosen, you are prompted for the hostname and the port number. The hostname is the name of the machine on which the listener process is running. The port number is the listening location for the listener. The default port is 1521 (see Figure 3.7).

FIGURE 3.7 Oracle Net Manager Hostname and Port Number screen

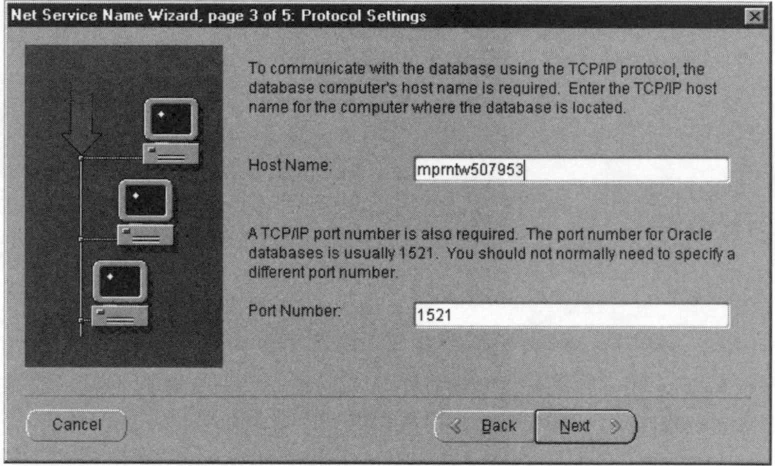

Choose the Service Name

The next step is to define the service name. For Oracle9*i*, the service name does not have to be the same as the `ORACLE_SID` because a database can have multiple service names defined for it. In Oracle9*i*, the service name is normally the same as the global database name. This is the service name that is supplied to the listener, so the listener has to be listening for this service. You can also choose whether this service is for Oracle8*i* or later databases or Oracle8 and previous databases. There is also a choice that allows you to select the connection type from one of these choices: Database Default, Shared Server, and Dedicated Server. Figure 3.8 shows an example of the Oracle Net Manager Service Name screen.

FIGURE 3.8 Oracle Net Manager Service Name screen

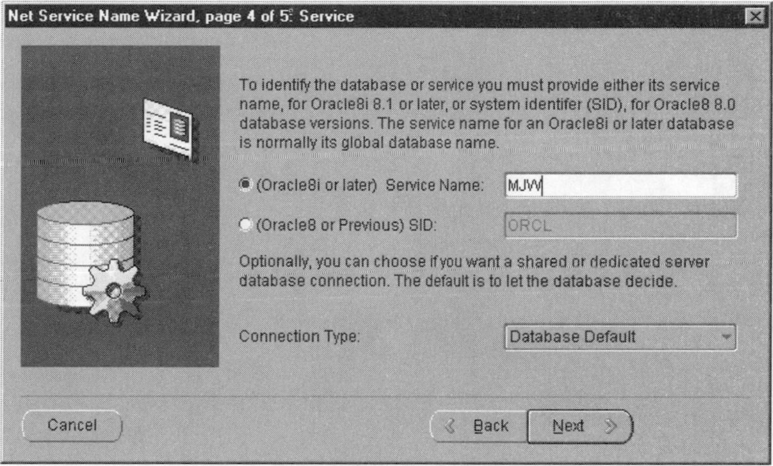

Test the Net Service Name Connection

The last step is to test the net service name. This test will verify that all of the connection information entered is correct. Press the Test button to test the network connection. Figure 3.9 displays an example of the Oracle Net Manager test network connection form.

The test connection will try to connect to the database with a username of Scott and a password of tiger by default. If your connection fails, check to see if you have a Scott/tiger user. You can change which login to test with by clicking the Change Login button in the Test Connection screen. You can also create the user Scott by running a script called `scott` located in the `$ORACLE_HOME/rdbms/admin` directory on Unix or `%ORACLE_HOME%\rdbms\admin` on Windows NT/2000.

FIGURE 3.9 Oracle Net Manager test network connection form

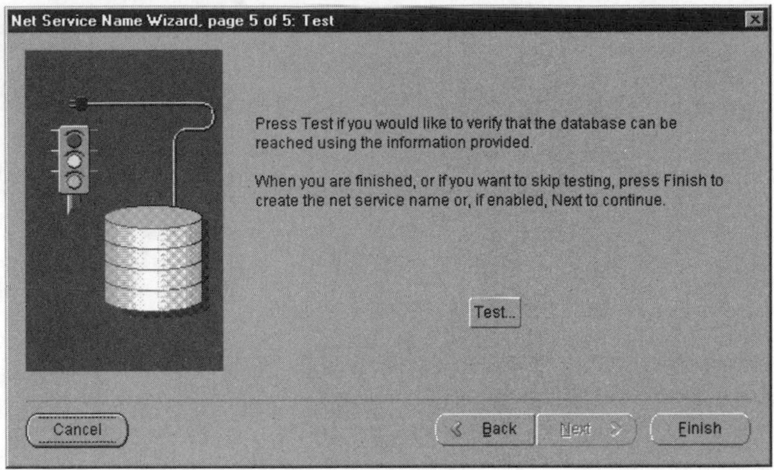

If everything is correct, you should see a result similar to Figure 3.10.

FIGURE 3.10 Oracle Net Manager `tnsnames.ora` wizard test result screen

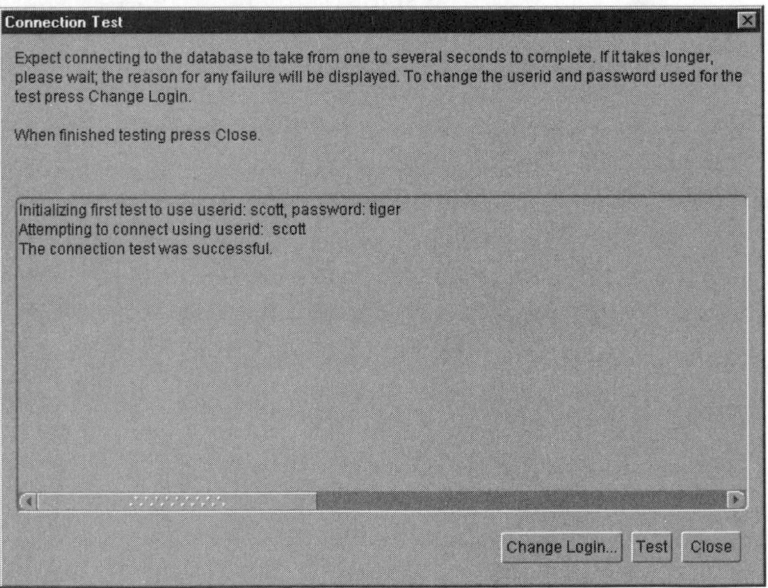

After you have completed all of this, you must save your changes by choosing Save Network Configuration from the File menu. This creates and saves the `tnsnames.ora` file.

Contents and Structure of the *tnsnames.ora* File

Here is an example of the `tnsnames.ora` file that you created above:

```
# D:\ORACLE\ORA90\NETWORK\ADMIN\TNSNAMES.ORA
# Configuration
# File:D:\Oracle\Ora90\NETWORK\ADMIN\tnsnames.ora
# Generated by Oracle Net Manager

DBA =
  (DESCRIPTION =
    (ADDRESS_LIST =
      (ADDRESS = (PROTOCOL = TCP)(HOST = gr99c0073)
      (PORT = 1521))
    )
    (CONNECT_DATA =
      (SERVICE_NAME = DBA)
    )
  )
```

Table 3.1 summarizes the parameters in the `tnsnames.ora` file.

TABLE 3.1 `tnsnames.ora` Parameters

Parameter	Description
`Description`	Starts connect descriptor section of file.
`Address_list`	Starts a list of all connect descriptor address information.
`Address`	Specifies connect descriptor for net service name.
`Protocol`	Specifies protocol used, such as TCP/IP.

TABLE 3.1 tnsnames.ora Parameters *(continued)*

Parameter	Description
Host	Specifies name of the machine where listener is running. An IP address can also be specified in TCP/IP.
Port	Specifies listening location of listener specific to TCP/IP protocol.
Connect_data	Starts the services section for this net service name.
Service_name	Replaces the SID parameter from older releases of Oracle. Defines what service to connect to. Can be the same as the ORACLE_SID or set to the global database name. Databases can now be referred to by more than a single service name.

Troubleshooting Client-Side Connection Problems

The client must be able to contact both the computer where the Oracle server is located and the listener listening for connections to the Oracle server. The client must also be able to resolve the net service name. Let's take a look at the checks that need to be performed on the client to verify connectivity to the Oracle server.

- Can the client contact the server?
- Can the client see the listener?
- Verify localnaming configuration files.
- Do multiple client network configuration files exist?
- Check network file locations.
- Check the NAMES.DIRECTORY_PATH parameter.
- Check the NAMES.DEFAULT_DOMAIN parameter.
- Check the client protocol adapters.
- Are there any common client-side error codes?

Check Client/Server Contact

Make sure the client can see the host computer. If you are using TCP/IP, you can attempt to ping the host computer. Simply type **ping** and the name of the host. If the host is not found, try using the IP address of the host computer instead of the hostname. If this works, the problem may be that your `hosts` file is not correct or your domain Name Server does not recognize the host computer name. For example, you could ping a computer with the hostname of gr99c0073 as follows:

```
C:\>ping gr99c0073

Pinging gr99c0073 [127.1.10.1] with 32 bytes of data:

Reply from 127.1.10.1: bytes=32 time<10ms TTL=128
Reply from 127.1.10.1: bytes=32 time<10ms TTL=128
Reply from 127.1.10.1: bytes=32 time<10ms TTL=128
Reply from 127.1.10.1: bytes=32 time<10ms TTL=128
```

Check Client/Listener Contact

Next, check to see if the client can contact the listener. You can use a utility called *tnsping* to verify this. `tnsping` is an Oracle utility that attempts to contact an Oracle listener. It works similarly to ping in that you can enter a net service name and the number of times to contact the listener. This utility verifies that the client can contact the listener. However, it does not verify that the client can actually connect to the Oracle server. You can also specify a number of attempts. In the example below, three attempts are made to contact the PROD database.

```
C:\>tnsping PROD  3

TNS Ping Utility for 32-bit Windows: Version 8.1.5.0.0 -
Production on 19-FEB-00
 21:18:25

(c) Copyright 1997 Oracle Corporation.  All rights
reserved.
```

```
Attempting to contact
(ADDRESS=(PROTOCOL=TCP)(HOST=gr0073)(PORT=1521))
OK (270 msec)
OK (40 msec)
OK (30 msec)
```

The tnsping utility shows how long the round trip took to contact the listener. This information can also assist you in uncovering the connection problem, as the accompanying sidebar reveals.

Real World Scenario

The Mysterious Timeout Problem

I have used tnsping to help troubleshoot some very interesting connection problems. One such problem involved a client who was experiencing intermittent connection timeouts. Sometimes the client could connect, but other times the client received a timeout error. The client also reported that it always took an inordinate amount of time to log in to the Oracle server.

This problematic client machine happened to be sitting adjacent to another client machine that had no connection or timeout problems whatsoever. I ran some connection tests with tnsping and discovered that the client having problems took on average 3000 milliseconds to connect to the listener while the other client took only 30 milliseconds. Both clients were using the same network routes to connect to the server.

After further investigation, I discovered that the machines were using different implementations of TCP/IP. This was causing the intermittent timeout problems. With the help of the tnsping utility, I was able to narrow down the problem to a difference in the client machine configurations.

Verify Localnaming Configuration Files

If the client is using the localnaming method for net service name resolution, check the entries in the tnsnames.ora file. Make sure the entries are syntactically correct and that there is an entry for the net service name. Also make sure the protocol is correct.

Look for Multiple Client Network Configuration Files

Make sure that all copies of these files are identical. Normally there should only be one copy of the client-side networking files like `tnsnames.ora` and `sqlnet.ora`. In some situations, such as when you are using other Oracle tools (such as Oracle Developer), these products get installed on a client in a separate `ORACLE_HOME` directory and have their own copies of the network files. This can make it necessary for a client to have more than one copy of the networking files.

Check Network File Locations

One of the most common problems I have encountered is clients moving network files and not setting the `TNS_ADMIN` environmental variable to the new file location. Oracle expects the `tnsnames.ora` and `sqlnet.ora` files to be in the default location. If it cannot locate the files and you have not set `TNS_ADMIN`, you receive an ORA-12154 error. Below is an example of this error. You also receive this error if the supplied net service name is invalid.

```
D:\ORACLE\ORA81\NETWORK\ADMIN>sqlplus system/
manager@Database Administrator

SQL*Plus: Release 9.0.1.0.0 - Production on Sat
Oct 19 21:40:12 2001

(c) Copyright 1999 Oracle Corporation.  All rights
 reserved.

ERROR:
ORA-12154: TNS:could not resolve service name
```

If you decide to move network files, be sure to set the `TNS_ADMIN` environmental variable to the location of the files. Oracle first searches the default location for the files and then searches the `TNS_ADMIN` location for the files.

Check *NAMES.DIRECTORY_PATH*

Make sure that the client has the proper names resolution setting. The `NAMES.DIRECTORY_PATH` parameter in the `sqlnet.ora` file controls the order in which the client resolves net service names. If the parameter is not set, the default is localnaming, Oracle Internet Directory, and then hostnaming.

If this parameter is set incorrectly, the client may never check the appropriate names resolution type. For example, if you are using localnaming and the parameter is set to `HOSTNAMES`, the `tnsnames.ora` file will never be used to resolve the net service name. You will receive an ORA-12154 "Cannot Resolve Service Name" error.

Check *NAMES.DEFAULT_DOMAIN*

`NAMES.DEFAULT_DOMAIN` is another common error. It was more common in older releases of Oracle because the parameter defaulted to `WORLD`. Check the client `sqlnet.ora` file to see if the parameter is set. If the parameter has a value and you are using unqualified net service names, the parameter value is appended to the end of the net service name. An unqualified service name is a service name that does not contain domain information.

For example, if you entered **Sqlplus matt/casey@PROD**, and the `NAMES.DEFAULT_DOMAIN` was set to `WORLD`, Oracle would append `WORLD` to the net service name; as a result, Oracle will pass the command as `sqlplus matt/casey@PROD.WORLD`. You will receive an ORA-12154 "Cannot Resolve Service Name" error if the service name should not include the `.WORLD` domain extension. You use this parameter only if you are using a hierarchical naming convention.

Check Client Protocol Adapters

Verify that the appropriate protocol adapters have been installed on the client. You can invoke the Universal Installer and check the client setup. Look for the listing of client protocol adapters installed.

Check for Client-Side Error Codes

Here is a summary of some of the common client-side Oracle errors that you may encounter.

```
ORA-12154 "TNS: could not resolve service name"
ORA-12198 "TNS: could not find path to destination"
ORA-12203 "TNS: Unable to connect to destination"
```

```
ORA-12533 "TNS: illegal address parameters"
ORA-12541 "TNS: No listener"
```

ORA-12154 Means that the client cannot find the service listed in the `tnsnames.ora` file. Some of the causes of this are described above, such as the file is not in the proper directory, or the `TNS_ADMIN` variable is not specified or specified incorrectly.

ORA-12198 or ORA-12203 Mean that the client found an entry for the service in the `tnsnames.ora` file but the service specified was not found. Check to make sure that the service specified in the `tnsnames.ora` file actually points to a valid database service.

ORA-12533 Means you have configured the `ADDRESS` section of the `tnsnames.ora` file incorrectly. Check to make sure the syntax is correct or re-create the definition using the Oracle Net Manager tool.

ORA-12541 Means that the client contacted a server that does not have a listener running on the specified port. Make sure that the listener is started on the server and that the listening port specifications on the client and the server match.

Summary

The names resolution methods available for clients include hostnaming, localnaming, and Oracle Internet Directory. Hostnaming, which can only be used if you are using TCP/IP, is mainly used for very simple Oracle networks. Localnaming is the most popular of the names resolution methods, and it uses the `tnsnames.ora` file, which is typically located on each client, to resolve net service names. The client looks up the net service name in the `tnsnames.ora` file and uses the resulting connect descriptor information to connect to the Oracle server. The hostnaming and localnaming methods are configured using the Oracle Net Manager. Oracle Internet Directory Services is a Lightweight Directory Access Protocol (LDAP) compliant server that provides for centralized management of Oracle database connection identifier information. The Oracle Internet Directory replaces Oracle Names Server as the preferred method of centralized administration of database services.

It is important to know how to troubleshoot connection problems. You should know the general format and content of the `tnsnames.ora` and `sqlnet.ora` files to be able to identify syntax errors. You should know where these files reside on the client. You should understand how the various names resolution methods work. You should become familiar with the tools that can be used, such as the TCP/IP-supplied `ping` utility and the Oracle-supplied `tnsping` utility to assist you when troubleshooting these problems. Finally, you should familiarize yourself with the most common Oracle errors that can occur as a result of connection problems.

This chapter covered the second main area of configuring the Oracle network environment. Configuration of the Oracle servers and clients covers the most common areas of network management for the database administrator. In fact, once client connectivity has been established, most of your networking tasks have been completed. In the next chapter on Oracle Shared Server, you will see how you can vary how you serve client connection requests and the reasons you may choose to use this option. But this still will not change the basic setup work that was discussed in this chapter and the previous one.

Exam Essentials

Define the three Oracle client-side names resolution options. You should be able to define the three Oracle client-side names resolution options. You should know under what situations you would use localnaming, hostnaming, and Oracle Internet Directory.

Define the prerequisites for using the hostnaming method. You should know how to configure this method using the Oracle Net Manager, and you should be able to understand the connection process when you use this method. You will also need to be able to define the parameter that you may have to add to the `listener.ora` file when you use this method. In addition, you should understand what the `HOSTS` file is.

Use the Oracle Net Manager. You should be able to use the Oracle Net Manager to configure the `sqlnet.ora` file on the client. You should understand the meaning of the `NAMES.DEFAULT_DOMAIN` and `NAMES.DIRECTORY_PATH` parameters within the `sqlnet.ora` file.

Define the localnaming method. In addition to knowing the meaning of the localnaming method and what it does, you need to understand how to use the Oracle Net Manager to configure this names resolution method. You should understand the primary file used in the localnaming method, the `tnsnames.ora` file.

Define the contents and structure of the `tnsnames.ora` file. You should be able to define what the `tnsnames.ora` file is, the various sections of the file, and how the file is used. You should understand the contents of the `tnsnames.ora` file so that you can identify syntax problems with the structure of entries in the file. You should be familiar with the common locations of this file and how to set the `TNS_ADMIN` parameter to override the default location of this and the other client-side network files.

Define and correct client-side errors. You need to be able to understand the types of client-side connection errors that can occur. You should be able to define these errors and understand the situations in which a client might encounter these errors.

Key Terms

Before you take the exam, be certain you are familiar with the following terms:

hostnaming method	ping
localnaming method	`TNS_ADMIN`
`NAMES.DIRECTORY_PATH`	`tnsnames.ora`
net service name	`tnsping`

Review Questions

1. What are the ways in which a client may resolve a net service name? (Choose all that apply.)

   A. Localnaming

   B. Hostnaming

   C. Globalnaming

   D. Oracle Internet Directory

2. When configuring a client, what file must be present to accomplish localnaming?

   A. `lsnrctl.ora`

   B. `names.ora`

   C. `tnsnames.ora`

   D. `sdns.ora`

   E. None of the above

3. Which of the following is a prerequisite to hostnaming?

   A. You must use `tnsnames.ora` on the client.

   B. You must be using TCP/IP.

   C. You must have an Oracle Internet Directory present.

   D. You must have a `sqlnet.ora` file present on the client.

   E. None of the above.

4. Which of the following statements about `tnsnames.ora` is *false*?

   A. It is used to resolve an Oracle service name.

   B. It can exist on the client.

   C. It is used for localnaming.

   D. It does not support the TCP/IP protocol.

5. Which entry in the `sqlnet.ora` file would use localnaming resolution before other name resolution types?

   A. `NAMES.DIRECTORY_PATH=(TNSNAMES,LDAP,HOSTNAME)`

   B. `NAMES.SEARCH_PATH=(TSNAMES,HOSTNAME,LDAP)`

   C. `NAMES.DIRECTORY_PATH=(HOSTNAME,LDAP,TNSNAMES)`

   D. `NAMES.SEARCH_PATH=(HOSTNAME,TNSNAMES,LDAP)`

6. Which option in the Oracle Net Manager is used to configure `tnsnames.ora`?

   A. Profile

   B. Listeners

   C. `tnsnames`

   D. Net service names

   E. Service Naming

7. The user Bob with the password *apple* needs to connect to the DBA service. Which one of the following connection statements would work?

   A. `sqlplus apple/bob@DBA`

   B. `sqlplus bob/apple@DBA`

   C. `sqlplus DBA@bob/apple`

   D. `sqlplus bob\apple@DBA`

   E. `sqlplus bob/apple#DBA`

8. Which phrase best completes the following sentence? A net service name is ____________.

   A. The name of the `ORACLE_SID`

   B. The database name

   C. Another name for a database location on my network

   D. The same as my `DB_NAME init.ora` setting

   E. None of the above

9. Which section of the tnsnames.ora file contains the parameter SERVICE_NAME?

   A. Address

   B. Connect_Data

   C. Host

   D. Description

10. A DBA wants to perform a check of connectivity to a specific Oracle listener from a client. The service name is mjw. Which of the following commands could this be done with?

    A. ping mjw

    B. trcasst mjw

    C. tnsping mjw

    D. None of the above

11. The DBA manages a large network of servers with many Oracle9*i* instances configured on each server. The business would like to centralize the Oracle services into a common location for ease of maintenance. Which of the following would be the best choice for centralized naming services?

    A. Hostnaming

    B. Localnaming

    C. Oracle Names Server

    D. Oracle Internet Directory

12. A client receives the following error message:

    ORA-12154 "TNS: could not resolve service name"

    Which of the following could be possible causes of the error? (Choose all that apply.)

    A. The listener is not running on the Oracle server.

    B. The user typed in an invalid service name.

    C. The user supplied the correct service name but the service name is misspelled in the tnsnames.ora file.

    D. The listener is not configured to listen for this service.

13. Which parameter, if present in the `sqlnet.ora` file, gets appended to the service name if the user supplies an unqualified service name when requesting a connection?

    A. `NAMES.DEFAULT_PATHNAMES`

    B. `NAMES.DEFAULT_DOMAIN`

    C. `NAMES.SERVICE_NAME`

    D. `NAMES.CONNECTION_NAME`

14. In which situation would an administrator choose to use hostnaming?

    A. The administrator has a complex network with many instances to manage.

    B. The administrator is interested in minimal client-side configuration.

    C. The administrator does not want to use the Oracle Net Manager.

    D. The administrator wants to use a `tnsnames.ora` file to contain the configuration settings.

    E. None of the above.

15. What portion of the `tnsnames.ora` file specifies the name or IP address of the server where the listener process is listening?

    A. `CONNECT_DATA`

    B. `PORT`

    C. `SERVICE_NAME`

    D. `HOST`

16. Which of these statements is *false* about hostnaming?

    A. TCP/IP must be used.

    B. Hostnames are resolved through an external naming service.

    C. Connection Manager can be used with hostnaming.

    D. The user needs only to provide the name of the host to get connected.

17. Which phrase best completes the following sentence? The network protocol __________.

    A. Is installed by default by the Oracle Installer

    B. Is another name for the Oracle protocol adapters

    C. Is not necessary for doing client/server connections

    D. Needs to be present for client/server connections

18. Which of the following is the utility that you can use to test the network connections across TCP/IP?

    A. `trcasst`

    B. `lsnrctl`

    C. `namesctl`

    D. Ping

    E. None of the above

19. If the Oracle instance has not been dynamically registered with the listener, and hostnaming is being used, what `listener.ora` parameter needs to be set?

    A. `GLOBAL_DATABASE`

    B. `DATABASE_NAME`

    C. `GLOBAL_DNAME`

    D. `GLOBAL_DBNAME`

20. Which section of the `tnsnames.ora` file is correct?

    A. `(ADDRESS =(PROTOCOL = TCP)(HOST = MIL02ORA)`
    `(PORT = 1521))`

    B. `(ADDRESS= (HOST=MIL02ORA) (PORT=1521)(PROTOCOL=TCP))`

    C. `(ADDRESS=(PROTOCOL=TCP, HOST=MIL02ORA,PORT=1521))`

    D. `(ADDRESS=(PROTOCOL=TCP) (HOST=MIL02ORA,PORT=1521))`

Answers to Review Questions

1. A, B, D. Oracle uses service names in networks in much the same way it uses synonyms in the database. Service names provide location transparency and hide the complexity of connect string information. There are three ways to configure Oracle Net to accomplish this: hostnaming, localnaming, and Oracle Internet Directory. You can set a global name for the database connect string, but you would do that in the context of one of these three names resolution solutions.

2. C. Localnaming is more often referred to as `TNSNAMES` naming because we use the `tnsnames.ora` file to resolve a service name. There is no such file as `lsnrctl.ora`, and the `sdns.ora` file is a file that was used with the Oracle Names Server, which is being replaced by the Oracle Internet Directory.

3. B. Hostnaming is typically used in small installations with few Oracle databases. This is an attractive option when the DBA wants to minimize client-side configuration. One of the prerequisites of hostnaming is that you must use TCP/IP.

4. D. A `tnsnames.ora` file is configured when we want to use localnaming, and it typically exists on the client workstation. It is also used to resolve a service name. The `tnsnames.ora` file used in localnaming does indeed support the TCP/IP protocol.

5. A. The DBA has the capability of modifying the search path for resolving an Oracle service name. If you want to first check for local naming resolution, you would use `NAMES.DIRECTORY_PATH` and make `TNSNAMES` the first choice in the list; therefore, A is the correct answer.

6. E. The Service Naming icon is used to configure the `tnsnames.ora` file. The Profile icon is used to configure `sqlnet.ora`, and the Listeners icon is used to configure `listener.ora`. A good knowledge of the Oracle Net Manager interface will definitely help you succeed on the OCP exam.

7. B. When we specify a connection to the database via SQL*Plus, the syntax is `sqlplus userid/password@service_name`. All of the other choices would result in a failed connection attempt.

8. C. Net service names resolve to locations somewhere in the enterprise. It may not necessarily be the same as the `ORACLE_SID` or the database name. This means the correct answer is C.

9. B. The `SERVICE_NAME` parameter is new in Oracle9*i* and is part of the `Connect_Data` portion of the `tnsnames.ora` file.

10. C. The `tnsping` command is used to check connectivity between a client and an Oracle listener. Ping can be used to check TCP/IP connectivity to a given host and `trcasst` is an Oracle utility used to format the contents of Oracle network trace files.

11. D. Oracle Internet Directory is Oracle's preferred centralized naming service. Oracle Names Server is still supported, but only for backwards compatibility.

12. B, C. If the user supplies a service name that is not contained in the `tnsnames.ora` file, this would cause this error. Problems with the `tnsnames.ora` file can cause this error to occur too. Listener problems would not cause this error to occur.

13. B. An enterprise may have many domains, each with its own services. In a hierarchical naming model, service names may be the same across domains. To differentiate between service names, the `NAMES.DEFAULT_DOMAIN` parameter is appended to a service that does not contain a domain name. For example, if a user specifies `DBA` and `NAMES.DEFAULT_DOMAIN=GR.COM`, the resultant service name to be searched for is `DBA.GR.COM`.

14. B. Hostnaming is used in situations in which there are few overall databases to administer and you want to minimize client-side configuration. Complex networks would probably be candidates for the Oracle Internet Directory Services. The Oracle Net Manager can be used to configure any of the name resolution possibilities and `tnsnames.ora` files are used for localnaming.

15. D. The HOST specifies the name of the server to contact. The PORT specifies the location of where the listener is listening on the HOST. CONNECT_DATA specifies the database service to connect to. SERVICE_NAME is the name of the actual database service.

16. C. Advanced networking options, like Oracle Connection Manager, are not available when you use the hostnaming method.

17. D. All network data is transported from a client to a database server by an underlying network protocol. This protocol needs to be in place for Oracle Net to function correctly. Protocols are independent of the Oracle software and are not the same as the Oracle protocol adapters. The adapters are what allow Oracle Net to talk to the underlying protocol.

18. D. Protocols come with tools that allow you to test network connectivity. One such utility for TCP/IP is ping. The user supplies either an IP address or a hostname to the ping utility. It then searches the network for this address. If it finds one, it will display information on data that is sent and received and how quickly it found this address. The other choices are Oracle-supplied utilities.

19. D. The GLOBAL_DBNAME parameter needs to be set in the listener.ora file if the instance has not been dynamically registered with the listener.

20. A. Review the syntax and formatting of the network files. All of the other syntax examples are incorrect.

Configuring the Shared Server Option

ORACLE9*i*: DBA FUNDAMENTALS II EXAM OBJECTIVES COVERED IN THIS CHAPTER:

- ✓ **Identify the components of the Oracle Shared Server.**
- ✓ **Describe the Oracle Shared Server architecture.**
- ✓ **Configure the Oracle Shared Server.**
- ✓ **Identify and explain usefulness of related dictionary views.**

Exam objectives are subject to change at any time without prior notice and at Oracle's sole discretion. Please visit Oracle's Certification website (`http://www.oracle.com/education/certification/`) for the most current exam objectives listing.

As the number of users connecting to Oracle services in the enterprise grows, the system requirements of the servers increase—particularly the memory and process requirements. This chapter discusses the *Oracle Shared Server option* (formerly known as Oracle Multithreaded Server) and its benefits. In addition, you will learn the steps of the connection process, how to configure the Shared Server option, and how user requests are processed in a shared server configuration. You will also learn how to manage the shared server environment using various Oracle data dictionary views and how to configure clients to request dedicated connections when you are connecting to an Oracle database configured with Shared Server. Finally, you will learn where to find information to assist you in tuning the Shared Server.

It is important for the database administrator to understand the Oracle Shared Server architecture and how and when it is appropriate to utilize this feature. When used properly, this feature can help alleviate problems with servers that are being taxed in terms of the number of processes running on the server. When the Shared Server is configured properly, it can help stave off system upgrades that may have seemed imminent, thus saving the organization time and money.

Shared Server Configuration

Shared Server is an optional configuration of the Oracle server that allows the server to support a larger number of concurrent connections without increasing physical resource requirements. This is accomplished by sharing resources among groups of users.

Dedicated Server versus Shared Server

If you have ever gone to a very upscale restaurant, you may have had your own personal waiter. The waiter is there to greet you and escort you to your seat. The waiter will take your order for food and drinks and even help in the preparation of your order. No matter how many other patrons enter the restaurant, your waiter is responsible for serving only your requests. Therefore, your service is very consistent—if the person is a good waiter.

A *dedicated server* environment works in much the same way. Every client connection has an associated dedicated server process on the machine where the Oracle server exists. No matter how many other connections are made to the server, you always have the same dedicated server responsible for processing only your requests. You utilize the services of that server process until you disconnect from the Oracle server.

Most restaurants tend to be more like shared servers. When you walk in, you are assigned a waiter or waitress, but they may have many other tables they are responsible for serving. This is good for the restaurant because they can serve more customers without increasing the staff. It may be fine for you as well, if the restaurant is not too busy and the waiter or waitress is not responsible for too many tables. Also, if most of the orders are small, the staff can keep up with the requests and the service will be as good as if you had your own personal waiter.

In the diner, things work slightly differently; here, the waitress takes your order and places it on a turnstile. If the diner has multiple cooks, the order is picked up from the turnstile and prepared by one of the available cooks. When the cook completes the preparation of the dinner, it is placed in a location where the waitress can pick it up and bring it back to your table.

This is how a shared server environment works. In a shared server environment, clients share processes on the Oracle server. These shared processes are called *dispatchers*. Dispatchers are like the waiter or waitress in the diner. A dispatcher can be responsible for taking the orders of many clients.

When you request something from the server, it is the dispatcher's responsibility to take your request and place it in a location called a *request queue*. The request queue functions like the turnstile in the diner analogy. There is one request queue where all of the dispatcher processes place their client requests. The request queue is a structure contained in the System Global Area (SGA).

Shared server processes, like cooks in a diner, are responsible for fulfilling the client requests. The shared server process executes the request and places the result into an area of the SGA called a *response queue*. Every dispatcher has its own response queue. The dispatcher picks up the completed request from the response queue and returns the results back to the client. Figure 4.1 depicts the processing steps for a Shared Server request shown here:

1. The client passes a request to the dispatcher serving it.
2. The dispatcher places the request on a request queue in the SGA.
3. One of the shared server processes executes the request.
4. The shared server places the completed request on the dispatchers' response queue of the SGA.
5. The dispatcher picks up the completed request from the response queue.
6. The completed request is passed back to the client.

FIGURE 4.1 Request processing in Shared Server

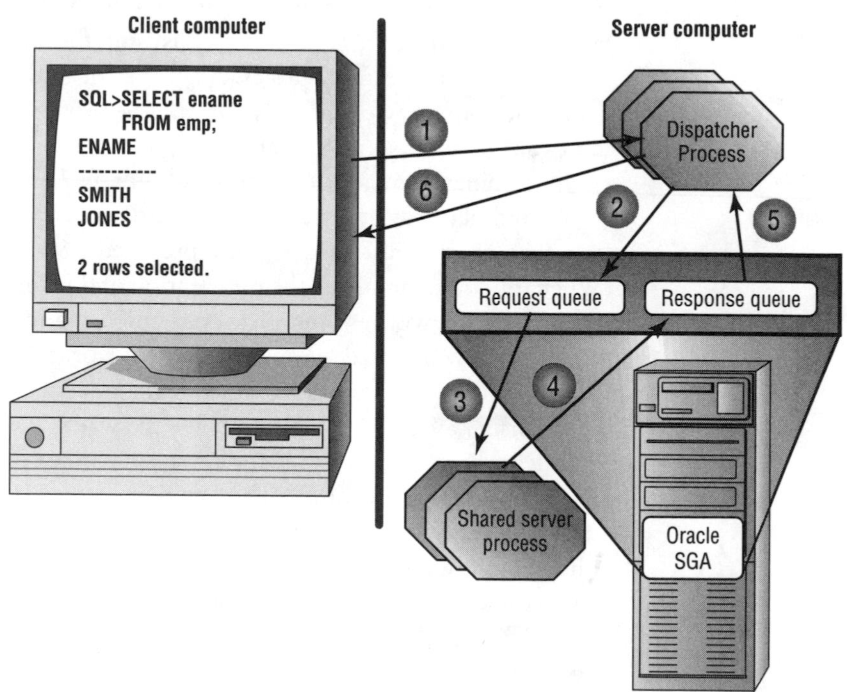

Advantages of Shared Server

A shared server is used in situations where server resources, such as memory and active processes, become constrained. People tend to throw more hardware at problems like these; this will likely remedy the problem, but it may be an unnecessary expense.

If your system is experiencing these problems, Shared Server allows you to support the same or greater number of connections without additional hardware requirements. As a result, Shared Server tends to decrease the overall memory and process requirements on the server.

An average dedicated connection takes roughly two to four megabytes of memory. A shared server connection takes about two megabytes of memory. As you can see, there will be some overall memory reduction. Also, because clients are sharing processes, the total number of processes is reduced. These translate into resource savings on the server.

Shared Server is also required to take advantage of certain network options, such as connection concentration when using Oracle Connection Manager.

Applications Suited to Shared Server

Shared Server is suitable for "high think" applications. High think applications are comprised of small transactions with natural pauses in the transaction patterns. These types of applications are good candidates for shared server connections. An example of a high think application would be an order entry system. Order entry systems tend to have small transactions with natural pauses in the work pattern of entering the information.

Drawbacks of Shared Server

Applications that generate a significant amount of network traffic or result in large result sets are not good candidates for shared server connections. Think of the diner analogy from the previous discussion. Your service is fine until two parties of 12 people show up. All of a sudden, the waitress is overwhelmed with work from these two other tables and your service begins to suffer. The same thing would happen in a shared server environment. If requests for large quantities of information start going to the dispatchers, the dispatchers can become overwhelmed by these large requests, and you may see performance suffer for the other clients connected to the dispatcher. This, in turn, will increase your response times. Dedicated processes better serve these types of applications.

There are some functions that are not allowed when you are using a shared server connection. You cannot start up, shut down, or perform certain kinds of recovery of an Oracle server when you are connected via a shared server.

Scalability versus Performance

Shared Server is a scalability enhancement option, not a performance enhancement option. If you are looking for an increase of performance, Shared Server is not what you should be configuring. Only use Shared Server if you are experiencing the system constraint problems discussed earlier. You will always have equal or better performance in a dedicated server environment.

Oracle Server Changes in a Shared Server Environment

When Shared Server is configured, Oracle adds two new types of structures to the SGA: request queues and response queues. These structures do not exist in a dedicated server environment. There is one request queue for all dispatchers but each dispatcher has its own response queue. So if you have four dispatchers, there would be one request queue and four response queues. The request queue is a location in the SGA where the dispatcher places client requests. A shared server process executes each request, and then it places the completed request in the dispatchers' response queue.

You have to configure the number of dispatcher and shared server processes that you want to start with when the instance starts; you also have to configure the maximum number of each of these structures. Later, you will see how to determine the starting number of dispatchers and shared server processes.

In a dedicated environment, each dedicated server has a memory segment called a *Program Global Area (PGA)*. The PGA is an area of memory where information about each client session is maintained. This information includes bind variables, cursor information, and the client's sort area. In a shared server environment, this information is moved from the PGA to an area of the SGA called the *User Global Area (UGA)*. You can configure a special area of the SGA called the *Large Pool* to accommodate the bulk of the UGA. In older releases of Oracle, the entire UGA was stored in the Shared Pool. As of

Oracle8, the majority of the UGA can be stored in the Large Pool. You will see how to configure the Large Pool later. Figure 4.2 shows how the SGA and PGA structures differ between a dedicated and a shared server environment.

FIGURE 4.2 SGA dedicated server versus Shared Server

Dedicated server SGA

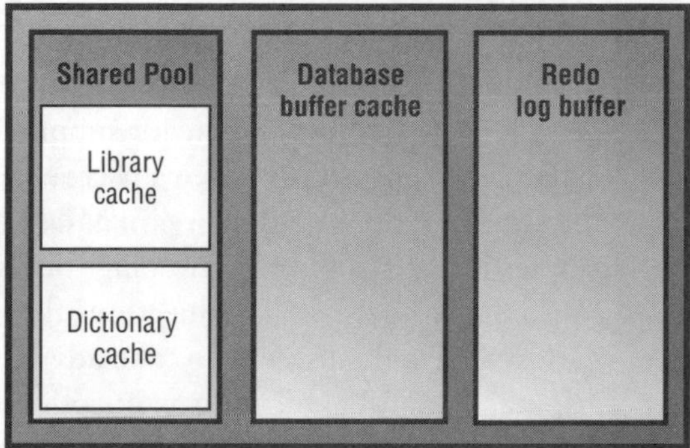

Shared Server SGA

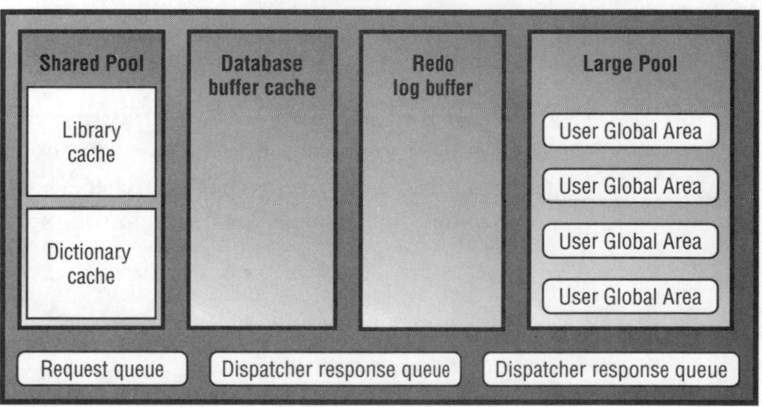

Dedicated server PGA

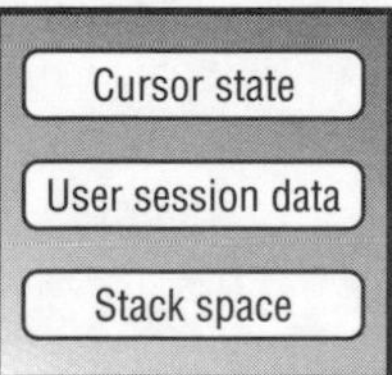

Shared Server PGA

Stack space

Each connection being serviced by a dispatcher is bound to a shared memory segment and forms a *virtual circuit*. The shared memory segment is utilized by the dispatcher to manage communications between the client and the Oracle server. The shared server processes use the virtual circuits to send and receive information to the appropriate dispatcher process.

The Role of the Listener in a Shared Server Environment

The listener plays an important role in the shared server environment. It is the listener that is responsible for supplying the client with the address of the dispatcher to connect to when a user requests connections to a shared server. The Oracle background process PMON notifies the listener as to which dispatcher is responsible for servicing this virtual circuit. The listener is then aware of the number of connections the dispatcher is managing. This information allows the listener to take advantage of dispatcher load balancing. Dispatcher load balancing was introduced in Oracle8*i*.

Load balancing allows the listener to make intelligent decisions about which dispatcher to redirect client connections to so that no one dispatcher becomes overburdened. When the listener receives a connection request, it looks at the current connection load for each dispatcher and redirects the client connection request to the least loaded dispatcher. By doing so, the listener ensures that connections are evenly distributed across dispatchers. When a client connection terminates, the listener is updated to reflect the change in the number of connections the dispatcher is handling. Figure 4.3 depicts the steps of the shared server connection process shown here:

1. The dispatcher processes are spawned when an instance is started.
2. The client contacts the Oracle server after resolving the service name.
3. The server redirects the client connection to the least busy dispatcher.
4. The dispatcher process manages the client server request.
5. PMON registers connection information with the listener.

FIGURE 4.3 Shared server connection process

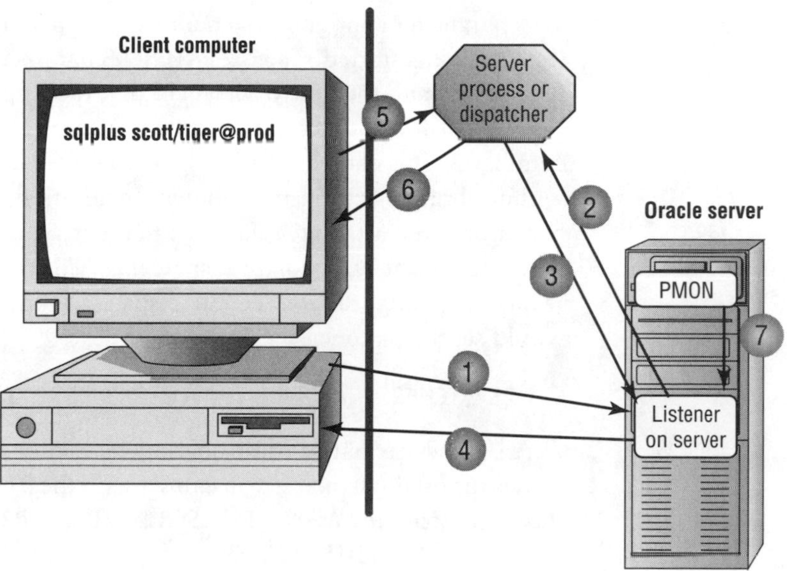

Configuring the Shared Server Option

Shared Server requires additional parameters in the `init.ora` file. These parameters identify the number and type of dispatchers, the number of shared servers, and the name of the database that you want to associate with the Shared Server.

As of Oracle9*i*, parameter names have been modified to eliminate the leading "MTS" prefix. For example, `MTS_DISPATCHERS` is now simply `DISPATCHERS`. These parameters are depreciated but still supported for backward compatibility.

DISPATCHERS Parameter

This parameter configures the number of dispatchers that should start when the instance is started. The DISPATCHERS parameter specifies the number of dispatchers and the type of protocol that the dispatchers can respond to.

You can add additional dispatchers dynamically using the ALTER SYSTEM command. This command allows you to increase the number of dispatchers without bringing the instance down. In addition, this command has a number of optional attributes. The two main attributes are the number of dispatchers and the protocol the dispatcher will listen for. For example, say you wanted to configure three TCP/IP dispatchers and two IPC dispatchers. You would set the parameter as follows:

```
DISPATCHERS = "(PRO=TCP)(DIS=3)(PRO=IPC)(DIS=2)"
```

All of the attributes for this parameter can be abbreviated. Table 1.1 shows the other attributes you can set with the DISPATCHERS parameter. Of the three attributes, ADDRESS, DESCRIPTION, or PROTOCOL, only one needs to be specified for a DISPATCHERS definition.

TABLE 4.1 Summary of DISPATCHER Attributes

Attribute	Abbreviations	Description
ADDRESS	ADD or ADDR	Specifies the network protocol address of the endpoint on which the dispatchers listen.
CONNECTIONS	CON or CONN	The maximum number of network connections per dispatcher. The default value varies by operating system.
DESCRIPTION	DES or DESC	The network description of the endpoint where the dispatcher is listening, including the protocol being listened for.
DISPATCHERS	DIS or DISP	The number of dispatchers to start when the instance is started. The default is 1.

TABLE 4.1 Summary of DISPATCHER Attributes *(continued)*

Attribute	Abbreviations	Description
LISTENER	LIS or LIST	The address of the listener that PMON sends connection information to.
PROTOCOL	PRO or PROT	The network protocol for the dispatcher to listen for.
SESSIONS	SES or SESS	The maximum number of network sessions allowable for this dispatcher.

Determining the Number of Dispatchers to Start

The number of dispatchers you start will vary depending on your particular configuration. Your operating system may place a limit on the number of connections that one dispatcher can handle. Consult your operating system documentation to obtain this information.

Use the following formula as a guide when you are deciding how many dispatchers to initially configure:

```
Number of Dispatchers = CEIL  (maximum number of
concurrent sessions / connections per dispatcher)
```

For example, if you have 200 concurrent TCP/IP connections, and you want each dispatcher to manage 20 concurrent connections, you would need 10 dispatchers. You would set your DISPATCHERS parameter as follows:

```
DISPATCHERS = "(PRO=TCP)(DIS=10)"
```

You can determine the number of concurrent connections by querying the V$SESSION view. This view shows you the number of clients currently connected to the Oracle server. Here is an example of the query:

```
SQL> select sid,serial#,username,server,program from
v$session
  2* where sid > 6
```

```
      SID    SERIAL# USERNAME   SERVER    PROGRAM
--------- ---------- ---------- --------- ---------------
        7         13      SCOTT DEDICATED SQLPLUS.EXE
        8         12      SCOTT DEDICATED SQLPLUS.EXE
        9          4     SYSTEM DEDICATED SQLPLUS.EXE
```

In this example, you see three users connected to the server, and their SIDs begin with the number 7. This is because in the SQL statement, you can ignore the first six sessions. These entries refer to the background processes such as PMON and SMON. If you took a sampling of this view over a typical work period, you would get an idea of the average number of concurrent connections for your system. You would then use this number as a guide when you established the starting number of dispatchers.

Managing the Number of Dispatchers

You can start additional dispatchers or remove dispatchers dynamically using the `ALTER SYSTEM` command. You can start any number of dispatchers up to the `MAX_DISPATCHERS` setting. Here is an example of adding three TCP/IP dispatchers to a system configured with two TCP/IP dispatchers:

```
ALTER SYSTEM SET DISPATCHERS="(PRO=TCP)(DIS=5)";
```

Notice that you set the number to the total number of dispatchers you want, not the number of dispatchers you want to add.

MAX_DISPATCHERS Parameter

Set this parameter to the maximum number of dispatchers you anticipate needing for the Oracle server. This number cannot be set dynamically. The maximum number of processes a dispatcher could run concurrently is operating system dependent. Use the following formula to set this parameter:

```
MAX_DISPATCHERS = (maximum number of concurrent sessions/
connections per dispatcher)
```

Here is an example of the parameter:

```
MAX_DISPATCHERS = 5
```

SHARED_SERVERS Parameter

This parameter specifies the number of shared servers to start when the Oracle instance is started. This parameter can be altered dynamically with the ALTER SYSTEM command. You must set this parameter to at least 1 for Oracle to use shared server connections. A setting of 0 or no setting means shared servers will not be used. This parameter can be changed dynamically, so even if shared servers are not configured when the instance starts, they can be configured without bringing the Oracle instance down and restarting it.

The number of servers necessary will vary depending on the type of activities your users are performing. Generally, for the types of high think applications that will be using shared server connections, 15 to 20 connections per shared server should be adequate. If your users are going to require larger result sets or are doing more intensive processing, then you will want to reduce this ratio.

Here is an example of the parameter:

```
SERVERS = 3
```

SHARED_SERVER_SESSIONS Parameter

This parameter specifies the total number of shared server sessions that are allowable for the Oracle instance. This parameter is derived from the lesser of CIRCUITS or SESSIONS - 5. For example if CIRCUITS is set to 10 and SESSIONS is set to 20, then SHARED_SERVER_SESSIONS would be equal to 10 because this is the lesser of the 2 values. This is a derived value and would not be set in the init.ora file manually.

Managing the Number of Shared Servers

You can start additional shared servers or reduce the number of shared servers dynamically using the ALTER SYSTEM command. You can start any number of shared servers up to the MAX_SERVERS setting. Here is an example of adding three additional shared servers to a system initially configured with two shared servers:

```
ALTER SYSTEM SET SHARED_SERVERS = 5;
```

Notice that you set the number to the total number of shared servers you want, not the number of shared servers you want to add.

MAX_SERVERS Parameter

Set this parameter to the maximum number of shared servers you anticipate needing for the Oracle server. This number cannot be set dynamically. Generally, you should set this parameter to accommodate your heaviest work times.

Here is an example of the parameter:

```
MAX_SERVERS = 5
```

CIRCUITS Parameter

This parameter manages the total number of virtual circuits allowed for all incoming and outgoing network sessions. This is a static parameter and defaults to the value of the SESSIONS init.ora parameter. This parameter does influence the total size of the SGA at system startup.

Here is an example of the parameter:

```
CIRCUITS = 200
```

Starting the Instance and Managing Shared Server

After you have completed the configuration work in the init.ora file, you will need to restart your database. Once you have restarted your database, you should query the V$ views to see if the instance has started the shared servers and the dispatcher processes. Later in this chapter, we will discuss the various data dictionary views used to manage Shared Server.

Registering Dispatcher Information with the Listener

When Shared Server is started, PMON registers dispatcher information with the listener. You can query the listener to see this registered information. The listener will keep track of the current connection load across all of the dispatchers. This information is necessary so that the listener can take advantage of dispatcher load balancing.

Real World Scenario

Troubleshooting Shared Server Startup Problems

If you have problems starting the instance, chances are that you have a problem with one of the Oracle Net files. If you receive an error that states the DISPATCHERS parameter is incorrect, make a backup of all of your Oracle Net files, such as `tnsnames.ora` and `listener.ora`, and re-create these files using the Oracle Net Manager. Most problems we have experienced with the Shared Server can be traced back to modifications made to these files without using Oracle Net Manager. Even cutting and pasting service information to create new service definitions can cause problems. After you have re-created your files, try to restart your instance.

Displaying Information about Shared Server Connections Using *lsnrctl*

You can use the `lsnrctl` command line utility to see information about the dispatcher processes. Use the *lsnrctl services* query to view information about dispatchers. The example below shows a listener listening for two TCP/IP dispatchers. Notice that the listing displays how many connections each dispatcher is managing, the listening location of the dispatcher, and the process ID of the dispatcher. This example has three active connections, two dispatcher D000s and one dispatcher D001.

```
D:\>lsnrctl services

LSNRCTL for 32-bit Windows: Version 9.0.1.1.1 - Production
on 03-OCT-2001 20:50:35

Copyright (c) 1991, 2001, Oracle Corporation.  All rights
reserved.

Connecting to
(DESCRIPTION=(ADDRESS=(PROTOCOL=TCP)(HOST=mprntw507953)
(PORT=1521)))
Services Summary...
```

```
Service "MJW" has 2 instance(s).
  Instance "MJW", status UNKNOWN, has 1 handler(s) for
this service...
    Handler(s):
      "DEDICATED" established:0 refused:0
         LOCAL SERVER
  Instance "MJW", status READY, has 3 handler(s) for this
service...
    Handler(s):
      "DEDICATED" established:0 refused:0 state:ready
         LOCAL SERVER
      "D001" established:11 refused:1 current:1 max:1002
state:ready
         DISPATCHER <machine: MPRNTW507953, pid: 352>

(ADDRESS=(PROTOCOL=tcp)(HOST=mprntw507953.cmg.com)
(PORT=1038))
      "D000" established:15 refused:3 current:2 max:1002
state:ready
         DISPATCHER <machine: MPRNTW507953, pid: 117>

(ADDRESS=(PROTOCOL=tcp)(HOST=mprntw507953.cmg.com)
(PORT=1036))
The command completed successfully
```

Data Dictionary Views for Shared Server

The data dictionary provides views you can query to gather information about the Shared Server environment. These views provide information about the number of dispatchers and shared servers configured, the activity among the shared servers and dispatchers, the activity in the request and response queue, as well as the clients that are connected with shared server connections. The data dictionary views are described in the following sections. For a complete listing of all of the column definitions for the V$ views, consult the *Oracle9i Database Reference Release 1* (9,0.1) Part Number A90190-02.

V$DISPATCHER Dictionary View

The V$DISPATCHER view contains information about the dispatchers. You can collect information about the dispatchers' activity, the number of connections the dispatchers are currently handling, and the total number of connections each dispatcher has handled since instance startup. Here is a sample output from the V$DISPATCHER view:

```
 SQL> select name,status,messages,idle,busy,bytes,breaks
from 2  v$dispatcher

NAME STATUS   MESSAGES    IDLE BUSY  BYTES BREAKS
---- ------ --------- ------- ---- ------ ------
D000 WAIT         168  389645  108  12435      0
D001 WAIT          94  389668   48   6940      0
```

V$DISPATCHER_RATE Dictionary View

The V$DISPATCHER_RATE view shows statistics for the dispatchers, such as the average number of bytes processed, the maximum number of inbound and outbound connections, and the average rate of bytes processed per client connection. The columns in the table that begin with CUR show current statistics. Columns that begin with AVG or MAX show historical statistics taken at some time interval. The time interval is typically measured in hundredths of a second. The scale measurement periods used for each of the column types is contained in the columns that begin with SCALE. This information can be useful when you are taking load measurements for the dispatchers. Here is a sample of the output from this view.

```
SQL>select name,cur_event_rate,cur_msg_rate,
    cur_svr_byte_rate from v$dispatcher_rate

NAME CUR_EVENT_RATE CUR_MSG_RATE CUR_SVR_BYTE_RATE
---- -------------- ------------ -----------------
D000             12            0                 0
D001             14            0                 1
```

V$QUEUE Dictionary View

The V$QUEUE dictionary view contains information about the request and response queues. The information deals with how long requests are waiting in the queues. This information is valuable when you are trying to determine if more shared servers are needed. The following example shows the COMMON request queue and two response queues:

```
SQL> select * from v$queue;

PADDR    TYPE           QUEUED      WAIT    TOTALQ
-------- ---------- --------- --------- ---------
00       COMMON              0         0       152
03C6C244 DISPATCHER          0         0        91
03C6C534 DISPATCHER          0         0        71
```

V$CIRCUIT Dictionary View

V$CIRCUIT displays information about Shared Server virtual circuits, such as the volume of information that has passed between the client and the dispatcher and the current status of the client connection. The SADDR column displays the session address for the connected session. This can be joined to the V$SESSION view to display information about the user to whom this connection belongs. Here is a sample output from this view:

```
SQL> select circuit,dispatcher,server,waiter WTR,
   2 status,queue,bytes from v$circuit;

CIRCUIT  DISPATCH SERVER   WTR STATUS QUEUE  BYTES SADDR
-------- -------- -------- --- ------ ------ ----- ------
03E2A624 03C6C244 00       00  NORMAL NONE   47330 03C7AB68
03E2A724 03C6C534 03C6BC64 00  NORMAL SERVER 43572 03C79BE8
```

V$SHARED_SERVER Dictionary View

This view contains information about the shared server processes. It displays information about the number of requests and the amount of information processed by the shared servers. It also indicates the status of the shared server (i.e., whether it is active or idle).

```
SQL> select name,status,messages,bytes,idle,busy,
     requests from v$shared_server;
```

```
NAME STATUS MESSAGES  BYTES  IDLE   BUSY  REQUESTS
---- ------ -------- ----- -----  ----  --------
S000 EXEC        372 86939 98472   300       175
S001 EXEC         26 9851  98703    38        13
```

V$SHARED_SERVER_Monitor Dictionary View

This view contains information that can assist in tuning the Shared Server. This includes the maximum number of concurrent connections attained since instance startup and the total number of servers started since instance startup. The query below shows an example of output from the V$SHARED_SERVER view.

```
SQL> select maximum_connections "MAX CONN",maximum_
sessions "MAX SESS", servers_started "STARTED" from
v$shared_server_monitor;

MAX CONN MAX SESS  STARTED
-------- --------- --------
115      120       10
```

V$SESSION Dictionary View

This view contains information about the client session. The SERVER column indicates whether this client is using a dedicated session or a dispatcher. The listing below shows an example of the V$SESSION view displaying the server information. This listing ignores any rows that do not have a username to avoid listing information about the background processes. Notice that user Scott has a server value of SHARED. This means Scott is connected to a dispatcher. The SYSTEM user is connected using a local connection because the status is NONE. If a user connected using a dedicated connection, the status would be DEDICATED.

```
SQL> select username,program,server from v$session
     where username is not null;

USERNAME         PROGRAM          SERVER
---------------  --------------   ---------
SYSTEM            SQLPLUS.EXE      NONE
SCOTT             SQLPLUS.EXE      SHARED
```

V$MTS Dictionary View

This view contains information about the configuration of the dispatchers and shared servers. This includes the maximum number of connections for each dispatcher, the number of shared servers that have been started and stopped, and the highest number of shared servers that have been active at the same time. This view gives you an indication of whether more shared server processes should be started. The sample below shows output from this view:

```
SQL> select MAX_CONNECTIONS MAX_CONN, SERVERS_STARTED
SRV_STARTED, SERVERS_TERMINATED SRV_TERM,
SERVERS_HIGHWATER SRV_HW
FROM V$MTS;

MAX_CONN SRV_STARTED SRV_TERM SRV_HW
-------- ----------- -------- ------
      60           0        0      2
```

The V$MTS view is identical in content to the V$SHARED_SERVER_MONITOR view. V$MTS was the name for this view at Oracle8*i* release and is still available for reference.

Requesting a Dedicated Connection in a Shared Server Environment

You can have Shared Server and dedicated servers connecting to a single Oracle server. This is advantageous in situations where you have a mix of activity on the Oracle server. Some users may be well suited to shared server connections while other types of users may be better suited to use dedicated connections.

By default, if Shared Server is configured, a client is connected to a dispatcher unless the client explicitly requests a dedicated connection. As part of the connection descriptor, the client has to send information requesting a dedicated connection. Configure this option using the Oracle Net Manager. Clients may request this type of connection if the names resolution method is localnaming. This option cannot be used with hostnaming.

Configuring Dedicated Connections When Localnaming Is Used

If you are using localnaming, you want to add a parameter to the service name entry in the `tnsnames.ora` file. The parameter `(SERVER=DEDICATED)` is added to the DBA net service name. The SERVER parameter can also be abbreviated as SRVR. Here is an example of the entry in the `tnsnames.ora` file.

```
# D:\ORACLE\ORA90\NETWORK\ADMIN\TNSNAMES.ORA Configuration
# File:D:\Oracle\Ora90\NETWORK\ADMIN\tnsnames.ora
# Generated by Oracle Net Manager

DBA =
  (DESCRIPTION =
    (ADDRESS_LIST =
      (ADDRESS = (PROTOCOL = TCP)(HOST = weishan)
(PORT = 1521))
    )
    (CONNECT_DATA =
      (SERVICE_NAME = DBA)
      (SRVR = DEDICATED)   Request a dedicated connection
for DBA
    )
  )
```

Tuning the Shared Server Option

Before tuning the Shared Server, you should examine the performance of the dispatchers and the shared server processes. You want to make sure that you have enough dispatchers so that clients are not waiting for dispatchers to respond to their requests, and you want to have enough shared server processes so that requests are not waiting to be processed. You also want to configure the Large Pool SGA memory area. The Large Pool is used to store the UGA. The UGA takes the place of the PGA that is used for dedicated servers.

The Large Pool is designed to allow the database to request large amounts of memory from a separate area of the SGA. Before the database had a Large

Pool design, memory allocations for Shared Server came from the Shared Pool. This caused Shared Server to compete with other processes updating information in the Shared Pool. The Large Pool alleviates the memory burden on the Shared Pool and enhances performance of the Shared Pool.

Configure the Large Pool

You can configure the Large Pool by setting the parameter LARGE_POOL_SIZE in the init.ora file. This parameter can be set to a minimum of 300KB and a maximum of at least 2GB; the maximum setting is operating system dependent. When a default value is used, Oracle adds 250KB per session for each shared server if the DISPATCHERS parameter is specified. If you do not configure a Large Pool, Oracle will place the UGA into the Shared Pool. Because of this, you should configure a Large Pool when using Shared Server so that you don't affect the performance of the Shared Pool. Here is an example of setting the LARGE_POOL_SIZE parameter in the init.ora file:

```
LARGE_POOL_SIZE = 50M
```

You can see how much space is being used by the Large Pool by querying the V$SGASTAT view. The free memory row shows the amount available in the Large Pool and the session heap row shows the amount of space used in the Large Pool. Here is a listing that shows an example of the query:

```
SQL> select * from v$sgastat where pool = 'Large Pool';

POOL        NAME                           BYTES
----------- -------------------------- ---------
large pool  free memory                   251640
large pool  session heap                   48360
```

Sizing the Large Pool

The Large Pool should be large enough to hold information for all of your shared server connections. Generally, each connection will need between one and three megabytes of memory, but this depends on that client's type of activity. Clients that do a great deal of sorting or open many cursors will use more memory.

You can gauge how much memory shared server connections are using by querying the V$SESSTAT view. This view contains information about memory utilization per user. The query below shows how to measure the maximum amount of memory for all shared server sessions since the instance was started. You can use this as a guide to determine how much memory you should allocate for the Large Pool. This example shows that the maximum amount of memory used for all shared server sessions is around 240KB:

```
select sum(value) "Max MTS Memory Allocated"from v$sesstat
ss, v$statname st
where name = 'session uga memory max'and ss.statistic#
=st.statistic#;

Max MTS Memory Allocated
------------------------
                  244416
```

Determine Whether You Have Enough Dispatchers

The dispatcher processes can be monitored by querying the V$DISPATCHER view. This view contains information about how busy the dispatcher processes are. Query this view to determine whether it will be advantageous to start more dispatchers.

The sample query below runs against the V$DISPATCHER view to show what percentage of the time dispatchers are busy:

```
Select name, (busy / (busy + idle))*100
"Dispatcher % busy Rate"
From V$DISPATCHER

Protocol           Dispatcher % Busy Rate
------------       ---------------------------
D000                .00070079
D001                .0059
```

These dispatchers show very little busy time. If dispatchers are busy more than 50 percent of the time, you should consider starting more dispatchers. This can be done dynamically with the ALTER SYSTEM command. Add one or two more dispatchers and monitor the busy rates of the dispatchers to see if they fall below 50 percent.

Determine How Long Users Are Waiting for Dispatchers

To measure how long users are waiting for the dispatchers to execute their request, look at the combined V$QUEUE and V$DISPATCHER views. See the listing below for an example:

```
SELECT decode(sum(totalq),0,'No Responses',
                Sum(wait)/sum(totalq)) "Average Wait time"
FROM V$QUEUE q, V$DISPATCHER d
WHERE q.type = 'DISPATCHER'
AND q.paddr = d.paddr;

Average Wait Time
------------------
  .0413
```

The average wait time for dispatchers is a little more than four hundredths of a second. Monitor this measure over time. If the number is consistently increasing, you should consider adding more dispatchers.

Determine Whether You Have Enough Shared Servers

You can monitor shared servers by using the V$SHARED_SERVER and V$QUEUE dictionary views. The shared servers are responsible for executing client requests and placing the requests in the appropriate dispatcher response queue.

The measurement you are most interested in is how long client requests are waiting in the request queue. The longer the request remains in the queue, the longer the client will wait for a response. The following statement will tell you how long requests are waiting in the queue:

```
Select decode(totalq,0,'No Requests') "Wait Time",
Wait/totalq || ' hundredths of seconds'
"Average Wait time per request"
from V$QUEUE
where type = 'COMMON'
```

```
Wait Time Average Wait time per request
-------- ------------------------------------
.023132   hundredths of a second
```

The average wait time in the request queue is a little more than two hundredths of a second. Monitor this measure over time. If the number is consistently increasing, you should consider adding more shared servers.

Summary

The Shared Server is a configuration of the Oracle server that allows you to support a greater number of connections without the need for additional resources. It is important to understand the shared server option because it can stave off potentially unnecessary hardware upgrades when you are faced with the problem of the number of processes your server can manage.

In this configuration, user connections share processes called dispatchers. Dispatchers replace the dedicated server processes in a dedicated server environment. The Oracle server is also configured with shared server processes that can process the requests of many clients.

The Oracle server is configured with a single request queue in which dispatchers place the client requests that the shared servers will take and process. The shared server processes put the completed requests in the appropriate dispatcher's response queue. The dispatcher then sends the completed request back to the client. These request and response queues are structures added to the SGA.

There are a number of parameters that are added to the `init.ora` file to configure Shared Server. Dispatchers and shared servers can be added dynamically after the Oracle server has been started. You can add more shared servers and dispatchers up to the maximum value specified.

There are several `V$` views that are used to monitor Shared Server. The information contained in these views pertains to dispatchers, shared server processes, and the clients that are connected to the dispatcher processes.

You can use the `V$` views to tune the Shared Server. It is most important to measure how long clients are waiting for dispatchers to process their requests and how long it is taking before a shared server processes the client requests. These factors may lead to increasing the number of shared server and dispatcher processes. You also want to monitor the usage of the Large Pool.

Exam Essentials

Define Oracle Shared Server. It will be important for you to be able to list the advantages of Shared Server versus a dedicated server and when it is appropriate to consider either option.

Understand the architecture of the Oracle Shared Server. Be able to summarize the steps that a client takes to initiate a connection with a shared server and the processes behind those steps. You should understand what happens during client request processing and outline the steps involved.

Understand the changes that are made in the SGA and the PGA. Make sure you understand that in a Shared Server environment many of the PGA structures are moved in the Large Pool inside of the SGA. This means that the SGA will become larger and the Large Pool will need to be configured in the `init.ora` file.

Know how to configure the Oracle Shared Server. You should be able to define the meaning of each of the parameters involved in the configuration of Oracle Shared Server. You should know what parameters can be dynamically modified and what parameters require the Oracle instance to be restarted to take effect.

Know how to configure clients running in Shared Server mode. You should be able to configure clients that need to have a dedicated connection to Oracle if it is running in Shared Server mode.

Know what views to use to monitor the Shared Server performance. It is important that you be able to use the available V$ views to monitor and tune the shared server and know how to adjust settings when necessary.

Key Terms

Before you take the exam, be certain you are familiar with the following terms:

- dedicated server
- dispatchers
- Large Pool
- load balancing
- `lsnrctl` services
- Oracle Shared Server option
- Program Global Area (PGA)
- request queue
- response queue
- shared server processes
- User Global Area (UGA)
- virtual circuit

Review Questions

1. All of the following are reasons to configure the server using Shared Server *except*:

   A. There is a reduction of overall memory utilization.

   B. The system is predominantly used for decision support with large result sets returned.

   C. The system is predominantly used for small transactions with many users.

   D. There is a reduction of the number of idle connections on the server.

2. Which of the following is *true* about Shared Server?

   A. Dedicated connections cannot be made when Shared Server is configured.

   B. Bequeath connections are not possible when Shared Server is configured.

   C. The database can be started when connected via Shared Server.

   D. The database cannot be stopped when connected via Shared Server.

3. The administrator wants to allow a user to connect via a dedicated connection into a database configured in Shared Server mode. Which of the following lines would accomplish this?

   A. `(SERVER=DEDICATED)`

   B. `(CONNECT=DEDICATED)`

   C. `(INSTANCE=DEDICATED)`

   D. `(MULTITRHEADED=FALSE)`

   E. None of the above

4. In what file would you find the shared server configuration parameters?

   A. `listener.ora`

   B. `mts.ora`

   C. `init.ora`

   D. `tnsnames.ora`

   E. `sqlnet.ora`

5. Which of the following is one of the components of Shared Server?

   A. Shared user processes

   B. Checkpoint processes

   C. Dispatcher processes

   D. Dedicated server processes

6. The DBA wants to put the database in Shared Server mode. In what file will modifications be made?

   A. `tnsnames.ora`

   B. `cman.ora`

   C. `names.ora`

   D. `init.ora`

7. What choice in the Oracle Net Manager allows for the configuration of Shared Server?

   A. Local

   B. Service Naming

   C. Listeners

   D. Profile

   E. None of the above

8. The DBA wants two TCP/IP dispatchers and one IPC dispatcher to start when the instance is started. Which line will accomplish this?

   A. `dispatchers=(protocol=tcp)(dispatchers=2) (protocol=IPC)(dispatchers=1)dispatchers=(protocol= tcp)(dispatchers=2) (protocol=IPC)(dispatchers=1)`

   B. `dispatchers="(protocol=tcp)(dispatchers=2) (protocol=IPC)(dispatchers=1)"`

   C. `dispatchers_start=(protocol=tcp)(dispatchers=2) (protocol=IPC)(dispatchers=1)`

   D. `dispatchers_start=(pro=tcp)(dis=2) (pro=IPC)(dis=1)`

9. What is the piece of shared memory that client connections are bound to during communications via Shared Server called?

   A. Program Global Area

   B. System Global Area

   C. Virtual Circuit

   D. Database Buffer Cache

   E. None of the above

10. What is the first step the dispatcher should take after it has received a request from the user?

    A. Pass the request to a shared server.

    B. Place the request in a request queue in the PGA.

    C. Place the request in a request queue in the SGA.

    D. Process the request.

11. Dispatchers have all of the following characteristics *except*:

    A. Dispatchers can be shared by many connections.

    B. More dispatchers can be added dynamically with the `ALTER SYSTEM` command.

    C. A dispatcher can listen for multiple protocols.

    D. Each dispatcher has its own response queue.

12. When configured in Shared Server mode, which of the following is contained in the PGA?
    A. Cursor state
    B. Sort information
    C. User session data
    D. Stack space
    E. None of the above

13. Which of the following is *false* about shared servers?
    A. Shared servers can process requests from many users.
    B. Shared servers receive their requests directly from dispatchers.
    C. Shared servers place completed requests on a dispatcher response queue.
    D. The SERVERS parameter configures the number of shared servers to start at instance startup.

14. Which of the following is *not* a step in the processing of a shared server request?
    A. Shared servers pass information back to the client process.
    B. Dispatchers place information in a request queue.
    C. Users pass requests to a dispatcher.
    D. The dispatcher picks up completed requests from its response queue.
    E. None of the above.

15. When you are configuring Shared Server, which initialization parameter would you likely need to increase?
    A. `DB_BLOCK_SIZE`
    B. `DB_BLOCK_BUFFERS`
    C. `SHARED_POOL_SIZE`
    D. `BUFFER_SIZE`
    E. None of the above

16. Which of the following is *false* about request queues?

    A. They reside in the SGA.

    B. They are shared by all of the dispatchers.

    C. Each dispatcher has its own request queue.

    D. The shared server processes remove requests from the request queue.

17. The DBA is interested in gathering information about users connected via shared server connections. Which of the following is the view that would contain this information?

    A. `V$USERS`

    B. `V$QUEUE`

    C. `V$SESS_STATS`

    D. `V$CIRCUIT`

    E. None of the above

18. What is the process that is responsible for notifying the listener after a database connection is established?

    A. SMON

    B. DBWR

    C. PMON

    D. LGWR

19. The DBA is interested in gathering performance and tuning related information for the shared server processes. The DBA should start by querying which of the following views?

    A. `V$USERS`

    B. `V$CIRCUIT`

    C. `V$SHARED_SERVER_MONITOR`

    D. `V$SESS_STATS`

20. What command can be executed to give details about the number of sessions connected via Shared Server?

A. `mtslsnr check`

B. `lsnrctl mts`

C. `lsnrctl status`

D. `lsnrctl services`

E. None of the above

Answers to Review Questions

1. B. Shared Server is a scalability option of Oracle. It provides a way to increase the number of supported user processes while reducing the overall memory usage. This configuration is well suited to high-volume, small transaction-oriented systems with many users connected. Because users share processes, there is also an overall reduction of the number of idle processes. It is not well suited for large data retrieval type applications like decision support.

2. D. Users can still request dedicated connections in a shared server configuration. Bequeath and dedicated connections are one and the same. The database cannot be stopped or started when a user is connected over a shared server connection.

3. A. A user must explicitly request a dedicated connection when a server is configured in Shared Server mode. Otherwise, the user will get a shared server connection. The correct parameter is `(SERVER=DEDICATED)`.

4. C. The shared server configuration parameters exist in the `init.ora` file on the Oracle server machine.

5. C. In Shared Server, users connect to a pool of shared resources called dispatchers. A client connects to the listener and the listener redirects the request to a dispatcher. The dispatchers handle all of the user requests for the session. Many users can share dispatchers.

6. D. Because the database has to be configured in Shared Server mode, changes have to be made to the `init.ora` file. The other choices are also configuration files, but none of them are used to configure Shared Server.

7. E. This is one of the tricky questions again! Many options and files can be configured by the Oracle Net Manager, including `tnsnames.ora` and `sqlnet.ora`. But because Shared Server is a characteristic of the database server and not of the network, Oracle Net Manager is not used to configure it.

8. B. Back to syntax again! The DISPATCHERS parameter of the `init.ora` file is used to configure dispatchers, so the correct answer is option B. All of the other choices are invalid parameters.

9. C. The System Global Area is the shared memory segment Oracle obtains on instance startup. The Program Global Area is an area of memory used primarily during dedicated connections. The Database Buffer Cache is actually a component of the Program Global Area. Virtual Circuits are the shared memory areas to which clients bind.

10. C. Once a dispatcher receives a request from the user process, it places the request on the request queue. Remember that in a shared server environment, a request can be handled by a shared server process. This is made possible by placing the request and user information in the SGA.

11. C. Many users can connect to dispatchers, and dispatchers can be added dynamically. Also, each dispatcher does have its own response queue. The only one of these options that is false is option C because dispatchers can listen for only one protocol. Multiple dispatchers can be configured so that each is responsible for different protocols.

12. D. A small PGA is maintained even though most of the user-specific information is moved to the SGA (specifically called the UGA in the Shared Pool or the Large Pool). The only information left in the reduced PGA is stack space.

13. B. Shared servers can process requests from many users. The completed requests are placed into the dispatchers' response queues. The servers are configured with the SERVERS parameter. However, shared servers do not receive requests directly from dispatchers. The requests are taken from the request queue.

14. A. Study the steps of what happens during a request via Shared Server. Dispatchers receive requests from users and place the requests on request queues. Only dispatchers interact with client processes. Shared servers merely execute the requests and place the results back on the dispatcher's response queue.

15. C. Shared Server requires a shift of memory away from individual session processes to the SGA. More information has to be kept in the SGA (in the UGA) within the Shared Pool. A Large Pool can also be configured and would probably be responsible for the majority of the SGA space allocation. But, because that was not a choice, option C is the correct answer. The block size and block buffers settings do not affect Shared Server.

16. C. Request queues reside in the SGA, and there is one request queue per instance. This is where shared server processes pick up requests that are made by users. Dispatchers have their own response queues but they *share* a single request queue.

17. D. There are several `V$` views that can be used to manage the Shared Server. `V$QUEUE` gives information regarding the request and response queues. `V$USERS` and `V$SESS_STATS` are not valid views. `V$CIRCUIT` will give information about the users who are connected via shared server connections, and it will provide the necessary information.

18. C. The PMON process is responsible for notifying the listener after a client connection is established. This is so that the listener can keep track of the number of connections being serviced by each dispatcher.

19. C. The `V$SHARED_SERVER_MONITOR` view can be queried to view information about the maximum number of connections and sessions, the number of servers started and terminated, and the server high-water mark. These numbers can help determine whether the DBA should start more shared servers.

20. C. Dispatchers register with listeners so that when a listener redirects a connection to a dispatcher, the listener knows how many active connections the dispatcher is serving. The `lsnrctl status` command summarizes the number of connections established, connections currently active, and other valuable information regarding Shared Server. The `lsnrctl services` command only gives a summary of dispatchers, not any details about connections.

Backup and Recovery Overview

ORACLE9*i*: DBA FUNDAMENTALS II EXAM OBJECTIVES COVERED IN THIS CHAPTER:

- ✓ Describe the basics of database backup, restore and recovery.
- ✓ List the types of failure that may occur in an Oracle environment.
- ✓ Define a backup and recovery strategy.

Exam objectives are subject to change at any time without prior notice and at Oracle's sole discretion. Please visit Oracle's Certification website (`http://www.oracle.com/education/certification/`) for the most current exam objectives listing.

Backup and recovery in an Oracle database environment can be simple or complex depending on the requirements of the business environment the database is supporting. Oracle provides methods for supporting such environments, and each of these methods requires different levels of complexity for backup and recovery operations.

First of all, there are multiple types of failures that may occur in an Oracle database environment. Each of these can result in different types of recovery operations. You must understand these types of failure in order to make the correct recovery decisions.

Once you understand Oracle backup and recovery and the possible types of Oracle database failures, you will be able to create a backup and recovery strategy. When you are determining this strategy, you need to consider a number of issues. First of all, keep in mind that in order for backup and recovery to be successful, everyone from the technical team through management must understand the requirements and the effects of the backup and recovery strategy. After this strategy is agreed upon and in place, a disaster recovery plan can be created based upon this strategy. When you are creating your disaster recovery plan, it's important that you understand the options for high availability, as well as the options for configuring your database for recoverability. After you have successfully created this plan, the final step is to test it.

This chapter takes you step-by-step through the basic principles of backup and recovery: it introduces you to the types of failures that may occur, and to the backup and recovery strategy. In the end, you should be comfortable with your knowledge of what is involved in the Oracle backup, restore, and recovery process. You should understand enough about the different types of failures so that you can identify the appropriate course of action to implement in a recovery situation. This level of understanding will not only make your job as a DBA easier, but it should also make it much more comfortable.

Database Backup, Restoration, and Recovery

If you understand and can identify the aspects of the Oracle database that are required for normal operation, you will understand what must be backed up, restored, and recovered.

The Oracle database is made up of a set of physical structures that must be present and consistent for the database to function normally. At a minimum, these physical structures consist of data files, redo logs, control files, and initialization files.

If any of these files are not present, the database may not start up or it may halt during normal operations. All of these files must be backed up on a regular basis to disk, tape, or both. Such a backup can consist of a user-managed backup or Recovery Manager (RMAN)-based backup. A *user-managed backup* consists of any custom backup; such a backup is usually performed in an OS script such as a Unix shell script or the DOS-based batch script. These scripts execute database commands and OS commands to copy the necessary database files to disk or tape. An *RMAN-based backup* is performed by the Oracle recover manager utility, which is part of the Oracle software. RMAN backups are performed by executing standard RMAN commands or scripts.

Both of these backups can be used to restore the necessary database files from disk or tape to the desired location. The *restore* process consists of copying the database files from tape or disk to a desired location so that database recovery can begin.

The *recovery* process consists of starting the database and making it consistent using a complete or partial backup copy of some of the physical structures of the database. Recovery has many options depending on the type of backups that are performed. We will discuss the different types of recovery in user-managed and RMAN-based situations in later chapters.

Types of Failure in Oracle Environments

There are two major categories of database failures: *non-media failures* and *media (disk) failures*. Non-media failures consist of four types of failures, which are typically less critical in nature. Media failures have only one type of failure, which is generally more critical in nature—the inability to read or write from a database file.

Non-Media Failures

This type of failure is made up of statement failures, process failures, instance failures, and user errors, and it is almost always less critical than a media failure. In most cases, statement, process, and instance failures are automatically handled by Oracle and require no DBA intervention. User error can require a manual recovery performed by the DBA.

Statement failure consists of a syntax error in the statement, and Oracle usually returns an error number and description. *Process failure* occurs when the user program fails for some reason, such as when there is an abnormal disconnection or a termination. The process monitor (PMON) process usually handles cleaning up the terminated process. *Instance failure* occurs when the database instance abnormally terminates due to a power spike or outage. Oracle handles this automatically upon start-up by reading through the current online redo logs and applying the necessary changes back to the database. *User error* occurs when a table is erroneously dropped or data is erroneously removed.

Media, or Disk, Failures

These failures are the most critical. A media failure occurs when the database fails to read or write from a file that it requires. For example, a disk drive could fail, a controller supporting a disk drive could fail, or a database file could be removed, overwritten, or corrupted. Each type of media failure that occurs requires a different method for recovery.

The basic steps you should take to perform media recovery are as follows:

1. Determine which files will need to be recovered: data files, control files, and/or redo logs.
2. Determine which type of media recovery is required: complete or incomplete, opened database, or closed database. (You will learn more about these types of recovery in later chapters.)
3. Restore backups of the required files: data files, control files, and offline redo logs (archived logs) necessary to recover.

4. Apply offline redo logs (archived logs) to the data files.
5. Open the database at the desired point, depending on whether you are performing a complete or an incomplete recovery.
6. Perform frequent testing of the process. Create a test plan of typical failure scenarios.

Defining a Backup and Recovery Strategy

To create a solid *backup and recovery strategy*, you must keep in mind six major requirements:

- The amount of data that can be lost in the event of a database failure
- The length of time that the business can go without the database in the event of a database failure
- Whether the database can be offline to perform a backup, and if so, the length of time that it can remain offline
- The types of resources available to perform backup and recovery
- The procedures for undoing changes to the database, if necessary
- The cost of buying and maintaining hardware and performing additional backups versus the cost of replacing or re-creating the data lost in a disaster

All of these requirements must clearly be understood before you plan a backup and recovery strategy.

Losing Data in a Database Failure

The amount of data that can be lost in a failure helps determine the backup and recovery strategy that gets implemented. For instance, if losing a week's worth of data in the event of failure is tolerable, then a weekly backup may be a possible option. On the other hand, if no data can be lost in the event of failure, then weekly backups would be out of the question and backups would need to be performed daily.

Surviving without the Database in a Database Failure

If the company database were to fail during an outage, how long would it take for the business to be negatively affected? Generally, this question can be answered by management. If all data is entered manually by data entry, the downtime could be relatively long without hurting the business operations. The business could potentially operate normally by generating orders or forms that could be entered into the database later. This type of situation could have minimal effect on the business.

On the other hand, a financial institution that sends and receives data electronically 24 hours a day can't afford to be down for any time at all, and if it were, business operations would most definitely be impaired. The electronic transactions could be unusable until the database was recovered.

After you determine how long the business could survive without a database, you can use the *mean time to recovery (MTTR)* to figure out the average amount of time the database could be down if it were to fail. The MTTR is the average time it takes to recover from certain types of failure. You should record each type of failure that is tested so that you can then determine an average recovery time. The MTTR can help determine mean recovery times for different failure scenarios. You can document these times during your testing cycles.

Performing an Offline Backup

To determine whether it is possible to perform a database backup if the database is offline or shut down, you must first know how long the database can afford to be out of commission.

For example, if the database is being used with an Internet site that has national or international access, or if it is being used with a manufacturing site that works two or three shifts across different time zones and has nightly batch processing, then it would have to be available 24 hours a day. In this case, the database would always need to remain online, with the exception of scheduled downtimes for maintenance. In this case, an online backup, or *hot backup*, would need to be performed. This type of backup is done when the database is online or running.

Businesses that don't require 24-hour availability and do not have long batch processing activities in the evening could potentially afford to have the database offline on regular nightly intervals for an offline backup, or *cold backup*. In this scenario, each site should conduct their own backup tests with factors unique to their environment to determine how long it would take to perform a cold backup. If the database downtime is acceptable for that site, then a cold backup could be a workable solution.

Knowing Your Backup and Recovery Resources

The personnel, hardware, and software resources available to the business also affect the backup and recovery strategy. Personnel resources would include at least adequate support from a database administrator (DBA), system administrator (SA), and operator. The DBA would be responsible for the technical piece of the backup, such as user-managed scripts or Recovery Manager (RMAN) scripts. A user-managed backup is an OS backup written in an OS scripting language, such as the Korn shell in the Unix OS. RMAN is an automated tool from Oracle that can perform the backup and recovery process. The SA would be involved in some aspects of the scripting, tape backup software, and tape hardware. The operator might be involved in changing tapes and ensuring that the proper tape cycles are followed.

The hardware resources could include an automated tape library (ATL), a stand-alone tape drive, adequate staging disk space for scripted hot backups and exports, adequate archived log disk space, and third disk mirrors. Many storage subsystem hardware vendors are offering their own third disk mirror options or equivalents. These options create disk copies of 100 gigabytes and greater in just a few minutes. All types of disk subsystems should be at least mirrored or use some form of Redundant Array of Inexpensive Disks (RAID), such as RAID 5, where performance is not compromised.

The software resources could include backup software, scripting capabilities, and tape library software. The Oracle RMAN utility comes with the Oracle9*i* Server software and is installed when selecting all components of Oracle9*i* Enterprise Server.

The technical personnel, the DBA and SA at a minimum, are generally responsible for informing the management of the necessary hardware and software to achieve the desired recovery goals.

RAID is essentially fault tolerance that protects against individual disk crashes. There are multiple levels of RAID. RAID 0 implements disk striping without redundancy. RAID 1 is standard disk mirroring. RAID 2–5 offer some form of parity-bit checking on separate disks. RAID 5 has become the most popular in recent years, with many vendors offering their own enhancements to RAID 5 for increased performance. RAID 0 + 1 has been a longtime fault-tolerance and performance favorite for Oracle database configurations. This is due to redundancy protection and strong write performance. However, with the new RAID 5 enhancements (performed by some storage array vendors to include large caches or memory buffers), the write performance has improved substantially. RAID 0 + 1 and RAID 5 both can be viable configurations for Oracle databases.

Undoing Changes to the Database

There are three primary ways of undoing changes to the database; one is a manual approach, the other two methods use Oracle features to undo the data.

- Manually—by reexecuting code or rebuilding tables
- Using Oracle LogMiner to recover dropped objects
- Using a new Oracle9*i* feature called Flashback Query

Whether it is possible to undo changes to the database with the manual approach depends on the sophistication of the code releases and the configuration management control for the application in question.

If the configuration control is highly structured with defined release schedules, then undoing changes may not be necessary. A highly structured release schedule would reduce the possibility of data errors or dropped database objects.

On the other hand, if the release schedule tends to be unstructured, the potential for data errors from developers can be higher. It is a good idea to prepare for these issues in any case. A full export can be done periodically, which would give the DBA a static copy of all the necessary objects within a database. Although exports have limitations, they can be useful for repairing data errors because individual users and tables can be extracted from the export file. Additionally, individual tablespace backups can be performed more frequently on high-use tablespaces.

Oracle LogMiner was first introduced in Oracle8/8*i*. This utility rebuilds data from redo log–generated transactions. LogMiner allows you to rebuild erroneously dropped tables by performing a series of steps that include building an external data dictionary and identifying the transactions that must be reloaded. LogMiner is run by using Procedural Language SQL (PL/SQL) procedures to build the LogMiner utility. Table 5.1 describes the PL/SQL procedures involved with using LogMiner. The Data Manipulation Language (DML) can be seen in the `v$logmnr_contents` table after the PL/SQL procedures have been executed.

TABLE 5.1 LogMiner PL/SQL Procedures

PL/SQL Procedure	Purpose
`sys.dbms_logmnr_d.build`	Builds data dictionary
`dbms_logmnr.add_logfile`	Accesses desired redo log file
`dbms_logmnr.start_logmnr`	Begins using LogMiner session

Oracle Flashback Query is a new feature to Oracle9*i*. This feature allows a user to access past versions of dictionary tables. This feature works by generating a picture of data as it was in the past by using undo data. This is performed by identifying all data that has been modified since undo was created and retained against the retention policy. Then the corresponding undo data is retrieved.

The Flashback Query feature is performed by executing the PL/SQL `dbms_flashback` package. Further, Automatic Undo Management must be enabled by setting the `init.ora` file to the `UNDO_MANAGEMENT = AUTO` parameter. There also must be an undo tablespace parameter designated, such as `UNDO_TABLESPACE = UNDOTBS`. This must be set in the `init.ora` before the Flashback Query can be used. The parameter that controls the length of retention of the Flashback Query is called `UNDO_RETENTION`. This parameter may be set with `UNDO_RETENTION = n` with *n* being an integer value in seconds.

Flashback Query cannot query data that is greater than five days old. This is true even if the `UNDO_RENTENTION` parameter is set to a value greater than five days old.

Weighing the Costs

Additional hardware is usually needed to perform adequate testing and failover for critical databases. When this additional hardware is unavailable, the risk of an unrecoverable database failure is greater.

The cost of the additional hardware should be weighed against the cost of re-creating the lost data in the event of an unrecoverable database failure. This type of cost comparison will cause the management team to identify the steps necessary to manually re-create lost data, if this can be done.

Once the steps for re-creating lost data are identified and the associated costs are determined, these costs can be compared to the cost of additional hardware. This additional hardware would be used for testing backups and as a system failover if a production server was severely damaged.

Testing a Backup and Recovery Plan

One of the most important (but also most overlooked) components of the recovery plan is testing. Testing should be done before and after the database that you are supporting is in production. Testing validates that your backups are working, and gives you the peace of mind that recovery will work when a real disaster occurs.

You should document and practice scenarios of certain types of failures so that you are familiar with them, and you should make sure that the methods to recover from these types of failures are clearly defined. At a minimum, you should document and practice the following types of failures:

- Loss of a system tablespace
- Loss of a nonsystem tablespace
- Loss of a current online redo log
- Loss of the whole database

Testing recovery should include recovering your database to another server, such as a test or development server. The cost of having additional servers available on which to perform testing can be intimidating for some businesses, and it can be one deterrent for adequate testing. Test servers are absolutely necessary, however, and businesses that fail to perform this requirement can be at risk of severe data loss or an unrecoverable situation.

One way that you can test recovery is to create a new development or testing environment and recover the database to a development or test server in support of a new software release. Database copies are often necessary to support new releases of the database and application code prior to moving it to production. RMAN provides the `DUPLICATE` command in support of this. Manual OS tools in Unix, such as `ufsrestore`, `tar`, and `cpio` from tape or copying from a disk staging area, are often used for scripted backups.

Real World Scenario

Driving Adequate Testing with the Service Level Agreement

Let's look at this real-life example to determine how much testing is enough for recovery preparation.

Many companies try to reduce implementation and support costs by not allocating sufficient resources for testing. In this particular case, a manufacturing company is trying to determine how much testing is enough to get by. Up until this point, this company had performed all of its data processing on a mainframe-customized environment, so the customized Oracle database environment is new to them. As a result, when the company switched to an Oracle-based environment, they did not set up a service level agreement with the information technology (IT) department so that their database environment would be maintained properly.

Because they lacked this service level agreement from customers of the database, they didn't have the instrument necessary to drive the testing, nor did they have the necessary resources to perform the testing. Their reasoning for this lack of resources was based on the premise that testing is a costly effort, and the results of it may never be needed. In this case, it was hard for the company to justify the expense of resources (IT staff and equipment) to perform testing. What this company was not aware of was that, at a minimum, certain recovery tests should be performed to validate the backup process and to train the database administration staff for certain common failures.

Also, because there was no service agreement with the database customers, there was never a formalized testing strategy to support the recovery of the database. As a result, within one year after the company converted their manufacturing environment to a custom Oracle-based solution, there was an outage. As a result, the company experienced a corrupt online redo log, but because the company had a customized hot backup strategy, a backup was available.

It wasn't immediately apparent to those working on the problem that the failure was due to a corrupt redo log. As a result, over six hours was wasted by the DBA group before the problem was accurately diagnosed. Once it was, the staff was not sure of the exact type of recovery to perform. Because of this, more time was wasted and more anxiety was created than necessary. Finally, the problem was diagnosed with the help of Oracle Support, who determined that the company would need to perform an incomplete recovery prior to the identified corruption point in the online redo log.

With a service level agreement from the database customers and the IT department, a formalized set of expectations would have been set. These expectations could have lead to the proper testing of the database. As a result, most of these problems could have been reduced.

Summary

Oracle provides numerous options for backup and recovery, which support varying business requirements. These options are founded on some basic principles of database file structures required in the backup, restore, and recovery processes. One of these principles is that the necessary Oracle database file structures are backed up on a regular basis so that if necessary, the restore and recovery of these files can be performed.

There are two major categories of failure: non-media and media based failures. Understanding these types of failure within these categories will allow you to develop a backup and recovery strategy. The result of this strategy is how you will respond in a failure situation to best meet the situation at hand.

It is important to have a solid of understanding of the backup, restore, and recovery processes of an Oracle database. Equally important is having an understanding of the types of failures or problems that could cause you to recover a database. Without understanding the importance and appropriate course of action to take for certain failures, significant down time or mistakes can occur. Making sure the database is open and available for use is one of the most important responsibilities of the DBA.

Exam Essentials

Identify the failure categories. Make sure you are aware of non-media and media failures. A media failure is more serious because it is a hardware failure or corruption, and it will prevent the user from reading from or writing to a database file. A non-media failure is usually less serious because recovering from this type of failure is usually easy.

Identify the different types of non-media failure. The four failure types are statement failure, process failure, instance failure, and user error. You should be aware of how each of these failure types is initiated.

Understand the multiple ways to undo user errors. Identify the three ways to undo user errors in the database. Undoing user errors is performed manually (rebuilding lost code or data, or importing objects), by using LogMiner to restore transactions from archived log files, and by using the Flashback Query feature to query data based on the undo information.

Understand the media recovery process. The media recovery process includes restoring physical database files that are impacted by media failure and applying archived logs to roll the restored files forward to a determined point in time.

Understand the difference between user-managed and RMAN backups and recovery. A traditional, user-managed backup and recovery is customized in an OS scripting language so that it can call database commands and perform OS commands. A RMAN backup and recovery is created by using the RMAN utility.

Identify the requirements for a backup and recovery strategy. Be able to understand the general concept of a backup and recovery strategy so that you are aware of the unique planning required to recover a database to meet your customers' requirements.

Key Terms

Before you take the exam, be certain you are familiar with the following terms:

- backup and recovery strategy
- cold backup
- hot backup
- instance failure
- instance recovery
- mean time to recovery (MTTR)
- media (disk) failures
- non-media failures
- process failure
- recovery
- Recovery Manager (RMAN)
- restore
- RMAN-based backup
- statement failure
- user error
- user-managed backup

Review Questions

1. What is a type of non-media failure? (Choose all that apply.)

   A. Process failure

   B. Crashed disk drive with data files that are unreadable

   C. Instance failure

   D. User error

   E. Statement failure

2. Why is it important to get management to understand and agree with the backup and recovery plan? (Choose all that apply.)

   A. So that they understand the benefits and costs of the plan.

   B. So that they understand the plan's effects on business operations.

   C. It's not important for management to understand.

   D. So that they give approval of the plan.

3. What are some of the reasons why a DBA might test the backup and recovery strategy?

   A. To validate the backup and recovery process

   B. To stay familiar with certain types of failures

   C. To practice backup and recovery

   D. To build duplicate production databases to support new releases

   E. All of the above

4. What method of undoing transactions in the database requires reading archived log information?

   A. Flashback Query

   B. Fastback Query

   C. LogMiner

   D. Export/Import data

5. Why should backup and recovery testing be done?

   A. To practice your recovery skills

   B. To validate the backup and recovery process

   C. To get MTTR statistics

   D. To move the database from the production server to the test server

   E. All of the above

6. What method of undoing transactions in the database requires the database parameter `UNDO_MANAGEMENT = AUTO`?

   A. Flashback Query

   B. LogMiner

   C. Manual rebuilding data

   D. Parallel query

7. At a minimum, what backup and recovery tests should be performed?

   A. Recovery from the loss of a system tablespace

   B. Recovery from the loss of a nonsystem tablespace

   C. Full database recovery

   D. Recovery from the loss of an online redo log

   E. All of the above

8. List all the methods used to protect against erroneous changes to the database without performing a full database recovery. (Choose all that apply.)

   A. Tablespace backups of high-usage tablespaces

   B. Control file backups

   C. Exports

   D. Multiplexed redo logs

9. A user-managed backup best describes the following:
   A. An RMAN-based backup
   B. An export of the database
   C. A hot backup only
   D. A custom backup using OS and database commands

10. An offline backup would be best performed on what type of business environment?
   A. A database that has transactional activity 24 hours a day
   B. A database that has transactional activity 12 hours a day and batch processing the other 12 hours
   C. A database that has transactional activity 12 hours only
   D. A database that has transactional activity 18 hours and data mart data extraction the other 6 hours

11. Which IT professionals will most likely be involved in the technical aspects of the backup and recovery strategy? (Choose all that apply.)
   A. Database administrator (DBA)
   B. Management
   C. System administrator (SA)
   D. Application developer

12. Undoing database changes can be more easily performed when the following is a general business practice:
   A. Software configuration management is tightly enforced.
   B. Developers modify the production code without DBA knowledge.
   C. Limited testing of production code is performed before it is implemented.
   D. Ad hoc DML statements are performed in production databases.

13. Statement failure is when which of the following occurs?

    A. A user accidentally drops a table.

    B. A user writes an invalid SQL command.

    C. A user deletes the wrong data.

    D. A user export is performed.

14. The wrong data in a table gets deleted by mistake. This type of error or failure is called a(n):

    A. Statement error

    B. User error

    C. Instance failure

    D. Media failure

15. What new feature in Oracle9*i* is used to view data based on the undo records?

    A. LogMiner

    B. Fastback Query

    C. Flashback Query

    D. Export

Answers to Review Questions

1. A, C, D, E. A media failure occurs when a database file cannot be read or written to. All other types of failures are non-media failures.

2. A, B, D. Management needs to understand the backup and recovery plan so that the plan can be tailored to meet the business operational requirements. Furthermore, by understanding the plan, management can better gauge the benefits and costs of decisions that they are about to make.

3. E. All are relevant reasons to test a backup and recovery strategy.

4. C. The LogMiner utility reads archived redo logs to reconstruct previously run information. This information can be used to undo changes to the database.

5. E. All answers are potential reasons to perform backups, the most important being that testing validates the backup and recovery process.

6. A. The Flashback Query requires that the UNDO_MANAGEMENT parameter be set to AUTO so that undo information automatically gets recorded in the designated undo tablespace.

7. E. All of the options are backup and recovery tests that should be performed.

8. A, C. Tablespace backups of high-usage tablespaces and exports of the whole database or high-usage tables can provide protection against erroneous changes without doing a full database recovery.

9. D. A user-managed backup is the term used for backing up an Oracle database using either an OS script such as a Unix shell script or a Windows batch file in conjunction with database commands.

10. C. A database that is being accessed 24 hours a day will not be a candidate for a offline backup because the database must be shut down.

11. A, C. The DBA and SA will most likely be involved in the technical aspects of the backup and recovery strategy because they are in charge of the technical areas required to perform the recovery operation.

12. A. Code and data modifications should be tightly enforced either by a software configuration management tool or by a manual process. This provides an audit trail of modifications that are made to the database. There is a better chance of undoing errors with this information.

13. B. A statement error occurs when a user writes an incorrect SQL command. The Oracle database will not process invalid commands during the parse phase of evaluating the SQL command; instead, it will return an error.

14. B. A user error occurs when a user performs some action within the database that they didn't want to do.

15. C. The Flashback Query feature is new to Oracle9*i*. This feature uses undo transactions to rebuild queries.

Instance and Media Recovery Structures

ORACLE9*i*: DBA FUNDAMENTALS II EXAM OBJECTIVES COVERED IN THIS CHAPTER:

- ✓ **Describe the Oracle processes, memory structures, and files relating to recovery.**
- ✓ **Identify the importance of checkpoints, redo log files, and archived log files.**
- ✓ **Describe ways to tune instance recovery.**

Exam objectives are subject to change at any time without prior notice and at Oracle's sole discretion. Please visit Oracle's Certification website (`http://www.oracle.com/education/certification/`) for the most current exam objectives listing.

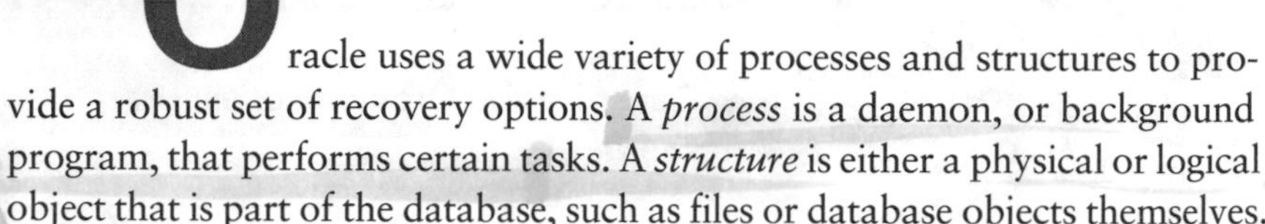

Oracle uses a wide variety of processes and structures to provide a robust set of recovery options. A *process* is a daemon, or background program, that performs certain tasks. A *structure* is either a physical or logical object that is part of the database, such as files or database objects themselves.

The processes consist of log writer (LGWR), system monitor (SMON), process monitor (PMON), checkpoint (CKPT), and archiver (ARCn). The available structures include redo logs, rollback segments, control files, and data files. You were introduced to these terms in Chapter 5, "Backup and Recovery Overview." This chapter provides further detail, including how different combinations of these processes and structures are used to recover from different kinds of failures.

This chapter also introduces methods you can use to tune instance recovery, including the ability to set approximate limits on the length of time needed to recover from instance failure. We will discuss and provide examples of these methods.

In order to understand the backup and recovery process, you must first understand processes and structures. This knowledge will help you, as the DBA, make real-life decisions about backup and recovery situations. For example, if you understand how the database physical structures get synchronized, you will be able to make sense of the recovery process. If you truly understand how processes and structures interact with backup and recovery procedures, you are on the road to having a solid understanding of the backup and recovery process.

Oracle Recovery Processes, Memory Components, and File Structures

Oracle recovery processes, memory components, and file structures all work together during recovery in order to maintain the physical integrity of the database. Oracle recovery processes interact with Oracle memory components to coordinate data blocks that are written to disk. These blocks of data reside in memory for faster access at different times of database operations. As these memory structures change, coordination with the physical and logical structures occurs so that the database can remain consistent.

Basically, recovery processes coordinate what blocks (and other information) need to be read (or modified from the data blocks in memory) and then written to disk or to the physical and logical structures in the form of online redo logs, archived logs, or data files. Each process has specific tasks that it fulfills.

These physical and logical structures are like memory structures in that they are made up of data blocks. But the *physical structures* are static structures that consist of files in the OS file system. Data blocks and other information are written to these physical structures to make them consistent. The *logical structures* are temporarily used to hold parts of information for intermediate time periods, or until the processes can permanently record the appropriate information in the physical structures.

Recovery Processes

Oracle has five major processes related to recovery. These processes include log writer, system monitor, process manager, checkpoint, and archiver. Let's look at each of these processes in more detail.

Log writer (LGWR) The *log writer (LGWR)* process writes redo log entries from the redo buffers. A *redo log entry* is any change, or *transaction,* that has been applied to the database, committed or not. (To *commit* means to save or permanently store the results of the transaction to the database.) The LGWR process is mandatory and is started by default when the database is started.

System monitor (SMON) The *system monitor (SMON)* process performs a varied set of functions. SMON is responsible for instance recovery, and it also performs temporary segment cleanup. It is a mandatory process and is started by default when the database is started.

Process monitor (PMON) The *process monitor (PMON)* process performs recovery of failed user processes. This is a mandatory process and is started by default when the database is started.

Checkpoint (CKPT) The *checkpoint (CKPT)* process performs checkpointing in the control files and data files. *Checkpointing* is the process of stamping a unique counter in the control files and data files for database consistency and synchronization. In Oracle7, the LGWR would also perform checkpointing if the CKPT process wasn't present. As of Oracle8, however, the CKPT process was made mandatory and was started by default. This is continued in Oracle9*i*.

Archiver (ARCn) The *archiver (ARCn)* process performs the copying of the online redo log files to archived log files. The ARCn process is enabled only if the `init.ora` file's parameter `LOG_ARCHIVE_START` is set to `TRUE` or with the `ARCHIVE LOG START` command. This isn't a mandatory process.

In the Windows 2000/XP environments, the processes are threads of the main Oracle executable. In the Unix environment, an example of each of these processes can be seen by typing the Unix command **`ps -ef | grep`** ***`<$ORACLE_SID>`***. *$ORACLE_SID* is a Unix environment variable that identifies the Oracle system identifier. In this case, *`$ORACLE_SID`* is `orc9`.

```
oracle@octilli:~ > ps -ef|grep orc9
oracle    2077     1  0 00:26 ?        00:00:00 ora_pmon_orc9
oracle    2079     1  0 00:26 ?        00:00:00 ora_dbw0_orc9
oracle    2081     1  0 00:26 ?        00:00:00 ora_lgwr_orc9
oracle    2083     1  0 00:26 ?        00:00:00 ora_ckpt_orc9
oracle    2085     1  0 00:26 ?        00:00:00 ora_smon_orc9
oracle    2087     1  0 00:26 ?        00:00:00 ora_reco_orc9
oracle    2097     1  0 00:26 ?        00:00:00 ora_arc0_orc9
```

Memory Structures

There are two Oracle memory structures relating to recovery: log buffers and data block buffers. The *log buffers* are the memory buffers that record the changes, or transactions, to data block buffers before they are written to online redo logs or disk. Online redo logs record all changes to the database, whether the transactions are committed or rolled back.

The *data block buffers* are the memory buffers that store all the database information. A data block buffer stores mainly data that needs to be queried, read, changed, or modified by users. The modified data block buffers that have not yet been written to disk are called *dirty buffers*. At some point, Oracle determines that these dirty buffers must be written to disk. When this happens, a checkpoint occurs.

Both Oracle memory structures can be viewed in a number of ways. The most common method is by performing a SHOW SGA command from SQL. This displays all of the memory sizes of the database that you are connected to. See the following example:

```
oracle@octilli:/oracle/admin/orc9/pfile > sqlplus /nolog

SQL*Plus: Release 9.0.1.0.0 - Production on Tue Sep 25
00:38:13 2001

(c) Copyright 2001 Oracle Corporation.  All rights
reserved.

SQL> connect /as sysdba
Connected.
SQL> show sga

Total System Global Area  235693104 bytes
Fixed Size                   279600 bytes
Variable Size             167772160 bytes
Database Buffers           67108864 bytes
Redo Buffers                 532480 bytes
SQL>
```

When you look at this code example, you will see that the database buffers are approximately 67MB, and the redo buffers are approximately 512KB. When the SHOW SGA command is run, the data block buffers are referred to as *database buffers*, and the log buffers are referred to as *redo buffers*. These values are extremely small and are suitable for a sample database or for testing. Data block buffers can be about 100MB to 300MB for average-sized databases with a few hundred users.

In this System Global Area (SGA) output, Variable Size pertains to the SHARED_POOL and LARGE_POOL values in the init.ora file. The SHARED_POOL value stores parsed versions of SQL and PL/SQL so that it may be reused. The LARGE_POOL value provides large memory sizes for shared servers session memory as well as backup and recovery operations. The `init.ora` file's `DBWR_IO_SLAVES` and `BACKUP_TAPE_IO_SLAVES` parameters are examples of backup and recovery operations that will use the `LARGE_POOL` memory. In the SGA output above, `Fixed Size` pertains to a few less-critical parameters in the `init.ora`.

File Structures

The Oracle file structures relating to recovery include the online redo logs, archived logs, control files, data files, and parameter files. The redo logs consist of files that record all the changes to the database. The archived logs consist of files that are copies of the redo logs; these exist so that a historical record of all the changes made to the database can be utilized if necessary. Control files are binary files that contain the physical structure of the database, such as operating system filenames of all files that make up the database. Data files are physical structures of the database that make up a logical structure called a tablespace. All data is stored within some type of object within a tablespace. Parameter files are the files that contain the initialization parameters for the database. These are the files that set the initial settings or values of database resources when the database is started. Let's look at each of these in more detail.

Redo Logs

The *redo logs* consist of files that record all of the changes to the database. Recording all changes is one of the most important activities in the Oracle database from the recovery standpoint. The redo logs get information written to them before all other physical structures in the database. The purpose of the redo log is to protect against data loss in the event of a failure.

The term *redo log* includes many subclassifications. Redo logs consist of *online redo logs*, *offline redo logs* (also called archived logs), *current online redo logs*, and *non-current online redo logs*. Each is described below.

Online redo logs Logs that the log buffers are writing to in a circular fashion. These logs are written and rewritten.

Offline redo logs, or archived logs Copies of the online redo logs before they are written over by the LGWR.

Current online redo logs Logs that are currently being written to and therefore are considered active.

Non-current redo logs Online redo logs that are not currently being written to and therefore are inactive.

Each database has at least two sets of online redo logs, but Oracle recommends at least three sets. You will see why when we discuss archived logs in the next section. Redo logs record all the changes that are made to the database; these changes result from the LGWR writing out log buffers to the redo logs at particular events or points in time.

As mentioned previously, redo logs are written in a circular fashion. That is, if there are three sets of logs, log 1 gets written to first until it is full. Then Oracle moves to log 2, and it gets written to until it is full. Then Oracle moves to log 3, and it gets written to until it is full. Oracle then goes back to log 1, writes over the existing information, and repeats this process over again. Here is a listing of the logs from the `V$LOGFILE` view.

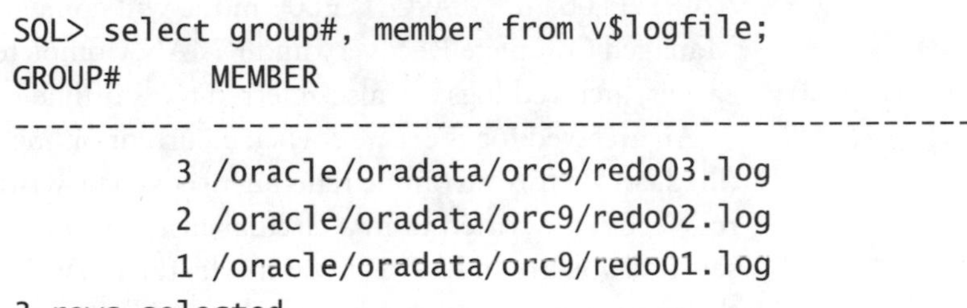

```
SQL> select group#, member from v$logfile;
GROUP#     MEMBER
---------- ------------------------------------------
         3 /oracle/oradata/orc9/redo03.log
         2 /oracle/oradata/orc9/redo02.log
         1 /oracle/oradata/orc9/redo01.log
3 rows selected.
```

Figure 6.1 shows an example of the circular process of redo file generation, which writes to one log at a time, starting with log 1, then log 2, then log 3, and then back to log 1 again.

FIGURE 6.1 The circular process of redo file generation

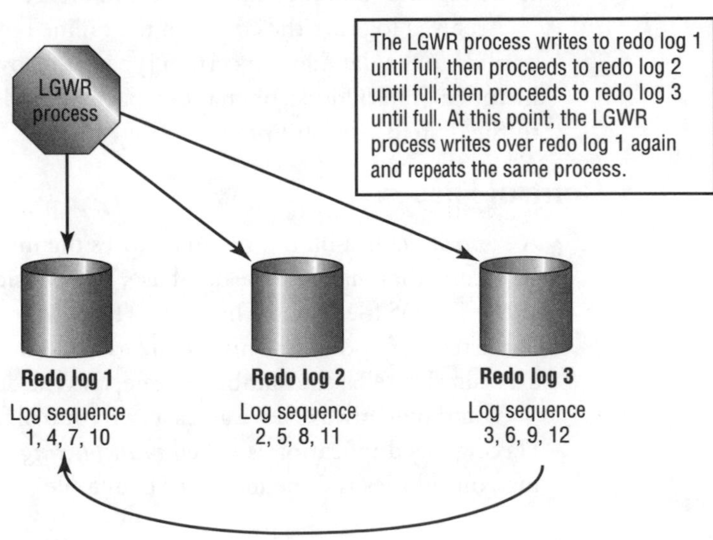

Redo logs contain values called *system change numbers (SCNs)* that uniquely identify each committed transaction in the database. SCNs are like a clock of events that have occurred in the database, and they are one of the major synchronization elements in recovery. Each data-file header and control file is synchronized with the current highest SCN.

Archived Logs

Archived logs are non-current online redo logs that have been copied to a new location offline. This location is the value of the `init.ora` file's `LOG_ARCHIVE_DEST` parameter. Archived logs are created if the database is in `ARCHIVELOG` *mode* rather than `NOARCHIVELOG` *mode*. A more detailed explanation of `ARCHIVELOG` and `NOARCHIVELOG` mode will come in Chapter 10, "User-Managed Complete Recovery and RMAN Complete Recovery." As noted earlier, archived logs are also referred to as offline redo logs.

An archived log is created when a current online redo log is completed or filled, and before an online redo log needs to be written to again. Remember, redo logs are written to in a circular fashion. If there are only two redo log sets and you are in `ARCHIVELOG` mode, the LGWR may have to wait or halt the writing of information to redo logs while an archived log is being copied. If it doesn't, the LGWR process would overwrite the archive information, making the archived log useless. If at least three redo log groups are available, the archived log will have enough time to be created and not cause the LGWR to wait for an available online redo log. This is under *average transaction* volumes. Some large or transaction-intensive databases may have 10 to 20 log sets to reduce the contention on redo log availability.

Archived logs are the copies of the online redo logs; the archived logs get applied to the database in certain types of recovery. Archived logs build the historical transactions, or changes, back in the database to make it consistent to the desired recovery point.

Control Files

A *control file* is a binary file that stores the information about the physical structures that make up the database. The physical structures are OS objects, such as all OS filenames. The control file also stores the highest SCN to assist in the recovery process. This file stores information about the backups if you are using RMAN, the database name, and the date the database was created.

You should always have at least two control files on different disk devices. Having this duplication is called *multiplexing* your control files. Multiplexing control files is done in an `init.ora` file's `CONTROL_FILES` parameter.

Every time a database is mounted, the control file is accessed to identify the data files and redo logs that are needed for the database to function. All new physical changes to the database get recorded in the control file by default.

Data Files

Data files are physical files stored on the file system. All Oracle databases have at least one data file, but usually more. Data files are where the physical and the logical structures meet. *Tablespaces* are logical structures and are made up of one or more data files. All logical objects reside in tablespaces. *Logical objects* are those that do not exist outside of the database, such as tables, indexes, sequences, and views.

Data files are made up of blocks. These *data blocks* are the smallest unit of measure in the database. The logical objects, such as tables and indexes, are stored in the data blocks, which reside in the data files.

The first block of every file is called a *header block*. The header block of the data file contains information such as the file size, block size, and associated tablespace. It also contains the SCN for recovery purposes.

Here is the output from the V$DATAFILE view, showing the data files that make up a sample database.

```
SQL> select file#, status, substr(name,0,50) from v$datafile;

     FILE# STATUS  SUBSTR(NAME,0,50)
---------- ------- --------------------------------------------------
         1 SYSTEM  /oracle/product/9.0.1/oradata/orc9/system01.dbf
         2 ONLINE  /oracle/product/9.0.1/oradata/orc9/undotbs01.dbf
         3 ONLINE  /oracle/product/9.0.1/oradata/orc9/cwmlite01.dbf
         4 ONLINE  /oracle/product/9.0.1/oradata/orc9/drsys01.dbf
         5 ONLINE  /oracle/product/9.0.1/oradata/orc9/example01.dbf
         6 ONLINE  /oracle/product/9.0.1/oradata/orc9/indx01.dbf
         7 ONLINE  /oracle/product/9.0.1/oradata/orc9/tools01.dbf
         8 ONLINE  /oracle/product/9.0.1/oradata/orc9/users01.dbf

8 rows selected.

SQL>
```

Parameter Files

There are two parameter files that make up the file structures of the Oracle9*i* database. The *parameter file* is the file that contains the initialization parameters of the database that are used upon startup. The standard parameter file, called *init<ORACLE_SID>.ora*, contains parameters required for instance startup. The ORACLE_SID equals the name of the oracle system identifier or database name. This parameter file is ASCII and can be edited.

The second parameter file, called *spfile<ORACLE_SID>.ora*, is the server parameter file that stores persistent parameters that are required for instance startup and those that are modified when the database is started. The server parameter file is stored in binary format, which is a new feature in Oracle9*i*.

Either of these files can be used to start the Oracle database, but the `spfile.ora` files are the default for starting the database. If these files are not found, then the `init.ora` files are used.

The default locations for these files are in the following directory structures. We will demonstrate both Unix and Windows NT/2000 locations.

Unix	`$ORACLE_HOME/dbs`
Windows NT/2000	`%ORACLE_HOME%\database`

Checkpoints, Redo Logs, and Archived Logs

Now that you have a basic understanding of the various Oracle processes, file structures, and memory structures used for recovery, it's time to see how these interrelate. As you learned earlier, checkpoints, redo logs, and archived logs are significant to all aspects of recovery.

The *checkpoint* is an event that determines the synchronization or consistency of all transactions on disk. The checkpoint is implemented by storing a unique number—the SCN (again, this stands for *system change number*)—in the control files, header of the data files, online redo logs, and archived logs.

The checkpoint is performed by the CKPT process. One of the ways a checkpoint is initiated is by the data block writer (DBWR) process. The DBWR process initiates a checkpoint by writing all modified data blocks in the data buffers (dirty buffers) to the data files. After a checkpoint is performed, all committed transactions are written to the data files.

If the instance were to crash at this point, only new transactions that occurred after this checkpoint would need to be applied to the database to enable a complete recovery. Therefore, the checkpoint process determines which transactions from the redo logs need to be applied to the database in the event of a failure and subsequent recovery. Remember that all transactions, whether committed or not, get written to the redo logs.

Other methods that cause a checkpoint to occur include any of the following commands: ALTER SYSTEM SWITCH LOGFILE, ALTER SYSTEM CHECKPOINT LOCAL, ALTER TABLESPACE BEGIN BACKUP, and ALTER TABLESPACE END BACKUP.

SCNs are recorded within redo logs at every log switch, at a minimum. This is because a checkpoint occurs at every log switch. Archived logs have the same SCNs recorded within them as the online redo logs because the archived logs are merely copies of the online redo logs.

Let's look at an example of how checkpointing, online redo logs, and archived logs are all interrelated. First, the ALTER TABLESPACE BEGIN BACKUP command is used to begin an online backup of a database.

An *online backup*, also called a *hot backup,* occurs while the database is still available or running. See Chapter 9, "User-Managed and RMAN-based Backups," for a more detailed explanation of a hot backup.

The ALTER TABLESPACE BEGIN BACKUP command is followed by an OS command to copy the files, such as cp in Unix. Then, the command ALTER TABLESPACE END BACKUP is used to end the hot backup. As we just discussed, these ALTER TABLESPACE commands also cause a checkpoint to occur. The following is an example of the data file data01.dbf for the tablespace DATA being backed up:

```
SQL> connect /as sysdba
Connected.
SQL> alter tablespace data begin backup;
Tablespace altered.
SQL> ! cp data01.dbf /stage/data01.dbf
SQL> alter tablespace data end backup;
Tablespace altered.
SQL>
```

Note that the tablespace DATA was put in backup mode, and then the OS command was executed, copying the data file `data01.dbf` to the new directory `/stage`, where it awaits writing to tape. Finally, the tablespace DATA was taken out of backup mode. These steps are repeated for every tablespace in the database. This is a simplified example of a hot backup.

If a hot backup was taken on Sunday at 2 A.M., and the database crashed on Tuesday at 3 P.M., then the last checkpoint would have been issued after all the data files were backed up. This backup would be the last checkpointed disk copy of the database. Therefore, all the archived logs generated after the 2 A.M. backup was completed would need to be applied to the checkpointed database to bring it up to 3 P.M. Tuesday, the time of the crash. When you are making a hot backup of the database, you are getting a copy of the database that has been checkpointed for each data file. In this case, each data file has a different SCN stamped in the header and each will need all applicable redo log entries made with a greater SCN applied to the data file to make the database consistent.

Ways to Tune the Instance Recovery

As we've previously discussed in Chapter 5, "Backup and Recovery Overview," *instance failure* is when the Oracle database instance abnormally terminates due to something like a power outage or a shutdown abort. *Instance recovery* is the automatic process that the Oracle database performs to ensure that the database is functioning properly and the data is consistent. This is also known as the *roll forward and roll backward process*. Upon startup of the Oracle database after an instance failure, Oracle reads the current online redo log and applies all the changes in that redo log to the database. Any uncommitted changes are then rolled back. Thus, the database is made consistent from the time of the outage.

The concept of defining an approximate set time for the instance recovery process is called bounded time recovery. *Bounded time recovery* means that the DBA controls or puts bounds on the time it takes for an instance to recover after instance failure. These bounds are controlled by using two initialization parameters.

There are two primary initialization parameters that will speed up the instance recovery process. The first parameter is called FAST_START_MTTR_TARGET. This parameter makes the database writer (DBW0 background process) write dirty blocks faster and at a predefined pace to meet agreed-upon recovery timeframes. This parameter can be set from 0 to 3600 seconds.

The second parameter is called FAST_START_PARALLEL_ROLLBACK. This parameter determines the maximum number of processes that can exist for performing a parallel rollback. This parameter is useful when there are long running transactions involved in the instance recovery process. This causes the rollback aspect of instance recovery to process faster. This parameter can be set as HIGH, LOW, and FALSE. The following are sample init.ora file parameters:

```
fast_start_mttr_target                         = 300
fast_start_parallel_rollback                   = LO
```

There are three V$ sys user views that can be queried to monitor these parameters. These views are V$INSTANCE_RECOVERY, V$FAST_START_SERVERS, and V$FAST_START_TRANSACTIONS. Below is an example of the V$INSTANCE_RECOVERY view, which can be used to monitor and determine the length of recovery for the FAST_START_MTTR_TARGET parameter. TARGET_MTTR and ESTIMATED_MTTR show the estimated time in seconds to recover the database in the advent of an instance failure at that given time.

```
SQL*Plus: Release 9.0.1.0.0 - Production on Mon Sep 24
23:14:36 2001

(c) Copyright 2001 Oracle Corporation.  All rights
reserved.


Connected to:
Oracle9i Enterprise Edition Release 9.0.1.0.0 - Production
With the Partitioning option
JServer Release 9.0.1.0.0 - Production

SQL> select target_mttr,estimated_mttr from v$instance_
recovery;
```

```
TARGET_MTTR ESTIMATED_MTTR
----------- --------------
         29             17

SQL>
```

Real World Scenario

Instance Recovery in a Distributed Database Environment

Let's look at a real-life example to determine the circumstances that can cause data loss even though Oracle *instance recovery* accounts for all data loss properly.

A small manufacturing company generates their manufacturing information on an Oracle database. This database keeps track of raw materials, work in progress, and finished products. In order to complete the work required of it, the database needs to be available throughout the three shifts that the company runs to meet customer demand.

For financial purposes, on a regular basis, information from this manufacturing database is transferred to the financial database on another server. This is done through a variety of out-of-database transfers, which leaves the data exposed until it meanders its way back into the financial database.

In the midst of one of these transfers, the company experiences a severe power spike, which causes the servers to reboot. As a result, instance failure occurs on each database because data was in the process of being transferred from the manufacturing database to the financial database when the power spike occurred. In addition, the database transfer mechanism did not recover the data in transit.

At this point, the experienced database administrator can see that the issue here is a loosely distributed database environment. This could result from the company using different vendors for manufacturing and financial applications with customized application program interfaces (APIs).

Now that the power spike is over, the system administrator must get the servers restarted and the database administrator needs to validate that the databases are available again. When this is done, the administrators find out that the manufacturing database thinks that the data has been transferred to financial database, but the data never actually made it into the financial database before the instance failure.

As a result, the databases are out of synchronization with each other and the data inconsistencies must be manually tracked down. The analysts and business people must determine what did or didn't make it to the appropriate database by a series of ad hoc SQL statements.

Summary

The recovery structures and processes available in Oracle allow significant recovery options for the DBA. These recovery structures consist of files, processes, memory buffers, and logical objects that reside in the database. In addition to these recovery structures, this chapter also identified the file structures—redo logs, archived logs, control files, data files, and parameter files—and the processes, which are PMON, SMON, LGWR, CKPT, and ARCn. It then discussed the memory structures, which consist of log buffers and data buffers. All of these structures play different roles in the recovery process, and they can be used for different types of recovery.

This chapter also described the checkpoint concept. During this discussion, you learned the importance of SCNs and how these identifiers help determine the consistency of the transactions that have been applied to the database.

In addition, you viewed the three main initialization parameters that you will need to tune the instance recovery process. It is through these that the DBA can constrain the time of the recover process to certain approximate limits. These parameters can be monitored by a series of V$ sys views.

This chapter lays the groundwork for making decisions in the backup and recovery process for later chapters and the real world. It is vital that you understand how the file structures and process that are discussed in this chapter function to make the database consistent or inconsistent in a failure situation. These topics can be thought of as the building blocks of the backup and recovery processes.

Exam Essentials

Identify the Oracle background processes involved in recovery. There are five background processes involved with recovery. These processes are as follows: log writer (LGWR) writes redo logs, system monitor (SMON) is involved with instance recovery, process monitor (PMON) performs recovery of process failure, checkpoint (CKPT) performs checkpointing of database files, and archiver (ARCn) copies online redo logs to archived logs.

Identify the Oracle memory structures that are involved in recovery. There are two memory structures involved in the recovery process. The log buffers are the memory buffers that record changes to redo logs, and the data block buffers store all the cached data, which is queried and modified by users.

Identify the Oracle file structures involved in recovery. The file structures related to recovery include the online redo logs, archived logs, control files, data files, and parameter files. These files make up the physical components of the Oracle database.

Understand the checkpoint process. The checkpoint process interacts with redo logs, archived logs, and data file headers to synchronize the database with SCNs. Checkpoints occur due to log switches, dirty block buffers, system commands, and initialization parameters.

Understand the difference between archived logs and redo logs. Redo logs contain transactional log information that will get written over. Archived logs are copies of the redo logs before the redo logs are written over. Archived logs are used to recover the database.

Identify the fast instance recovery techniques. You should understand the concept of bound time instance recovery and be able to use initialization parameters to define recovery time and to monitor this process with the V$ sys views. The two initialization parameters that help define instance recovery are FAST_START_MTTR_TARGET and FAST_START_PARALLEL_ROLLBACK.

Key Terms

Before you take the exam, be certain you are familiar with the following terms:

- archived log
- archiver (ARCn)
- bounded time recovery
- checkpoint (CKPT)
- checkpointing
- commit
- control file
- current online redo log
- data block buffer
- data block
- data file
- database buffer
- dirty buffer
- header block
- hot backup
- `init<ORACLE_SID>.ora`
- instance failure
- instance recovery
- log buffer
- log writer (LGWR)
- logical object
- logical structure
- multiplexing
- non-current online redo log
- offline redo log
- online backup
- online redo log
- `ORACLE_SID`
- parameter file
- physical structure
- process
- process monitor (PMON)
- redo buffer
- redo log entry
- redo log
- roll forward and roll backward process
- `spfile<ORACLE_SID>.ora`
- structure
- system change number (SCN)
- system monitor (SMON)
- tablespace
- transaction

Review Questions

1. What command must the DBA execute to initiate an instance recovery?

   A. `RECOVER DATABASE`

   B. `RECOVER INSTANCE`

   C. `RECOVER TABLESPACE`

   D. No command is necessary.

2. What process is in charge of writing data to the online redo logs?

   A. Log buffer

   B. ARCn

   C. Data buffers

   D. LGWR

3. What are the file structures related to recovery? (Choose all that apply.)

   A. Redo logs

   B. Archived logs

   C. Log buffers

   D. Data files

4. What file structure consists of a binary file that stores information about all the physical components of the database?

   A. Redo log

   B. Data file

   C. Control file

   D. Archived logs

5. Which of the following are processes associated with recovery? (Choose all that apply.)

   A. PMON

   B. SMON

   C. ARC*n*

   D. DBWR

6. In Oracle9*i*, which process is responsible for performing checkpointing?

   A. SMON

   B. PMON

   C. LGWR

   D. CKPT

7. Which of the following are memory structures? (Choose all that apply.)

   A. Rollback segments

   B. Log buffers

   C. Data block buffers

   D. Data files

8. What type of shutdown requires an instance recovery upon startup?

   A. `SHUTDOWN NORMAL`

   B. `SHUTDOWN IMMEDIATE`

   C. `SHUTDOWN TRANSACTIONAL`

   D. `SHUTDOWN ABORT`

9. What events trigger a checkpoint to take place? (Choose all that apply.)

   A. CKPT

   B. `SHUTDOWN NORMAL`

   C. `SHUTDOWN IMMEDIATE`

   D. Log switch

10. What procedure is responsible for stamping the SCN to all necessary physical database structures?

    A. Read-consistent image

    B. Checkpointing

    C. Commits

    D. Rollbacks

11. The dirty buffers get written to disk when what event occurs?

    A. A commit occurs.

    B. A rollback occurs.

    C. Checkpoint occurs.

    D. `SHUTDOWN ABORT` occurs.

12. What database process is *not* mandatory or present at startup of the database?

    A. PMON

    B. CKPT

    C. SMON

    D. ARCn

13. What is the primary background process responsible for instance recovery?

    A. PMON

    B. LGWR

    C. SMON

    D. ARCn

14. What is a redo log that is being actively written to called?

    A. Online archived log

    B. Current online redo log

    C. Online redo log

    D. Offline redo log

15. What is a redo log that is not currently being written to and is instead copied to a new location called?

    A. Online archived log

    B. Current online redo log

    C. Offline redo log

    D. Online redo log

16. Which file structure joins the physical structures of the database to the logical database structure?

    A. Table

    B. Control file

    C. Redo log

    D. Data file

17. Which memory structure is responsible for temporarily storing redo log entries?

    A. Large pool

    B. Database buffers

    C. Log buffers

    D. Shared pool

18. What is having more than one control file called?

    A. Multiple control files

    B. Duplicating control files

    C. Multiplexing control files

    D. Duplexing control files

19. What event happens when a log switch occurs?

    A. An archived log is created.

    B. A checkpoint occurs.

    C. All transactions are committed.

    D. All pending transactions are committed.

20. What is a physical structure that is new to Oracle9*i*?

A. All parameter files

B. Multiplexed control files

C. `init.ora`

D. `spfile.ora`

Answers to Review Questions

1. D. The instance recovery is automatic.

2. D. The LGWR, or log writer process, writes changes from the log buffers to the online redo logs.

3. A, B, D. Redo logs, archived logs, and data files are all file structures that are associated with recovery. Log buffers are memory structures.

4. C. The control file is a binary file that stores all the information about the physical components of the database.

5. A, B, C. PMON, SMON, and ARCn are all associated with some part of the recovery process. PMON recovers failed processes, SMON assists in instance recovery, and ARCn generates archived logs used to recover the database. The DBWR writes data to the data files when appropriate.

6. D. The CKPT process performs all the checkpointing. This process starts by default.

7. B, C. There are only two memory structures related to recovery: log buffers and data block buffers.

8. D. `SHUTDOWN ABORT` requires an instance recovery upon startup because the data files are not checkpointed during shutdown.

9. B, C, D. The `SHUTDOWN NORMAL` and `SHUTDOWN IMMEDIATE` events checkpoint all necessary physical database structures. Switching log files forces a checkpoint of all necessary physical database structures. The CKPT process is responsible for initiating or performing the checkpoint; it doesn't cause it.

10. B. Checkpointing is the procedure initiated by the CKPT process, which stamps all the data files, redo logs, and control files with the latest SCN.

11. C. A checkpoint causes dirty buffers to be flushed to disk. A SHUTDOWN NORMAL or SHUTDOWN IMMEDIATE causes a checkpoint on shutdown, but a SHUTDOWN ABORT doesn't force a checkpoint. This is why instance recovery is necessary upon startup. A rollback and commit do not cause a checkpoint.

12. D. The ARCn process is not a required at startup. This process is only used if the database is running in archive mode.

13. C. The SMON process is responsible for the majority of instance recovery.

14. B. A current online redo log is a log that is being written to by the LGWR process.

15. C. Archived logs are offline redo logs. These are redo logs that are copied to a new location before the LGWR writes over them.

16. D. The data file is a physical structure that makes up a logical tablespace.

17. C. The log buffers are responsible for temporarily holding log entries that will be written to the redo logs.

18. C. You should always have more than one control file to protect against the loss of one. This practice is called multiplexing control files.

19. B. A log switch forces a checkpoint immediately as part of the synchronization process for recovery.

20. D. The `spfile.ora` parameter file is new to Oracle9*i*. The `init.ora` file has been around since the beginning of the Oracle database, but the `spfile.ora` file is a new binary initialization file.

Configuring the Database Archiving Mode

ORACLE9*i*: DBA FUNDAMENTALS II EXAM OBJECTIVES COVERED IN THIS CHAPTER:

- ✓ **Describe the differences between Archivelog and Noarchivelog modes.**
- ✓ **Configure a database for Archivelog mode.**
- ✓ **Enable automatic archiving.**
- ✓ **Perform manual archiving of logs.**
- ✓ **Configure multiple archive processes.**
- ✓ **Configure multiple destinations, including remote destinations.**

Exam objectives are subject to change at any time without prior notice and at Oracle's sole discretion. Please visit Oracle's Certification website (`http://www.oracle.com/education/certification/`) for the most current exam objectives listing.

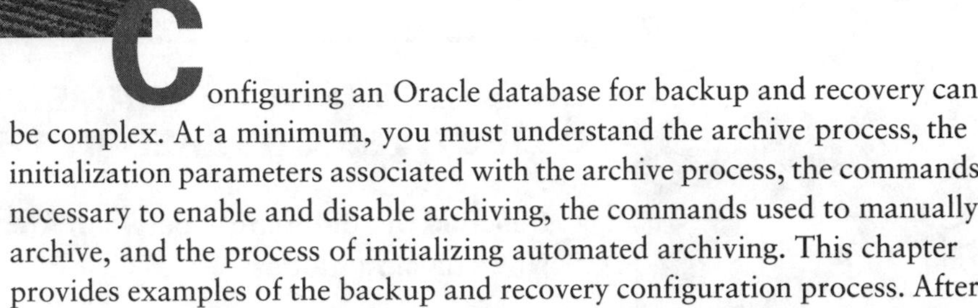

Configuring an Oracle database for backup and recovery can be complex. At a minimum, you must understand the archive process, the initialization parameters associated with the archive process, the commands necessary to enable and disable archiving, the commands used to manually archive, and the process of initializing automated archiving. This chapter provides examples of the backup and recovery configuration process. After reading this chapter, you should be comfortable with this process.

In Chapter 6, "Instance and Media Recovery Structures," you learned about the file and memory structures involved with Oracle backup and recovery. Two of these structures are covered in more detail within this chapter—specifically, the archiver process and the archived logs that this process generates.

The archiver and archived logs are the key components you need for the backup and recovery process. Archived logs make it possible for a complete recovery to be conducted. In addition, the archiver or archivers are responsible for creating archived logs so that they are available in the event of a failure. It is important that you understand how to configure the database for archiving and that you need to provide multiple copies of archived logs to reduce the damage caused by failure situations.

Choosing *ARCHIVELOG* Mode or *NOARCHIVELOG* Mode

One of the most fundamental backup and recovery decisions that a DBA will make is whether to operate the database in `ARCHIVELOG` mode or `NOARCHIVELOG` mode. As you learned earlier, the redo logs record all the transactions that have occurred in a database, and the archived logs are copies of these redo logs. So, the archived logs contain the historical changes, or transactions, that occur in the database. Operating in ARCHIVELOG mode means that the database will generate archived logs; operating in NOARCHIVELOG mode means that the database will not generate archived logs. This section discusses the differences between ARCHIVELOG and NOARCHIVELOG mode.

ARCHIVELOG Mode

In *ARCHIVELOG mode*, the database generates archived log files from the redo logs. This means that the database makes copies of all the historical transactions that have occurred in the database. Here are other characteristics of operating in ARCHIVELOG mode:

- Performing *online (hot) backups* is possible. This type of backup is done when the database is up and running. Therefore, a service outage is not necessary to perform a backup. The ALTER TABLESPACE *<TABLESPACE_NAME>* BEGIN BACKUP command is issued to perform hot backups. After this command is issued, an OS copy can take place on each tablespace's associated data files. When the OS copy is complete, an ALTER TABLESPACE *<TABLESPACE_NAME>* END BACKUP command must be issued. These commands must be executed for every tablespace in the database.
- A complete recovery can be performed. This is possible because the archived logs contain all the changes up to the point of failure. All logs can be applied to a backup copy of the database (hot or cold backup). This would apply to all the transactions up to the time of failure. Thus, there would be no data loss or missing transactions.
- Tablespaces can be taken offline immediately.
- Increased disk space is required to store archived logs, and increased maintenance is associated with maintaining this disk space.

NOARCHIVELOG Mode

In *NOARCHIVELOG mode*, the database does not generate archived log files from the redo logs. This means that the database is not storing any historical transactions from such logs. Instead, the redo logs are written over each other as needed by Oracle. As a result, the only transactions that can be used in the event of instance failure are in the current redo logs. Operating in NOARCHIVELOG mode has the following characteristics:

- In most cases, a complete restore cannot be performed. This means that a loss of data will occur. The last cold backup will need to be used for recovery.
- The database must be shut down completely for a backup, which means the database will be unavailable to the users of the database during that time. This means that only a cold backup can be performed.
- Tablespaces cannot be taken offline immediately.
- Additional disk space and maintenance is not needed to store archived logs.

Understanding Recovery Implications of *NOARCHIVELOG*

The recovery implications associated with operating a database in NOARCHIVELOG mode are important. A loss of data usually occurs when the last consistent full backup is used for a recovery. Therefore, to reduce the amount of data lost in the event of a failure, frequent cold backups need to be performed. This means that the database could be unavailable to users on a regular basis.

Now that you are familiar with the problems associated with this mode, let's look at examples of when it would not make sense to use NOARCHIVELOG mode and when it would.

Imagine that Manufacturing Company A's database must be available for 24 hours a day to support three shifts of work. This work consists of entering orders, bills of lading, shipping instructions, and inventory adjustments. The shifts are as follows: day shift, 9 A.M. to 5 P.M.; swing shift, 5 P.M. to 1 A.M.; and night shift, 1 A.M. to 9 A.M. If this database is shut down for a cold backup from midnight to 2 A.M., then the night shift and swing shift would be unable to use it during that period. As a result, a NOARCHIVELOG backup strategy would not be workable for Manufacturing Company A.

On the other hand, if Manufacturing Company B's database must be available only during the day shift, from 9 A.M. to 5 P.M., then backups could be performed after 5 P.M. and before 9 A.M. without affecting users. Thus, the DBA could schedule the database to shut down at midnight and perform the backup for two hours. The database would be restarted before 9 A.M., and there would be no interference with the users' work. In the event of a failure, there would be a backup from each evening, and only a maximum of one day's worth of data would be lost. If one day's worth of data loss were acceptable, this would be a workable backup and recovery strategy for Manufacturing Company B.

These examples show that in some situations, operating in NOARCHIVELOG mode makes sense. But there are recovery implications that stem from this choice. One implication is that a loss of data will occur in the event of a failure. Also, there are limited choices on how to recover. The choice is usually to restore the whole database from the last consistent whole backup while the database was shut down (cold backup).

Configuring a Database for *ARCHIVELOG* Mode and Automatic Archiving

Once the determination has been made to run the database in ARCHIVELOG mode, the database will need to be configured properly. You can do this to a new database during database creation or to an existing database via Oracle commands. After the database is in ARCHIVELOG mode, you will most likely configure automatic archiving. *Automatic archiving* frees the DBA up from the manual task of archiving logs with commands before the online redo logs perform a complete cycle.

Setting *ARCHIVELOG* Mode

ARCHIVELOG mode can be set during the database creation or by using the ALTER DATABASE ARCHIVELOG command. The database must be mounted, but not open, in order to execute this command. This command stays in force until it is turned off by using the ALTER DATABASE NOARCHIVELOG command. The database must be mounted, but not open, in order to execute this command as well.

The redo log files will be archived to the location specified by the *LOG_ARCHIVE_DEST* parameter in the init.ora file. By default, the database is in manual archiving mode. This means that as the redo logs become full, the database will hang until the DBA issues the ARCHIVE LOG ALL command, which archives all the online redo log files not yet archived. Figure 7.1 shows a database configured for ARCHIVELOG mode.

FIGURE 7.1 A database configured for ARCHIVELOG mode

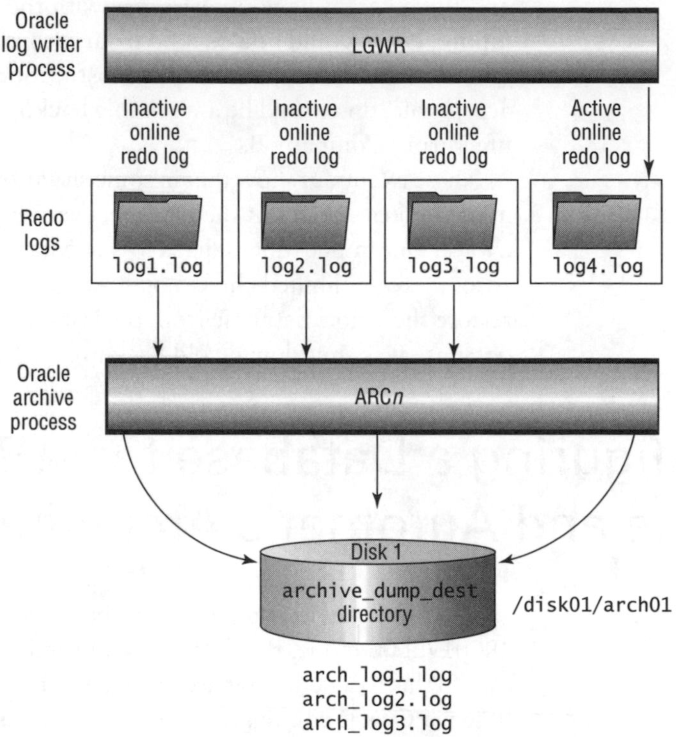

Let's look at an example of how to tell whether the database is in ARCHIVELOG or NOARCHIVELOG mode. You will need to run SQL*Plus and execute the following SQL statement that queries from one of the V$ views. Alternatively, you can perform OS commands, such as `ps –ef |grep arch` in Unix, that check the process list to see whether the ARC*n* process is running. This process does the work of copying the archived logs from the redo logs.

This example shows ARCHIVELOG mode using the V$ views:

```
oracle@octilli:~ > sqlplus /nolog

SQL*Plus: Release 9.0.1.0.0 - Production on Tue Sep 25
19:08:25 2001

(c) Copyright 2001 Oracle Corporation.  All rights
reserved.
```

```
SQL> connect /as sysdba

Connected.

SQL> select name,log_mode from v$database;

NAME      LOG_MODE
--------- ------------
ORC9      ARCHIVELOG

SQL>
```

This example shows NOARCHIVELOG mode using the V$ views:

```
oracle@octilli:~ > sqlplus /nolog

SQL*Plus: Release 9.0.1.0.0 - Production on Tue Sep 25
19:08:25 2001

(c) Copyright 2001 Oracle Corporation.  All rights
reserved.

SQL> connect /as sysdba

Connected.

SQL> select name,log_mode from v$database;

NAME      LOG_MODE
--------- ------------
ORC9      NOARCHIVELOG

SQL>
```

The following is an example of using the Unix OS command `ps -ef |grep arch` to see whether the archiver process is running. This is more indirect than the V$ table output, but if the archiver process is running, then the database would have to be in ARCHIVELOG mode.

```
oracle@octilli:~ > ps -ef|grep arc
oracle    2097     1  0 00:26 ?          00:00:00 ora_arc0_orc9
oracle    4468  4327  0 19:34 pts/3      00:00:00 grep arc
oracle@octilli:~ >
```

A couple of methods exist for determining the location of the archived logs. The first is to execute the SHOW PARAMETER command and the second is to view the init.ora file. An example of using the SHOW PARAMETER command to display the value of LOG_ARCHIVE_DEST is as follows:

```
SQL> show parameters log_archive_dest

NAME                                 TYPE        VALUE
------------------------------------ ----------- --------------------
log_archive_dest                     string      oracle/admin/orc9/arch
log_archive_dest_1                   string
log_archive_dest_10                  string
log_archive_dest_2                   string
log_archive_dest_3                   string
log_archive_dest_4                   string
log_archive_dest_5                   string
log_archive_dest_6                   string
log_archive_dest_7                   string
log_archive_dest_8                   string
log_archive_dest_9                   string
log_archive_dest_state_1             string      enable
log_archive_dest_state_10            string      enable
log_archive_dest_state_2             string      enable
log_archive_dest_state_3             string      enable
log_archive_dest_state_4             string      enable
log_archive_dest_state_5             string      enable
log_archive_dest_state_6             string      enable
log_archive_dest_state_7             string      enable
log_archive_dest_state_8             string      enable
log_archive_dest_state_9             string      enable
SQL>
```

An example of viewing a partial `init.ora` file to display the LOG_ARCHIVE_DEST is listed here:

```
######################################################################
# Partial Sample of Init.ora File
######################################################################

###########################################
# Archive Logging
###########################################
log_archive_start=true
log_archive_dest=/oracle/admin/orc9/arch
log_archive_format=archorc9_%s.log
```

Setting Automatic Archiving

To configure a database for automatic archiving, you must perform a series of steps:

1. Edit the `init.ora` file and set the *LOG_ARCHIVE_START* parameter to TRUE. This will automate the archiving of redo logs as they become full.
2. Shut down the database and restart the database by using the command STARTUP MOUNT.
3. Use the ALTER DATABASE ARCHIVELOG command to set ARCHIVELOG mode.
4. Open the database with the ALTER DATABASE OPEN command.

To verify that the database is actually archiving, you should execute the ALTER SYSTEM SWITCH LOGFILE command. After you execute this command, check the OS directory specified by the parameter LOG_ARCHIVE_DEST to validate that archived log files are present. You can also execute the ARCHIVE LOG LIST command to display information that confirms the database is in ARCHIVELOG mode and automatic archival is enabled.

Now let's walk through this process.

1. First, edit the `init.ora` file and change the parameter LOG_ARCHIVE_START to TRUE. As a result, the database will be in automatic ARCHIVELOG mode. See the example `init.ora` file below.

```
########################################################################
# Partial Sample of Init.ora File
########################################################################

############################################
# Archive Logging
############################################
log_archive_start=true
log_archive_dest=/oracle/admin/orc9/arch
log_archive_format=archorc9_%s.log
```

2. Next, run the following commands in SQL:

```
SQL> shutdown
SQL> startup mount
SQL> alter database archivelog;
SQL> alter database open;
```

The automatic archival feature has now been enabled for this database. To verify that the database has been configured correctly, you can perform the following checks.

1. First, perform an ALTER SYSTEM SWITCH LOGFILE. This will need to be done *n* + 1 times, where *n* is the number of redo logs in your database.

```
SQL> alter system switch logfile;
```

2. Next, perform a directory listing of the archive destination in LOG_ARCHIVE_DEST. The Unix command pwd displays the current working directory, and `ls` shows the contents of the directory.

```
oracle@octilli:/oracle/admin/orc9/arch > ls -ltr
total 276
-rw-r-----    1 oracle   dba         133632 Sep 25 00:27 archorc9_3.log
-rw-r-----    1 oracle   dba         125952 Sep 25 00:28 archorc9_4.log
-rw-r-----    1 oracle   dba           1024 Sep 25 00:28 archorc9_5.log
-rw-r-----    1 oracle   dba           1536 Sep 25 00:28 archorc9_6.log
```

```
-rw-r-----    1 oracle   dba         1024 Sep 25 00:28 archorc9_7.log
oracle@octilli:/oracle/admin/orc9/arch >
```

The other way to verify that the automatic archival feature has been enabled is to execute the ARCHIVE LOG LIST command, which displays the status of these settings (as is shown here).

```
SQL> archive log list;
Database log mode              Archive Mode
Automatic archival             Enabled
Archive destination            /oracle/admin/orc9/arch
Oldest online log sequence     6
Next log sequence to archive   8
Current log sequence           8
SQL>
```

If you enable ARCHIVELOG mode but forget to enable the automatic archival by not editing the init.ora and changing the LOG_ARCHIVE_START to TRUE, the database will hang when it gets to the last available redo log. You will need to perform manual archiving as a temporary fix or to shut down and start up the database after changing the LOG_ARCHIVE_START parameter.

Real World Scenario

Providing Adequate Space for Archive Logging

The additional disk space necessary for ARCHIVELOG mode is often overlooked or underestimated. For average databases, you should have enough space to keep at least one or two days of archived logs online. In order to estimate the correct size of such files, you will need to estimate the volume during peak transaction volume periods. Peak times are typically when the heaviest transactional activity or batch activity occurs.

This estimated size is multiplied by how many log_archive_dest_n locations are set up. If you perform nightly hot backups on your system, one or two days of online archived logs should meet most of your recovery requirements from the archived log perspective.

But if the archive process doesn't have enough disk space to write archived logs, the database will hang or stop all activity. This hung state will remain until you make more space available by moving older archived logs off your system, by compressing log files, or by setting up an automated job that will remove logs after they have been written to tape. You must be careful not to misplace or delete archived logs when trying to free up space for the archive process. Remember these archived logs could be required in a recovery situation.

Manually Archiving Logs

The *manual archiving* of logs consists of enabling the database for ARCHIVELOG mode and then manually executing the ARCHIVE LOG ALL command from SQL. The init.ora parameter LOG_ARCHIVE_START must be set to FALSE to disable automatic archival. The next step is to put the database in ARCHIVELOG mode by performing the following commands:

```
SQL> shutdown
SQL> startup mount
SQL> alter database archivelog;
SQL> alter database open;
```

Now you are ready to perform manual archiving of redo logs by using

```
SQL> archive log all;
```

or

```
SQL> archive log next;
```

The ARCHIVE LOG ALL command will archive all redo logs available for archiving, and the ARCHIVE LOG NEXT command will archive the next group of redo logs.

Using *init.ora* Parameters for Multiple Archive Processes and Locations

The capability to have more than one archived log destination and multiple archivers was first introduced in Oracle8. In Oracle8*i* and 9*i*, more than two destinations can be used, providing even greater archived log redundancy.

The main reason for having multiple destinations for archived log files is to eliminate any *single point of failure*. For example, if you were to lose the disk storing the archived logs before these logs were backed up to tape, the database would be vulnerable to data loss in the event of a failure. If the disk containing the archived logs was lost, then the safest thing to do would be to run a backup. This would ensure that no data would be lost in the event of a database crash from *media failure*. Having only one archived log location is a single point of failure for the backup process. Hence, Oracle has provided multiple locations, which can be on different disk drives, so that the likelihood of archived logs being lost is significantly reduced. See Figure 7.2, which demonstrates ARCHIVELOG mode with multiple destinations.

In addition to reducing the potential archived log loss, one of the multiple locations can be remote. The remote location supports the Oracle standby database, which is an option that can be configured to protect a computing site from a disaster. Let's go over a brief explanation of this option and why it can require remote archived log capabilities.

The Oracle standby database can require archived logs to be moved to a remote server, which is running a copy of the production database. This copy of the production database is in a permanent recovery situation with archived logs from the production database regularly being applied to the standby database.

There are certain initialization parameters that can be used to assure that the archived logs get moved to remote locations. These initialization parameters will be covered in more detail in the upcoming section "Remote Archived Log Locations."

FIGURE 7.2 ARCHIVELOG mode with multiple destinations

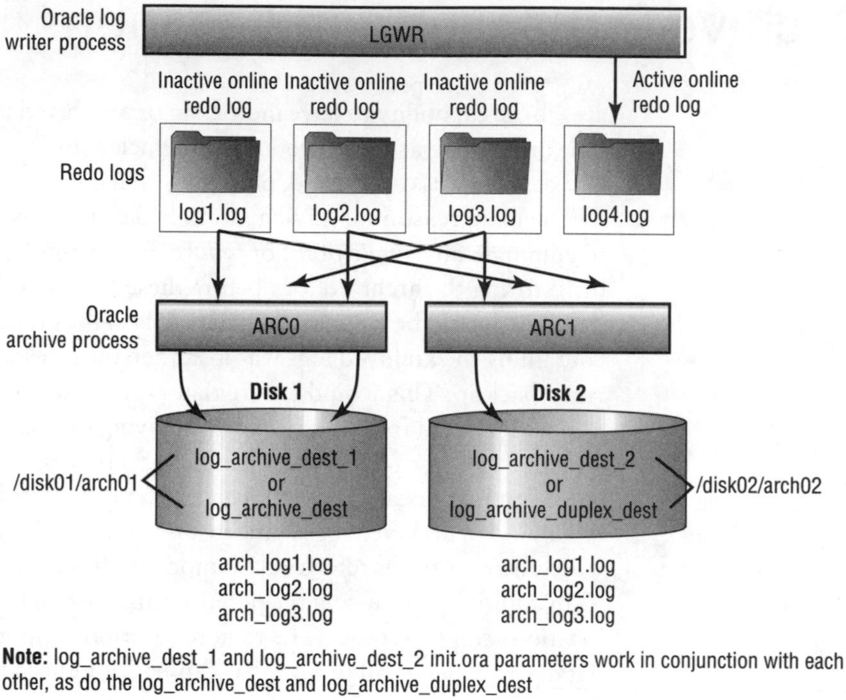

Multiple Archive Processes and Locations

Having multiple archive processes can make the archived log creation process faster. If significant volumes of data are going through the redo logs, the archiver can be a point of contention. This means that redo logs could wait or delay database activity while trying to write out an archived log. Furthermore, the archiver has more work to do if the database is writing to multiple destinations. Thus, multiple archive processes can do the extra work to support the additional archive destinations.

To implement these new features, the database must be in ARCHIVELOG mode. (To set the database to ARCHIVELOG mode, perform the steps shown earlier in the section entitled "Configuring a Database for ARCHIVELOG mode and Automatic Archiving.") To verify that the database is in ARCHIVELOG mode, either run an ARCHIVE LOG LIST command or query the V$DATABASE view, as shown earlier.

To configure a database for multiple archive processes and LOG_ARCHIVE_DESTs, you use two sets of init.ora parameters.

The first set is based on the destination parameter, which has been slightly changed to LOG_ARCHIVE_DEST_*N* (where *N* is a number from 1 to 10). The values for these parameters LOG_ARCHIVE_DEST_1 and LOG_ARCHIVE_DEST_2 are as follows: 'LOCATION = /ORACLE/ADMIN/ORC9/ARCH1', 'LOCATION = /ORACLE/ADMIN/ORC9/ARCH2', and 'LOCATION = /ORACLE/ADMIN/ORC9/REMOTE_ARCH3'. The first set of parameters is listed below in init.ora.

```
###############################################
# Archive Logging
###############################################
log_archive_start=true
#log_archive_dest=/oracle/admin/orc9/arch
log_archive_dest_1='location=/oracle/admin/orc9/arch1'
log_archive_dest_2='location=/oracle/admin/orc9/arch2'
log_archive_dest_3='location=/oracle/admin/orc9/arch_remote3'
log_archive_max_processes=3
log_archive_format=archorc9_%s.log
```

After these parameters are changed or added, then you will need to start up the database to use the new parameters. These new dump locations will then be in effect.

The second set of parameters are *LOG_ARCHIVE_DEST = </SOME/DIRECTORY/LOCATION>* and *LOG_ARCHIVE_DUPLEX_DEST = </SOME/DIRECTORY/LOCATION>*. The following example uses LOG_ARCHIVE_DEST = /ORACLE/ADMIN/ORC9/ARCH1 and LOG_ARCHIVE_DUPLEX_DEST = /ORACLE/ADMIN/ORC9/ARCH2. The main difference in this approach is that you use these parameters if you are going to have only two locations or want to use the same init.ora parameter format supported in 8.0.*x*. These parameters are mutually exclusive with LOG_ARCHIVE_DEST_*N* mentioned in the previous example. This second set of parameters can be seen below in the init.ora parameter values.

```
###############################################
# Archive Logging
###############################################
log_archive_start=true
log_archive_dest=/oracle/admin/orc9/arch1
log_archive_duplex_dest=/oracle/admin/orc9/arch2
```

```
log_archive_max_processes=2
log_archive_format=archorc9_%s.log
```

This second method of mirroring archived logs is designed to mirror just one copy of the log files, whereas the first method can mirror up to 10 copies, one of which can be a remote database.

Remote Archived Log Locations

With all remote transactions, there is a greater degree of potential problems. In order to deal with these potential transaction problems, Oracle has developed some specific commands for remote archive destinations. Among these, there are a couple of commands and initialization parameters that determine whether the logs are required to reach the remote location and whether they are required to retry unsuccessful sends.

LOG_ARCHIVE_MIN_SUCCEED_DEST=*N* is the initialization parameter that determines how many of the 10 maximum archive destinations must successfully receive an archived log before the online redo logs can be written over. If this is not met, the database will hang.

The first parameters specify whether the destinations are mandatory or optional log archive destinations. When you use the MANDATORY parameter, destinations will require log files to arrive at the remote location; if these files don't arrive, the database generating these logs will hang. When you use the OPTIONAL parameter, the opposite of the MANDATORY parameter, if a log does not make it to remote location, the database will continue processing without hanging.

The REOPEN command causes failed archive destinations to be retried after a certain period of time. Below is an example of this command and the parameters previously mentioned. Note that the REOPEN example uses a service-entered destination for use in standby database mode.

```
LOG_ARCHIVE_DEST_1="LOCATION=/oracle/admin/tst9/arch1 MANDATORY"
LOG_ARCHIVE_DEST_2="LOCATION=/oracle/admin/tst9/arch2 OPTIONAL"
LOG_ARCHIVE_DEST_3="SERVICE=euro_fin_db_V9.0.1 REOPEN=60"
```

Make sure each LOG_ARCHIVE_DEST_*N* and LOG_ARCHIVE_DUPLEX_DEST is on a different physical device. The main purpose of these new parameters is to allow a copy of the files to remain intact if a disk were to crash.

Summary

The Oracle backup and recovery capability is full featured and robust. It provides many options that support a wide variety of backup and recovery situations. In this chapter, you have seen how to configure an Oracle database for backup and recovery. You have learned the ramifications of operating in ARCHIVELOG as opposed to NOARCHIVELOG mode, and vice versa, and how that choice affects the backup and recovery process. You have seen examples of how the `init.ora` parameters control the destinations and automation of the archive logging. Finally, you walked through an example that enabled ARCHIVELOG mode and automatic archival of logs in the database.

A solid understanding of the archived log process is fundamental to the backup and recovery process. The decision to enable archive logging has major implications on a DBA's ability to recover the database. In addition, certain recovery options that will be covered in upcoming chapters are dependent on whether or not you have enabled ARCHIVELOG mode. Make sure you understand the reasons for enabling or not enabling the archived log process because this knowledge will benefit you during OCP testing, as well as in real life situations.

Exam Essentials

Identify the differences between ARCHIVELOG and NOARCHIVELOG modes. You should know the differences between having the database generate archived logs or not. Make sure that you aware of the impact that the ARCHIVELOG and NOARCHIVELOG modes have on the backup and recovery process.

Know how to configure a database in ARCHIVELOG mode. Be able to explain how to configure a database so that it will generate archived logs. You should also be able to identify the commands and initialization parameters involved in this process.

Know how to configure the database for automatic archiving. Be able to identify the initialization parameter `LOG_ARCHIVE_START = TRUE`, which is used to enable automatic archiving.

Demonstrate how to perform manual archiving. Know how to use the required commands to generate archive logs manually.

Understand how to configure a database for multiple archive destinations. Know the two different methods of initialization parameters: ARCHIVE_DEST_LOG_*N* and ARCHIVE_LOG_DEST_DUPLEX. You should also understand the differences between each of these methods, such as remote archive logging and the number of locations.

Understand how to configure multiple archive processes. To configure multiple archive processes, you must be familiar with the initialization parameter that configures the database for multiple archive log processes.

Understand the commands and initialization parameters involved with remote archiving. You should be comfortable with the commands that affect remote archival, such as MANDATORY, OPTIONAL, and REOPEN. You should also be familiar with the initialization parameters, such as LOG_ARCHIVE_MIN_SUCCEED_DEST, and how they affect the remote archive process.

Key Terms

Before you take the exam, be certain you are familiar with the following terms:

- ARCHIVELOG mode
- automatic archiving
- LOG_ARCHIVE_DEST
- LOG_ARCHIVE_START
- manual archiving
- media failure
- NOARCHIVELOG mode
- online (hot) backups
- single point of failure

Review Questions

1. What state does the database need to be in to enable archiving?

   A. Opened

   B. Closed

   C. Mounted

   D. Unmounted

2. What are some of the issues the DBA should be aware of when the database is running in `ARCHIVELOG` mode?

   A. Whether they have the ability to perform a complete recovery

   B. Whether they have to shut down the database to perform backups

   C. Whether they have the ability to perform an incomplete recovery

   D. Whether this mode will cause increased disk space utilization

3. Which of the choices below are ways in which you can change the destination of archived log files? (Choose all that apply.)

   A. Change the `LOG_ARCHIVE_DEST_`*n* `init.ora` parameter.

   B. Configure the control file.

   C. Change the `LOG_ARCHIVE_DEST` `init.ora` parameter.

   D. Change the `LOG_ARCHIVE_DUMP` `init.ora` parameter.

4. What is the maximum number of archived log destinations that is supported?

   A. 1

   B. 2

   C. 5

   D. 10

5. What type of database backup requires a shutdown of the database? (Choose all that apply.)

   A. A database in ARCHIVELOG

   B. A database in NOARCHIVELOG

   C. Hot backup (online backup)

   D. Cold backup (offline backup)

6. List all the methods of determining that the database is in ARCHIVELOG mode. (Choose all that apply.)

   A. Query the V$DATABASE view.

   B. See whether the ARC*n* process is running.

   C. Check the value of the LOG_ARCHIVE_DEST parameter.

   D. View the results of the ARCHIVE LOG LIST command.

7. You are the DBA for a manufacturing company that runs three shifts a day and performs work 24 hours a day on the database, taking orders, performing inventory adjustments, and shipping products. Which type of backup should you perform? (Choose all that apply.)

   A. Hot backup in ARCHIVELOG mode

   B. Cold backup in ARCHIVELOG mode

   C. Online backup in NOARCHIVELOG mode

   D. Online backup in ARCHIVELOG mode

8. What init.ora parameter allows no more than two archive log destinations?

   A. ARCHIVE_LOG_DEST_*N*

   B. ARCHIVE_LOG_DEST_DUPLEX

   C. LOG_ARCHIVE_DEST_DUPLEX

   D. LOG_ARCHIVE_DUPLEX_DEST

9. What `init.ora` parameter allows no more than 10 archive log destinations?

   A. ARCHIVE_LOG_DEST_*N*

   B. ARCHIVE_LOG_DEST_DUPLEX

   C. LOG_ARCHIVE_DEST_DUPLEX

   D. LOG_ARCHIVE_DUPLEX_DEST

   E. LOG_ARCHIVE_DEST_*N*

10. What `init.ora` parameter allows remote archive log destinations?

    A. ARCHIVE_LOG_DEST

    B. ARCHIVE_LOG_DEST_DUPLEX

    C. LOG_ARCHIVE_DEST_*N*

    D. LOG_ARCHIVE_DUPLEX_DEST

11. What command is necessary to perform manual archiving?

    A. MANUAL ARCHIVE ALL

    B. ARCHIVE MANUAL

    C. LOG ARCHIVE LIST

    D. ARCHIVE LOG ALL

12. What is required to manually archive the database?

    A. The database running in ARCHIVELOG mode.

    B. LOG_ARCHIVE_START is set to TRUE.

    C. MANUAL_ARCHIVE is set to TRUE.

    D. Nothing.

13. What command is necessary to perform manual archiving?

    A. ARCHIVE LOG NEXT

    B. ARCHIVE LOG LIST

    C. ARCHIVE ALL LOG

    D. ARCHIVE ALL

14. What will happen to the database if ARCHIVELOG mode is enabled, but the LOG_ARCHIVE_START command is not set to TRUE? (Choose all that apply.)

    A. The database will perform with problems.

    B. The database will hang until the archived logs are manually archived.

    C. The database will not start because of improper configuration.

    D. The database will work properly until all online redo logs have been filled.

15. Which of the following is true about NOARCHIVELOG mode?

    A. The database must be shut down completely for backups.

    B. Tablespaces must be taken offline before backups.

    C. The database must be running for backups.

    D. The database may be running for backups, but it isn't required.

16. Which initialization parameter determines how many of the archived log destinations must be successfully written to before the online redo logs may be written over?

    A. ARCHIVE_MINIMUM_SUCCEED

    B. LOG_ARCHIVE_MINIMUM_SUCCEED

    C. LOG_ARCHIVE_MIN_SUCCEED_DEST

    D. ARCHIVE_MIN_SUCCEED_DEST

17. What parameter will allow the database to keep on processing if an archived log does not arrive at a log archive destination?

A. REOPEN

B. MANDATORY

C. OPTIONAL

D. UNSUCCESSFUL

18. What parameter will cause failed archived log transfers to retry after a determined period of time?

A. MANDATORY

B. OPTIONAL

C. REOPEN

D. RETRY

19. How can you identify whether the database is in ARCHIVELOG mode or not? (Choose all that apply.)

A. You can use the ARCHIVE LOG LIST command.

B. You can select * from V$DATABASE.

C. You can use the ARCHIVELOG LIST command.

D. You can select * from V$LOG.

20. Complete recovery can be performed when what is true about the database?

A. It is in ARCHIVELOG mode.

B. It is in NOARCHIVELOG mode.

C. Manual archive logging is enabled.

D. Automatic archive logging is enabled.

Answers to Review Questions

1. C. The database must be in MOUNT mode to enable archive logging.

2. D. The database will use more space because of the creation of archived logs.

3. A, C. The archive destination is controlled by the LOG_ARCHIVE_DEST init.ora parameter and by issuing ALTER SYSTEM commands when the database is running.

4. D. The maximum number of archive destinations is controlled by the LOG_ARCHIVE_DEST_*N* init.ora parameter. It will support up to 10 locations.

5. B, D. A database in NOARCHIVELOG mode will not support backups without a shutdown of the database, and a cold backup is a backup taken when the database is offline or shut down.

6. A, B, D. The V$DATABASE view shows whether the database is in ARCHIVELOG or NOARCHIVELOG mode, the ARC*n* process indirectly determines that the archiver is running, and the ARCHIVE LOG LIST command shows whether archiving is enabled. Checking the value of the LOG_ARCHIVE_DEST parameter indicates only whether there is a directory to contain the archived logs, not whether the database is in ARCHIVELOG mode.

7. A, D. A hot backup and online backup are synonymous. A cold backup and offline backup are synonymous. A hot backup can be run only in ARCHIVELOG mode (so the backup method in answer C doesn't exist). A hot backup can be run while the database is running; therefore, it does not affect the availability of the database. Because this database must have 24-hour availability, a hot or online backup would be appropriate.

8. D. The LOG_ARCHIVE_DUPLEX_DEST parameter allows for the second archive destination. Also, this parameter must be used in conjunction with the LOG_ARCHIVE_DEST parameter for the first archive log destination.

9. E. The LOG_ARCHIVE_DEST_*N* allows up to 10 locations.

10. C. LOG_ARCHIVE_DEST_*N* allows up to 10 locations. One of these locations can be remote, that is, not on the same server.

11. D. The ARCHIVE LOG ALL command is responsible for manually generating archived logs. The ARCHIVE LOG NEXT command will also archive logs manually, but it will only archive the next archived log in the sequence as opposed to all of the archived logs. The database must also be in ARCHIVELOG mode.

12. A. The database running in ARCHIVELOG mode is a requirement for performing manual or automatic archiving. This means that the database must be restarted with STARTUP MOUNT and then the command ALTER DATABASE ARCHIVELOG must be executed. Then the database should be opened for normal use.

13. A. The ARCHIVE LOG NEXT command will archive the next group of redo logs.

14. B, D. The database will hang after all the online redo logs have been filled, but it will work properly as long as there are unfilled online redo logs.

15. A. The database must be shut down completely for backups. If the database is open and a backup is taken, the backup will be invalid.

16. C. The LOG_ARCHIVE_MIN_SUCCEED_DEST parameter determines how many of the log archive destinations must be successfully written to before the online redo logs can be overwritten.

17. C. The OPTIONAL parameter will allow the database to continue processing even when the online redo logs have been filled and the archived log still has not arrived at the log archive destination.

18. C. The REOPEN parameter will cause failed archived log transfers to retry after a determined period of time.

19. A, B. The ARCHIVE LOG LIST command can be executed from within SQL*Plus and will display whether or not the database is in ARCHIVELOG mode. Selecting from V$DATABASE will also show this information.

20. A. When the database is in ARCHIVELOG mode, complete recovery can be performed. What mode to use is one of the most significant decisions you can make about backup and recovery of your database.

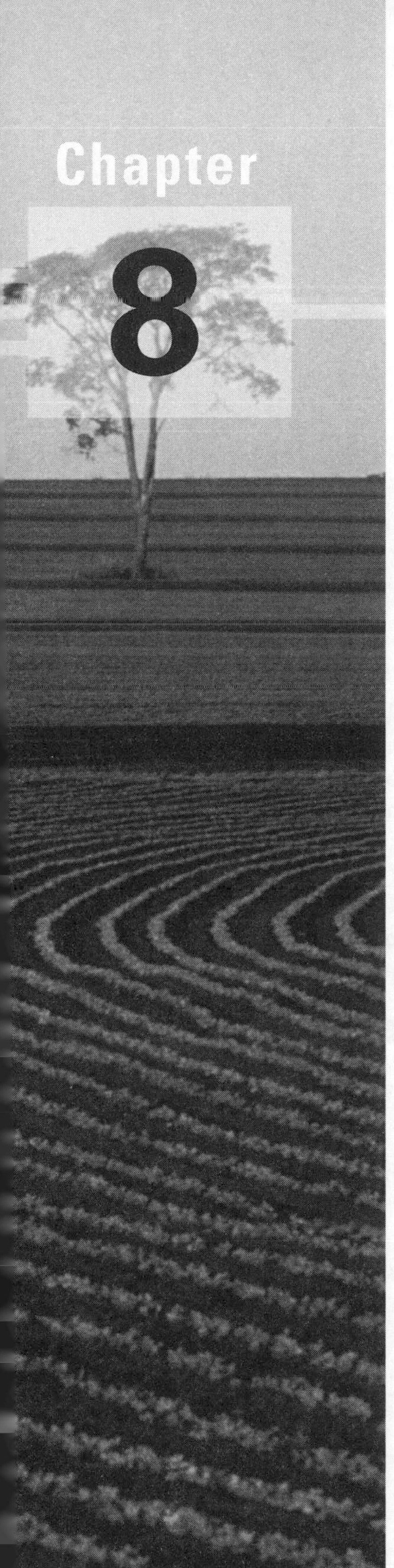

Oracle Recovery Manager Overview and Configuration

ORACLE9*i*: DBA FUNDAMENTALS II EXAM OBJECTIVES COVERED IN THIS CHAPTER:

- ✓ **Identify the features and components of RMAN.**
- ✓ **Describe the RMAN repository and control file usage.**
- ✓ **Describe channel allocation.**
- ✓ **Describe the Media Management Library interface.**
- ✓ **Connect to RMAN without the recovery catalog.**
- ✓ **Configure the RMAN environment.**

Exam objectives are subject to change at any time without prior notice and at Oracle's sole discretion. Please visit Oracle's Certification website (`http://www.oracle.com/education/certification/`) for the most current exam objectives listing.

This chapter provides an overview of RMAN, including the capabilities and components of the RMAN tool. The RMAN utility attempts to move away from the highly customized OS backup scripts (user-managed) discussed in earlier chapters, to a highly standardized backup and recovery process. Thus, as of Oracle version 8, you can reduce backup and recovery mistakes associated with the highly customized OS backup scripts used before RMAN's release.

In this chapter, you will walk through a practical example of connecting to the RMAN utility without using the optional, but recommended, recovery catalog. We will also demonstrate multiple ways to configure the RMAN environment to automate and set up manual RMAN settings.

Each of the topics covered in this chapter is important; you can apply this knowledge to your real-world DBA work in addition to your preparations for the test. When you know how to use the RMAN repository, channel allocation, and MML, and you can configure the RMAN environment, you will be better able to utilize RMAN in your organization.

Identifying Features of Oracle Recovery Manager (RMAN)

Oracle Recovery Manager (RMAN) has many features that can be used to facilitate the backup and recovery process. This tool comes in both GUI and command-line versions. In general, RMAN performs and standardizes the backup and recovery process, and by doing this, it can reduce mistakes made by DBAs during this process. A list of some of the major RMAN features follows:

Backs up databases, tablespaces, data files, control files, and archived logs The RMAN tool is capable of backing up Oracle databases in multiple ways to allow for flexibility in backup and recovery methods.

Compresses backups by determining which blocks have changed and backing up only those blocks One way RMAN improves performance of the backup is by compressing backups. RMAN identifies blocks that have changed and only backs up those blocks. Also, empty blocks are not backed up.

Performs incremental backups RMAN has the ability to perform incremental and full backups. Incremental backups include only the changes that have been made since the last backup. This type of backup can improve performance by allowing you to take a full backup one day a week and incremental backups on the rest of the days.

Provides scripting capabilities to combine tasks One way RMAN can improve the efficiency of your backup, restoration, and recovery operations is by allowing RMAN commands to be scripted. The scripts can consist of multiple RMAN commands that can be stored within the recovery catalog. These scripts can be called and executed to perform tasks repetitively.

Logs backup operations RMAN has the ability to log the status of backups as they progress. This information is stored in log and trace files.

Integrates with third-party tape media software The RMAN tool has APIs with many third-party tape media software. These allow RMAN to be executed within other non-Oracle backup utilities and to be integrated in a common backup strategy for an organization.

Provides reports and lists of catalog information Information about backups that is stored within the recovery catalog can be queried with RMAN `LIST` and `REPORT` commands. These commands provide useful ways to display information.

Stores information about backups in a catalog within an Oracle database Information about backups is stored in the recovery catalog. This information can be retrieved at a later date or whenever desired.

Offers performance benefits, such as parallel processing of backup and restore operations Backup and restore operations can be set in parallel. This can split workloads onto different tape heads and disk devices, which will improve performance.

Creates duplicate databases for testing and development purposes Duplicate databases can be created from RMAN backups and can be used for testing purposes.

Tests whether backups can be restored successfully RMAN provides the `VALID` commands that will check to see whether the backup is valid.

Determines whether backups are still available in media libraries RMAN provides the CROSSCHECK command to determine if the backup media and catalog information match.

Figure 8.1 illustrates some of the differences between RMAN and the customized backup scripts and commands used in the earlier chapters.

FIGURE 8.1 Differences between backup scripts and the RMAN utility

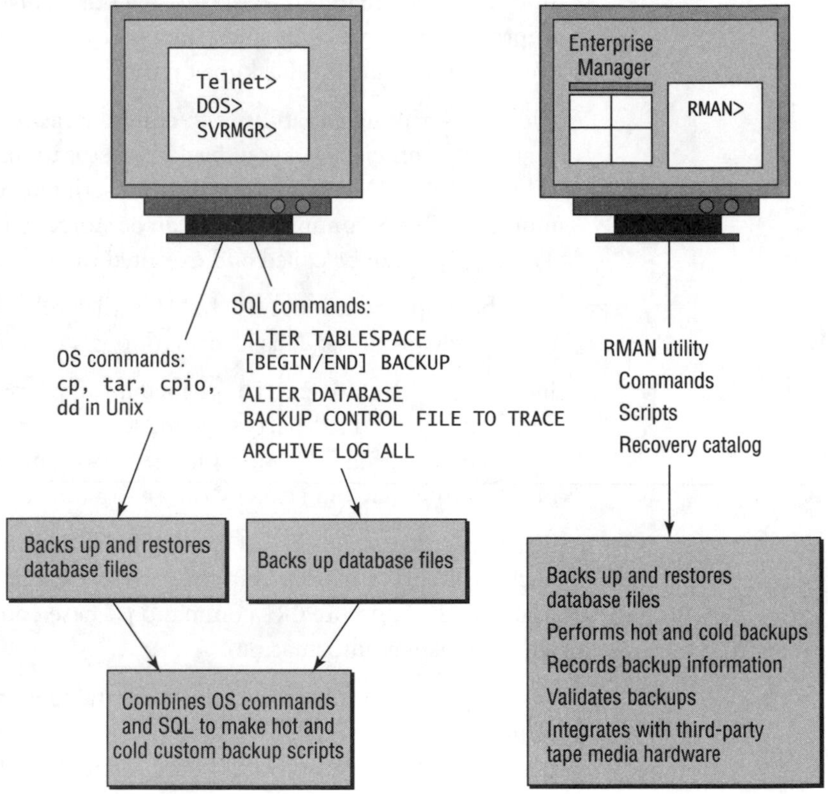

Exploring RMAN Components

The main components of RMAN are GUI or command-line access, the optional recovery catalog, the RMAN commands and scripting, and tape media connectivity. These components enable a DBA to automate and standardize the backup and recovery process. Each component is described below:

GUI or command-line access method This method provides access to Recovery Manager, which in turn provides access to RMAN. The GUI method spawns off of server sessions that connect to the *target database*—the database targeted by RMAN for backup or recovery actions. GUI access is provided through the *Oracle Enterprise Manager (OEM)* tool, which is a DBA tool that performs backups, exports/imports, data loads, performance monitoring/tuning, job and event scheduling, and standard DBA management, to mention a few. Command-line access can be run in a standard Unix Telnet or X Windows session as well as in a DOS shell in the Windows environment.

Optional recovery catalog This special data dictionary of backup information is stored in a set of tables, in much the same way that the data dictionary stores information about databases. The recovery catalog provides a method for storing information about backups, restores, and recoveries. This information provides status updates on the success or failure of backups, the OS backup, data file copies, tablespace copies, control file copies, archived log copies, full database backups, and the physical structures of a database.

RMAN commands These commands enable different actions to be performed that facilitate the backup and restoration of the database. These commands can be organized logically into scripts, which can then be stored in the recovery catalog database. The scripts can be reused for other backups, thus keeping consistency among different target database backups.

Tape media connectivity This component provides a method for interfacing with various third-party tape hardware vendors to store and track backups in *automated tape libraries (ATLs)*. An ATL is a large tape cabinet that stores many tapes and can write to multiple tapes at the same time to improve performance. ATLs use robotic arms to load, unload, and store tapes. By default, Oracle provides media management libraries (MML) for the Legato Storage Management (LSM) software, which manages an ATL device.

Figure 8.2 shows an example of how the RMAN utilities' components fit together to form a complete backup and recovery package.

FIGURE 8.2 The components of RMAN

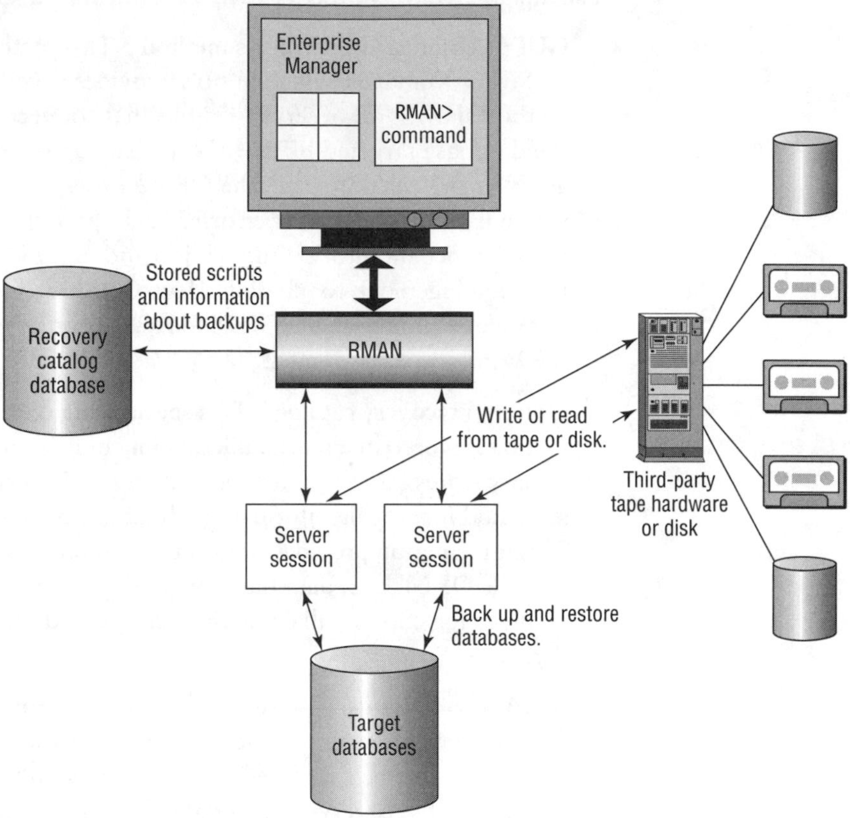

Storing Information Using the RMAN Repository and Control Files

The RMAN utility uses two methods to store information about the target databases that are backed up. Each method is called the *RMAN repository*. When RMAN uses the first method, it accesses an optional RMAN catalog or recovery catalog of information about backups. In the second method, it accesses the necessary information about backups in the target database's control file. If the optional recovery catalog database is not used, then the target database's control file will be used as the RMAN repository. The information that RMAN needs to function in the recovery catalog database or in the target database's control file is also called the RMAN repository. The target database's control is always updated, whether the catalog is used or not. In the next paragraph, we will discuss the recovery catalog as the RMAN repository for storing information, and then we will list the commands you can use in this method. Following this list, we will focus on using the control file as the RMAN repository.

Oracle recommends that you store RMAN backup data in the recovery catalog database as opposed to in the control file of the target database. If you store the data in this manner, the RMAN utility will have full functionality. This recovery catalog database is another Oracle database that has special RMAN catalog tables that store metadata about backups in much the same way that a data dictionary stores data about objects in the database. When this database is used, activities such as cross checking backups and available tapes can be performed. Also, using this method, backup scripts can be created and stored in the recovery catalog database for later use. This database can also be backed up so that the information it contains is made safe. We will discuss the recovery catalog database in more detail in Chapter 13, "Recovery Catalog Creation and Maintenancc."

Before we move on to discuss the second method in more detail, take a look at these commands. They are allowed only if you use the RMAN recovery catalog as the RMAN repository.

- `CREATE CATALOG`
- `UPGRADE CATALOG`
- `DROP CATALOG`
- `CREATE SCRIPT`
- `DELETE SCRIPT`
- `REPLACE SCRIPT`
- `PRINT SCRIPT`
- `LIST STORED FILES`
- `LIST INCARNATION`
- `REGISTER DATABASE`
- `REPORT SCHEMA AT TIME`
- `RESET DATABASE`
- `RESYNC CATALOG`

As mentioned earlier, the RMAN utility also enables you to connect to a target database without using this recovery catalog database. Though this approach is not recommended by Oracle, it does have its uses. (For instance, you might use this approach if the overhead of creating and maintaining the recovery catalog were too great for your organization.)

If you use RMAN without the recovery catalog, you are storing most of the necessary information about each target database in the target database's control file, which serves as the RMAN repository. Thus, you must manage the target database's control file to support this data. The `init.ora` file's `CONTROL_FILE_RECORD_KEEP_TIME` parameter determines how long information that can be used by RMAN is kept in the control file. The default value for this parameter is 7 days, but it can be as many as 365 days. The greater the number, the larger the control file becomes so that it can store more information. The control file can only be as large as the OS allows, so be aware of this. The information that is stored within the control file is stored in the *reusable sections*. These sections can grow if the value of the `CONTROL_FILE_RECORD_KEEP_TIME` parameter is 1 or more. The reusable sections are made up of the following categories:

- Archived log
- Backup data file
- Backup redo log
- Copy corruption
- Deleted object
- Offline range
- Backup corruption
- Backup piece
- Backup set
- Data file copy
- Log history

Describing Channel Allocation

Channel allocation is a method you can use to connect RMAN and target databases. While you are doing this, you can also determine the type of I/O device that the server process will use to perform the backup or restore operation. Figure 8.3 displays this example. The I/O device can be either tape or disk (in Figure 8.3, you can see both).

FIGURE 8.3 Channel allocation

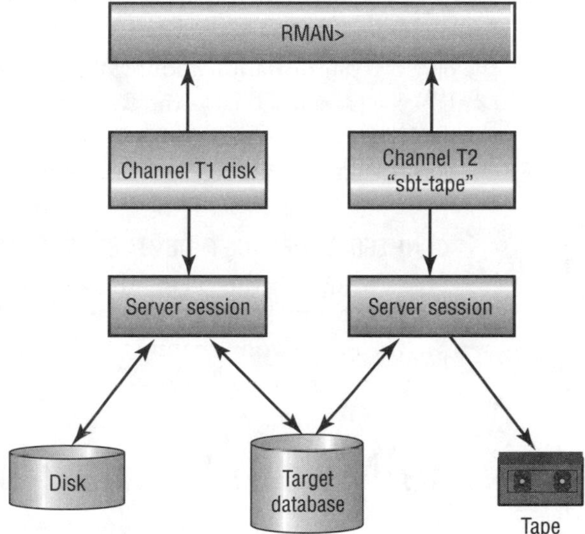

Channels can be allocated manually or automatically.

Manual channel allocation is performed any time you issue the `ALLOCATE CHANNEL` command, which starts a server process on the server of the target database. To manually write to a disk file system, you would use the `ALLOCATE CHANNEL` *<channel name>* `TYPE DISK` command. Similarly, to write to a tape backup system, you would use the `ALLOCATE CHANNEL` *<channel name>* `TYPE 'SBT_TAPE'` command. These are the most common manual channel allocation usages.

Automatic channel allocation is performed when you set the RMAN configuration at the RMAN command prompt. You do this by using the `CONFIGURE DEFAULT DEVICE` or `CONFIGURE DEVICE` command. This type of allocation is automatic when you are executing the `BACKUP`, `RESTORE`, or `DELETE` commands. By using the `CONFIGURE` commands you can eliminate the need to use the `ALLOCATE CHANNEL <channel name> TYPE DISK` or `'SBT_TAPE'` command every time you perform a `BACKUP`, `RESTORE`, or `DELETE`. The complete listing of automatic channel allocation commands is as follows:

- `CONFIGURE DEVICE TYPE PARALLELISM`
- `CONFIGURE DEFAULT DEVICE TYPE`

- CONFIGURE CHANNEL DEVICE TYPE
- CONFIGURE CHANNEL *n* DEVICE TYPE

There are some default naming conventions for the disk and tape device types—ORA_MAINT_DISK_*n* and ORA_SBT_TAPE_*n*. The example below shows the default device type set to DISK and parallelism set to 1. This means that if you don't allocate a channel manually, you will get the parameters listed below.

```
RMAN> show all;
RMAN configuration parameters are:
...
CONFIGURE DEFAULT DEVICE TYPE TO DISK; # default
CONFIGURE DEVICE TYPE DISK PARALLELISM 1; # default

RMAN>
```

Exploring the Media Management Library Interface

The media management library (MML) interface is an API that interfaces RMAN and different hardware vendors' ATLs.

All tape hardware vendors that wish to work with Oracle RMAN will make their own MML. This is necessary because most tape hardware devices are proprietary and require different program calls. The MML is then linked in with the Oracle database kernel so that the RMAN server process and MML can read and write the Oracle data to the tape device. Figure 8.4 describes this concept.

Oracle provides a third-party media management library (MML) that is included in its software installation by default with RMAN. This MML is used with Legato Storage Manager (LSM) software, which will manage an automated tape library (ATL).

FIGURE 8.4 MML and RMAN server process

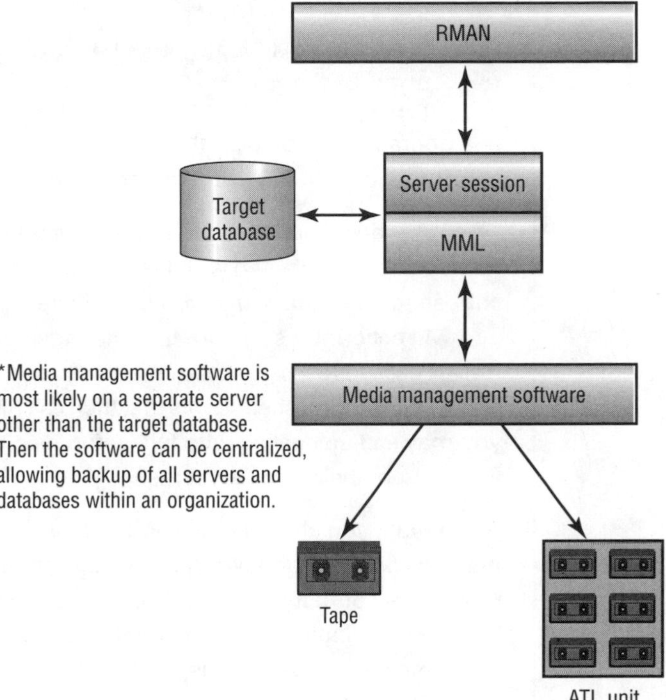

When you set up the MML with RMAN, you need to use OS commands to replace an existing shared library with the new media management vendor's library. Here is a generic example of this being done in the Unix environment.

1. If an old `libobk.so` symbolic link already exists in `$ORACLE_HOME/lib`, then remove it before installing the media manager. For example:

   ```
   oracle@octilli:/oracle/product/9.0.1/rdbms/lib > rm
   libobk.so
   ```

2. There are two ways to access the new media management library from the vendor. Either create a symbolic link,

   ```
   oracle@octilli: >  ln -s /vendor/lib/oracle_lib.so
   $ORACLE_HOME/rdbms/lib/libobk.so
   ```

   or move the library into the `$ORACLE_HOME/lib` directory.

   ```
   oracle@octilli: >   mv /vendor/lib/oracle_lib.so
   $ORACLE_HOME/rdbms/lib/libobk.so
   ```

Real World Scenario

Configuring and Using the Media Manager Vendor Software

In your role as a DBA, you have configured RMAN and made sure that it is operational. You also have a backup script and method that you feel comfortable with. But you are not out of the woods, yet.

This is because there is often a whole new setup, configuration, usage, and testing effort associated with the software and hardware solutions that you choose to integrate with RMAN. For instance, if you interface with an ATL, you will encounter software that manages the tapes, and most likely, the RMAN backups as well. In some cases, these software solutions can be simple agents performing shell scripts that then call RMAN scripts. But in some cases, you may end up dealing with full-featured software applications that execute RMAN from their own GUI screens.

As a result, you should make sure that you plan for the extra time you will need to configure and work with these software tools. You will also need to take into account the time you will need to work with system administrators, backup coordinators, and other database administrators to assure that your complete backup package is properly implemented.

Connecting to RMAN without a Recovery Catalog

In order to connect to the target database in RMAN, you must set the `ORACLE_SID` to the appropriate target database. In this example, it is `orc9`. This example uses the `oraenv` shell script provided by Oracle with the *9i* database software to change database environments. Next, you initiate the RMAN utility. Once the RMAN utility is started, issue the `CONNECT TARGET` command with the appropriate `SYSDBA` privileged account. This performs the connection to the target database.

Let's walk through this step by step:

1. Set the ORACLE_SID to the appropriate target database that you wish to connect to.

   ```
   oracle@octilli:/oracle/product/9.0.1/bin > . oraenv
   ORACLE_SID = [orc9] orc9
   ```

2. Execute the RMAN utility by typing **RMAN** and pressing Enter.

   ```
   oracle@octilli:/oracle/product/9.0.1/bin > rman

   Recovery Manager: Release 9.0.1.0.0 - Production

   (c) Copyright 2001 Oracle Corporation.  All rights
   reserved.

   RMAN>
   ```

3. Issue the CONNECT TARGET command with the appropriate DBA privileged account.

   ```
   RMAN> connect target /

   connected to target database: ORC9 (DBID=3960695)

   RMAN>
   ```

Here are two other methods of connecting to the target database without the recovery catalog:

```
oracle@octilli:~ > rman target / nocatalog
```

and

```
oracle@octilli:~ > rman target SYS/CHANGE_ON_INSTALL@tst9
NOCATALOG
```

Configuring the RMAN Environment

Configuring the RMAN environment consists mainly of executing the CONFIGURE command at some point while you are using the RMAN prompt.

The existing configuration can be seen by executing the SHOW ALL command, as we did in the "Describing Channel Allocation" section earlier. Let's start by first looking at the output from the SHOW ALL command in the target database TST9.

```
RMAN> show all;

using target database controlfile instead of recovery
catalog
RMAN configuration parameters are:
CONFIGURE RETENTION POLICY TO RECOVERY WINDOW OF 5 DAYS;
CONFIGURE BACKUP OPTIMIZATION OFF; # default
CONFIGURE DEFAULT DEVICE TYPE TO DISK; # default
CONFIGURE CONTROLFILE AUTOBACKUP OFF; # default
CONFIGURE CONTROLFILE AUTOBACKUP FORMAT FOR DEVICE TYPE
DISK TO '%F'; # default
CONFIGURE DEVICE TYPE DISK PARALLELISM 1; # default
CONFIGURE DATAFILE BACKUP COPIES FOR DEVICE TYPE DISK TO
1; # default
CONFIGURE ARCHIVELOG BACKUP COPIES FOR DEVICE TYPE DISK TO
1; # default
CONFIGURE MAXSETSIZE TO UNLIMITED; # default
CONFIGURE SNAPSHOT CONTROLFILE NAME TO '/oracle/product/
9.0.1/dbs/snapcf_tst9.ft

RMAN>
```

Now let's look at a specific example of what happens while you are configuring the AUTOBACKUP control file. This process begins when you execute the CONFIGURE CONTROLFILE AUTOBACKUP ON command at the RMAN prompt, as shown here:

```
RMAN> configure controlfile autobackup on;

new RMAN configuration parameters:
CONFIGURE CONTROLFILE AUTOBACKUP ON;
new RMAN configuration parameters are successfully stored

RMAN>
```

If you want to revert to the default entry for the AUTOBACKUP control file or some other configuration setting, you can use the CLEAR command, as demonstrated here:

```
RMAN> configure controlfile autobackup clear;

old RMAN configuration parameters:
CONFIGURE CONTROLFILE AUTOBACKUP ON;
RMAN configuration parameters are successfully reset to
default value

RMAN>
```

There are other configuration parameters that can be used in RMAN. Each of these configuration parameters can be used in a similar way as the previous configuration example. The other configuration parameters can be broken into the following major categories:

- Configuring automatic channels
- Configuring the AUTOBACKUP control file
- Configuring the backup retention policy
- Configuring the maximum size of backup sets
- Configuring backup optimization
- Configuring the number of backup copies
- Configuring tablespaces for exclusion from whole database backups
- Configuring the snapshot control file location

Summary

This chapter discussed the features and capabilities of the RMAN utility. From it, you should have gotten a sense of some of the basic functions of RMAN. You should have learned how RMAN can be used with or without the recovery catalog and in what environments this practice would be most beneficial. In addition, you learned what the effects of using RMAN on the control file would be if you are not using the recovery catalog. You also learned of manual and automatic channel allocation and explored specific examples of each.

Each of the topics covered in this chapter will be covered on the test. Having an understanding of the components and features of RMAN is important for both testing and the workplace. When you know how to work with the RMAN repository, use channel allocation and the MML, and configure the RMAN environment, you will be able to make appropriate decisions when you implement and use RMAN in the workplace. This level of understanding will definitely be beneficial in the testing process.

Exam Essentials

Name the components of RMAN. The different components that make up RMAN include the GUI access through Oracle Enterprise Manager, the RMAN command line capabilities, Media Management support, and the optional recovery catalog database.

Know how to configure RMAN to store backup information without a recovery catalog. You will need to configure the control file so that it will store information about backups. You would do this by setting the `CONTROL_FILE_RECORD_KEEP_TIME` parameter.

Understand the RMAN repository or target database control file limitations. Not all the commands are available to you if you use RMAN repository to access your target database's control file rather than your own database's RMAN catalog. Be aware of these commands.

Define channel allocation. You'll need to understand what channel allocation is and the two I/O devices it can be connected to: tape and disk. You should also know that there are two types of channel allocation: automatic and manual.

Configure the RMAN environment. Be able to use the `CONFIGURE` command and the parameters necessary to configure this environment. Also, be aware that you can configure the NLS settings and media management layer in the OS.

Describe the media management library interface. Be familiar with the media management library and know that it is a library created by tape hardware vendors to link RMAN with their unique hardware devices and software.

Be able to connect to RMAN without the recovery catalog. You should know how to set the database environment ORACLE_SID to the correct target database you would like to back up.

Key Terms

Before you take the exam, be certain you are familiar with the following terms:

automated tape library (ATL)

automatic channel allocation

channel allocation

manual channel allocation

Oracle Enterprise Manager (OEM)

Oracle Recovery Manager (RMAN)

reusable section

RMAN repository

target database

Review Questions

1. Does the RMAN utility require the use of the recovery catalog?

   A. The recovery catalog is required.

   B. The recovery catalog is not required.

   C. The recovery catalog is required if it is stored in the same database as the target database.

   D. The recovery catalog is not required if it is stored in the same database as the target database.

2. What are some of the capabilities of the RMAN utility? (Choose all that apply.)

   A. Backs up databases, tablespaces, data files, control files, and archived logs

   B. Compresses backups

   C. Provides scripting capabilities

   D. Tests whether backups can be restored

   E. All of the above

3. What type of interface does the RMAN utility support? (Choose all that apply.)

   A. GUI through Oracle Enterprise Manager

   B. Command-line interface

   C. Command line only

   D. GUI through Oracle Enterprise Manager only

4. What actions can be performed within the RMAN utility? (Choose all that apply.)

   A. Start up target database.

   B. Shut down target database.

   C. Grant roles to users.

   D. Create user accounts.

5. The tape media management library (MML) enables RMAN to perform which of the following? (Choose all that apply.)

   A. Interface with third-party tape hardware vendors.

   B. Use third-party automated tape libraries (ATLs).

   C. Write to any tape.

   D. Write to disk.

6. Which of the following commands is used in automatic channel allocation?

   A. `ALLOCATE CHANNEL C1 TYPE DISK`

   B. `ALLOCATE CHANNEL C1 TYPE 'SBT_TAPE'`

   C. `CONFIGURE DEFAULT DEVICE TYPE`

   D. `CONFIGURE DEFAULT TYPE DEVICE`

7. Which of the following commands are examples of those used in the manual channel allocation process? (Choose all that apply.)

   A. `ALLOCATE CHANNEL T1 TYPE DISK`

   B. `ALLOCATE CHANNEL T1 TYPE 'SBT_TAPE'`

   C. `CONFIGURE DEFAULT DEVICE TYPE`

   D. `CONFIGURE DEFAULT TYPE DEVICE`

8. Which of the following media management libraries are provided with most RMAN installations?

   A. MMLs that support Legato Storage Manager software.

   B. MMLs that support Disk.

   C. MMLs are not supplied.

   D. MMLs are not necessary for proprietary tape hardware.

9. Which of the following commands would you use to set the default parallelism for a RMAN session?

   A. `SET DEVICE TYPE PARALLELISM`

   B. `CONFIGURE DEVICE TYPE PARALLELISM`

   C. `INSTALL DEVICE TYPE PARALLELISM`

   D. `CONFIG DEVICE TYPE PARALLELISM`

10. Which of the following commands cannot be used without a recovery catalog? (Choose all that apply.)

    A. `RESYNCH CATALOG`

    B. `RESET DATABASE`

    C. `REPLACE SCRIPT`

    D. `LIST INCARNATION`

    E. All of the above

11. Which of the following commands best describes manual channel allocation? (Choose all that apply.)

    A. `CONFIGURE DEFAULT DEVICE TYPE`

    B. `CONFIGURE CHANNEL DEVICE TYPE`

    C. `ALLOCATE CHANNEL <channel_name> TYPE 'SBT_TAPE'`

    D. `ALLOCATE CHANNEL <channel_name> TYPE DISK`

12. Which of the following commands automatically backs up the control file?

    A. `SET CONTROLFILE AUTOBACKUP ON`

    B. `CONFIGURE CONTROLFILE AUTOBACKUP ON`

    C. `CONFIGURE CONTROLFILE AUTO ON`

    D. `CONFIGURE CONTROLFILE AUTOBACKUP TRUE`

13. Which of the following files best describes the default media management library for Unix?

    A. `libobk.sl`

    B. `libobk.so`

    C. `obklib.so`

    D. `libmml.so`

14. Study the following command and then choose the option that best describes what this command does.

    `RMAN> connect target /`

    A. Connects to the recovery catalog

    B. Connects to the target database

    C. Connects to the target database and the recovery catalog

    D. Connects to neither the target database nor the recovery catalog

15. What is the maximum size for the RMAN repository if the recovery catalog is not being used?

    A. Dependent on OS file size limitations

    B. No limits

    C. 2 gigabytes

    D. 4 gigabytes

Answers to Review Questions

1. B. The recovery catalog is optional regardless of the configuration of the target database. It is used to store information about the backup and recovery process in much the same way that the data dictionary stores information about the database.

2. E. All answers are capabilities of the RMAN utility.

3. A, B. The RMAN utility can be run in GUI mode via the use of Oracle Enterprise Manager or through a command-line interface on the server.

4. A, B. The RMAN utility can start and stop a target database. Database objects and users' accounts are not created with the RMAN utility.

5. A, B. The tape media library enables RMAN to interface with other tape hardware vendors and use their automated tape library systems. Writing to disk and tape can still be performed by using special tape libraries.

6. C. The `CONFIGURE DEFAULT DEVICE TYPE` command is used during automatic channel allocation. The `CONFIGURE DEFAULT TYPE DEVICE` command is incorrect and the other examples are manual channel allocation examples.

7. A, B. Both examples with `ALLOCATE CHANNEL` as a part of the command are examples of manual channel allocation. The other examples, C and D, are not manual channel allocation.

8. A. The MMLs that are installed with most RMAN installations support the Legato Storage Manager.

9. B. The `CONFIGURE DEVICE TYPE PARALLELISM` command will set a default parallelism value.

10. E. None of these commands can be used unless you have implemented the recovery catalog.

11. C, D. Both of these options are methods of manual channel allocation. SBT_TAPE supports tape allocation and DISK supports disk allocation.

12. B. The CONFIGURE CONTROLFILE AUTOBACKUP ON command will configure the control file to be automatically backed up.

13. B. The libobk.so file is the default media management library. This must be replaced or pointed to whatever vendor is being used.

14. B. This command connects to the target database.

15. A. The RMAN repository is the target database control file if the recovery catalog is not being used. The size of any file is dependent on the OS in which it resides.

User-Managed and RMAN-Based Backups

ORACLE9*i*: DBA FUNDAMENTALS II EXAM OBJECTIVES COVERED IN THIS CHAPTER:

- ✓ Describe user-managed backup and recovery operations.
- ✓ Discuss backup issues associated with read tablespaces.
- ✓ Perform closed database backups.
- ✓ Perform open database backups.
- ✓ Back up the control file.
- ✓ Perform cleanup after a failed online backup.
- ✓ Use the DBVERIFY utility to detect corruption.
- ✓ Identify types of RMAN specific backups.
- ✓ Use the RMAN BACKUP command to create sets.
- ✓ Back up the control file.
- ✓ Back up the archived redo log files.
- ✓ Use the RMAN COPY command to create image copies.

Exam objectives are subject to change at any time without prior notice and at Oracle's sole discretion. Please visit Oracle's Certification website (`http://www.oracle.com/education/certification/`) for the most current exam objectives listing.

A *physical backup* is a copy of the physical database files, and it can be performed in two ways. The first is through the Recovery Manager (RMAN) tool that Oracle provides. The second way is by performing a user-managed, or non-RMAN, backup. This chapter focuses on both types of backup.

The user-managed backup has been used for years to back up the Oracle database. The OS backup script is a totally customized solution, and therefore, it has the variations and inconsistencies associated with custom solutions. This backup usually consists of an OS backup created with a scripting language, such as Korn shell or Bourne shell in the Unix environment, or batch commands in the Windows NT/2000/XP environment.

Even though the user-managed backup has been historically helpful, the current trend shows that most larger database sites are now using RMAN to conduct their backups. The reason for this is because of RMAN's extended capabilities and because it can be used consistently regardless of platform.

However, the OS backup is still useful to the DBA. You can use it to train yourself so that you understand the physical backup fundamentals. Further, many storage subsystem providers still utilize user-managed backups in conjunction with third mirror capabilities to expedite large backups in a short period of time. (A *third mirror*, or third mirroring equivalents, offers a way to separate a third copy of the disk mirror at the hardware level. This third copy is made into a backup that can be copied to tape.) After you have learned as much as you can from the user-managed backup, move on to RMAN, which builds on these fundamentals.

In this chapter, you will learn the various physical backup methods with both user-managed backups and RMAN backups.

User-Managed Backup and Recovery Operations

As mentioned, different sites customize their user-managed backups and recovery operations to suit different requirements. This customization is possible because this type of backup is generally a script written in a Unix shell or using Windows NT/2000/XP batch commands. As a result, these user-managed backups and recovery operations must be managed as custom code, and significant testing must be conducted to validate their functionality.

This description shows both the benefits and drawbacks of using this type of backup. Though this ability to customize can allow user-managed backups to be designed for unique situations in addition to significant testing and validation, such customizations could cause errors that could invalidate the entire backup or recovery process.

Despite such possible side effects, user-managed backups have been in use for many years in the Oracle environment. In addition to their broad usage, these backups also provide the building blocks you need to understand the entire Oracle backup and recovery process (including RMAN). This is why every DBA should be comfortable with user-managed backup and recovery operations. This knowledge will allow them to make the correct decisions in a failure situation whether the site is using user-managed or RMAN-based backup and recovery.

Working with Read-Only Tablespaces

The backup and recovery of a *read-only tablespace* requires unique procedures in certain situations. The backup and recovery process changes depending on the state of the tablespace at the time of backup and the time of recovery, and the state of the control file. This section discusses the implications of each of these situations.

A backup of a *read-only tablespace* requires different procedures from those used in a backup of a *read-write tablespace*. The read-only tablespace is, as its name suggests, marked read-only; in other words, all write activity is disabled. Therefore, the system change number (SCN) does not change after the tablespace has been made read-only, as long as it stays read-only. This means that after a database failure, no recovery is needed for a tablespace marked read-only if the tablespace was read-only at the time of the backup. The read-only tablespace could simply be restored and no archived logs would get applied during the recovery process. If a backup is restored that contains a tablespace that was in read-write mode at the time of the backup but is in read-only at the time of failure, then a recovery would need to be performed. This is because changes would be made during read-write mode. Archived logs would be applied up until the tablespace was made read-only.

The state of the control file also affects the recovery process of read-only tablespaces. During recovery of a backup control file, or recovery when there is no current control file, read-only tablespaces should be taken offline or you will get an ORA-1233 error. The control file cannot be created with a read-only tablespace online. The data file or data files associated with the read-only tablespace must be taken offline before the recovery command is issued. After the database is recovered, the read-only tablespace can be brought online. We will look at examples of the recovery of read-only tablespace in Chapter 10, "User-Managed Complete Recovery and RMAN Complete Recovery."

Understanding Closed and Opened Database Backups

A *closed backup* is a backup of a database that is not in the opened state. Usually this means that the database is completely shut down. This kind of backup is also called a cold, or offline, backup. An *opened backup* is a backup of a database in the opened state. In this state, the database is completely available for access. An opened backup is also called a hot, or online, backup.

The main implication of a closed backup is that the database is unavailable to users until the backup is complete. One of the preferable prerequisites of doing a cold backup is that the database should be shut down with the `NORMAL` or `IMMEDIATE` options so that the database is in a consistent state. In other words, the database files are stamped with the same SCN at the same point in time. This is called a *consistent backup*. Because no recovery information in the archived logs needs to be applied to the data files, no recovery is necessary for a consistent, closed backup. Figure 9.1 is an example of a closed backup.

FIGURE 9.1 Physical backup utilizing the cold, offline, or closed backup approach in Unix

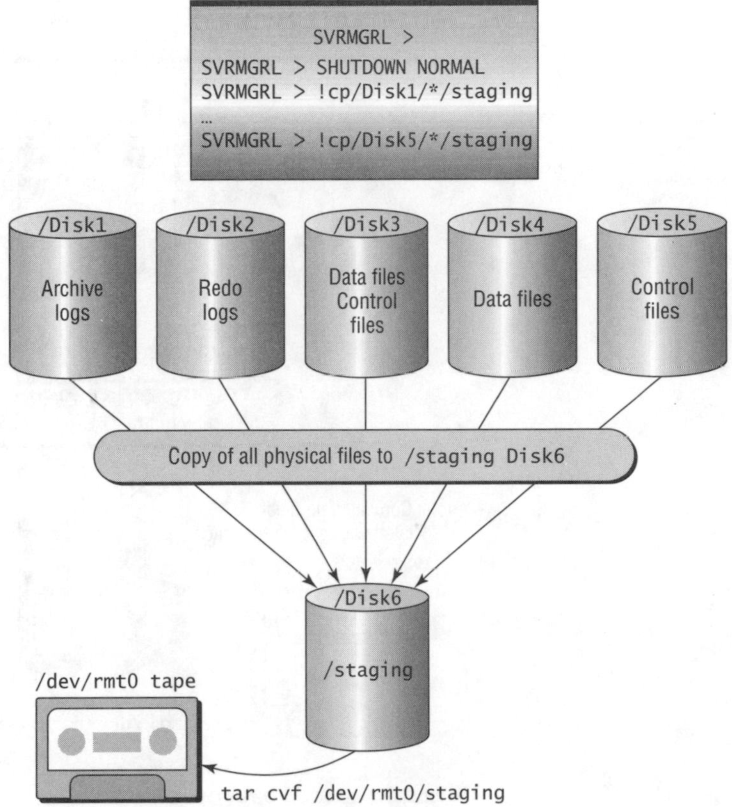

The main implication of an opened backup is that the database is available to users during the backup. The backup is accomplished with the command `ALTER TABLESPACE` <*TABLESPACE_NAME*> `BEGIN BACKUP`, an OS copy command, and the command `ALTER TABLEPACE` <*TABLESPACE_NAME*> `END BACKUP`. Refer back to Chapter 7, "Configuring the Database Archiving Mode" for a more detailed discussion of hot backups. Figure 9.2 is an example of an opened backup.

FIGURE 9.2 Physical backup utilizing the hot, online, or opened backup approach in Unix

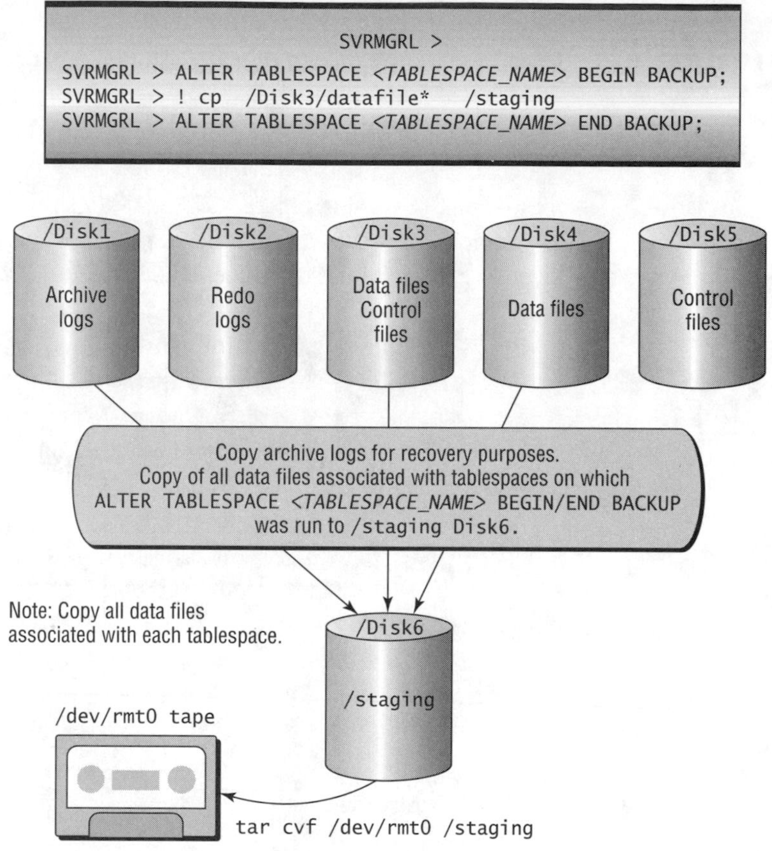

During an opened backup, the database is in an inconsistent state; in other words, the SCN information for the data files and control files is not necessarily consistent. Therefore, this is referred to as an *inconsistent backup*. This requires recovery of the data files by applying archived logs to bring the data files to a consistent state.

Performing Closed and Opened Database Backups

A closed backup and *opened backup* are performed in a similar manner—by executing OS copy commands. The closed backup can be performed just like a standard OS backup after the database has been shut down. Basically, the closed backup just makes a copy of all the necessary physical files that make up the database; these include the data files, online redo logs, control files, and parameter files.

The opened backup is also executed by issuing OS copy commands. These commands are issued between an `ALTER TABLESPACE` *<TABLESPACE_NAME>* `BEGIN BACKUP` command and an `ALTER TABLESPACE` *<TABLESPACE_NAME>* `END BACKUP` command. The opened backup requires only a copy of the data files. The `ALTER TABLESPACE` *<TABLESPACE_NAME>* `BEGIN BACKUP` command causes a checkpoint to the data file or data files in the tablespace. This causes all dirty blocks to be written to the data file, and the data-file header is stamped with the SCN consistent with those data blocks. All other changes occurring in the data file from Data Manipulation Language (DML), such as `INSERT`, `UPDATE`, and `DELETE` statements, get recorded in the data files and redo logs in almost the same way as during normal database operations. However, the data-file header SCN does not get updated until the `ALTER TABLESPACE` *<TABLESPACE_NAME>* `END BACKUP` command gets executed and another checkpoint occurs. To distinguish what blocks are needed in a recovery situation, Oracle writes more information in the redo logs during the period that the `ALTER TABLESPACE` *<TABLESPACE_NAME>* `BEGIN BACKUP` command is executed.

This is one reason why data files are fundamentally different from other Oracle database files, such as redo logs, control files, and `init.ora` files, when it comes to backups. Redo logs, control files, and `init.ora` files can be copied with standard OS copy commands without performing any preparatory steps such as the `ALTER TABLESPACE` *<TABLESPACE_NAME>* commands. This is completely true in the Unix environment. This is partially true in the Windows NT/2000/XP environment because of the locking that is performed on open files.

Even though hot backups can be performed at any time when the database is opened, it is a good idea to perform hot backups when there is the lowest DML activity. This will prevent excessive redo logging, which could impair database performance.

Here are the steps you need to take to perform a closed database backup:

1. Shut down the database that you want to back up. Make sure that a `SHUTDOWN NORMAL`, `IMMEDIATE`, or `TRANSACTIONAL` command is used, and not a `SHUTDOWN ABORT`.

```
oracle@octilli:/opt/oracle > sqlplus /nolog
```

```
SQL*Plus: Release 9.0.1.0.0 - Production on Sat Sep 29
00:11:37 2001

(c) Copyright 2001 Oracle Corporation.  All rights
reserved.

SQL> connect /as sysdba
Connected.
Database closed.
Database dismounted.
ORACLE instance shut down.
```

2. Once the database is shut down, perform an OS copy of all the data files, parameter files, and control files to a disk or a tape device. In Unix, perform the following commands to copy the data files, parameter files, and control files to a disk staging location where they await copy to tape.

```
cp /oracle/product/9.0.1/oradata/*.dbf  /staging/cold
  #   datafiles
cp /oracle/admin/orc9/pfile/*  /staging/cold
  #   INIT.ora files
cp /oracle/oradata/*.ctl  /staging/cold
  #   control files location 1
cp /oracle/product/9.0.1/oradata/*.ctl  /staging/cold
  #   control files location 2
cp /oracle/oradata/orc9/*.log  /staging/cold
  #   online redo logs group 1
```

3. Restart the database and proceed with normal database operations.

```
SQL> startup;
```

Here are the steps you would use to perform an opened database backup. The database is available to users during these operations, although the response time for users may be decreased depending on what tablespace is being backed up.

1. To determine all the tablespaces that make up the database, query the V$TABLESPACE and V$DATAFILE dynamic views. The following is the SQL statement that identifies tablespaces and their associated data files.

```
select a.TS#,a.NAME,b.NAME from
v$tablespace a, v$datafile b
where a.TS#=b.TS#;
```

2. Determine what all the data files are that make up each tablespace. Each tablespace can be made up of many data files. All data files associated with the tablespace need to be copied when the tablespace is in backup mode. Perform the above query by connecting to SQLPLUS.

```
oracle@octilli:~ > sqlplus /nolog

SQL*Plus: Release 9.0.1.0.0 - Production on Sat Sep 29 10:44:22
2001

(c) Copyright 2001 Oracle Corporation.  All rights reserved.

SQL>
SQL> connect /as sysdba
Connected.

SQL>  select a.TS#,a.NAME,b.NAME from
            v$tablespace a, v$datafile b
      where a.TS#=b.TS#;

  TS# NAME       NAME
----- ---------- ----------------------------------------------
    0 SYSTEM     /oracle/product/9.0.1/oradata/orc9/system01.dbf
    1 UNDOTBS    /oracle/product/9.0.1/oradata/orc9/undotbs01.dbf
    2 CWMLITE    /oracle/product/9.0.1/oradata/orc9/cwmlite01.dbf
    3 DRSYS      /oracle/product/9.0.1/oradata/orc9/drsys01.dbf
    4 EXAMPLE    /oracle/product/9.0.1/oradata/orc9/example01.dbf
    5 INDX       /oracle/product/9.0.1/oradata/orc9/indx01.dbf
    7 TOOLS      /oracle/product/9.0.1/oradata/orc9/tools01.dbf
    8 USERS      /oracle/product/9.0.1/oradata/orc9/users01.dbf
```

3. Put the tablespaces in backup mode.

```
SQL> alter tablespace users begin backup;
Tablespace altered.
```

4. Perform an OS copy of each data file associated with the tablespace in backup mode.

```
SQL> ! cp /oracle/product/9.0.1/oradata/orc9/
users01.dbf /staging/cold
```

5. End backup mode for the tablespace.

```
SQL> alter tablespace users end backup;
Tablespace altered.
```

These series of commands can be repeated for every tablespace and associated data file that make up the database. The database must be in ARCHIVELOG mode to execute the ALTER TABLESPACE *<TABLESPACE_NAME>* BEGIN and END backup commands. Typically, this type of backup is done with a scripting language in Unix or a third-party GUI utility in the Windows environment. Using Unix shell scripts, a list of data files and tablespaces are dumped to a file listing and parsed into svrmgr and cp commands so that all tablespaces and data files are backed up together.

During an opened or closed backup, it is a good idea to get a backup control file, all archived logs, and a copy of the parameter files. These can be packaged with data files so that all necessary or potentially necessary components for recovery are grouped together. This is called a *whole database backup.*

Identifying User-Managed Control-File Backups

There are two types of user-managed control-file backups. The first type is performed by executing a command that creates a binary copy of the existing control file in a new directory location. For example, the following command performs a binary copy of the control file.

```
SQL> alter database backup controlfile to
  '/staging/control.ctl.bak';
```

The second type of control-file backup creates an ASCII copy of the current control file as a trace file in the USER_DUMP_DEST location. The USER_DUMP_DEST parameter should be set in your init.ora file. In a configuration compliant with Optimal Flexible Architecture (OFA), this will be the udump directory. The backup of the control file can be performed by executing the following command:

```
SQL> alter database backup controlfile to trace;
```

The output of the trace file looks like this:

```
/oracle/admin/orc9/udump/ora_4976.trc
Oracle9i Enterprise Edition Release 9.0.1.0.0 - Production
With the Partitioning option
JServer Release 9.0.1.0.0 - Production
ORACLE_HOME = /oracle/product/9.0.1
System name:   Linux
Node name:   octilli
Release:   2.4.4-4GB
Version:   #1 Fri May 18 14:11:12 GMT 2001
Machine:   i686
Instance name: orc9
Redo thread mounted by this instance: 1
Oracle process number: 13
Unix process pid: 4976, image: oracle@octilli (TNS V1-V3)

*** SESSION ID:(8.7) 2001-09-29 00:29:20.499
*** 2001-09-29 00:29:20.499
# The following commands will create a new control file
and use it
# to open the database.
# Data used by the recovery manager will be lost.
Additional logs may
# be required for media recovery of offline data files.
Use this
# only if the current version of all online logs are
available.
STARTUP NOMOUNT
CREATE CONTROLFILE REUSE DATABASE "ORC9" NORESETLOGS
ARCHIVELOG
    MAXLOGFILES 50
    MAXLOGMEMBERS 5
    MAXDATAFILES 100
```

```
    MAXINSTANCES 1
    MAXLOGHISTORY 226
LOGFILE
  GROUP 1 '/oracle/oradata/orc9/redo01.log'  SIZE 100M,
  GROUP 2 '/oracle/oradata/orc9/redo02.log'  SIZE 100M,
  GROUP 3 '/oracle/oradata/orc9/redo03.log'  SIZE 100M
# STANDBY LOGFILE
DATAFILE
  '/oracle/product/9.0.1/oradata/orc9/system01.dbf',
  '/oracle/product/9.0.1/oradata/orc9/undotbs01.dbf',
  '/oracle/product/9.0.1/oradata/orc9/cwmlite01.dbf',
  '/oracle/product/9.0.1/oradata/orc9/drsys01.dbf',
  '/oracle/product/9.0.1/oradata/orc9/example01.dbf',
  '/oracle/product/9.0.1/oradata/orc9/indx01.dbf',
  '/oracle/product/9.0.1/oradata/orc9/tools01.dbf',
  '/oracle/product/9.0.1/oradata/orc9/users01.dbf'
CHARACTER SET WE8ISO8859P1
;
# Recovery is required if any of the datafiles are
restored backups,
# or if the last shutdown was not normal or immediate.
RECOVER DATABASE
# All logs need archiving and a log switch is needed.
ALTER SYSTEM ARCHIVE LOG ALL;
# Database can now be opened normally.
ALTER DATABASE OPEN;
# Commands to add tempfiles to temporary tablespaces.
# Online tempfiles have complete space information.
# Other tempfiles may require adjustment.
ALTER TABLESPACE TEMP ADD TEMPFILE '/oracle/product/9.0.1/
oradata/orc9/temp01.dbf' REUSE;
# End of tempfile additions.
```

The control-file backup to ASCII can be used as part of a common technique of moving production databases to test and development servers. This technique can be useful for testing backups.

Cleaning Up after Failed Online Backups

Online backups, whether they are user-managed or RMAN-based, perform the same database commands. One of these commands, the ALTER TABLESPACE *<tablespace name>* BEGIN BACKUP command, results in tablespaces being placed into backup mode. When the required data file(s) is completely copied, the ALTER TABLESPACE *<tablespace name>* END BACKUP command is then executed.

If there is a problem before the tablespace is taken out of backup mode, the tablespace may cause problems during recovery or it may lock up the next backup. If the database is shutdown with a tablespace in backup mode, the database will not start without taking the associated data files out of backup mode. Sometimes RMAN may have problems if the next scheduled backup attempts to place the tablespace in backup mode when it is already in backup mode. This will cause the next RMAN backup to fail or hang while it is trying to place the tablespace in backup mode.

If an online backup fails, all tablespace associated data files should be checked to make sure that they are not in backup mode. This can be done by checking the V$BACKUP view. The following example shows that one data file is in backup mode. The tablespace associated with data file 4 should be taken out of backup mode. This tablespace should be identified and then altered out of backup mode with ALTER TABLESPACE *<tablespace_name>* END BACKUP. See the example below:

1. First, check to see if any data file is active; if one is, this means that the tablespace and its associated data files are in backup mode. In this case, data file number 4 is in backup mode because the status is ACTIVE.

```
select * from v$backup;

     FILE# STATUS                CHANGE# TIME
---------- ------------------ ---------- ---------
         1 NOT ACTIVE                  0
         2 NOT ACTIVE                  0
         3 NOT ACTIVE                  0
         4 ACTIVE                 279174 29-SEP-01
         5 NOT ACTIVE                  0
         6 NOT ACTIVE                  0
         7 NOT ACTIVE                  0
         8 NOT ACTIVE             278815 29-SEP-01
```

```
8 rows selected.

SQL>
```

2. Next, find what tablespace is associated with data file 4 by executing the following SQL query. Note that data file 4 and tablespace 3 are associated with the DRSYS tablespace.

```
select substr(b.name,0,10) name,a.file#,a.ts#,status
from v$datafile a, v$tablespace b
where a.ts#=b.ts#
order by file#;

NAME            FILE#        TS# STATUS
---------- ---------- ---------- -------
SYSTEM              1          0 SYSTEM
UNDOTBS             2          1 ONLINE
CWMLITE             3          2 ONLINE
DRSYS               4          3 ONLINE
EXAMPLE             5          4 ONLINE
INDX                6          5 ONLINE
TOOLS               7          7 ONLINE
USERS               8          8 ONLINE

8 rows selected.
```

3. Next, take this tablespace out of backup mode by executing the following command. Then query the V$BACKUP view again to verify that the data file status is not active.

```
alter tablespace DRSYS end backup;

Tablespace altered.


select * from v$backup;
```

```
     FILE# STATUS                CHANGE# TIME
---------- ------------------ ---------- ---------
         1 NOT ACTIVE                  0
         2 NOT ACTIVE                  0
         3 NOT ACTIVE                  0
         4 NOT ACTIVE             279174 29-SEP-01
         5 NOT ACTIVE                  0
         6 NOT ACTIVE                  0
         7 NOT ACTIVE                  0
         8 NOT ACTIVE             278815 29-SEP-01

8 rows selected.
```

Real World Scenario

Checking the Backup before Shutdown

Because RMAN backups called by Media Management vendor's software are conducted in the background, they tend to be forgotten. Another reason these backups may be forgotten is because rather than the DBA conducting them, such backup-related tasks may be executed and controlled by the backup coordinator, who may reside within the systems administrators group. As a result, when the backup terminates for some reason, you may not know about it, unless you have good communication set up. As a result, the backup may terminate in such a way that it leaves the database partially in backup mode with some tablespaces and the associated data files still active, or it leaves jobs incomplete and hanging in the recovery catalog.

What happens when the database goes down when a tablespace is in backup mode? If this happens, the data file is not checkpointed so that it is consistent with the rest of the database. Therefore, when the database is restarted, the data file is marked as inconsistent and in need of recovery. This situation can come as an unwanted surprise when you are bouncing the database for some reason.

You can remedy this situation without recovery by issuing the `ALTER DATAFILE '<datafile name>' END BACKUP` command to fix this. However, this situation can be avoided in the first place if you check the `V$BACKUP` view to validate that it is safe to shut down the database before you do so.

The DBVERIFY Utility

The Oracle *DBVERIFY utility* is executed by entering **dbv** at the command prompt. This utility has six parameters that can be specified at execution. The parameters are FILE, START, END, BLOCKSIZE, LOGFILE, and FEEDBACK. Table 9.1 describes these parameters.

TABLE 9.1 DBVERIFY Parameters

Parameter	Description	Default Value for Parameter
FILE	Data file to be verified by the utility.	No default parameter
START	Starting block to begin verification.	First block in the data file
END	Ending block to end verification.	Last block in the data file
BLOCKSIZE	Block size of database. This should be the same as the init.ora parameter DB_BLOCK_SIZE.	2048
LOGFILE	Log file to store the results of running the utility.	No default parameter
FEEDBACK	Displays the progress of the utility by displaying a dot for each number of blocks processed.	0

This help information can also be seen by executing the DBV HELP=Y command. See the following example:

```
oracle@octilli:/db01/oracle/tst9 > dbv help=y

DBVERIFY: Release 9.0.1.0.0 - Production on Tue Oct 9
00:06:48 2001

(c) Copyright 2001 Oracle Corporation.  All rights
reserved.
```

```
Keyword     Description                       (Default)
----------------------------------------------------
FILE        File to Verify                    (NONE)
START       Start Block                      (First Block of
File)
END         End Block                         (Last Block of
File)
BLOCKSIZE   Logical Block Size                (2048)
LOGFILE     Output Log                        (NONE)
FEEDBACK    Display Progress                  (0)
PARFILE     Parameter File                    (NONE)
USERID      Username/Password                 (NONE)
SEGMENT_ID  Segment ID (tsn.relfile.block) (NONE)
oracle@octilli:/db01/oracle/tst9 >
```

To run the DBVERIFY utility, the BLOCKSIZE parameter must match your database block size, or the following error will result:

```
oracle@octilli:/db01/oracle/tst9 > dbv file=data01.dbf

DBVERIFY: Release 9.0.1.0.0 - Production on Tue Oct 9
00:12:55 2001

(c) Copyright 2001 Oracle Corporation.  All rights
reserved.


DBV-00103: Specified BLOCKSIZE (2048) differs from actual
(8192)
oracle@octilli:/db01/oracle/tst9 >
```

Once the BLOCKSIZE parameter is set to match the database block size, the DBVERIFY utility can proceed. There are two ways to run this utility: without the LOGFILE parameter specified, and with it specified.

Let's walk through each of these examples. First, this is what it looks like without the LOGFILE parameter set:

```
oracle@octilli:/db01/oracle/tst9 > dbv file=data01.dbf
BLOCKSIZE=8192
```

```
DBVERIFY: Release 9.0.1.0.0 - Production on Tue Oct 9
00:10:53 2001

(c) Copyright 2001 Oracle Corporation.  All rights
reserved.

DBVERIFY - Verification starting : FILE = data01.dbf


DBVERIFY - Verification complete

Total Pages Examined         : 6400
Total Pages Processed (Data) : 0
Total Pages Failing   (Data) : 0
Total Pages Processed (Index): 0
Total Pages Failing   (Index): 0
Total Pages Processed (Other): 1
Total Pages Processed (Seg)  : 0
Total Pages Failing   (Seg)  : 0
Total Pages Empty            : 6399
Total Pages Marked Corrupt   : 0
Total Pages Influx           : 0
oracle@octilli:/db01/oracle/tst9 >
```

The following code demonstrates the DBVERIFY utility with the `LOGFILE` parameter set. The results of this command are written to the file `data01.log` and not to the screen. This can be displayed by editing the log file.

```
oracle@octilli:/db01/oracle/tst9 >dbv file=data01.dbf
BLOCKSIZE=8192 LOGFILE=data01.log

DBVERIFY: Release 9.0.1.0.0 - Production on Tue Oct 9
00:14:13 2001

(c) Copyright 2001 Oracle Corporation.  All rights
reserved.


oracle@octilli:/db01/oracle/tst9 >
```

Identifying RMAN-Specific Backups

There are three types of backups that are supported by the RMAN utility:

- Full or incremental
- Opened or closed
- Consistent or inconsistent

Each is described in the following sections.

Full or Incremental Backups

The full and incremental backups are differentiated by how the data blocks are backed up in the target database. The *full backup* backs up all the data blocks in the data files, modified or not. An *incremental backup* backs up only the data blocks in the data files that were modified since the last incremental backup.

The full backup cannot be used as part of an incremental backup strategy. The baseline backup for an incremental backup is a level 0 backup. A level 0 backup is a full backup at that point in time. Thus, all blocks, modified or not, are backed up, allowing the level 0 backup to serve as a baseline for future incremental backups. The incremental backups can then be applied with the baseline, or level 0, backup to form a full backup at some time in the future. The benefit of the incremental backup is that it is quicker, because not all data blocks need to be backed up.

There are two types of incremental backups: differential and cumulative, both of which back up only modified blocks. The difference between these two types of incremental backups is in the baseline database used to identify the modified blocks that need to be backed up.

The *differential incremental backup* backs up only data blocks modified since the most recent backup at the same level or lower. A differential incremental backup will determine which level 1 or level 2 backup has occurred most recently and back up only blocks that have changed since that backup. The differential incremental backup is the default incremental backup.

The *cumulative incremental backup* backs up only the data blocks that have changed since the most recent backup of the next lowest level—*n* – 1 or lower (with *n* being the existing level of backup). For example, if you are performing a level 2 cumulative incremental backup, the backup will copy data blocks only from the most recent level 1 backup. If no level 1 backup is available, then it will back up all data blocks that have changed since the most recent level 0 backup.

Full backups do not mean the whole or complete database was backed up. In other words, a full backup can back up only part of the database and not all data files, control files, and logs.

Opened or Closed Backups

The opened and closed backups are differentiated by the state of the target database being backed up. The RMAN *opened backup* occurs when the target database is backed up while it is opened or available for use. This is similar to the non-RMAN hot backup that was demonstrated earlier in this chapter.

The RMAN *closed backup* occurs when the target database is mounted but not opened. This means the target database is not available for use during this type of backup. This is similar to the non-RMAN cold backup that was demonstrated earlier in this chapter.

Consistent or Inconsistent Backups

The consistent and inconsistent backups are differentiated by the state of the SCN in data file headers and in the control files. The *consistent backup* is a backup of a target database that is mounted but not opened and was shut down with either a `SHUTDOWN IMMEDIATE`, `SHUTDOWN TRANSACTIONAL`, or `SHUTDOWN NORMAL` option, but not the `SHUTDOWN ABORT` option. Also, the database must not have crashed prior to being mounted. This means that the SCN information in the data files matches the SCN information in the control files.

The *inconsistent backup* is the backup of the target database when it is opened but crashed prior to mounting, or when it was shut down with the `SHUTDOWN ABORT` option prior to mounting. This means that the SCN information in the data files does not match the SCN information in the control files.

Using RMAN's *BACKUP* and *COPY* Commands

There are two main backup sources that can be the basis for the RMAN recovery process: image copies and backup sets.

Image copies are actual copies of the database files, archived logs, or control files, and they are not stored in a special RMAN format—they can be stored only on disk. An image copy in RMAN is equivalent to an OS copy command such as cp or dd in Unix, or the COPY command in Windows NT/2000/XP. Thus, no RMAN restore processing is necessary to make image copies usable in a recovery situation. This can improve the speed and efficiency of the restore and recovery process in some cases. An image copy is performed by executing the RMAN *COPY* command.

On the other hand, database files in *backup sets* are stored in a special RMAN format and must be processed with the RESTORE command before these files are usable. This can take more time and effort during the recovery process. Let's take a look at an example of using the BACKUP command, and then we will look at the RMAN COPY command in more detail.

Using RMAN *BACKUP* to Create Sets

The RMAN *BACKUP* command is used to perform a backup that creates a backup set.

When you are using the BACKUP command, the target database should be mounted or opened. You must manually allocate a channel for the BACKUP command to use during the backup process. Below is an example of this command in action. In this example, you are backing up the USERS tablespace and the current control file to a backup set.

```
oracle@octilli:/oracle/product/9.0.1/bin > rman

Recovery Manager: Release 9.0.1.0.0 - Production

(c) Copyright 2001 Oracle Corporation.  All rights
reserved.

RMAN> connect target

connected to target database: ORC9 (DBID=3960695)
RMAN> run
2> {allocate channel ch1 type disk;
3> backup tablespace users
4> include current controlfile;}

using target database controlfile instead of recovery catalog
```

```
allocated channel: ch1
channel ch1: sid=12 devtype=DISK

Starting backup at 30-SEP-01
channel ch1: starting full datafile backupset
channel ch1: specifying datafile(s) in backupset
input datafile fno=00008 name=/oracle/product/9.0.1/
oradata/orc9/users01.dbf
including current controlfile in backupset
channel ch1: starting piece 1 at 30-SEP-01
channel ch1: finished piece 1 at 30-SEP-01
piece handle=/oracle/product/9.0.1/dbs/01d5bspm_1_1
comment=NONE
channel ch1: backup set complete, elapsed time: 00:00:08
Finished backup at 30-SEP-01
released channel: ch1
```

You cannot include archived logs and data files in a single backup. In other words, you will need to use the BACKUP command for the database or tablespace backup, and you will need to use it again for archived logs.

The BACKUP command has multiple options that can be specified. These options control performance, formatting, file sizes, and types of backups, to mention a few. Below are Tables 9.2 and 9.3, which describe the complete list of the BACKUP command's options and formats.

TABLE 9.2 BACKUP Command Options

Option	Description
FULL	Causes the server session to copy all used blocks from data files into the backup set. The only blocks that do not get copied are blocks that have never been used. All archived log and redo log blocks are copied when the archived logs are designated for backup.
INCREMENTAL LEVEL INTEGER	Causes the server session to copy data blocks that have been modified since the last incremental *n* backup where *n* is any integer from 1 to 4.

TABLE 9.2 BACKUP Command Options *(continued)*

Option	Description
FILESPERSET INTEGER	Determines how many files are in a backup set. When this option is used, the number of data files is compared to a determined number of files that are being backed up per channel allocated, and it takes the lower of the two. Using this option is another method for performing parallel backups.
DISKRATIO INTEGER	Forces RMAN to group data files in backup sets that are spread across a determined number of disk drives.
SKIP OFFLINE| READONLY | INACCESSIBLE	Excludes some data files or archived redo logs from the backup set. Some of the files it excludes include offline data files, read-only data files, or inaccessible data files and archived logs.
MAXSETSIZE INTEGER	Specifies the maximum size of the backup set. Bytes are the default unit of measure, but kilobytes (K), megabytes (M), and gigabytes (G) can also be used.
DELETE INPUT	Deletes input files when the backup set has been created. This option should only be used when backing up archived logs, data file copies, or backup sets. This is equivalent to using the CHANGE and DELETE command for all input files.
INCLUDE CURRENT CONTROLFILE	Creates a copy of the current control file and places it into each backup set.

TABLE 9.3 BACKUP Command Formats

Format	Description
%c	Specifies the copy number of the backup piece within the set of duplexed backup pieces.
%d	Specifies the database name.

TABLE 9.3 BACKUP Command Formats *(continued)*

Format	Description
%n	Specifies the database name, padded on the right with *n* characters equal to a length of 8 characters.
%p	Specifies the backup piece number within the backup set. This number starts at 1 and increases by 1 for each backup piece created.
%s	Specifies the backup number. This number starts at 1 and increases by 1 for each backup piece created.
%t	Specifies the backup set time stamp. The combination of %s and %t can be used to form a unique name for a backup set.
%u	Specifies an 8-character name that combines a compressed version of the backup set number and the time the backup set was created.
%U	This format parameter is equivalent to %u_%p_%c.

Using RMAN *COPY* to Create Image Copies

In this example, we will utilize the RMAN COPY command to create an image copy of various database files. In this example, you are backing up the system data file and the current control file as image copies to the /staging directory.

```
RMAN> run { allocate channel ch1 type disk;
2> copy
3> datafile 1 to '/staging/system01.dbf' ,
4> current controlfile to '/staging/control.ctl';}

allocated channel: ch1
channel ch1: sid=12 devtype=DISK

Starting copy at 30-SEP-01
channel ch1: copied datafile 1
output filename=/staging/system01.dbf recid=1
stamp=441840852
```

```
channel ch1: copied current controlfile
output filename=/staging/control.ctl
Finished copy at 30-SEP-01
released channel: ch1
```

Backing Up the Control File

A control file backup can be performed through the RMAN utility by executing the CURRENT CONTROLFILE command. Below is a brief example of using this command within the RMAN utility after being connected to the appropriate target database and RMAN catalog database.

In the following example, note that the TAG command is being used to name the backed up control file controlfile_thurs within the recovery catalog. As you might guess from this name, the TAG command is used to assign a meaningful, logical name to backups or image copies. By performing this task, this command allows you to find backups more easily in LIST outputs. The TAG command name can also be used in SWITCH and RESTORE commands.

```
RMAN> run {
2> allocate channel ch1 type disk;
3> backup
4> format 'cf_t%t_s%s_p%p'
5> tag controlfile_thurs
6> (current controlfile);
7> release channel ch1;
8> }

allocated channel: ch1
channel ch1: sid=11 devtype=DISK

Starting backup at 05-OCT-01
channel ch1: starting full datafile backupset
channel ch1: specifying datafile(s) in backupset
including current controlfile in backupset
channel ch1: starting piece 1 at 05-OCT-01
```

```
channel ch1: finished piece 1 at 05-OCT-01
piece handle=/oracle/product/9.0.1/dbs/cf_t442286312_s7_p1
comment=NONE
channel ch1: backup set complete, elapsed time: 00:00:02
Finished backup at 05-OCT-01

released channel: ch1

RMAN>
```

Backing Up the Archived Redo Logs

Another important part of a complete database backup is including the archived logs. Without the archived redo logs, you cannot roll forward from online backups. Below is an example of a complete database backup file that includes the archived redo logs. In this example, the first activity that is performed is the backing up of the database. Next, all the redo logs that can be archived are flushed to archived logs in the filesystem. After that, the archived logs are backed up in the RMAN catalog by using the `BACKUP ARCHIVELOG ALL` command; this command backs up all available archived logs in the filesystem. Below is a brief example of using this command as it is used in complete database backup.

```
run {
    allocate channel c1 type disk;
    allocate channel c2 type disk;
    backup database;
    backup (archivelog all);
     }
```

Summary

User-managed backups have been commonplace at Oracle sites for years. This type of backup mainly consists of OS-based commands, such as those produced from Korn or Bourne shells in the Unix environment. In the Windows environment, user-managed backups are available through the use of third-party GUI tools and batch commands. More recently, RMAN backups have become more popular with many sites (since the release of RMAN in Oracle8).

The fundamentals of backing up an Oracle database can be seen clearly when you analyze an OS-based backup. Some of these basic techniques are utilized in the hot, or opened, backup examples, and some are used in cold, or closed examples. If you have a solid understanding of these concepts, you should fully understand the backup process with RMAN-based backups.

RMAN-based backups can perform the same functions as user-managed backups. But RMAN backups tend to be more standardized as a result of their use of a common command set. We demonstrated some of the commands that are involved in performing various backup operations within RMAN in this chapter.

User-managed and RMAN-based backups are the two primary methods of backing up databases. You will be responsible for at least one of these types of backups, if not both, in a real-world DBA job. Understanding how to perform user-managed backup and recovery is a necessary prerequisite for understanding RMAN-based backup and recovery. This knowledge will help you understand what RMAN is trying to do and improve upon.

Exam Essentials

Understand user-managed backup and recovery. User-managed backup and recovery is a traditional process that uses OS and database commands to backup and recover the database.

Know the backup issues that are associated with read-only tablespaces. Read-only tablespaces have special requirements for backup. If the tablespace was read-only at the time of backup, no recovery is needed, but if it was read-write, then recovery is needed.

Identify the differences between open and closed backups. A closed backup is taken when the database is offline or has been shut down using all modes other than `SHUTDOWN ABORT`. In an open backup, the database is online or available during the backup process. You should also be familiar with the database commands that must be performed against the opened database before data files can be copied.

Identify the different types of user-managed control file backups. The two formats of control file backups are binary format and ASCII format.

Understand what needs to be cleaned up after an online backup fails. The V$BACKUP view can be used to see the status of the data files after a failed online backup. The V$BACKUP view shows whether a data file is ACTIVE or INACTIVE in the backup process.

Understand how the DBVERIFY utility works to detect corruption. The DBVERIFY utility works on online and offline data files to identify corrupted blocks.

Identify the types of RMAN-specific backups. The three types of RMAN backups are full/incremental, open/closed, and consistent/inconsistent.

Understand the difference between backup sets and image copies. Backup sets are backups that are stored in a specific RMAN format; image copies are just backups of actual database files in the same format as the OS. You should also be familiar with the BACKUP command options and formats.

Know how to use RMAN commands to backup control files and archived redo logs. You should know how to use all of the necessary RMAN commands with the proper syntax to backup control files and archived logs.

Key Terms

Before you take the exam, be certain you are familiar with the following terms:

BACKUP

backup sets

closed backup

consistent backup

COPY

cumulative incremental backup

DBVERIFY utility

differential incremental backup

full backup

image copies

inconsistent backup

incremental backup

opened backup

physical backup

read-only tablespace

read-write tablespace

third mirror

whole database backup

Review Questions

1. Which type of backup most closely represents an opened backup? (Choose all that apply.)

   A. Online backup

   B. Offline backup

   C. Hot backup

   D. Cold backup

2. In the event of a database failure that requires a full database restore, how would you perform a recovery for a read-only tablespace? (Choose all that apply.)

   A. No recovery is necessary, if the restored copy was made when the tablespace was read-only.

   B. You would recover by applying redo log entries to the read-only tablespace, regardless of the state of the tablespace copy.

   C. You would recover by applying redo log entries to the read-only tablespace if the tablespace was in read-write mode at the time of the backup used for the restore.

   D. You would recover by applying redo log entries to the read-only tablespace if the tablespace was in read-only mode at the time of the backup used for the restore.

3. What type of backup is consistent?

   A. Online backup

   B. Opened backup

   C. Hot backup

   D. Cold backup

4. What type of backup is inconsistent? (Choose all that apply.)

   A. Cold backup

   B. Online backup

   C. Opened backup

   D. Closed backup

5. If a read-only tablespace is restored from a backup when the data file is read-only, what type of recovery is necessary?

   A. Data file recovery

   B. Tablespace recovery

   C. Database recovery

   D. No recovery is needed.

6. What are valid ways to back up a control file while the database is running? (Choose all that apply.)

   A. Back up to trace file

   B. Back up to binary control file

   C. OS copy to tape

   D. Back up to restore file

7. Which of the following statements is true about a user-managed backup?

   A. This type of backup is conducted using the RMAN utility.

   B. A user-managed backup can be customized using a combination of OS and database commands.

   C. A user-managed backup is a new type of backup in Oracle9*i*.

   D. A user-managed backup is one of the backup options within RMAN.

8. If a tablespace was backed up shortly after it was made read-only, what would need to be done with archived logs during a recovery of that tablespace?

   A. All archived logs would need to be applied.

   B. Only the archived logs that were added after the backup would need to be applied.

   C. Only the archived logs that were added before the backup would need to be applied.

   D. No archived logs would need to be applied.

9. Which of the following is a true statement about a RMAN image copy?

   A. It can be backed up to tape or disk.

   B. It can be backed up to disk only.

   C. It can be backed up to tape only.

   D. It can be copied to tape only.

10. A cold backup requires the database to be in what condition? (Choose all that apply.)

    A. `ARCHIVELOG` mode

    B. `NOARCHIVELOG` mode

    C. The database must be started.

    D. The database cannot contain any read-only tablespaces.

11. To perform an open or hot backup, what state must the database be in?

    A. `ARCHIVELOG` mode

    B. `NOARCHIVELOG` mode

    C. Shutdown

    D. Automatic archiving must be enabled.

12. Hot backups are best run when what is occurring in the database?
    A. Heavy DML activity
    B. Heavy batch processing
    C. The database is being shut down.
    D. Low DML activity

13. What method can be used to clean up a failed online or hot backup?
    A. Shutting down the database
    B. Querying `V$TABLESPACE`
    C. Querying `V$BACKUP`
    D. Querying `V$DATAFILE`

14. What utility can be used to check to see if a data file has block corruption?
    A. DBVALIDATE
    B. DBVERIFY
    C. DBVERIFIED
    D. DBVALID

15. Which of the following are types of RMAN backups? (Choose all that apply.)
    A. Open and closed backups
    B. Full and incremental backups
    C. Consistent and inconsistent backups
    D. Control file backups

Answers to Review Questions

1. A, C. An opened backup is performed when the database is opened or available for access (online). A hot backup and online backup are synonymous.

2. A, C. In a read-only tablespace, the SCN doesn't change or if it does, none of the changes get applied. So if the backup of the tablespace was taken when the tablespace was read-only, no recovery would be necessary. On the other hand, if the backup was taken when the database was read-write, then redo logs would need to be applied. The redo logs in this case would also contain the command that puts the tablespace into read-only mode.

3. D. A cold backup ensures that all the SCNs in the data files are consistent for a single point in time.

4. B, C. Opened and online backups both back up the data files with different SCNs in the headers, which makes recovery necessary during a restore operation.

5. D. No recovery is needed because the tablespace was read-only during backup and at the time of failure.

6. A, B. Backing up both to a trace file and to a binary control file are valid backups of the control file. The other references are made up.

7. B. A user-managed backup is a customizable backup that uses OS and database commands, and it is usually written in some sort of native scripting language.

8. D. No archived logs would need to be applied because the tablespace was backed up after it was made read-only.

9. B. An image copy can be backed up only to disk.

10. A, B. A cold backup occurs when the database is shutdown. The database can be in `ARCHIVELOG` mode or `NOARCHIVELOG` mode.

11. A. The database must be in ARCHIVELOG mode. Archiving can be set to manual or automatic.

12. D. More transactional activity gets written to redo logs when a tablespace is in backup mode. It is a good idea to do hot backups when you have the lowest transactional activity.

13. C. It is a good idea to query V$BACKUP to check to see if any data files are being actively backed up. If they are, you can execute ALTER TABLESPACE <tablespace_name> END BACKUP to change the status from ACTIVE to INACTIVE.

14. B. The DBVERIFY utility is used to check whether or not a data file has any block corruption.

15. A, B, C. Open and closed, full and incremental, and consistent and inconsistent backups are the different type of RMAN backups.

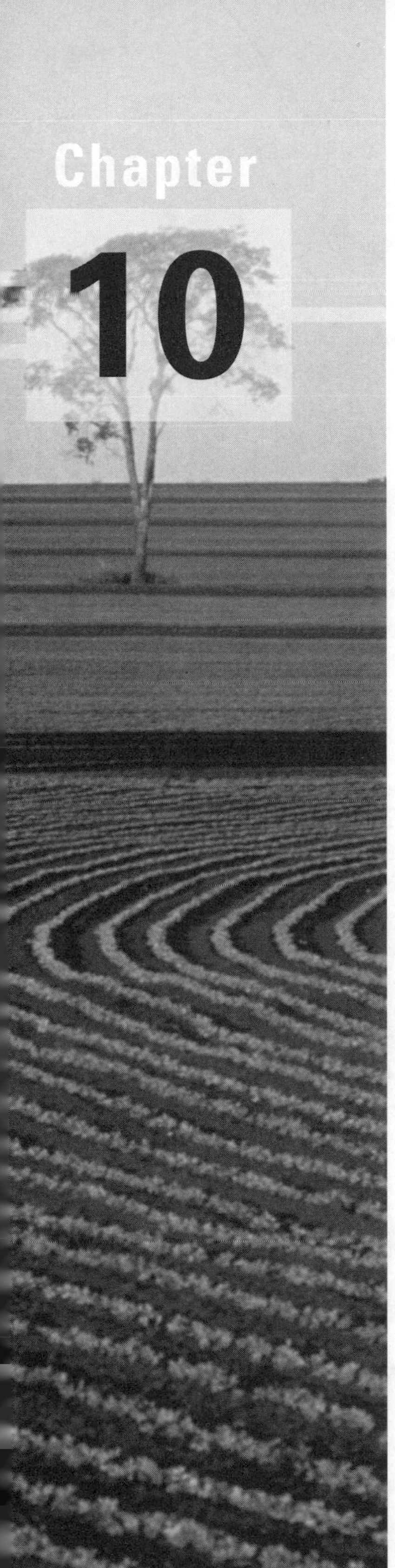

User-Managed Complete Recovery and RMAN Complete Recovery

ORACLE9*i*: DBA FUNDAMENTALS II EXAM OBJECTIVES COVERED IN THIS CHAPTER:

- ✓ Describe media recovery.
- ✓ Perform recovery in Noarchivelog mode.
- ✓ Perform complete recovery in Archivelog mode.
- ✓ Restore datafiles to different locations.
- ✓ Relocate and recover a tablespace by using archived redo log files.
- ✓ Describe read-only tablespace recovery.
- ✓ Describe the use of RMAN for restoration and recovery.

Exam objectives are subject to change at any time without prior notice and at Oracle's sole discretion. Please visit Oracle's Certification website (`http://www.oracle.com/education/certification/`) for the most current exam objectives listing.

In this chapter, we will focus on media failures and how to recover from them. There are two methods that can be used to recover from media failures: user-managed recovery and RMAN-based recovery. This chapter uses examples to demonstrate the differences between each type.

As we have discussed in previous chapters, the mode you decide to operate in, whether ARCHIVELOG mode or NOARCHIVELOG mode, determines the recovery options that you can perform. This chapter covers these options and the modes in which you operate in further detail. You will also become familiar with examples of both ARCHIVELOG mode and NOARCHIVELOG mode media recoveries using both user-managed and RMAN methods of recovery. In addition to this detailed discussion of recovery methods, you also will look at recovery situations in which the relocation of files is required, and you will learn how to handle read-only tablespace recovery in different situations.

Media recoveries are critical tasks in the testing process and workplace. How media recovery situations are handled depends on the DBA performing the recovery. You can improve your ability to perform such recoveries by testing various media recovery situations so that you have a degree of confidence. As a result of this practice, when you need to perform a media recovery, your uncertainties will be significantly reduced. Testing media recovery situations will also prepare you for the real-life situations that you will experience as a DBA.

Defining Media Recovery

Media recovery is a type of recovery used for recovering any currently used data file, control file, or online redo log file that becomes unavailable. The data file or control file may become unavailable for a number of reasons—it may have been lost, deleted, or moved from its original location, or it may have been damaged by data corruption or a hardware failure. All of these situations result in the Oracle database not being able to read or write to this file.

When a situation requiring media recovery occurs, the DBA must restore the unavailable file or files. If the database is in ARCHIVELOG mode, you must then recover these files by applying archived logs to the restored files. This will make the restored files as current as the rest of the database files.

Recovering Using *NOARCHIVELOG* and *ARCHIVELOG* Modes

One of the most significant backup and recovery decisions a DBA can make is whether to operate in ARCHIVELOG mode or NOARCHIVELOG mode. The outcome of this decision dramatically affects the backup and recovery options available.

When the database is in *ARCHIVELOG mode*, it generates historical changes in the form of offline redo logs, or archived logs. That is, the database doesn't write over the online redo logs until a copy is made, and this copy is called an offline redo log, or archived log. These logs can be applied to backups of the data files to recover the database up to the point of a failure. Figure 10.1 illustrates complete recovery in ARCHIVELOG mode.

When the database is in *NOARCHIVELOG mode*, it does not generate historical changes; as a result, there is no archive logging. In this mode, the database writes over the online redo logs without creating an archived log. Thus, no historical information is generated and saved for later use. Figure 10.2 illustrates incomplete recovery in NOARCHIVELOG mode. Even though this is called a complete recovery, the recovery process will be missing transactions because you are not generating archived logs to be applied in the recovery process.

FIGURE 10.1 Complete recovery in ARCHIVELOG mode for media failure on January 28th

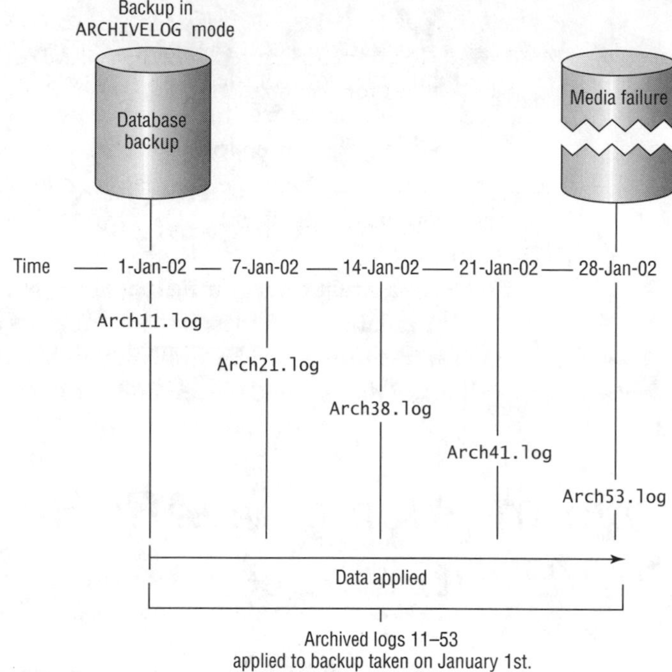

FIGURE 10.2 Complete recovery in NOARCHIVELOG mode for media failure on January 28th (transactions lost)

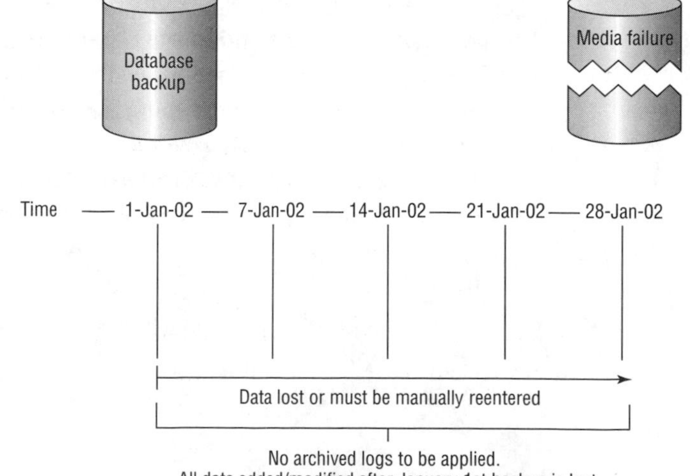

A significant type of failure is a media failure because in most cases, it requires that you restore all or some of the data files and the application of the redo logs during recovery. As discussed in Chapter 6, " Instance and Media Recovery Structures," media failure occurs when a database file cannot be accessed for some reason. The usual reason is a disk crash or controller failure.

Real World Scenario

The Dangers of Media Failures and Recovery

A media failure is generally considered the most dangerous type of failure and it is the most touchy to recover from as well. The severity of this type of failure may vary from a lost or accidentally removed data file to a severe hardware failure.

No matter what type of media failure the DBA is handling, they must contribute more analysis and thought to a media failure then they would to most other failure situations, such as those associated with instance recovery or basic user error. In fact, in certain situations, a severe hardware failure could cause a significant amount of the physical database to be relocated to a new filesystem. And in some cases, new filesystems may need to be re-created and properly configured for stripe, load, and redundancy. This can be a difficult task to perform when the database is down, especially if minimal downtime cannot be tolerated by the users. In less demanding environments, the database may remain unavailable for an excessive period of time.

A case in point is a small nonprofit organization that lost a disk controller for its financial database application. As in many small companies, this organization was concerned about keeping IT costs to a minimum. As a result, most resources that had been purchased were in use, such as servers and disk space. Another result of this policy was that extra capacity, such as multiple controllers to disk arrays, was not always purchased in an effort to reduce costs.

Because of this, when the disk controller was lost, the financial instance was unavailable until a new disk controller could be purchased, delivered, and installed in the disk storage array. This application was unavailable for one business day until the hardware was successfully installed and the database was successfully restored and recovered.

Media failure requires database recovery. If the database is in ARCHIVELOG mode, *complete recovery* can be performed. This means that a backup can be restored to the affected filesystem, and archived logs can be applied up to the point of failure. Thus, no data is lost.

If the database is in NOARCHIVELOG mode, however, a complete recovery cannot be performed without some transactions being lost. This means that a backup can be restored to the affected filesystem, but there won't be any archived logs or historical changes saved. Thus, the database will have only the transactions that were available at the time of the backup. If backups were scheduled every night, the business would only lose one day's worth of transactions. If backups were scheduled weekly, on the other hand, the business would lose one week's worth of transactions. The end result is that, in almost all cases, some data will be lost. This is a complete recovery of the database but the database does not contain all the transactions up to the failure point. The end result is that the database will be similar to an *incomplete recovery*, which will be covered in Chapter 11, "User-Managed and RMAN-Based Incomplete Recovery." The differences are that an incomplete recovery will be intentionally stopped before all the transactions are applied to the database, and an incomplete recovery requires the database to be in ARCHIVELOG mode and some other specific actions to be performed.

Performing User-Managed Recovery in *NOARCHIVELOG* Mode

This is an example of a user-managed recovery when the database is in NOARCHIVELOG mode. In this case, the database cannot be completely recovered. The database is available all day during the week. Every Saturday, the database is shut down, and a complete, *cold backup* (offline backup) is performed. The database is restarted when this activity is completed.

Diagnosing the Failure

On Wednesday morning, there is a lost or deleted data file in the database. The error received upon startup is as follows:

```
SQL> startup
ORACLE instance started.
Total System Global Area                    19504528 bytes
Fixed Size                                     64912 bytes
Variable Size                               16908288 bytes
Database Buffers                             2457600 bytes
Redo Buffers                                   73728 bytes
```

```
Database mounted.
ORA-01157: cannot identify/lock data file 4 - see
  DBWR trace file
ORA-01110: data file 4:
  '/db01/ORACLE/tst9/users01.dbf'
```

Because you are operating in NOARCHIVELOG mode, you must perform a full database restore from the previous weekend. You cannot perform a tablespace or data file recovery in NOARCHIVELOG mode because you have no ability to roll back and roll forward historical changes. There are no archived logs to apply to the data file to make the data file current with the rest of the database. Data entered into the database on Monday, Tuesday, and Wednesday are lost and must be reentered, if possible.

To perform the database restore, you will need to copy all the data files, online redo logs, and control files from the last Saturday backup and perform a full database restore. You will then copy these files back to their original locations.

Step-by-Step Recovery

To recover a lost data file when you are operating in NOARCHIVELOG mode, take the following steps:

1. Perform a *cold backup* of the database to simulate the Saturday backup. The following is a sample script, which performs a cold backup by shutting down the database and copying the necessary data files, redo logs, and control files.

```
# User-managed backup script
# Cold backup script for tst9
#
echo ''
echo 'starting cold backup...'
echo ''
# Script to stop database!
./stopdb_tst9.sh

echo ''
echo 'tst9 shutdown...'
echo ''
echo 'clean up last backup in staging directory'
```

```
rm /staging/cold/tst9/*
rm /staging/cold/tst9/*
echo ''
echo 'copying files to staging...'
echo ''
cp /db01/oracle/tst9/* /staging/cold/tst9/.
cp /db02/oracle/tst9/* /staging/cold/tst9/.
cp /oracle/admin/tst9/arch/* /staging/cold/tst9/.
echo ''
echo 'tst9 starting up.......'
echo ''
# Script to startup database!
./startdb_tst9.sh
```

2. Validate that the user TEST's objects exist in the USERS tablespace. This is the tablespace that you will remove to simulate a lost or deleted data file.

```
SQL> select username, default_tablespace,
 temporary_tablespace from dba_users
;
USERNAME         DEFAULT_TABLESPACE  TEMPORARY_TABLESPACE
---------------- ------------------- --------------------
SYS              SYSTEM              TEMP

SYSTEM           TOOLS               TEMP

OUTLN            SYSTEM              SYSTEM

DBSNMP           SYSTEM              SYSTEM

TEST             USERS               TEMP

5 rows selected.
SQL>
```

3. Create a table and insert data to simulate data being entered after Saturday's cold backup. This is the data that would be entered on Monday

through Wednesday, before the failure, but after the cold backup. The user TEST was created before the cold backup with a default tablespace of USERS. The account has connect and resource privileges.

```
SQL> connect test/test
SQL> create table t1 (c1 number, c2 char (50));
Statement processed.
SQL> insert into t1 values (1, 'This is a test!');
1 row processed.
SQL> commit;
Statement processed.
SQL>
```

4. Verify the data file location of the USERS tablespace. Then remove or delete this file.

```
SQL> select name from v$datafile;
NAME
-----------------------------------------
/db01/ORACLE/tst9/system01.dbf
/db01/ORACLE/tst9/rbs01.dbf
/db01/ORACLE/tst9/temp01.dbf
/db01/ORACLE/tst9/users01.dbf
/db01/ORACLE/tst9/tools01.dbf
/db01/ORACLE/tst9/data01.dbf
/db01/ORACLE/tst9/indx01.dbf
7 rows selected.
SQL>

rm /db01/ORACLE/tst9/users01.dbf
```

5. Start the database and verify that the "cannot identify/lock data file" error occurs.

```
[oracle@DS-LINUX tst9]$ sqlplus /nolog

SQL*Plus: Release 9.0.1.0.0 - Production on Thu Nov 1
21:04:10 2001
```

```
(c) Copyright 2001 Oracle Corporation.  All rights
reserved.

SQL> connect / as sysdba
Connected.
SQL> startup
ORACLE instance started.
Total System Global Area                    19504528 bytes
Fixed Size                                     64912 bytes
Variable Size                               16908288 bytes
Database Buffers                             2457600 bytes
Redo Buffers                                   73728 bytes
Database mounted.
ORA-01157: cannot identify/lock data file 4 -
  see DBWR trace file
ORA-01110: data file 4:
  '/db01/ORACLE/tst9/users01.dbf'
```

6. Shut down the database to perform a complete database restore. The database must be shut down to restore a cold backup.

```
SQL> shutdown
ORA-01109: database not open
Database dismounted.
ORACLE instance shut down.
SQL>
```

7. Perform a complete database restore by copying all data files, redo logs, and control files to their original locations.

```
cp /staging/cold/tst9/* /db01/ORACLE/tst9
```

8. Start the database and check to see whether the data entered after the cold backup is there. When you do, you will see that Table `t1` and the data do not exist. All data entered after the last backup will have to be reentered.

```
[oracle@DS-LINUX backup]$ sqlplus /nolog

SQL*Plus: Release 9.0.1.0.0 - Production on Thu Nov 1
21:04:10 2001
```

```
(c) Copyright 2001 Oracle Corporation.  All rights
reserved.

SQL> connect test/test
Connected.

SQL> select * from t1;
select * from t1
              *
ORA-00942: table or view does not exist
SQL>
```

Conclusions

The most notable observation about this scenario is that when the database is in NOARCHIVELOG mode, data is lost. All data entered after the backup, but before the failure, is lost and must be reentered. To recover it, you will have to shut down the database. Furthermore, you must restore the whole database instead of just the one data file that was lost or removed, which could increase the recovery time.

Performing User-Managed Complete Recovery in *ARCHIVELOG* Mode

In this example, the database is completely recovered because it is in ARCHIVELOG mode. This database is available 24 hours a day, 7 days a week, with the exception of scheduled maintenance periods. Every morning at 1 A.M., a *hot backup* is performed. The data files, archived logs, control files, backup control files, and `init.ora` files are copied to a staging directory, and from there, they are then copied to tape. The copy also remains on the disk until the next morning, when the hot backup runs again. This allows for quick access in the event of failure. When the backup runs again, the staging directory is purged and rewritten.

Diagnosing the Failure

On Wednesday morning, there is a lost or deleted data file in the database. The error received upon startup is as follows:

```
SQL> startup
ORACLE instance started.
```

```
Total System Global Area                    19504528 bytes
Fixed Size                                     64912 bytes
Variable Size                               16908288 bytes
Database Buffers                             2457600 bytes
Redo Buffers                                   73728 bytes
Database mounted.
ORA-01157: cannot identify/lock data file 4 -
  see DBWR trace file
ORA-01110: data file 4:
  '/db01/ORACLE/tst9/users01.dbf'
```

In this case, you are operating in ARCHIVELOG mode, so you only need to replace the damaged or lost file: /db01/oracle/tst9/users01.dbf. Then, with the database open, the archived logs can be applied to the database. This archived log action reapplies all the changes to the database; therefore, no data will be lost.

Step-by-Step Recovery

To recover the lost data file, take these steps:

1. Connect to user TEST and enter data in Table t1 in the tablespace USERS, which consists of the data file users01.dbf. This will simulate the data that is in the hot backup of the USERS tablespace.

```
[oracle@DS-LINUX backup]$ sqlplus /nolog

SQL*Plus: Release 9.0.1.0.0 - Production on Thu Nov 1
21:04:10 2001

(c) Copyright 2001 Oracle Corporation.  All rights
reserved.

SQL> connect test/test
Connected.
SQL> insert into t1 values (1,'This is test one -
  before hot backup');
1 row processed.
SQL> connect / as sysdba
SQL> commit;
Statement processed.
```

```
SQL> select username,default_tablespace from
     2> dba_users where username = 'TEST';
USERNAME                   DEFAULT_TABLESPACE
-------------------------- ----------------------------
TEST                       USERS
1 row selected.
```

2. Perform a hot backup of the USERS tablespace by placing it in backup mode. Proceed to copy the data file `users01.dbf` to a staging directory. Then, end the backup of the USERS tablespace.

```
SQL>
[oracle@DS-LINUX backup]$ sqlplus /nolog

SQL*Plus: Release 9.0.1.0.0 - Production on Thu Nov 1
21:04:10 2001

(c) Copyright 2001 Oracle Corporation.  All rights
reserved.

SQL> connect /as sysdba
Connected.
SQL> alter tablespace users begin backup;
Statement processed.
SQL> ! cp /db01/ORACLE/tst9/users01.dbf /stage
SQL> alter tablespace users end backup;
Statement processed.
SQL> alter system switch logfile;
Statement processed.
```

3. Connect to the user TEST and add more data to Table `t1`. This data is in rows 2 and 3. This data has been added after the backup of the `users01.dbf` data file, therefore, the data is not part of the data file copied earlier. After this is done, perform log switches to simulate normal activity in the database. This activates the archiver process to generate archived logs for the newly added data.

```
[oracle@DS-LINUX backup]$ sqlplus /nolog

SQL*Plus: Release 9.0.1.0.0 - Production on Thu Nov 1
21:04:10 2001
```

```
(c) Copyright 2001 Oracle Corporation.  All rights
reserved.

SQL> connect test/test
Connected.
SQL> insert into t1 values(2,'This is test two -
  after hot backup');
1 row processed.
SQL> insert into t1 values(3,'This is test three -
  after hot backup');
1 row processed.
SQL> commit;
Statement processed.
SQL> connect / as sysdba
Connected.
SQL> alter system switch logfile;
Statement processed.
SQL> alter system switch logfile;
Statement processed.
SQL> alter system switch logfile;
Statement processed.
SQL> alter system switch logfile;
Statement processed.
```

4. Verify the location of the data file of the USERS tablespace. Then remove or delete this file.

```
SQL> ! rm  /db01/ORACLE/tst9/users01.dbf
```

5. Shut down the database. Upon restarting, verify that the missing data file error occurs.

```
[oracle@DS-LINUX tst9]$ sql

SQL*Plus: Release 9.0.1.0.0 - Production on Thu Nov 1
21:04:10 2001

(c) Copyright 2001 Oracle Corporation.  All rights
reserved.
```

```
SQL> connect /as sysdba
Connected to an idle instance.
SQL> startup
ORACLE instance started.
Total System Global Area                   19504528 bytes
Fixed Size                                    64912 bytes
Variable Size                              16908288 bytes
Database Buffers                            2457600 bytes
Redo Buffers                                  73728 bytes
Database mounted.
ORA-01157: cannot identify/lock data file 4 -
  see DBWR trace file
ORA-01110: data file 4:
  '/db01/ORACLE/tst9/users01.dbf'
SQL>
```

6. Take the recovered data file offlinc. This will enable you to recover this data file and tablespace while the rest of the database is available for user access.

```
SQL> alter database datafile '/db01/oracle/tst9/
users01.dbf' offline;
Statement processed.
```

7. Restore the individual data file by copying the data file `users01.dbf` back to the original location.

```
[oracle@DS-LINUX tst9]$ cp /stage/users01.dbf /db01/
oracle/tst9
```

8. With the database open, begin the recovery process by executing the *RECOVER DATABASE* command. Then, apply all the available redo logs; this should result in a complete recovery. Finally, bring the data file online so that it is available for access by users.

```
SQL> connect /as sysdba
Connected.
SQL> recover datafile '/db01/ORACLE/tst9/users01.dbf';
ORA-00279: change 48323 generated at 03/29/00 22:04:25
  needed for thread 1
ORA-00289: suggestion :
  /oracle/admin/tst9/arch1/archtst9_84.log
```

```
ORA-00280: change 48323 for thread 1 is in sequence #84
Specify log: {<RET>=suggested | filename | AUTO |
CANCEL}
Log applied.
ORA-00279: change 48325 generated at 03/29/00 22:05:25
  needed for thread 1
ORA-00289: suggestion :
  /oracle/admin/tst9/arch1/archtst9_85.log
ORA-00280: change 48325 for thread 1 is in sequence #85
ORA-00278: log file
  '/oracle/admin/tst9/arch1/archtst9_84.log'
  no longer needed for this recovery

Specify log: {<RET>=suggested | filename | AUTO |
CANCEL}

Log applied.
ORA-00279: change 48330 generated at 03/29/00 22:08:41
  needed for thread 1
ORA-00289: suggestion :
  /oracle/admin/tst9/arch1/archtst9_86.log
ORA-00280: change 48330 for thread 1 is in sequence #86
ORA-00278: log file
  '/oracle/admin/tst9/arch1/archtst9_85.log'
  no longer needed for this recovery

Specify log: {<RET>=suggested | filename | AUTO |
CANCEL}

ORA-00279: change 48330 generated at 03/29/00 22:08:41
  needed for thread 1
ORA-00289: suggestion :
  /oracle/admin/tst9/arch1/archtst9_86.log
ORA-00280: change 48330 for thread 1 is in sequence #86
ORA-00278: log file
  '/oracle/admin/tst9/arch1/archtst9_85.log'
  no longer needed for this recovery
```

```
Specify log: {<RET>=suggested | filename | AUTO |
CANCEL}

Log applied.
Media recovery complete.
SQL>
SQL> alter database datafile
  '/db01/ORACLE/tst9/users01.dbf' online;
Statement processed.
```

9. Verify that there is no data loss, even though records 2 and 3 were added after the hot backup. The data for these records were applied from the offline redo logs (archived logs).

```
SQL> select * from t1;
C1         C2
---------- --------------------------------------------
         1 This is a test one - before hot backup
         2 This is a test two - after hot backup
         3 This is a test three - after hot backup
3 rows selected.
SQL>
```

Conclusions

The most notable observation about this scenario is that when the database is in ARCHIVELOG mode, no data is lost. All data entered after the hot backup into the USERS tablespace, but before the failure, is not lost. Only the data file users01.dbf must be restored, which takes less time than restoring *all* the data files. Therefore, by applying the archived logs during the recovery process, you can salvage all changes that occur after a hot backup of a data file.

Another equally important feature is that the database can remain open to users while the one tablespace and associated data file(s) are being recovered. This allows users to access data in other tablespaces of the database not affected by the failure.

Restoring Data Files to Different Locations

Restoring data files to a different location in both ARCHIVELOG mode and NOARCHIVELOG mode can be performed in a similar manner. The main difference is that like any NOARCHIVELOG mode recovery, the database in most cases cannot be completely recovered to the point of failure. The only time a database can be completely recovered in NOARCHIVELOG mode is when the database has not cycled through all of the online redo logs since the last complete backup.

To restore the files to a different location, you would perform an OS copy from the backup location to the new location, and then start the database at the mount stage. After that, you would update the control file with the ALTER DATABASE RENAME FILE command to designate the new location. Let's walk through this procedure.

1. Use OS commands to restore files to new locations.

```
cp /db01/oracle/tst9/data01.dbf /db02/oracle/tst9/
data01.dbf
```

2. Start up the database instance and mount the database.

```
oracle@octilli:~ > oraenv
ORACLE_SID = [tst9] ?
oracle@octilli:~ > sqlplus /nolog

SQL*Plus: Release 9.0.1.0.0 - Production on Mon Oct 29
23:26:23 2001

(c) Copyright 2001 Oracle Corporation.  All rights
reserved.
SQL> connect /as sysdba
Connected.
SQL> startup mount
ORACLE instance started.

Total System Global Area   75854976 bytes
Fixed Size                   279680 bytes
Variable Size              71303168 bytes
Database Buffers            4194304 bytes
```

```
Redo Buffers                        77824 bytes
Database mounted.
SQL>
```

3. Use the ALTER DATABASE RENAME FILE command to designate the new location.

```
SQL> ALTER DATABASE RENAME FILE
2> '/db01/oracle/tst9/data01.dbf' to
3> '/db02/oracle/tst9/data01.dbf';
```

4. Use the ALTER DATABASE OPEN command to open the database.

```
SQL>alter database open;
Database altered.
```

Relocate and Recover a Tablespace by Using Archived Redo Logs

In this example, during the recovery process, you will relocate a tablespace to a new filesystem by restoring the tablespace's data files to a new filesystem. You will use the RECOVER DATABASE command to determine which archived logs you will need to apply to the newly relocated data files. This type of recovery can be performed at the tablespace level or at the database level. If you perform it at the tablespace level, you will need to take the tablespace offline; at the database level, you will need to start and mount the database. Below is an example of this recovery procedure at the database level.

1. Set ORACLE_SID to ORCL, which is your target database, so that the database can be started or mounted with SQL*Plus.

```
oracle@octilli:~ > oraenv
ORACLE_SID = [tst9] ?
```

2. Run the appropriate user-managed script to back up the tst9 database to disk. This customized script shuts down the database and then copies the data files, control files, redo logs, and archived log files to a staging directory. After this is done, database tst9 is restarted.

```
# User-managed backup script
# Cold backup script for tst9
```

```
#
echo ''
echo 'starting cold backup...'
echo ''
# Script to stop database!
./stopdb_tst9.sh

echo ''
echo 'tst9 shutdown...'
echo ''
echo 'clean up last backup in staging directory'
rm /staging/cold/tst9/*
rm /staging/cold/tst9/*
echo ''
echo 'copying files to staging...'
echo ''
cp /db01/oracle/tst9/* /staging/cold/tst9/.
cp /db02/oracle/tst9/* /staging/cold/tst9/.
cp /oracle/admin/tst9/arch/* /staging/cold/tst9/.
echo ''
echo 'tst9 starting up........'
echo ''
# Script to startup database!
./startdb_tst9.sh
```

3. Now start up the database to demonstrate the `INDX` tablespace failure that will need to be restored, recovered, and relocated to the new filesystem.

```
oracle@octilli:/db01/oracle/tst9 > sqlplus /nolog

SQL*Plus: Release 9.0.1.0.0 - Production on Thu Nov 1
21:04:10 2001

(c) Copyright 2001 Oracle Corporation.  All rights
reserved.

SQL> connect /as sysdba
Connected to an idle instance.
```

```
SQL> startup mount
ORACLE instance started.

Total System Global Area   75854976 bytes
Fixed Size                   279680 bytes
Variable Size              71303168 bytes
Database Buffers            4194304 bytes
Redo Buffers                  77824 bytes
Database mounted.
SQL> alter database open;
alter database open
*
ERROR at line 1:
ORA-01157: cannot identify/lock data file 7 - see DBWR
trace file
ORA-01110: data file 7: '/db01/oracle/tst9/indx01.dbf'

SQL>
```

4. Next, shut down the database.

```
SQL> shutdown
ORA-01109: database not open

Database dismounted.
ORACLE instance shut down.
```

5. After this is accomplished, restore the backup `indx01.dbf` file from the online backup directory located in `/staging/cold/tst9/indx01.dbf` to the new filesystem `/db02/oracle/tst9`.

```
oracle@octilli:/staging/cold/tst9 > cp indx01.dbf /
db02/oracle/tst9/.
```

6. Next, start up and mount the database, and then use the RENAME command to update the control file with the `indx01.dbf` data file's new location.

```
SQL> startup mount
ORACLE instance started.
```

```
Total System Global Area   75854976 bytes
Fixed Size                   279680 bytes
Variable Size              71303168 bytes
Database Buffers            4194304 bytes
Redo Buffers                  77824 bytes
Database mounted.
SQL> alter database rename file
  2  '/db01/oracle/tst9/indx01.dbf' to
  3  '/db02/oracle/tst9/indx01.dbf';

Database altered.

SQL>
```

7. Then recover the database and apply the necessary archived logs to make the `indx01.dbf` data file in the `INDX` tablespace current. Then open the database.

```
SQL> recover database;
ORA-00279: change 153845 generated at 10/31/2001
23:12:23 needed for thread 1
ORA-00289: suggestion : /oracle/admin/tst9/arch/
archtst9_12.log
ORA-00280: change 153845 for thread 1 is in sequence
#12


Specify log: {<RET>=suggested | filename | AUTO |
CANCEL}

Log applied.
Media recovery complete.

SQL> alter database open;

Database altered.
```

8. Verify that the INDX tablespace and its associated data file have been moved from filesystem /db01/oracle/tst9 to /db02/oracle/tst9.

```
SQL> select name,status from v$datafile;

NAME                                  STATUS
------------------------------------- -------
/db01/oracle/tst9/system01.dbf        SYSTEM
/db01/oracle/tst9/rbs01.dbf           ONLINE
/db01/oracle/tst9/temp01.dbf          ONLINE
/db01/oracle/tst9/users01.dbf         ONLINE
/db02/oracle/tst9/tools01.dbf         ONLINE
/db01/oracle/tst9/data01.dbf          ONLINE
/db02/oracle/tst9/indx01.dbf          ONLINE
/db02/oracle/tst9/data02.dbf          ONLINE

8 rows selected.

SQL>
```

Describe Read-Only Tablespace Recovery

There are three scenarios that can occur with read-only tablespace recovery. These are as follows:

- Read-only backup and read-only recovery
- Read-only backup and read-write recovery
- Read-write backup and read-only recovery

The first scenario is the most straightforward because no recovery is needed. The SCN does not change because the tablespace is read-only. In this type of recovery, the only activity you need to do is restore the data files associated with the read-only tablespaces; thus no archived logs need to be applied.

The second scenario will require a more complex recovery process because the tablespace is being recovered to a read-write state in which the SCN number has changed or transactions have been made in the tablespace.

In this case, you would restore the tablespace from backup and apply archived logs from the point at which the table was made read-write.

The final scenario will also require recovery because the tablespace is restored in a read-write state and then recovered to read-only. In this case, you will need to restore the backup of the tablespace in read-write mode and apply archived logs up to the point where the tablespace was made read-only. You should always perform a backup after making a tablespace read-only because doing so eliminates the need to restore the tablespace.

Using RMAN for Restoration and Recovery

The restore and recovery considerations for using RMAN consist of how you will restore databases, tablespaces, data files, control files, and archived logs from RMAN. Restores and recoveries can be performed from backups on both disk and tape devices.

There are two main backup sources that can be the basis for the RMAN recovery process. These sources are image copies and backup sets. *Image copies* can be stored only on disk. Image copies are actual copies of the database files, archived logs, or control files and are not stored in a special RMAN format. An image copy in RMAN is equivalent to an OS copy command, such as `cp` or `dd` in Unix, or `COPY` in Windows NT/2000/XP.

In Oracle9*i*, the `RESTORE` command will determine the best available backup set or image copy to use in the restoration and the file will only be restored if a restoration is necessary. In prior Oracle versions, the files were always restored, even if it wasn't necessary.

The `RECOVER` command applies the necessary changes from the online redo logs and archived log files to recover the restored files. If you are using incremental backups, the online redo logs and archived log files will be applied to recover the database.

Performing RMAN Recovery in *NOARCHIVE* Mode

As the first example of using RMAN for restores and recoveries, you will restore a database in `NOARCHIVELOG` mode. To restore a database in this mode, you must first make sure that the database was shut down cleanly so that you are sure to get a consistent backup. This means the database should be shut down with a SHUTDOWN NORMAL, IMMEDIATE, or TRANSACTIONAL command, but the ABORT command should not be used. The database should then be started in MOUNT mode, but not opened. This is because the database files cannot be backed up when the database is opened and not in ARCHIVELOG mode.

Next, while in the RMAN utility, you must connect to the target database, which in our example, is tst9 in the Unix environment. Then you can connect to the recovery catalog in the rcat database.

Once you are connected to the proper target and catalog, you can execute the appropriate RMAN backup script. This script will back up the entire database. After this has been done, the database can be restored with the appropriate RMAN script. Finally, the database can be opened for use.

Let's walk through this example:

1. Set the ORACLE_SID to tst9, which is your target database, so that the database can be started in MOUNT mode with SQL*Plus.

```
oracle@octilli:~ > oraenv
ORACLE_SID = [tst9] ?
oracle@octilli:~ > sqlplus /nolog

SQL*Plus: Release 9.0.1.0.0 - Production on Mon Oct 29
23:36:19 2001

(c) Copyright 2001 Oracle Corporation.  All rights
reserved.

SQL> connect /as sysdba
Connected to an idle instance.
SQL> startup mount
ORACLE instance started.

Total System Global Area   75854976 bytes
Fixed Size                   279680 bytes
Variable Size              71303168 bytes
Database Buffers            4194304 bytes
Redo Buffers                  77824 bytes
SQL>
```

2. Start the RMAN utility at the command prompt and connect to the target and the recovery catalog database `rcat`.

```
oracle@octilli:~ > rman

Recovery Manager: Release 9.0.1.0.0 - Production

(c) Copyright 2001 Oracle Corporation.  All rights
reserved.

RMAN> connect target

connected to target database: tst9 (not mounted)

RMAN> connect catalog rman/rman@rcat

connected to recovery catalog database

RMAN>
```

3. Once you are connected to the target and recovery catalog, you can back up the target database to disk or tape. In this example, you choose disk. You give the database name a format of backupset unique identifier, and then you concatenate to the database name with the backupset number.

```
RMAN> run
2> {
3> allocate channel c1 type disk;
4> backup database format 'db_%u_%d_%s';
5> release channel c1;
6> }

allocated channel: c1
channel c1: sid=11 devtype=DISK

Starting backup at 29-OCT-01
channel c1: starting full datafile backupset
channel c1: specifying datafile(s) in backupset
```

```
including current controlfile in backupset
input datafile fno=00001 name=/db01/oracle/tst9/
system01.dbf
input datafile fno=00006 name=/db01/oracle/tst9/
data01.dbf
input datafile fno=00002 name=/db01/oracle/tst9/
rbs01.dbf
input datafile fno=00008 name=/db01/oracle/tst9/
data02.dbf
input datafile fno=00003 name=/db01/oracle/tst9/
temp01.dbf
input datafile fno=00004 name=/db01/oracle/tst9/
users01.dbf
input datafile fno=00007 name=/db01/oracle/tst9/
indx01.dbf
input datafile fno=00005 name=/db01/oracle/tst9/
tools01.dbf
channel c1: starting piece 1 at 29-OCT-01
channel c1: finished piece 1 at 29-OCT-01
piece handle=/oracle/product/9.0.1/dbs/db_0jd7r8e3_
TST9_19 comment=NONE
channel c1: backup set complete, elapsed time: 00:01:57
Finished backup at 29-OCT-01

released channel: c1
```

4. Once the backup has completed, the database may be restored. It must be mounted but not opened. In the restore script, choose three disk channels to utilize parallelization of the restore process. The *RESTORE DATABASE* command is responsible for the restore process within RMAN. No recovery is required because the database was in NOARCHIVELOG mode and the complete database was restored.

```
RMAN> run
{
allocate channel c1 type disk;
allocate channel c2 type disk;
allocate channel c3 type disk;
restore database;
}
```

5. Once the database has been restored, it can be opened and then shut down normally. At this point, a startup should be performed to make sure the restore process was successful.

```
SQL> alter database open;

Database altered.

SQL> shutdown
Database closed.
Database dismounted.
ORACLE instance shut down.

SQL> startup
ORACLE instance started.
Total System Global Area   75854976 bytes
Fixed Size                   279680 bytes
Variable Size              71303168 bytes
Database Buffers            4194304 bytes
Redo Buffers                  77824 bytes
Database mounted.
Database opened.
SQL>
```

Performing RMAN Complete Recovery in *ARCHIVELOG* Mode

As the second example of using RMAN for restores and recoveries, you will restore a database in ARCHIVELOG mode. In this case, the database can be mounted or opened. This is because the database files can be backed up when the database is opened and in ARCHIVELOG mode in a similar manner to the way the user-managed ALTER TABLESPACE *<tablespace_name>* BEGIN BACKUP command is used.

To perform this, you must connect to the target database (tst9 in the Unix environment in our example). Then you can connect to the recovery catalog in the rcat database.

Once you are connected to the proper target and catalog, you can execute the appropriate RMAN backup script. This script will back up the entire database. After this is done, you can restore the database with the appropriate RMAN script and then open it for use. Let's walk through this example:

1. Set the ORACLE_SID to tst9, which is your target database, so that the database can be started in MOUNT mode with SQL*Plus.

```
oracle@octilli:~ > oraenv
ORACLE_SID = [tst9] ?
oracle@octilli:~ > sqlplus /nolog

SQL*Plus: Release 9.0.1.0.0 - Production on Mon Oct 29
23:36:19 2001

(c) Copyright 2001 Oracle Corporation.  All rights
reserved.

SQL> connect /as sysdba
Connected to an idle instance.
SQL> startup mount
ORACLE instance started.

Total System Global Area   75854976 bytes
Fixed Size                   279680 bytes
Variable Size              71303168 bytes
Database Buffers            4194304 bytes
Redo Buffers                  77824 bytes
SQL>
```

2. Start the RMAN utility at the command prompt and connect to the target and the recovery catalog database rcat.

```
oracle@octilli:~ > rman

Recovery Manager: Release 9.0.1.0.0 - Production
```

```
(c) Copyright 2001 Oracle Corporation.  All rights
reserved.

RMAN> connect target

connected to target database: tst9 (not mounted)

RMAN> connect catalog rman/rman@rcat

connected to recovery catalog database

RMAN>
```

3. Once you are connected to the target and recovery catalog, you can back up the target database, including archived logs, to disk or tape. In this example, you choose disk. You give the database name a format of `db_%u_%d_%s`, which means that a `db_` will be concatenated to the backupset unique identifier and then concatenated to the database name with the backupset number.

```
RMAN> run
2> {
3> allocate channel c1 type disk;
4> backup database format 'db_%u_%d_%s';
5> backup format 'log_t%t_s%s_p%p'
6> (archivelog all);
7> }

allocated channel: c1
channel c1: sid=11 devtype=DISK

Starting backup at 30-OCT-01
channel c1: starting full datafile backupset
channel c1: specifying datafile(s) in backupset
including current controlfile in backupset
input datafile fno=00001 name=/db01/oracle/tst9/
system01.dbf
input datafile fno=00006 name=/db01/oracle/tst9/
data01.dbf
```

```
input datafile fno=00002 name=/db01/oracle/tst9/
rbs01.dbf
input datafile fno=00008 name=/db01/oracle/tst9/
data02.dbf
input datafile fno=00003 name=/db01/oracle/tst9/
temp01.dbf
input datafile fno=00004 name=/db01/oracle/tst9/
users01.dbf
input datafile fno=00007 name=/db01/oracle/tst9/
indx01.dbf
input datafile fno=00005 name=/db01/oracle/tst9/
tools01.dbf
channel c1: starting piece 1 at 30-OCT-01
channel c1: finished piece 1 at 30-OCT-01
piece handle=/oracle/product/9.0.1/dbs/db_0kd7tqts_
TST9_20 comment=NONE
channel c1: backup set complete, elapsed time: 00:01:48
Finished backup at 30-OCT-01

Starting backup at 30-OCT-01
current log archived
channel c1: starting archive log backupset
channel c1: specifying archive log(s) in backup set
input archive log thread=1 sequence=1 recid=8
stamp=442361669
input archive log thread=1 sequence=2 recid=9
stamp=442361872
input archive log thread=1 sequence=3 recid=10
stamp=442362056
input archive log thread=1 sequence=4 recid=11
stamp=442362297
input archive log thread=1 sequence=5 recid=12
stamp=442362415
input archive log thread=1 sequence=6 recid=13
stamp=442792220
input archive log thread=1 sequence=7 recid=14
stamp=443231077
input archive log thread=1 sequence=8 recid=15
stamp=444439517
```

```
input archive log thread=1 sequence=9 recid=16
stamp=444512889
input archive log thread=1 sequence=10 recid=17
stamp=444525609
channel c1: starting piece 1 at 30-OCT-01
channel c1: finished piece 1 at 30-OCT-01
piece handle=/oracle/product/9.0.1/dbs/log_t444525610_
s21_p1 comment=NONE
channel c1: backup set complete, elapsed time: 00:00:04
Finished backup at 30-OCT-01
released channel: c1
```

4. Once the backup has completed, the database may be restored and recovered. The database must be mounted but not opened. In the restore and recovery script, choose three disk channels to utilize parallelization of the restore process. This is not necessary, but it improves the restore and recovery time. The *RESTORE DATABASE* command is responsible for the restore process within RMAN; this command is required because the database was in ARCHIVELOG mode and these files need to be applied to the data files in order for a complete recovery to be performed. Finally, the database is opened.

```
RMAN> run
2> {
3> allocate channel c1 type disk;
4> allocate channel c2 type disk;
5> allocate channel c3 type disk;
6> restore database;
7> recover database;
8> alter database open;
9> }

allocated channel: c1
channel c1: sid=11 devtype=DISK

allocated channel: c2
channel c2: sid=12 devtype=DISK
```

```
allocated channel: c3
channel c3: sid=13 devtype=DISK

Starting restore at 30-OCT-01

channel c1: starting datafile backupset restore
channel c1: specifying datafile(s) to restore from
backup set
restoring datafile 00001 to /db01/oracle/tst9/
system01.dbf
restoring datafile 00002 to /db01/oracle/tst9/rbs01.dbf
restoring datafile 00003 to /db01/oracle/tst9/
temp01.dbf
restoring datafile 00004 to /db01/oracle/tst9/
users01.dbf
restoring datafile 00005 to /db01/oracle/tst9/
tools01.dbf
restoring datafile 00006 to /db01/oracle/tst9/
data01.dbf
restoring datafile 00007 to /db01/oracle/tst9/
indx01.dbf
restoring datafile 00008 to /db01/oracle/tst9/
data02.dbf
channel c1: restored backup piece 1
piece handle=/oracle/product/9.0.1/dbs/db_0kd7tqts_
TST9_20 tag=null params=NULL
channel c1: restore complete
Finished restore at 30-OCT-01

Starting recover at 30-OCT-01



starting media recovery
media recovery complete

Finished recover at 30-OCT-01
```

```
database opened
released channel: c3
released channel: c1
released channel: c2

RMAN>
```

5. Once the database has been restored, recovered, and opened, it should be shut down normally. A startup should be performed to make sure the restore process was successful.

```
SQL> shutdown
Database closed.
Database dismounted.
ORACLE instance shut down.

SQL> startup
ORACLE instance started.
Total System Global Area   75854976 bytes
Fixed Size                   279680 bytes
Variable Size              71303168 bytes
Database Buffers            4194304 bytes
Redo Buffers                  77824 bytes
Database mounted.
Database opened.
SQL>
```

Using RMAN to Restore Data Files to Different Locations

As the third example, you will restore and recover a data file by using RMAN. In this case, the database will also be in ARCHIVELOG mode because an individual data file will be backed up. As in the previous tablespace example, the database will be backed up while it is open.

First, within RMAN, you must perform the appropriate data file backup script. For this example, you will select the data file for the DATA tablespace. You will back up the current control file as an extra precaution.

Once the data file is backed up, you can begin the restore and recovery process. For this process, the database should be mounted, but not open. You will also need to use the SET NEWNAME command to identify the new data file location, and the SWITCH command to record the location change in the control file. With the database mounted, you can execute the appropriate RMAN script to restore and recover the data file. The steps are as follows:

1. Set ORACLE_SID to ORCL, which is your target database, so that the database can be started or mounted with SQL*Plus.

```
oracle@octilli:~ > oraenv
ORACLE_SID = [tst9] ?
```

2. Connect to RMAN, the target database, and the recovery catalog in one step.

```
oracle@octilli:~ > rman target / catalog rman/rman@rcat

Recovery Manager: Release 9.0.1.0.0 - Production

(c) Copyright 2001 Oracle Corporation.  All rights
reserved.

connected to target database: TST9 (DBID=1268700551)
connected to recovery catalog database
```

3. Run the appropriate RMAN script to back up the DATA data file to disk.

```
RMAN> run
2> {
3> allocate channel ch1 type disk;
4> backup
5> format '%d_%u'
6> (datafile '/db01/oracle/tst9/data02.dbf');
7> release channel ch1;
8> }

allocated channel: ch1
```

```
channel ch1: sid=12 devtype=DISK

allocated channel: ch1
channel ch1: sid=12 devtype=DISK

Starting backup at 30-OCT-01
channel ch1: starting full datafile backupset
channel ch1: specifying datafile(s) in backupset
input datafile fno=00008 name=/db01/oracle/tst9/
data02.dbf
channel ch1: starting piece 1 at 30-OCT-01
channel ch1: finished piece 1 at 30-OCT-01
piece handle=/oracle/product/9.0.1/dbs/TST9_0nd7tstb
comment=NONE
channel ch1: backup set complete, elapsed time:
00:00:01
Finished backup at 30-OCT-01

released channel: ch1

RMAN>
```

4. Once the data file has been backed up, you can restore and recover the data file with the appropriate RMAN script. The RMAN script uses the SET NEWNAME command to designate the new location of the data file that will be relocated; then database will be restored. Next, the SWITCH command will record the location change in the control file. Finally, the database will be recovered and opened.

```
RMAN> run
2> {
3> set newname for datafile 8 to '/db02/oracle/tst9/
data02.dbf';
4> restore database;
5> switch datafile all;
6> recover database;
7> alter database open;
8> }
```

```
executing command: SET NEWNAME

Starting restore at 30-OCT-01

allocated channel: ORA_DISK_1
channel ORA_DISK_1: sid=11 devtype=DISK
channel ORA_DISK_1: starting datafile backupset restore
channel ORA_DISK_1: specifying datafile(s) to restore
from backup set
restoring datafile 00001 to /db01/oracle/tst9/
system01.dbf
restoring datafile 00002 to /db01/oracle/tst9/rbs01.dbf
restoring datafile 00003 to /db01/oracle/tst9/
temp01.dbf
restoring datafile 00004 to /db01/oracle/tst9/
users01.dbf
restoring datafile 00005 to /db01/oracle/tst9/
tools01.dbf
restoring datafile 00006 to /db01/oracle/tst9/
data01.dbf
restoring datafile 00007 to /db01/oracle/tst9/
indx01.dbf
channel ORA_DISK_1: restored backup piece 1
piece handle=/oracle/product/9.0.1/dbs/db_0kd7tqts_
TST9_20 tag=null params=NULL
channel ORA_DISK_1: restore complete
channel ORA_DISK_1: starting datafile backupset restore
channel ORA_DISK_1: specifying datafile(s) to restore
from backup set
restoring datafile 00008 to /db02/oracle/tst9/
data02.dbf
channel ORA_DISK_1: restored backup piece 1
piece handle=/oracle/product/9.0.1/dbs/TST9_0nd7tstb
tag=null params=NULL
channel ORA_DISK_1: restore complete
Finished restore at 31-OCT-01

datafile 8 switched to datafile copy
```

```
input datafilecopy recid=32 stamp=444528057 filename=/
db02/oracle/tst9/data02.df
starting full resync of recovery catalog
full resync complete

Starting recover at 31-OCT-01
using channel ORA_DISK_1



starting media recovery
media recovery complete

Finished recover at 31-OCT-01

database opened

RMAN>
```

5. Once the database has been restored, shut it down normally. Then perform a startup to make sure the restore process was completed.

```
SQL> shutdown
SQL> startup
```

Use RMAN to Relocate and Recover a Tablespace Using Archived Logs

In this example, you will relocate a tablespace to a new filesystem during recovery. You can perform this using the SET NEWNAME and SWITCH commands that were mentioned earlier. In addition, the RECOVER command applies the necessary backup of data files and archived logs. The major difference between this process and that of relocating a data file is that the tablespace needs to be taken offline before the associated data files can be moved to a new location. The database, however, can be opened during this process. Below is an example of this procedure.

1. Set ORACLE_SID to ORCL, which is your target database, so that the database can be started or mounted with SQL*Plus.

```
oracle@octilli:~ > oraenv
ORACLE_SID = [tst9] ?
```

2. Connect to RMAN, the target database, and the recovery catalog in one step.

```
oracle@octilli:~ > rman target / catalog rman/rman@rcat

Recovery Manager: Release 9.0.1.0.0 - Production

(c) Copyright 2001 Oracle Corporation.  All rights
reserved.

connected to target database: TST9 (DBID=1268700551)
connected to recovery catalog database
```

3. Run the appropriate RMAN script to back up the tst9 database to disk.

```
RMAN> run
2> {
3> allocate channel c1 type disk;
4> backup database format 'db_%u_%d_%s';
5> backup format 'log_t%t_s%s_p%p'
6> (archivelog all);
7> }
```

4. Then issue the recovery script, which will utilize the SET NEWNAME, RESTORE, SWITCH, and RECOVER commands. Finally, bring the tablespace online.

```
RMAN> run
2> {
3> sql 'alter tablespace tools offline immediate';
4> set newname for datafile '/db01/oracle/tst9/
tools01.dbf' to
5> '/db02/oracle/tst9/tools01.dbf';
6> restore (tablespace tools);
7> switch datafile 5;
```

```
8> recover tablespace tools;
9> sql 'alter tablespace tools online';}

sql statement: alter tablespace tools offline immediate

executing command: SET NEWNAME

Starting restore at 31-OCT-01

allocated channel: ORA_DISK_1
channel ORA_DISK_1: sid=11 devtype=DISK
channel ORA_DISK_1: starting datafile backupset restore
channel ORA_DISK_1: specifying datafile(s) to restore
from backup set
restoring datafile 00005 to /db02/oracle/tst9/
tools01.dbf
channel ORA_DISK_1: restored backup piece 1
piece handle=/oracle/product/9.0.1/dbs/db_0kd7tqts_
TST9_20 tag=null params=NULL
channel ORA_DISK_1: restore complete
Finished restore at 31-OCT-01

datafile 5 switched to datafile copy
input datafilecopy recid=34 stamp=444610301 filename=/
db02/oracle/tst9/tools01.f
starting full resync of recovery catalog
full resync complete

Starting recover at 31-OCT-01
using channel ORA_DISK_1

starting media recovery
media recovery
archive log thread 1 sequence 16 is already on disk as
file /oracle/admin/tst9/arch/archtst9_16.log
archive log thread 1 sequence 17 is already on disk as
```

```
file /oracle/admin/tst9/arch/archtst9_17.log
archive log thread 1 sequence 18 is already on disk as
file /oracle/admin/tst9/arch/archtst9_18.log
archive log
filename=/oracle/admin/tst9/arch/archtst9_16.log
thread=1 sequence=6
media recovery complete

Finished recover at 31-OCT-01

sql statement: alter tablespace tools online
RMAN>
```

Summary

In this chapter, we emphasized media recoveries. We described the two methods of performing Oracle database recovery for media failures (user-managed and RMAN-based recoveries) and we performed specific examples of each.

In addition, we identified the differences between ARCHIVELOG mode and NOARCHIVELOG mode and we described the significant implications that each mode has on the backup and recovery process. We also showed examples of both ARCHIVELOG mode and NOARCHIVELOG mode recoveries using both user-managed and RMAN methods of recovery.

We then discussed read-only tablespace recovery and the three recovery scenarios associated with it. Each of these scenarios requires different recovery actions. We also performed both user-managed and RMAN-based recovery situations in which file relocation was required.

Media recoveries are an important topic in testing and in real work situations. How media recovery situations are handled depends on the confidence of the DBA performing the media recovery. You can obtain confidence by practicing media recoveries in all of the above-mentioned situations. Then, when you need to perform a media recovery, your uncertainties will have been significantly reduced. Such practice situations will also prepare you for testing and situations you will encounter as a DBA.

Exam Essentials

Understand media recovery. Media recovery is required when database files, such as data files, control files, or online redo logs, become unavailable. Such files can become unavailable because of hardware failure, corruption, or accidental removal.

Know the recovery differences between ARCHIVELOG and NOARCHIVELOG mode. In order to perform a complete recovery, the database must be in ARCHIVELOG mode. In NOARCHIVELOG mode, an incomplete recovery must be performed—otherwise all transactions after the last full backup to the point of failure will be lost.

Be familiar with the process of restoring data files to different locations. To restore data files to different locations, you must use the OS commands to copy files from the backup location to the new location. Then you will use the ALTER DATABASE RENAME FILE command to record the new data file locations in the control file.

List the read-only tablespace recovery scenarios. The three read-only recovery scenarios include read-only backup and read-only recovery, read-only backup and read-write recovery, and read-write backup and read-only recovery. You should understand how recovery varies in each of these scenarios.

Understand the commands necessary to perform RMAN restoration and recovery. The RESTORE command will determine the best available backup set or image copy to use in the restoration. The RECOVER command will apply the necessary changes from the online redo logs and archived logs as well as incremental backups (if used) to the restored files.

Understand RMAN recovery in ARCHIVELOG and NOARCHIVELOG mode. In NOARCHIVELOG mode, you use a RESTORE command of a consistent database but you don't use the RECOVER command. In ARCHIVELOG mode, both the RESTORE and RECOVER commands are used.

Use RMAN commands to restore data files to different locations. The SET NEWNAME command is used to name the new location of the data file, and the SWITCH command is used to update the control file with the new location. After this, the database is recovered.

Use RMAN commands to relocate and recover a tablespace using archived logs. The SET NEWNAME command is used to name the new location of the data file, and the SWITCH command is used to update the control file with the new location. Note that the tablespace must be taken offline to perform the recovery, and then it must be put back online when the recovery is complete while the database is still open.

Key Terms

Before you take the exam, be certain you are familiar with the following terms:

ARCHIVELOG mode	incomplete recovery
cold backup	media recovery
complete recovery	NOARCHIVELOG mode
hot backup	RECOVER DATABASE
image copies	RESTORE DATABASE

Review Questions

1. Which of these failure situations best describe a media failure and will require recovery? (Choose all that apply.)

   A. A deleted data file

   B. All control files deleted

   C. A failed disk controller with access to disks storing data files

   D. A disk drive crash on a non-mirrored storage array containing data files

   E. All of the above

2. In which of these modes must a database be in order for a complete database recovery up to the point of failure to be performed?

   A. `NOARCHIVELOG`

   B. `ARCHIVELOG`

   C. `Export`

   D. `LOG`

3. What is the type of recovery being performed when transactions are not applied and the database is `NOARCHIVELOG` mode?

   A. Complete recovery

   B. Partial recovery

   C. Incomplete recovery

   D. No recovery

4. What command is required to relocate files in a user-managed recovery?

   A. `ALTER DATABASE RENAME FILE`

   B. `SET NEWNAME`

   C. `ALTER DATABASE SET NEWNAME`

   D. `ALTER DATABASE NEWNAME FILE`

5. You make cold database backups including a read-only tablespace and then you make the tablespace read-write. Before the next weekly backup, the tablespace is made read-write and you need to perform recovery on that tablespace. What option must be performed?

   A. No recovery is needed because the tablespace was backed up read-only.

   B. No recovery is needed because the tablespace did not have many changes made in it after it was made read-write.

   C. Recovery is needed because the tablespace was made read-write and the backup was read-only.

   D. Restoring the read-only tablespace is all that is needed.

6. What RMAN command is required to recover a database in `NOARCHIVELOG` mode?

   A. `RESTORE`

   B. `RECOVER`

   C. `SET NEWNAME`

   D. `SWITCH`

7. What RMAN command is responsible for applying incremental backups and archived logs?

   A. `RESTORE`

   B. `RECOVER`

   C. `SET NEWNAME`

   D. `SWITCH`

8. When using `RMAN`, what mode does the database need to be in to perform a database restore and recovery?

   A. Opened

   B. Nomount

   C. Closed

   D. Mount

9. The `SWITCH` command is responsible for which of the following activities during the relocation process of database files?

   A. Renaming the location

   B. Updating the control file

   C. Moving the physical files

   D. Updating the files in the data dictionary

10. Which of the following recoveries doesn't require you to recover the database?

    A. Read-only tablespace backup and tablespace was read-only when recovered

    B. Read-only tablespace backup and tablespace was read-write when recovered

    C. Read-write tablespace backup and tablespace was read-only when recovered

    D. Read-write tablespace backup and tablespace was read-write when recovered

11. What are the read-only tablespace recovery scenarios? (Choose all that apply.)

    A. Read-only backup to read-only recovery

    B. Read-only backup to read-write recovery

    C. Read-write backup to read-write recovery

    D. Read-write backup to read-only recovery

12. What type of read-only recovery could the DBA avoid if they are following recommended procedures?

    A. Read-only backup to read-only recovery

    B. Read-only backup to read-write recovery

    C. Read-write backup to read-write recovery

    D. Read-write backup to read-only recovery

13. What is unique about a RMAN image copy?
    A. It can only back up data files.
    B. It can only back up to tape.
    C. It can only back up to disk.
    D. It cannot back up control files.

14. Which of the following is a true statement about a backup set?
    A. It is not stored in a special RMAN format.
    B. It can contain multiple data files.
    C. It can contain multiple data files and archived logs.
    D. It can only contain one data file per backup set.

15. Which RMAN command is responsible for copying files from the backup media?
    A. `RESTORE`
    B. `RENAME`
    C. `RECOVER`
    D. `SWITCH`

Answers to Review Questions

1. E. All these failures will require media recovery. Each failure will make a database file unavailable, which will mean that a restoration and recovery is needed.

2. B. Complete recovery up to the point of failure can only be performed when the database is in ARCHIVELOG mode.

3. A. Complete recovery in NOARCHIVELOG mode is the correct answer. Even though you are performing a complete recovery, not all transactions are being applied and there can be data missing. This is because the database is not in ARCHIVELOG mode or is not generating archived logs.

4. A. The ALTER DATABASE RENAME FILE command is used for user-managed backups.

5. C. Recovery is needed when a read-only tablespace is made read-write and the backup was taken when the tablespace was read-only. This means that the SCNs in the headers of the data files have changed and will need to be resynchronized with the rest of the database during the recovery process.

6. A. The RESTORE command is responsible for the recovery process when the database is in NOARCHIVELOG mode because no recovery is necessary.

7. B. The RECOVER command applies incremental backups and archived logs to the recovery process.

8. D. The database should be mounted to perform a database restore and recovery so that the control file can be read and the target database can be connected.

9. B. The SWITCH command is responsible for updating the control file with the new location of the files that have been moved.

10. A. When the tablespace is read-only for the backup and read-only during the recovery, no recovery is needed. The data files of the read-only tablespace can be restored because there is no change to the SCN of data file headers.

11. A, B, D. The scenarios for read-only tablespace recovery are read-only backup to read-only recovery, read-only backup to read-write recovery, and read-write backup to read-only recovery.

12. D. Every time you make a tablespace read-only, you should conduct a backup shortly thereafter. This eliminates the need to conduct a recovery in the read-write backup to read-only recovery scenario.

13. C. The RMAN image copy is similar to an OS copy. It can only be performed to disk.

14. B. A backup set can contain multiple data files within the same backup set, but it cannot contain data files and archived logs in the same backup set. A backup set is stored in a special RMAN format, unlike an image copy.

15. A. The `RESTORE` command is responsible for copying files from the backup media to the desired location.

User-Managed and RMAN-Based Incomplete Recovery

ORACLE9*i*: DBA FUNDAMENTALS II EXAM OBJECTIVES COVERED IN THIS CHAPTER:

- ✓ **Describe the steps of incomplete recovery.**
- ✓ **Perform an incomplete database recovery.**
- ✓ **Identify the loss of current online redo log files.**
- ✓ **Perform an incomplete database recovery using UNTIL TIME.**
- ✓ **Perform an incomplete database recovery using UNTIL SEQUENCE.**

Exam objectives are subject to change at any time without prior notice and at Oracle's sole discretion. Please visit Oracle's Certification website (`http://www.oracle.com/education/certification/`) for the most current exam objectives listing.

Incomplete database recovery requires an understanding of the redo log and ARCHIVELOG processes, the synchronization of the Oracle database, and the options allowed for performing an incomplete recovery. This chapter discusses the incomplete recovery process and the commands associated with each incomplete recovery option. It also includes an example that shows how to perform an incomplete recovery due to lost or corrupted current redo log files.

In addition to the user-managed incomplete recovery, this chapter demonstrates how to use RMAN for this process. The RMAN examples covered include how to use the `SET UNTIL TIME` and `UNTIL SEQUENCE` clauses.

Incomplete recovery is the only method of recovery for certain types of failures. It is important that you understand when and how to use incomplete recovery methods. Anytime there is a failure that will cause you not to apply all the changes back to the databases, you will need to use one of the incomplete recovery methods that will be discussed in this chapter.

Describing the User-Managed Incomplete Recovery

Incomplete recovery occurs when the database is not recovered entirely to the point at which the database failed. This is a partial recovery of the database in which some archived logs are applied to the database, but not all of them. With this type of recovery, only a portion of the transactions gets applied.

There are three types of incomplete media recovery:

- Cancel-based
- Time-based
- Change-based

Each of these options allows recovery to a point in time prior to the failure. The main reason why there are three options is so that the DBA can have better flexibility and control of where recovery is halted during the recovery process. Each of these options is described in detail in the next section.

Incomplete recovery is performed any time you don't want to apply all the archived and nonarchived log files that are necessary to bring the database up to the time of failure. As a result, the database is essentially not completely recovered; transactions remain missing. Figure 11.1 illustrates the different types of incomplete recovery.

FIGURE 11.1 Incomplete recovery in ARCHIVELOG mode for a media failure on January 28th

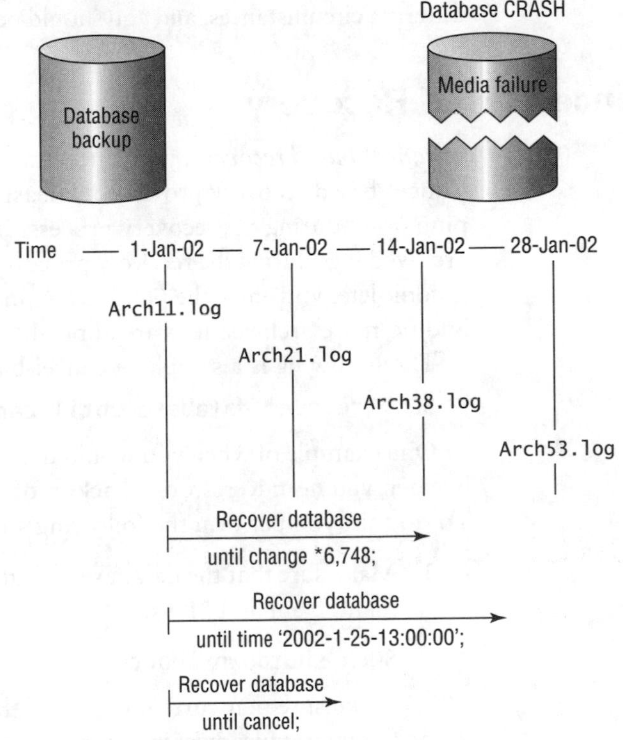

Incomplete recovery should be performed when the DBA wants or is required to recover the database prior to the point of time when the database failed. Some of the circumstances that might call for this type of recovery include data file corruption, redo log corruption, or the loss of a table due to user error.

In some cases, incomplete recovery is the only option available to you. In a failure situation that involves the loss or corruption of the current and inactive nonarchived redo log files, recovering the database without the transactions in these files is the only option. If a complete recovery were performed instead, the error would be reintroduced as a result of the recovery process.

Performing an Incomplete Database Recovery

This section details the three types of incomplete database recovery: cancel-based, time-based, and change-based. Each of these methods is used for different circumstances, and you should be aware of when each is appropriate.

Cancel-Based Recovery

In *cancel-based recovery,* you cancel the recovery before the point of failure. Cancel-based recovery provides the least flexibility and control of the stopping point during the recovery process. In this type of recovery, you apply archived logs during the recovery process. At some point before the recovery is complete, you enter the CANCEL command. At this point, recovery halts, and no more archived logs are applied.

The following is a sample of cancel-based incomplete recovery.

```
SQL> recover database until cancel;
```

One example of when you would use a cancel-based incomplete recovery is when you need to restore a backup of a lost data file from a hot backup. To do this, you perform the following steps:

1. Make sure that the database is shutdown by using the SHUTDOWN command from SQL*Plus.

   ```
   SQL> shutdown abort
   ```

2. Make sure that current copies of the data files, control files, and parameter files exist in case there are errors that arise during the recovery process. If these files exist, you will be able to restart the recovery process, if needed, without introducing any new errors that might have resulted from a previous failed recovery.

3. Make sure that a current backup exists because copied files from the current backup will replace the failed data files, online redo log files, or control files.

4. Restore the data files from the backup location to the proper location. You do this by issuing an operating system–specific command. In Unix, you would use a cp command, as in this example:

```
cp /stage/data01.dbf /oracle/database/tst9/data01.dbf
cp /stage/system01.dbf /oracle/database/tst9/system01.dbf
cp /stage/rbs01.dbf /oracle/database/tst9/rbs01.dbf
cp /stage/temp01.dbf /oracle/database/tst9/temp01.dbf
cp /stage/users01.dbf /oracle/database/tst9/users01.dbf
cp /stage/tools01.dbf /oracle/database/tst9/tools01.dbf
cp /stage/indx01.dbf /oracle/database/tst9/indx01.dbf
```

5. Start the database in MOUNT mode.

```
SQL> startup mount
```

6. Verify that all the data files you need to recover are online. The following query shows the status of each data file that is online (with the exception of the system data file, which is always online; status equals system).

```
SQL> select file#,status,enabled,name from v$datafile;
FILE#      STATUS  ENABLED    NAME

---------- ------- ---------- ------------------------

1 SYSTEM  READ WRITE /oracle/database/tst9/system01.dbf

2 ONLINE  READ WRITE /oracle/database/tst9/rbs01.dbf

3 ONLINE  READ WRITE /oracle/database/tst9/temp01.dbf

4 ONLINE  READ WRITE /oracle/database/tst9/users01.dbf

5 ONLINE  READ WRITE /oracle/database/tst9/tools01.dbf

6 ONLINE  READ WRITE /oracle/database/tst9/data01.dbf

7 ONLINE  READ WRITE /oracle/database/tst9/indx01.dbf

7 rows selected.
```

7. Perform an incomplete recovery by using the *UNTIL CANCEL* clause in the RECOVER DATABASE command.

   ```
   SQL> recover database until cancel;
   ```

8. Open the database with the RESETLOGS option.

   ```
   SQL>  alter database open resetlogs;
   ```

   You must use the RESETLOGS clause with the ALTER DATABASE OPEN command for all types of incomplete recovery. The *RESETLOGS* option ensures that the log files applied in recovery can never be used again by resetting the log sequence and rebuilding the existing online redo logs. This process permanently deactivates all transactions that exist in the nonarchived log files so that they can never be recovered. At the same time, it resynchronizes log files with the data files and control files. If these transactions were not purged, the log files would create bad archived logs. This is the main reason why a backup of the control file, data files, and redo logs should be done prior to performing an incomplete recovery.

9. Perform a new cold or hot backup of the database. Existing backups are no longer valid.

Remember, after the ALTER DATABASE OPEN RESETLOGS command is applied, the previous log files and backed-up data files are useless for this newly recovered database. This is because a gap exists in the log files. The old backup data files and logs can never again be synchronized with the database. Thus, a complete backup must be performed after an incomplete recovery of any type.

Real World Scenario

Using Incomplete Recovery to Move a Database

Recovery operations can be used as tools to perform activities other than the typical recovery from failure. For this reason, you need to be familiar with the backup and recovery features and capabilities associated with an incomplete recovery.

> Incomplete recovery options, such as the backup control file being used in conjunction with the `RECOVER DATABASE USING BACKUP CONTROLFILE UNTIL CANCEL` command, can be useful when you are trying to move databases from one location to another. When you use such options, you can move databases for any purpose, such as moving a database for testing, or just moving a database to a new server. You must make sure that if you are moving a database to a new server, the Oracle database software you are using and the OS on the new server are similar.
>
> This approach of moving databases is performed by taking the hot or cold backup of the database you want to move and moving the data files and initialization files to the new location. Then you would change the backup control file to location references of all the physical database files, such as redo logs and data files. After you have done this, you need to validate your `ORACLE_SID` and make sure that it is sourced to the correct database; you will then need to execute the backup control file at the SQL prompt as sysdba. This will generate a new database on a new server and in different locations. Please refer to the Oracle documentation for the exact steps to perform this task and always try this process in a test environment first.
>
> As a DBA, you will be responsible for setting up test database environments for numerous reasons. You will find that the ability to move and set up databases and applications on different servers for testing and upgrade purposes is a must-have skill. Every time there is any significant upgrade, it will need to be tested on a different environment than the production environment. This approach of moving data files and re-creating the control file works well for many testing and upgrading situations.

Time-Based Recovery

In *time-based recovery*, the DBA recovers the database to a point in time before the point of failure. Time-based recovery provides more flexibility and control than the cancel-based option does. The cancel-based option's granularity is the size of a redo log file; in other words, when you are applying a redo log file, you get all the transactions in that file, regardless of the time period over which that log was filled.

In time-based recovery, you apply archived logs to the database up to a designated point in time. This point could be in the middle of the archived log, but not necessarily apply to the whole archived log. After you have applied these logs, you can control the recovery process to a time prior to a fatal action in the database, such as data block corruption or the loss of a database object due to user error. Below is a sample of the time-based, incomplete recovery.

```
SQL> recover database until time '2001-9-30:22:55:00';
```

You can use the preceding example to restore lost data files and then use time-based recovery in place of cancel-based recovery. To do this, you restore all the necessary data files from a hot backup, as before. The only change is that you use the *UNTIL TIME* clause in step 7 instead of an `UNTIL CANCEL` clause, as shown here:

7. Perform an incomplete recovery by using the `UNTIL TIME` clause.

```
SQL> recover database until time '2001-9-30:22:55:00';
```

All other steps remain the same.

Change-Based Recovery

In *change-based recovery*, you recover to a *system change number (SCN)* before the point of failure. This type of incomplete recovery gives you the most control.

As you have already learned, the SCN is what Oracle uses to uniquely identify each committed transaction. The SCN is a number that orders the transactions consecutively in the redo logs as each transaction occurs. This number is also recorded in transaction tables within the rollback segments, control files, and data file headers. The SCN coordination between the transactions and these files synchronizes the database to a consistent state.

Each redo log is associated with a low and high SCN number. This SCN information can be seen in the *V$LOG_HISTORY* view below. Notice the low and high SCN numbers in the `FIRST_CHANGE#` and `NEXT_CHANGE#` columns for each log sequence or log file.

```
SQLWKS> select sequence#,first_change#,next_change#,first_
time
     2> from v$log_history where sequence# > 10326;

SEQUENCE#  FIRST_CHAN NEXT_CHANG FIRST_TIME
---------- ---------- ---------- --------------------
     10327   60731807   60732514 30-SEP-01
     10328   60732514   60732848 30-SEP-01
     10329   60732848   60747780 30-SEP-01
     10330   60747780   60748140 30-SEP-01
4 rows selected.
```

All transactions between these SCNs are included in these logs. Oracle determines what should be recovered by using the SCN information that is recorded in transaction tables within the rollback segments, control files, and data file headers.

To perform a change-based recovery, you can use the previous example of incomplete database recovery but utilize change-based recovery in place of cancel-based or time-based recovery. To do this, restore all the needed data files from a hot backup, and then just use the following step 7 instead of the one shown previously.

7. Perform an incomplete recovery by using the *UNTIL CHANGE* clause.

```
SQL> recover database until change 60747681;
```

Recovering after Losing Current Redo Logs

Incomplete recovery is necessary if there is a loss of the current and/or inactive nonarchived redo log files. If this scenario occurs, it means that you don't have all the redo log files up to the point of failure, so the only alternative is to recover prior to the point of failure.

Oracle has made improvements to compensate for this failure by giving you the ability to mirror copies of redo logs or to create group members on different filesystems.

Some common error messages that might be seen in the alert log are ORA-00255, ORA-00312, ORA-00286, and ORA-00334. Each of these error messages indicates a problem writing to the online redo log files.

To perform incomplete recovery after the redo log files have been lost, you do the following:

1. Start Server Manager and execute a `CONNECT INTERNAL` command.

```
SQL>  connect / as sysdba ;
```

2. Execute a `SHUTDOWN` command and copy all data files.

```
SQL>shutdown;
cp /stage/data01.dbf /oracle/database/tst9/data01.dbf
cp /stage/system01.dbf /oracle/database/tst9/system01.dbf
```

```
cp /stage/rbs01.dbf /oracle/database/tst9/rbs01.dbf
cp /stage/temp01.dbf /oracle/database/tst9/temp01.dbf
cp /stage/users01.dbf /oracle/database/tst9/users01.dbf
cp /stage/tools01.dbf /oracle/database/tst9/tools01.dbf
cp /stage/indx01.dbf /oracle/database/tst9/indx01.dbf
```

3. Execute a `STARTUP MOUNT` command to read the contents of the control file.

```
SQL>  startup mount;
```

4. Execute a `RECOVER DATABASE UNTIL CANCEL` command to start the recovery process.

```
SQL>  recover database until cancel;
```

5. Apply the necessary archived logs up to, but not including, the lost or corrupted log.

6. Open the database and reset the log files.

```
SQL>  alter database open resetlogs;
```

7. Switch the log files to see whether the new logs are working.

```
SQL>  alter system switch logfile;
```

8. Shut down the database.

```
SQL>  shutdown normal;
```

9. Execute `STARTUP` and `SHUTDOWN NORMAL` commands to validate that the database is functional by making sure that the alert logs after these commands are executed.

```
SQL>  startup;
SQL>  shutdown normal;
```

10. Perform a cold backup or hot backup.

If you need to recover archived logs from a different location, you can just change the `LOG_ARCHIVE_DEST` location to the new location of the archived log files. This may occur in a recovery situation in which you recover your archived logs from tape to a staging location on disk.

Performing an RMAN-Based Incomplete Recovery Using *UNTIL TIME*

In this example you will perform one type of incomplete recovery using RMAN. You will recover the database to a particular point in time. To do so, you will create a user, called TEST, and two tables with date and time data stored in them. You will then perform a database backup in ARCHIVELOG mode and recover to a time between 2:31, when the data was stored in the first table, and 3:59, when the data was stored in the second table. You accomplish all of this with the SET UNTIL TIME clause in RMAN; this clause is required to perform incomplete recovery. Thus, when the database is recovered, you should not see the second table's data. When the recovery is completed and validated, you will need to register the database in the recovery catalog. Let's walk through this example:

1. Source your ORACLE_SID to tst9, which is your target database, so that the database can be started in MOUNT or OPENED mode with SQL.

```
oracle@octilli:~ > . oraenv
ORACLE_SID = [tst9] tst9
oracle@octilli:~ >

SQL> startup mount
Oracle instance started
database mounted

Total System Global Area      75854976 bytes
Fixed Size                      279680 bytes
Variable Size                 71303168 bytes
Database Buffers               4194304 bytes

Or

SQL> startup mount
ORACLE instance started.
Total System Global Area   75854976 bytes
Fixed Size                   279680 bytes
```

```
Variable Size                          71303168 bytes
Database Buffers                        4194304 bytes
Redo Buffers                              77824 bytes
Database mounted.
SQL> alter database open;
```

2. Connect to RMAN, the target database, and the recovery catalog in one step.

```
oracle@octilli:~ > rman target / catalog rman/rman@rcat

Recovery Manager: Release 9.0.1.0.0 - Production

(c) Copyright 2001 Oracle Corporation.  All rights
reserved.

connected to target database: TST9 (DBID=1268700551)
connected to recovery catalog database

RMAN>
```

3. Create a user TEST and the two tables, which will be used throughout this example. Data will be added to the first table. The results of this data insertion can be seen in the SELECT statement.

```
SQL> create user test identified by test
     2> default tablespace users
     3> temporary tablespace temp;
Statement processed.
SQL> grant connect,resource to test;
Statement processed.
SQL> connect test/test
Connected.
SQL> create table t1 (c1 number, c2 char(50));
Statement processed.
SQL>insert into t1 values (1, to_char(sysdate,
  'HH:MI DD-MON-YYYY'));
SQL>commit;
SQL> create table t2 (c1 number, c2 char(50));
Statement processed.
```

```
SQL> connect system/manager
SQL> alter system switch logfile;
Statement processed.
SQL> select * from t1;
C1         C2
---------- ------------------------------------------
1          02:31 04-OCT-2001
1 row selected.
```

4. Back up the database.

```
RMAN> run {
2> allocate channel ch1 type disk;
3> backup database;
4> }

allocated channel: ch1
channel ch1: sid=10 devtype=DISK

Starting backup at 04-OCT-01
channel ch1: starting full datafile backupset
channel ch1: specifying datafile(s) in backupset
including current controlfile in backupset
input datafile fno=00001 name=/db01/oracle/tst9/
system01.dbf
input datafile fno=00006 name=/db01/oracle/tst9/
data01.dbf
input datafile fno=00002 name=/db01/oracle/tst9/
rbs01.dbf
input datafile fno=00003 name=/db01/oracle/tst9/
temp01.dbf
input datafile fno=00004 name=/db01/oracle/tst9/
users01.dbf
input datafile fno=00007 name=/db01/oracle/tst9/
indx01.dbf
input datafile fno=00005 name=/db01/oracle/tst9/
tools01.dbf
channel ch1: starting piece 1 at 04-OCT-01
piece handle=/oracle/product/9.0.1/dbs/02d5p88p_1_1
comment=NONE
```

```
channel ch1: backup set complete, elapsed time:
00:01:49
Finished backup at 04-OCT-01
```

5. Back up all archived log files.

```
RMAN> run {
    2> allocate channel ch1 type disk;
    3> backup
    4> format 'log_t%t_s%s_p%p'
    5> (archivelog all);
    6> }
```

6. Create the second table, `t2`, and add the date-time data to the table. This date-time is the same day, but at 3:59 in the afternoon. Assume that you have run some log switches to move the data to the archived logs.

```
SQL> connect test/test
Connected.
SQL>insert into t2 values (2, to_char(sysdate,
  'HH:MI DD-MON-YYYY'));
1 row processed.
SQL>commit;
SQL> select * from t2;
C1         C2
---------- ----------------------------------------
1          03:59 04-OCT-2001
1 row selected.
SQL> connect system/manager
SQL> alter system switch logfile;
SQL> alter system switch logfile;
```

7. Back up the archived logs to disk with the appropriate RMAN script.

```
RMAN> run {
    2> allocate channel ch1 type disk;
    3> backup
    4> format '/oracle/backups/log_t%t_s%s_p%p'
    5> (archivelog all);
    6> }
```

8. Restore the database to a point in time between 2:31 and 3:59. Then validate that you do not see the second table.

```
RMAN> run {
allocate channel ch1 type disk;
set until time 'OCT 04 2001 15:58:00';
restore database;
recover database;
sql 'alter database open resetlogs';
}

SQL> select * from t1;
C1          C2
-----------------------------------------------------
 1          02:31 04-OCT-2001
1 row selected.
SQL> select * from t2;
No rows selected.
SQL>
```

9. Once the database has been restored, it should be shut down normally. Then you should perform a startup to make sure the restore process was completed successfully.

```
SQL> shutdown
SQL> startup
```

10. Once the database has been validated, the database should be reregistered in the RMAN catalog. This must done every time there is an incomplete recovery and the `SQL 'ALTER DATABASE OPEN RESETLOGS';` command is performed. To reregister the database, you must be connected to the target database and the recovery catalog.

```
oracle@octilli:~ > rman target / catalog rman/rman@rcat

Recovery Manager: Release 9.0.1.0.0 - Production

(c) Copyright 2001 Oracle Corporation.  All rights
reserved.
```

```
connected to target database: TST9 (DBID=1268700551)
connected to recovery catalog database

RMAN> reset database;

database registered in recovery catalog
starting full resync of recovery catalog
full resync complete

RMAN>
```

A complete backup should be performed on any database that is opened with the RESETLOGS options because all previous archived logs are invalid with databases opened with these options.

Performing RMAN-Based Incomplete Recovery Using *UNTIL SEQUENCE*

In this example, you will perform another type of incomplete recovery using RMAN. You will recover the database to a particular log sequence number. To do this, you will need to use the SET UNTIL [LOGSEQ/SEQUENCE/SCN] clause to perform an incomplete recovery until a sequence point. In this example, you will recover to the log sequence just prior to a corrupt online redo log. When the recovery is completed and validated, you will need to register the database in the recovery catalog. Let's walk through this example:

1. Source ORACLE_SID to tst9, which is your target database, so that the database can be started in MOUNT or OPENED mode with SQL.

```
oracle@octilli:~ > . oraenv
ORACLE_SID = [tst9] tst9
oracle@octilli:~ >
```

```
SQL> startup mount
Oracle instance started
database mounted

Total System Global Area       75854976 bytes
Fixed Size                       279680 bytes
Variable Size                  71303168 bytes
Database Buffers                4194304 bytes


Or

SQL> startup mount
ORACLE instance started.
Total System Global Area   75854976 bytes
Fixed Size                   279680 bytes
Variable Size              71303168 bytes
Database Buffers            4194304 bytes
Redo Buffers                  77824 bytes
Database mounted.
SQL> alter database open;
```

2. Connect to RMAN, the target database, and the recovery catalog in one step.

```
oracle@octilli:~ > rman target / catalog rman/rman@rcat

Recovery Manager: Release 9.0.1.0.0 - Production

(c) Copyright 2001 Oracle Corporation.  All rights
reserved.

connected to target database: TST9 (DBID=1268700551)
connected to recovery catalog database

RMAN>
```

3. Create a user TEST and the two tables, which will be used throughout this example. Data will be added to the first table. The results of this data insertion can be seen in the SELECT statement.

```
oracle@octilli:~ > sqlplus /nolog

SQL*Plus: Release 9.0.1.0.0 - Production on Fri Oct 5
00:33:53 2001

(c) Copyright 2001 Oracle Corporation.  All rights
reserved.

SQL> connect /as sysdba
Connected.
SQL> archive log list;
Database log mode              Archive Mode
Automatic archival             Enabled
Archive destination            /oracle/admin/tst9/arch
Oldest online log sequence     262
Next log sequence to archive   264
Current log sequence           264
```

4. Back up the database and archive the log files.

```
RMAN> run {
2> allocate channel ch1 type disk;
3> backup database;
4> backup (archivelog all);
5> }

allocated channel: ch1
channel ch1: sid=9 devtype=DISK

Starting backup at 05-OCT-01
channel ch1: starting full datafile backupset
channel ch1: specifying datafile(s) in backupset
including current controlfile in backupset
input datafile fno=00001 name=/db01/oracle/tst9/
system01.dbf
```

```
input datafile fno=00006 name=/db01/oracle/tst9/
data01.dbf
input datafile fno=00002 name=/db01/oracle/tst9/
rbs01.dbf
input datafile fno=00003 name=/db01/oracle/tst9/
temp01.dbf
input datafile fno=00004 name=/db01/oracle/tst9/
users01.dbf
input datafile fno=00007 name=/db01/oracle/tst9/
indx01.dbf
input datafile fno=00005 name=/db01/oracle/tst9/
tools01.dbf
channel ch1: starting piece 1 at 05-OCT-01
channel ch1: finished piece 1 at 05-OCT-01
piece handle=/oracle/product/9.0.1/dbs/05d5petc_1_1
comment=NONE
channel ch1: backup set complete, elapsed time:
00:01:48
Finished backup at 05-OCT-01
Starting backup at 05-OCT-01
current log archived
channel ch1: starting archive log backupset
channel ch1: specifying archive log(s) in backup set
input archive log thread=1 sequence=257 recid=1
stamp=442278586
input archive log thread=1 sequence=258 recid=2
stamp=442278595
input archive log thread=1 sequence=259 recid=3
stamp=442278598
input archive log thread=1 sequence=260 recid=4
stamp=442278603
input archive log thread=1 sequence=261 recid=5
stamp=442278607
input archive log thread=1 sequence=262 recid=6
stamp=442284653
input archive log thread=1 sequence=263 recid=7
stamp=442285081
channel ch1: starting piece 1 at 05-OCT-01
channel ch1: finished piece 1 at 05-OCT-01
```

```
piece handle=/oracle/product/9.0.1/dbs/06d5pf0q_1_1
comment=NONE
channel ch1: backup set complete, elapsed time:
00:00:01
Finished backup at 05-OCT-01
released channel: ch1

RMAN>
```

5. In this case, there is a corrupt online redo log sequence number 264, so you will need to recover to log sequence number 263.

```
RMAN> run {
2> allocate channel ch1 type disk;
3> set until logseq=263 thread=1;
4> restore database;
5> recover database;
6> sql "alter database open resetlogs";
7> }

allocated channel: ch1
channel ch1: sid=11 devtype=DISK

executing command: SET until clause

Starting restore at 05-OCT-01

channel ch1: starting datafile backupset restore
channel ch1: specifying datafile(s) to restore from
backup set
restoring datafile 00001 to /db01/oracle/tst9/
system01.dbf
restoring datafile 00002 to /db01/oracle/tst9/rbs01.dbf
restoring datafile 00003 to /db01/oracle/tst9/
temp01.dbf
restoring datafile 00004 to /db01/oracle/tst9/
users01.dbf
restoring datafile 00005 to /db01/oracle/tst9/
tools01.dbf
```

```
restoring datafile 00006 to /db01/oracle/tst9/
data01.dbf
restoring datafile 00007 to /db01/oracle/tst9/
indx01.dbf
channel ch1: restored backup piece 1
piece handle=/oracle/product/9.0.1/dbs/04d5peg1_1_1
tag=null params=NULL
channel ch1: restore complete
Finished restore at 05-OCT-01

Starting recover at 05-OCT-01

starting media recovery

archive log thread 1 sequence 262 is already on disk as
file /oracle/admin/tst9/arch/archtst9_262.log
archive log filename=/oracle/admin/tst9/arch/archtst9_
262.log thread=1 sequence2
media recovery complete
Finished recover at 05-OCT-01

sql statement: alter database open resetlogs
released channel: ch1

RMAN>
```

6. Next, you can validate that the database was opened and the logs were reset, thus recovering before the corrupt log file sequence 263.

```
SQL> archive log list
Database log mode              Archive Mode
Automatic archival             Enabled
Archive destination            /oracle/admin/tst9/arch
Oldest online log sequence     0
Next log sequence to archive   1
Current log sequence           1
SQL>
```

7. Once the database has been restored, shut it down normally. Then perform a startup to make sure that the restore process was completed successfully.

```
SQL> shutdown
SQL> startup
```

8. Once the database has been validated, it should be reregistered in the RMAN catalog with the `RESET DATABASE` command. This must be done every time there is an incomplete recovery and the SQL `'ALTER DATABASE OPEN RESETLOGS';` command is performed. You must be connected to the target database and the recovery catalog.

```
oracle@octilli:~ > rman target / catalog rman/rman@rcat

Recovery Manager: Release 9.0.1.0.0 - Production

(c) Copyright 2001 Oracle Corporation.  All rights
reserved.

connected to target database: TST9 (DBID=1268700551)
connected to recovery catalog database

RMAN> reset database;

database registered in recovery catalog
starting full resync of recovery catalog
full resync complete

RMAN>
```

Summary

Incomplete recovery allows you to recover a database to before the point where the database failed, or to the last available transaction at the time of the failure. In other words, as a result of this type of recovery, the recovered database is missing transactions or is incomplete.

You might need to perform incomplete database recovery for various reasons. The type of failure that requires such a recovery might be in the database, such as a corruption error or a dropped database object. This means that recovery would need to stop short of using all the archived logs that are available to be applied. If it didn't, the failure could be reintroduced to the database as the transactions were being read from archived redo logs.

Another situation that might require an incomplete recovery is one in which your database has lost the current redo log files. Again, the reason this can only be solved with an incomplete recovery is because not all the previous transactions are available. At least one online log file is corrupted or lost.

The RMAN incomplete recovery process was also demonstrated with examples that used the `SET UNTIL TIME` and `SEQUENCE` commands.

Incomplete recovery is a key component for certain types of failure; as a result, to be properly prepared for the test you must understand this concept. In the workplace, you can use these concepts in routine maintenance activities like those in which you may be required to move databases from one server to another.

Exam Essentials

Identify the types of user-managed incomplete recovery. The three different types of user-managed incomplete recovery are cancel-based, time-based, and change-based recovery. Make sure you understand all three types.

Understand how to perform a user-managed incomplete recovery. You should know the commands that must be issued during the incomplete recovery process. These include `RECOVER DATABASE UNTIL CANCEL/TIME/CHANGE`.

Know how to perform an incomplete recovery that results from a loss of redo logs. To do this, you must know how to stop the recovery process prior to the missing or corrupt redo log. This is the only way you can recover a database that has this type of failure.

Understand how to use the RMAN `UNTIL TIME` command. In incomplete RMAN-based recovery, this command is used to stop the recovery prior to complete recovery based on a time of occurrence.

Know when to use the RMAN `UNTIL SEQUENCE` command. This command is used in incomplete RMAN-based recovery to stop the recovery before it becomes a complete recovery based on a sequence number such as log sequence, sequence, or SCN.

Key Terms

Before you take the exam, be certain you are familiar with the following terms:

cancel-based recovery

change-based recovery

incomplete recovery

`RESETLOGS`

system change number (SCN)

time-based recovery

`UNTIL CANCEL`

`UNTIL CHANGE`

`UNTIL TIME`

`V$LOG_HISTORY`

Review Questions

1. What are the three types of incomplete recovery? (Choose all that apply.)

   A. Change-based

   B. Time-based

   C. Stop-based

   D. Cancel-based

   E. Quit-based

2. Which type of incomplete recovery can be performed in NOARCHIVELOG mode?

   A. Change-based

   B. Time-based

   C. Stop-based

   D. Cancel-based

   E. None

3. You're a DBA and you have just performed an incomplete recovery. You neglected to perform a backup following the incomplete recovery. After a couple of hours of use, the database fails again due to the loss of a disk that stores some of your data files. What type of incomplete recovery can you perform?

   A. Change-based

   B. Stop-based

   C. Time-based

   D. Cancel-based

   E. None

4. What does Oracle use to uniquely identify each committed transaction in the log files?

   A. Unique transaction ID

   B. Static transaction ID

   C. System change number

   D. Serial change number

   E. Transaction change number

5. What type of recovery is necessary to execute the `ALTER DATABASE OPEN RESETLOGS` command? (Choose all that apply.)

   A. Complete recovery

   B. Incomplete recovery

   C. Cancel-based recovery

   D. Time-based recovery

6. What should be performed after the `ALTER DATABASE OPEN RESETLOGS` command has been applied?

   A. A recovery of the database

   B. A backup of the database

   C. An import of the database

   D. Nothing

7. What type of incomplete recovery gives the DBA the most control?

   A. Cancel-based

   B. Time-based

   C. Change-based

   D. All give equal control.

8. Which type of incomplete recovery gives the DBA the least control?

   A. Cancel-based

   B. Time-based

   C. Change-based

   D. All give equal control.

9. What command is used in an RMAN incomplete recovery?

   A. `SET SEQUENCE`

   B. `SET UNTIL TIME`

   C. `SET TIME`

   D. `SET CHANGE`

10. A reset command should be performed after what action in the database?

    A. The database is opened with the `RESETLOGS` option.

    B. There is a physical change to the recovery catalog.

    C. There is a physical change to the target database.

    D. The database has been completely recovered.

11. The RMAN change-based recovery has which of the following options? (Choose all that apply.)

    A. `LOGSEQ`

    B. `SEQLOG`

    C. `SEQUENCE`

    D. `SCN`

12. If you need to perform a user-managed recovery of a database and you stop the recovery before October 4th at 15:01:00, which command would be used?

    A. `SET UNTIL TIME 'OCT 04 2001 15:00:00'`

    B. `RECOVER UNTIL TIME  'OCT 04 2001 15:00:00'`

    C. `RECOVER DATABASE UNTIL TIME 'OCT 04 2001 15:00:00'`

    D. `RECOVER TABLESPACE UNTIL TIME 'OCT 04 2001 15:00:00'`

13. Which of the following situations will force an incomplete recovery?

    A. Loss of data file

    B. Corrupt data file

    C. Loss of an online redo log that has been archived

    D. Corrupt current online redo log

14. Which of the following is a common command that must be performed with all incomplete recoveries and not with complete recoveries?

    A. `RECOVER DATABASE`

    B. `RECOVER UNTIL CANCEL`

    C. `ALTER DATABASE OPEN RESETLOGS`

    D. `RESTORE DATABASE`

15. What information could be required in order for a change recovery to be performed? (Choose all that apply.)

    A. `SEQUENCE#`

    B. `FIRST_CHANGE#`

    C. `NEXT_CHANGE#`

    D. Information from `V$LOG_HISTORY`

    E. All of the above

Answers to Review Questions

1. A, B, D. Options A, B, and D all describe valid types of incomplete recovery. Options C and E are not incomplete recovery types.

2. E. Incomplete recovery cannot be performed in NOARCHIVELOG mode.

3. E. Incomplete recovery cannot be performed unless a new backup is taken after the first failure. All backups prior to an incomplete recovery are invalidated for use with any of the existing data files, control files, or redo logs.

4. C. The system change number, or SCN, uniquely identifies each committed transaction in the log files.

5. B, C, D. All forms of incomplete recovery require the use of the RESETLOGS clause during the ALTER DATABASE OPEN command. All redo logs must be reset to a new sequence number. This invalidates all prior logs to that database.

6. B. A backup of the database should be performed if the ALTER DATABASE OPEN RESETLOGS command has been applied.

7. C. Change-based recovery gives the DBA the most control of the incomplete recovery process because it allows the stopping point to be specified by the SCN number.

8. A. Cancel-based recovery applies the complete archived log before it cancels or stops the recovery process. Therefore, you cannot recover part of the transactions within the archived log as with change-based or time-based recovery.

9. B. RMAN time-based recovery applies the changes in an archived log up to the point in time reference specified in the SET UNTIL TIME command.

10. A. Anytime the database is opened with the RESETLOGS options, you will need to reset the target database in the recovery catalog.

11. A, C, D. There are three RMAN change options: `LOGSEQ`, `SEQUENCE`, and `SCN`. These are used with the `SET UNTIL` command.

12. C. The user-managed recovery of a database would be performed with the `RECOVER DATABASE UNTIL TIME 'OCT 04 2001 15:00:00'` command.

13. D. A corrupt current online redo will force an incomplete recovery because the transactions in that log will not be applied to the recovery process, and the database will need to be stopped before complete recovery by time, change, or cancel commands.

14. C. The `ALTER DATABASE OPEN RESETLOGS` command must be performed with all incomplete recoveries but it does not have to be performed with complete recoveries.

15. E. All options are information from the `V$LOG_HISTORY` view, which contain the log sequence number and SCN information.

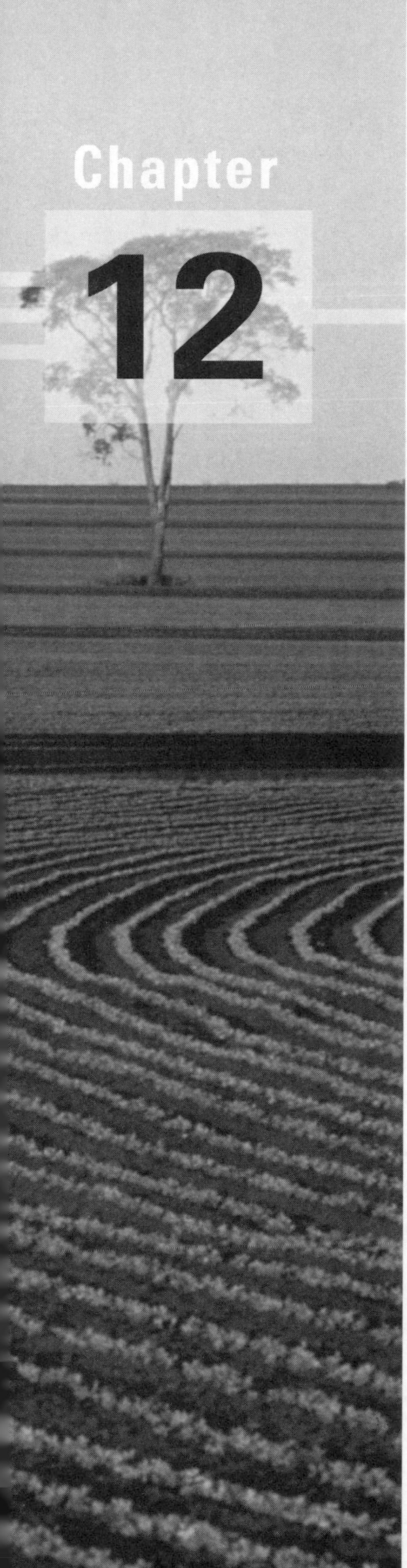

RMAN Maintenance

ORACLE9*i*: DBA FUNDAMENTALS II EXAM OBJECTIVES COVERED IN THIS CHAPTER:

- ✓ **Perform cross checking of backups and copies.**
- ✓ **Update the repository when backups have been deleted.**
- ✓ **Change the availability status of backups and copies.**
- ✓ **Make a backup or copy exempt from the retention policy.**
- ✓ **Catalog backups made with operating system commands.**

Exam objectives are subject to change at any time without prior notice and at Oracle's sole discretion. Please visit Oracle's Certification website (`http://www.oracle.com/education/certification/`) for the most current exam objectives listing.

This chapter discusses practical topics related to RMAN maintenance including recovery catalog information and information pertaining to backup media, whether disk or tape. The main emphasis of these RMAN features is on keeping the catalog synchronized with the backup media.

In addition to learning about catalog synchronization, you will become familiar with maintenance commands for multiple maintenance operations. For instance, you will learn about cross checking backups with the catalog entries, updating the catalog when you deleted a backup, changing the status of backups, and exempting a backup from the retention policy. Also, this chapter will also demonstrate how to catalog or copy OS files into the RMAN catalog.

The RMAN maintenance commands discussed in this chapter are required for testing, as well as day-to-day management of the RMAN tool. It is important that you know how to perform maintenance functions on the recovery catalog, the repository, and associated media sources so that RMAN will function properly in backup and recovery situations.

Performing Cross Checking of Backups and Copies

Cross checking backups and copies is a process that compares the recovery catalog information with the information contained on the actual media that contains the backup, such as tape or a file on disk. When cross checking is performed, there are cases in which the actual tape containing the backup is removed from the tape library and shipped off site. You can use the

CROSSCHECK command to check for this. When you use this command, notice that all of the backups are listed as available.

In the example illustrated here, we are using the disk media that contains the files, but tape media could also contain these files. In this example, the CROSSCHECK command is being used on the TST9 database. Notice the backup piece, stamp=4422842, is available here. Also note the special ALLOCATE CHANNEL FOR MAINTENANCE TYPE DISK command, which performs the CROSSCHECK command that is a maintenance activity.

```
RMAN> allocate channel for maintenance type disk;

allocated channel: ORA_MAINT_DISK_1
channel ORA_MAINT_DISK_1: sid=12 devtype=DISK

RMAN> crosscheck backup of database;

crosschecked backup piece: found to be 'AVAILABLE'
backup piece handle=/oracle/product/9.0.1/dbs/03d5pe6s_1_1
recid=2 stamp=4422842
crosschecked backup piece: found to be 'AVAILABLE'
backup piece handle=/oracle/product/9.0.1/dbs/04d5peg1_1_1
recid=3 stamp=4422846
crosschecked backup piece: found to be 'AVAILABLE'
backup piece handle=/oracle/product/9.0.1/dbs/05d5petc_1_1
recid=4 stamp=4422842
crosschecked backup piece: found to be 'AVAILABLE'
backup piece handle=/oracle/product/9.0.1/dbs/08d5rmrn_1_1
recid=7 stamp=4423588
crosschecked backup piece: found to be 'AVAILABLE'
backup piece handle=/oracle/product/9.0.1/dbs/0ad5rpmm_1_1
recid=9 stamp=4423618
crosschecked backup piece: found to be 'AVAILABLE'
backup piece handle=/oracle/product/9.0.1/dbs/0fd5rv49_1_1
recid=12 stamp=442363
crosschecked backup piece: found to be 'AVAILABLE'
backup piece handle=/oracle/product/9.0.1/dbs/0gd5rv49_1_1
recid=13 stamp=442364
```

In the next example, notice that the file that was renamed with a Unix OS command `mv` is now listed as `EXPIRED`. This means that the `EXPIRED` backup in catalog is not available on the media. Let's step through this process.

1. Rename the backup set file `03d5pe6s_1_1` to `03d5pe6s_1_1.old` so that the catalog does not recognize the filename as it is stored in the catalog database.

   ```
   oracle@octilli:/oracle/product/9.0.1/dbs > mv 03d5pe6s_
   1_1 03d5pe6s_1_1.old
   oracle@octilli:/oracle/product/9.0.1/dbs >
   ```

2. Next, reexecute the `CROSSCHECK` command and notice that the `03d5pe6s_1_1` backup set has expired.

   ```
   RMAN> crosscheck backup of database;

   crosschecked backup piece: found to be 'EXPIRED'
   backup piece handle=/oracle/product/9.0.1/dbs/03d5pe6s_
   1_1 recid=2 stamp=4422842
   crosschecked backup piece: found to be 'AVAILABLE'
   backup piece handle=/oracle/product/9.0.1/dbs/04d5peg1_
   1_1 recid=3 stamp=4422846
   crosschecked backup piece: found to be 'AVAILABLE'
   backup piece handle=/oracle/product/9.0.1/dbs/05d5petc_
   1_1 recid=4 stamp=4422842
   crosschecked backup piece: found to be 'AVAILABLE'
   backup piece handle=/oracle/product/9.0.1/dbs/08d5rmrn_
   1_1 recid=7 stamp=4423588
   crosschecked backup piece: found to be 'AVAILABLE'
   backup piece handle=/oracle/product/9.0.1/dbs/0ad5rpmm_
   1_1 recid=9 stamp=4423618
   crosschecked backup piece: found to be 'AVAILABLE'
   backup piece handle=/oracle/product/9.0.1/dbs/0fd5rv49_
   1_1 recid=12 stamp=442363
   crosschecked backup piece: found to be 'AVAILABLE'
   backup piece handle=/oracle/product/9.0.1/dbs/0gd5rv49_
   1_1 recid=13 stamp=442364

   RMAN>
   ```

Below is an example of how you would cross check a copy within the target database TST9. This is performed and functions similarly to the cross check of the backup set example that we previously went through using the CROSSCHECK BACKUP OF DATABASE command. In this case, you would use the CROSSCHECK COPY OF DATABASE command.

```
RMAN> crosscheck copy of database;

validation succeeded for datafile copy
datafile copy filename=/staging/cold/tst9/data01.dbf
recid=15 stamp=442429505

RMAN>
```

Updating the Repository When Backups Have Been Deleted

RMAN can mark a backup in the repository, which is either the recovery catalog or the control file, with a status of deleted. Remember that if you do not use the recovery catalog, the information about backups is stored in the target database's control file. Backups that have been marked in this manner will not appear in a list output when the recovery catalog is queried. RMAN uses a special command, ALLOCATE CHANNEL FOR DELETE TYPE DISK, to perform this maintenance activity. We will be using the CHANGE command and DELETE command in these examples.

This example shows the process of deleting part of a backup set and control file:

1. Designate a channel to work with the storage medium—a tape, in this example.

   ```
   RMAN> allocate channel for delete type tape;

   allocated channel: ORA_MAINT_TAPE_1
   channel ORA_MAINT_TAPE_1: sid=11 devtype=TAPE
   ```

2. Mark the backup set and a control file as deleted.

```
RMAN> change backupset 261 delete;


List of Backup Pieces
BP Key  BS Key  Pc# Cp# Status      Device Type Piece Name
------- ------- --- --- ----------- ----------- ----------
262     261     1   1   AVAILABLE   TAPE        /oracle/
product/9.0.1/dbs/02d5p1

Do you really want to delete the above objects (enter YES
or NO)? YES
deleted backup piece
backup piece handle=/oracle/product/9.0.1/dbs/02d5p88p_1_1
recid=1 stamp=4422789
```

3. When this has been done, you must release the channel so that it can be used by other jobs within RMAN.

```
RMAN> release channel;

released channel: ORA_MAINT_TAPE_1

RMAN>
```

Change the Availability Status of Backups and Copies

RMAN can mark a backup or copy as unavailable or available. This capability is used primarily to designate backups or to designate a copy that has been moved offsite or is being brought back onsite. The following example shows how a backup set can be made unavailable and can then be made available again. To do this, we will use the CHANGE, UNAVAILABLE, and AVAILABLE commands. The *CHANGE*, *UNAVAILABLE*, and *AVAILABLE* commands are used to make a backup set or copy unavailable or available in the recovery catalog. As in the previous examples, you must be connected to the target database and the recovery catalog before you can execute these commands.

1. Execute the CHANGE command to make a backup set unavailable.

```
RMAN> change backupset 283 unavailable;

changed backup piece unavailable
backup piece handle=/oracle/product/9.0.1/dbs/03d5pe6s_
1_1 recid=2 stamp=4422842
```

2. Execute the CHANGE command to make the backup set available again.

```
RMAN> change backupset 283 available;

allocated channel: ORA_DISK_1
channel ORA_DISK_1: sid=11 devtype=DISK
changed backup piece available
backup piece handle=/oracle/product/9.0.1/dbs/03d5pe6s_
1_1 recid=2 stamp=4422842

RMAN>
```

The next example shows how to make a copied file that has been cataloged unavailable. This will be done in the same manner as a backup set, but we will use the CHANGE DATAFILECOPY command.

1. First we will connect to RMAN and list all the copies in the database. Notice that column S (the status column) has a value of A for available.

```
oracle@octilli:~ > rman target / catalog rman/rman@rcat

Recovery Manager: Release 9.0.1.0.0 - Production

(c) Copyright 2001 Oracle Corporation.  All rights reserved.

connected to target database: TST9 (DBID=1268700551)
connected to recovery catalog database

RMAN> list copy of database;
```

```
List of Datafile Copies
Key     File S Completion CkpSCN Ckp Time  Name
------- ---- - ---------- ------ --------- ---------------------------
502     6    A 06-OCT-01  67540  05-OCT-01 staging/cold/tst9/data01.dbf
```

2. Next, change the data file with the CHANGE DATAFILECOPY command so that it becomes unavailable.

```
RMAN> change datafilecopy '/staging/cold/tst9/
data01.dbf' unavailable;

changed datafile copy unvailable
datafile copy filename=/staging/cold/tst9/data01.dbf
recid=15 stamp=442429505
```

3. Then use the LIST command to show that the copy is unavailable. This status (U for unavailable) can be seen in the S column.

```
RMAN> list copy of database;


List of Datafile Copies
Key     File S Completion CkpSCN Ckp Time  Name
------- ---- - ---------- ------ --------- ---------------------------
502     6    U 06-OCT-01  67540  05-OCT-01 staging/cold/tst9/data01.dbf

RMAN>
```

4. Now you can make the file available again by using the following command:

```
RMAN> change datafilecopy '/staging/cold/tst9/
data01.dbf' available;

allocated channel: ORA_DISK_1
channel ORA_DISK_1: sid=18 devtype=DISK
changed datafile copy available
datafile copy filename=/staging/cold/tst9/data01.dbf
recid=15 stamp=442429505
```

5. Now verify that the file is available. Again, notice the S column has a value of A.

```
RMAN> list copy of database;


List of Datafile Copies
Key     File S Completion CkpSCN Ckp Time  Name
------- ---- - ---------- ------ --------  ----------------------------
502     6    A 06-OCT-01  67540  05-OCT-01 staging/cold/tst9/data01.dbf

RMAN>
```

Make a Backup or Copy Exempt from the Retention Policy

To make a backup or copy that is excluded from the tape retention policy, you must perform certain RMAN commands. These commands involve the use of the CONFIGURATION parameters that can be seen in the examples below. *CONFIGURATION parameters* are similar to OS environment variables or settings, but these parameters are used for RMAN settings. These settings are used by all RMAN connections by default.

1. First, you must know what the RMAN configuration parameters are set to. You can do this by executing the SHOW ALL command.

```
RMAN> show all;

RMAN configuration parameters are:
CONFIGURE RETENTION POLICY TO REDUNDANCY 1; # default
CONFIGURE BACKUP OPTIMIZATION OFF; # default
CONFIGURE DEFAULT DEVICE TYPE TO DISK; # default
CONFIGURE CONTROLFILE AUTOBACKUP OFF; # default
CONFIGURE CONTROLFILE AUTOBACKUP FORMAT FOR DEVICE TYPE
DISK TO '%F'; # default
CONFIGURE DEVICE TYPE DISK PARALLELISM 1; # default
```

```
CONFIGURE DATAFILE BACKUP COPIES FOR DEVICE TYPE DISK
TO 1; # default
CONFIGURE ARCHIVELOG BACKUP COPIES FOR DEVICE TYPE DISK
TO 1; # default
CONFIGURE MAXSETSIZE TO UNLIMITED; # default
CONFIGURE SNAPSHOT CONTROLFILE NAME TO '/oracle/
product/9.0.1/dbs/snapcf_tst9.ft

RMAN>
```

2. Next, you should set the retention policy to a number of days. We will arbitarily set the retention to 10 days for this example. In real life, this value would be agreed upon by the IT management. The results of this assignment mean that the recovery catalog keeps backups for only 10 days. To set the retention policy, you will use the `CONFIGURE RETENTION POLICY TO RECOVERY WINDOW OF` *`N`* `DAYS` configuration setting.

```
RMAN> CONFIGURE RETENTION POLICY TO RECOVERY WINDOW OF
10 DAYS;

new RMAN configuration parameters:
CONFIGURE RETENTION POLICY TO RECOVERY WINDOW OF 10
DAYS;
new RMAN configuration parameters are successfully
stored
starting full resync of recovery catalog
full resync complete
```

3. Next, you should create a backup using the `KEEP` command. The `KEEP` command uses a defined time period or forever. In this example, we will use a set date or time of 01-DEC-02. This means that the database and logs will not expire until this date is reached even if the retention policy is set for only 10 days.

```
RMAN> run {
2> allocate channel c1 type disk;
3> backup database keep until time '01-DEC-02' logs;
4> backup (archivelog all) ;
5> release channel c1;
6> }
```

```
allocated channel: c1
channel c1: sid=9 devtype=DISK

Starting backup at 10-OCT-02
backup will be obsolete on date 01-DEC-02
archived logs required to recover from this backup will
expire when this backups
channel c1: starting full datafile backupset
channel c1: specifying datafile(s) in backupset
including current controlfile in backupset
input datafile fno=00001 name=/db01/oracle/tst9/
system01.dbf
input datafile fno=00006 name=/db01/oracle/tst9/
data01.dbf
input datafile fno=00002 name=/db01/oracle/tst9/
rbs01.dbf
input datafile fno=00008 name=/db01/oracle/tst9/
data02.dbf
input datafile fno=00003 name=/db01/oracle/tst9/
temp01.dbf
input datafile fno=00004 name=/db01/oracle/tst9/
users01.dbf
input datafile fno=00007 name=/db01/oracle/tst9/
indx01.dbf
input datafile fno=00005 name=/db01/oracle/tst9/
tools01.dbf
channel c1: starting piece 1 at 10-OCT-02
channel c1: finished piece 1 at 10-OCT-02
piece handle=/oracle/product/9.0.1/dbs/0hd68u54_1_1
comment=NONE
channel c1: backup set complete, elapsed time: 00:01:58
Finished backup at 10-OCT-02

Starting backup at 10-OCT-01
current log archived
channel c1: starting archive log backupset
channel c1: specifying archive log(s) in backup set
```

```
input archive log thread=1 sequence=1 recid=8
stamp=442361669
input archive log thread=1 sequence=2 recid=9
stamp=442361872
input archive log thread=1 sequence=3 recid=10
stamp=442362056
input archive log thread=1 sequence=4 recid=11
stamp=442362297
input archive log thread=1 sequence=5 recid=12
stamp=442362415
input archive log thread=1 sequence=6 recid=13
stamp=442792220
channel c1: starting piece 1 at 10-OCT-02
channel c1: finished piece 1 at 10-OCT-02
piece handle=/oracle/product/9.0.1/dbs/0id68u8u_1_1
comment=NONE
channel c1: backup set complete, elapsed time: 00:00:01
Finished backup at 10-OCT-02

released channel: c1

RMAN>
```

Real World Scenario

Multiple Backups Types on Your Tapes

Your tape backup device could be supporting multiple backups that may include both RMAN-based and normal filesystem backups. Most automated tape libraries (ATLs) and the software associated with them support filesystem backups as well as RMAN backups. This means that you could have each type of backup on a tape, especially because digital linear tapes (DLTs) will support large storage volumes—from 40–200 gigabytes per tape—which means that filesystem backups and RMAN backups could be interspersed on a single tape.

> You should be cognizant of this possibility. First of all, make sure that the tape cycle your organization uses supports the requirements of both the backup filesystem and RMAN that are needed for the longest period of time. For example, filesystem backups are needed for only one week—until the next complete filesystem backup is taken on the weekend. But some RMAN backups may be needed for up to a month in order to support business requirements. As a result, in this situation, you should store all the tapes for up to a month.

Catalog Backups Made with Operating System Commands

RMAN can catalog or store information in the catalog about OS-based backups. In a traditional hot backup, you would use the `ALTER TABLESPACE BEGIN BACKUP` command to do this. Then you would perform a `cp` command in Unix to copy the file to another place on the disk. This new location is then cataloged in RMAN. *Cataloging* means that the information in the recovery catalog is stored. Below is an example of how the `data01.dbf` data file is cataloged. This can be done for an entire database similar to how it is done for a user-managed backup.

1. Make a copy of the `data01.dbf` data file to a backup location.

```
oracle@octilli:~ > cp /db01/ORACLE/tst9/data01.dbf
   /staging/data01.dbf
```

2. Connect to the target database and recovery catalog.

```
oracle@octilli:~ > rman target / catalog rman/rman@rcat
```

3. Store the data file in the recovery catalog by executing the `CATALOG DATAFILECOPY` command.

```
RMAN> catalog datafilecopy '/staging/cold/tst9/
data01.dbf';

cataloged datafile copy
datafile copy filename=/staging/cold/tst9/data01.dbf
recid=15 stamp=442429505
RMAN>
```

Now that you have cataloged the file in the RMAN repository, you can query the repository with a variation of the LIST command. This LIST command will view all the cataloged information for the target database.

```
RMAN> list copy of database;

List of Datafile Copies
Key     File S Completion CkpSCN Ckp Time  Name
------- ---- - ---------- ------ --------  ----------------------------
502     6    A 06-OCT-01  67540  05-OCT-01 staging/cold/tst9/data01.dbf

RMAN>
```

Summary

In this chapter, we have demonstrated multiple RMAN maintenance commands and the uses of these commands. Essentially, they are used to keep your tape or disk backups synchronized with your catalog.

We also demonstrated how to perform RMAN maintenance operations that cross check catalog entries with the actual backup media, update the catalog for a deleted backup, change the status of backups and copies, and exempt a backup from the retention policy.

In addition, we noted special channel commands for maintenance operations and cataloged non-RMAN files, such as database data files, within the RMAN catalog.

RMAN maintenance commands are required for testing but are essential when you are trying to manage the RMAN environment in the workplace. This chapter is full of many commands that are used to perform such maintenance activities. Make sure that you understand the command syntax and how to use them. When you understand all of this, you should be comfortable when you are confronted with the problems that present themselves on the test and in the workplace.

Exam Essentials

Know how to cross check backups and copies. Cross checking compares the actual media (tape or disk) that contains the backups with the recovery catalog. The available and expired backup piece indicates that the cross check did or did not find a match between the catalog and media.

Update the repository when backups have been deleted. The commands that you must issue to update the repository when backups have been deleted include the `CHANGE BACKUPSET` *n* `DELETE` command, among others. You should also understand that the repository of backup information is the recovery catalog database if it is being used, and if it isn't, the repository is the target database's control file.

Be able to change the availability status of backups. The commands that you must issue to update the repository when backups have been deleted include `CHANGE BACKUPSET` *n* `UNAVAILABLE` and `CHANGE BACKUPSET` *n* `AVAILABLE`.

Be able to change the availability status of copies. The commands that you must issue to update the repository when copies have been deleted are `CHANGE DATAFILECOPY` *n* `UNAVAILABLE` and `CHANGE DATAFILECOPY` *n* `AVAILABLE`.

Make a backup or copy exempt from the retention policy. To make a backup or copy exempt, you will need to understand how commands such as `BACKUP DATABASE KEEP UNTIL TIME 'DATE TIME STAMP' LOGS` can be used to override configuration settings such as `CONFIGURE RETENTION POLICY TO RECOVERY WINDOW OF` *n* `DAYS`.

Catalog backups made with operating system commands. You should be able to catalog OS files into the database by using the `CATALOG DATAFILECOPY '/location/filename'` command.

Key Terms

Before you take the exam, be certain you are familiar with the following terms:

`AVAILABLE`	`CONFIGURATION` parameters
cataloging (`CATALOG` command)	cross checking (`CROSSCHECK` command)
`CHANGE`	`UNAVAILABLE`

Review Questions

1. The RMAN CROSSCHECK command requires the use of which of the following?
   A. Recovery catalog
   B. RMAN repository only
   C. Standard channel allocation
   D. Allocated channel for restore

2. What type of channel gets allocated for the CROSSCHECK command?
   A. c1
   B. t1
   C. MAINTENANCE
   D. Only sbt_tape

3. The CROSSCHECK command can only be performed on what type of backups? (Choose all that apply.)
   A. Backup pieces only
   B. Backup sets
   C. Copies
   D. Backup sets only

4. Which command is used to remove backup sets and copies from the recovery catalog?
   A. REMOVE
   B. UNAVAILBLE
   C. DELETE
   D. MARK UNSUABLE

5. What channel type is required for using the DELETE command?

A. DELETE

B. c1

C. MAINTENANCE

D. t1

6. The CHANGE AVAILABILITY command can be used on what type of backups? (Choose all that apply.)

A. Copies

B. User-managed backups

C. Backup sets

D. Cataloged backups

7. What is the status of an unavailable backup?

A. Unavailable

B. Deleted

C. U

D. UA

8. The RMAN retention policy is known as what?

A. Command

B. Report

C. List

D. CONFIGURATION parameter

9. The retention policy can be bypassed by what command?

   A. EXTEND

   B. KEEP

   C. EXEMPT

   D. UNLIMITED

10. What is the term for recording non-RMAN backup in the RMAN repository?

    A. OS file copies

    B. Backup sets

    C. Backup pieces

    D. Catalog backups

11. When a backup set is made unavailable, what commands must be used?

    A. CHANGE and UNAVAILABLE

    B. SET and UNAVAILABLE

    C. MAKE and UNAVALIBLE

    D. CHANGE and REMOVE

12. In order to delete a backup from disk, you must perform which of the following commands?

    A. ALLOCATE CHANNEL FOR REMOVE TYPE DISK

    B. ALLOCATE CHANNEL FOR DELETE TYPE DISK

    C. ALLOCATE CHANNEL FOR UNAVAILABLE TYPE DISK

    D. ALLOCATE CHANNEL TO DELETE TYPE DISK

13. Which of the following commands will set the retention policy for 7 days within RMAN?

    A. `CONFIGURE RETENTION POLICY TO RECOVERY PERIOD OF 7 DAYS;`

    B. `CONFIGURE RETENTION POLICY TO RECOVERY WINDOW OF 7 DAYS;`

    C. `CONFIGURE RETENTION POLICY TO RECOVERY TIME OF 7 DAYS;`

    D. `CONFIGURE RETENTION POLICY TO RECOVERY TIMEFRAME OF 7 DAYS;`

14. Which of the following commands will display the retention policy?

    A. `show retention plan`

    B. `display all`

    C. `show all`

    D. `display retention plan`

15. Which of the following commands will allow you to identify if the availability of a data file copy has changed?

    A. `LIST COPY OF DATABASE AVAILABILITY`

    B. `LIST COPY OF DATABASE`

    C. `LIST COPY OF AVAILABILITY`

    D. `LIST BACKUP OF AVAILBILITY`

Answers to Review Questions

1. A. The CROSSCHECK command requires the use of a recovery catalog. This is the backup information that must be checked with the recovery catalog to compare to the tape or disk media where the actual backups are stored.

2. C. The channel that gets allocated for CROSSCHECK command is a special channel for maintenance only. c1 and t1 are simply names of the channel devices.

3. B, C. The CROSSCHECK command can perform both backup sets and copies.

4. B. The DELETE command removes backup sets and copies for the catalog.

5. A. The allocate channel for delete is necessary when using the DELETE command. c1 and t1 are names of the channel devices.

6. A, C, D. The CHANGE AVAILABILITY command can be used on backup sets, copies, and cataloged backups that are file copies.

7. C. The status of unavailable is seen in the list command output and is U.

8. D. The retention policy is a parameter known as a CONFIGURATION parameter. There are many other configuration parameters.

9. B. The RMAN KEEP command causes backups to bypass or outlast a retention policy.

10. D. A catalog backup is a file that is backed up for an OS or a user-managed backup.

11. A. The command to make a backup set unavailable is CHANGE BACKUPSET <*backupset_number*> UNAVAILBLE.

12. B. The `ALLOCATE CHANNEL FOR DELETE TYPE DISK` command will allocate what is necessary before you can delete a backup within RMAN.

13. B. The correct command is `CONFIGURE RETENTION POLICY TO RECOVERY WINDOW OF 7 DAYS`. The other options are invalid syntax for the configuration parameters.

14. C. The `show all` command will display all configuration parameters in RMAN. One of these configuration parameters is the retention policy.

15. B. The `LIST COPY OF DATABASE` command will show status of A for available and U for unavailable.

Recovery Catalog Creation and Maintenance

ORACLE9*i*: DBA FUNDAMENTALS II EXAM OBJECTIVES COVERED IN THIS CHAPTER:

- ✓ **Describe the contents of the recovery catalog.**
- ✓ **Create the recovery catalog.**
- ✓ **Maintain the recovery catalog by using RMAN commands.**
- ✓ **Use RMAN to register, resynchronize, and reset a database.**
- ✓ **Query the recovery catalog to generate reports and lists.**
- ✓ **Create, store, and run scripts.**
- ✓ **Describe methods for backing up and recovering the recovery catalog.**

Exam objectives are subject to change at any time without prior notice and at Oracle's sole discretion. Please visit Oracle's Certification website (`http://www.oracle.com/education/certification/`) for the most current exam objectives listing.

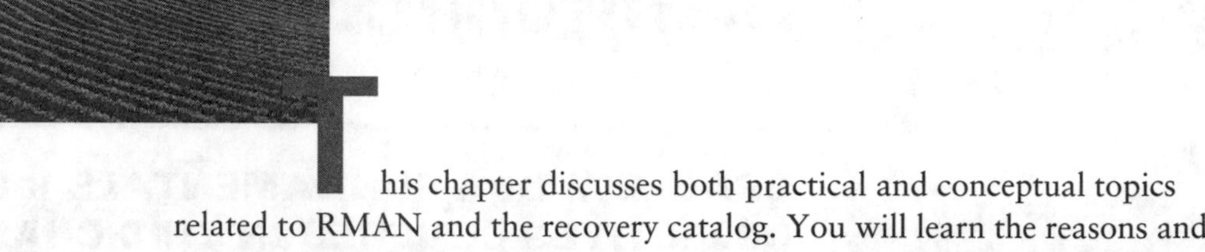

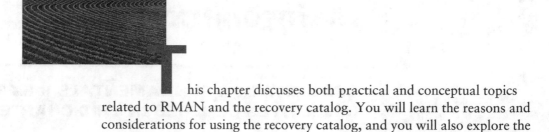

This chapter discusses both practical and conceptual topics related to RMAN and the recovery catalog. You will learn the reasons and considerations for using the recovery catalog, and you will also explore the components that make up this catalog.

This chapter focuses on the practical aspects of the recovery catalog, such as installation and configuration. You will use the RMAN commands introduced in this chapter to manage and maintain the recovery catalog, and you will learn how to create the reports and lists that provide information about the backup process. You will also work with scripts to perform assorted backup tasks and activities, similar to what you have already done with the OS hot and cold backup scripts. However, the scripts in this chapter are executed within the RMAN utility.

The topics covered in this chapter will all be required in both testing and real-world situations. The recovery catalog is a key component and allows for complete functionality of RMAN. Understanding how this information can be stored and utilized is key to performing well on the test and getting the most of RMAN in the workplace.

Considerations for Using the Recovery Catalog

Your decision to use the *recovery catalog* is one of the most significant decisions you make when you are using RMAN. The recovery catalog provides many more backup and recovery functions than using the target database's control file as the RMAN repository. For this reason, when you are using RMAN, Oracle recommends that you use the recovery catalog whenever possible.

The main considerations regarding the use of the recovery catalog are as follows:

- Some functionality is not supported unless the recovery catalog exists.
- You should create a separate catalog database.
- You must administer the catalog database like any other database in areas such as data growth and stored database objects such as scripts.
- You must back up the catalog database.
- You must determine whether you will keep each target database in a separate recovery catalog within a database.

Oracle recommends that you use the recovery catalog unless the process of maintaining and creating the catalog database requires too many resources for a site. (Any site that has an experienced and qualified DBA and system administrator should be able to maintain and create the catalog database.) If the database is small and not critical, however, using RMAN without the recovery catalog is acceptable and has been improved from previous Oracle versions.

You should store the recovery catalog on a separate server and filesystem than the one on which you store the target databases it is responsible for backing up. This prevents failures on the target database server and filesystem from affecting the recovery catalog for backup and recovery purposes.

Figure 13.1 shows the recovery catalog's association with the whole RMAN backup process.

FIGURE 13.1 RMAN utility interacting with the recovery catalog

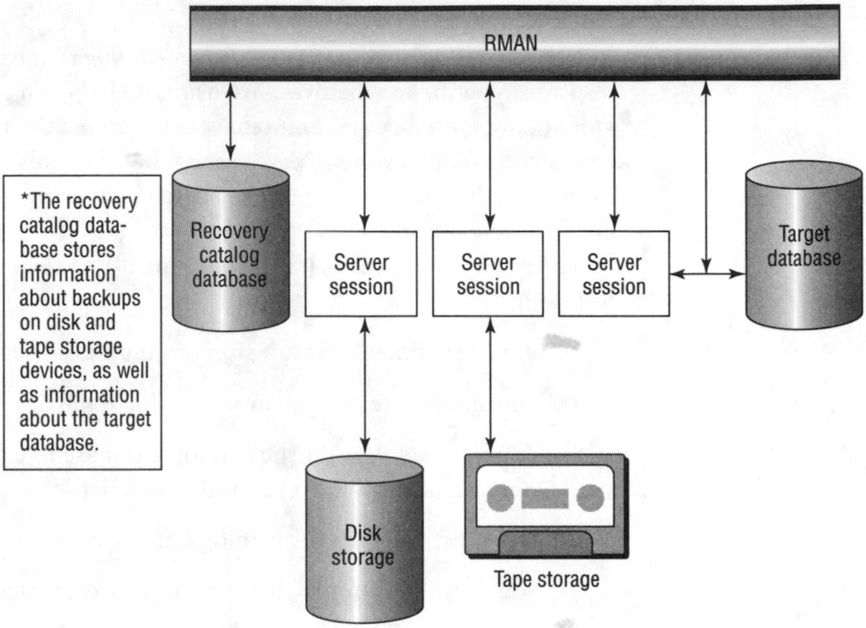

The Components of Recovery Catalog

The main components of the RMAN recovery catalog support the logging of the backup and recovery information in the catalog. This information is stored within tables, views, and other databases objects within an Oracle database. Backups are compressed for optimal storage.

Here is a list of the components contained in a recovery catalog:

- Backup and recovery information that is logged for long-term use from the target databases
- RMAN scripts that can be stored and reused
- Backup information about data files and archived logs
- Information about the physical makeup, or schema, of the target database

Creating a Recovery Catalog

As noted earlier, the *recovery catalog* is an optional feature of RMAN. The catalog is similar to the standard database catalog, in that it stores information about the recovery process as the database catalog stores information about the database.

RMAN can be run without the catalog. For this reason, the recovery catalog must be stored in its own database, preferably on a server other than the server where the target database resides. To enable the catalog, an account with CONNECT, RESOURCE, and RECOVERY_CATALOG_OWNER privileges must be created to hold the catalog tables. After this is done, the catalog creation script command must be executed as the database user RMAN connected to the RMAN utility.

Let's walk through the steps to create the recovery catalog. This example assumes that you have already built a database called `rcat` in which you plan to store the recovery catalog.

1. First, you must select the database where the recovery catalog will reside. This is not the target database. In this case, this RMAN database is being called `rcat`. In this situation, you will be using the `oraenv` shell script (provided by Oracle) to switch to other databases on the same server.

```
oracle@octilli:/oracle/product/9.0.1/bin > . oraenv
ORACLE_SID = [rcat] ?
oracle@octilli:/oracle/product/9.0.1/bin >
```

2. After you have completed the preceding step, you will need to create the user that will store the catalog. To do this, use the name RMAN with the password RMAN. Make DATA the default tablespace and TEMP the temporary tablespace.

```
oracle@octilli:~ > sqlplus /nolog

SQL*Plus: Release 9.0.1.0.0 - Production on Sat Sep 29
14:21:01 2001

(c) Copyright 2001 Oracle Corporation.  All rights
reserved.
```

```
SQL> connect /as sysdba
Connected.
SQL>
SQL> create user rman identified by rman
    2> default tablespace data
    3> temporary tablespace temp;
Statement processed.
```

3. Grant the appropriate permissions to the RMAN user.

```
SQL> grant connect,resource,recovery_catalog_owner
  to rman;
Statement processed.
SQL>
```

4. Then launch the RMAN tool.

```
oracle@octilli:/oracle/product/9.0.1/bin > rman

Recovery Manager: Release 9.0.1.0.0 - Production

(c) Copyright 2001 Oracle Corporation.  All rights
reserved.
```

5. Connect to the catalog with the user called RMAN that you created in step 2.

```
RMAN> connect catalog rman/rman

connected to recovery catalog database
recovery catalog is not installed
```

6. Finally, you can create the catalog by executing the following command and specifying the tablespace in which you want to store the catalog.

```
RMAN> create catalog tablespace data;

recovery catalog created

RMAN>
```

Oracle recommends the following space requirements for RMAN in tablespaces for one-year growth in the recovery catalog database: system tablespace, 90MB; rollback tablespace, 5MB; temp tablespace, 5MB; and the recovery catalog tablespace, 15MB.

Use RMAN Commands to Maintain the Recovery Catalog

There are multiple RMAN commands that will help you maintain the recovery catalog:

CROSSCHECK Identifies the differences between the catalog and the actual files on the media—either disk or tape.

DELETE Removes any file with which the `LIST` or `CROSSCHECK` command can operate.

DELETE EXPIRED Removes records of expired backups from the recovery catalog.

DELETE INPUT Used in conjunction with the `BACKUP` command in situations in which you have multiple archive destinations. If this is the case, then one archived log is copied and the other destinations are deleted.

CHANGE/KEEP/NOKEEP Alter the length of time you will keep a backup so that you can bypass a retention policy for a special backup.

Using RMAN to Register, Resynchronize, and Reset the Database

There are three other RMAN commands that perform initial setup and configuration operations on the recovery catalog. Essentially, these commands are less frequently used maintenance commands. These commands fall into these categories:

- Registering and unregistering the target database
- Resetting the recovery catalog
- Resynchronizing the recovery catalog

You should be familiar with these setup and configuration categories and the associated commands.

Registering and Unregistering the Target Database

Registering the target database is required so that RMAN can store information about the target database in the recovery catalog. This is the information that RMAN uses to properly back up the database.

Here is an example of registering a target database:

```
oracle@octilli:~ > rman target / catalog rman/rman@rcat

oracle@octilli:~ > . oraenv
ORACLE_SID = [tst9] ? orc9
oracle@octilli:~ > rman target / catalog rman/rman@rcat

Recovery Manager: Release 9.0.1.0.0 - Production

(c) Copyright 2001 Oracle Corporation.  All rights
reserved.

connected to target database: ORC9 (DBID=3960695)
connected to recovery catalog database

RMAN> register database;

database registered in recovery catalog
starting full resync of recovery catalog
full resync complete

RMAN>
```

By *unregistering* the target database, you remove the information necessary to back up the database. This task is not performed in the RMAN utility; instead, it is performed by executing a stored procedure as the recovery catalog's schema owner.

Here is an example of how you would unregister a target database:

1. You must get the DB_ID and DB_KEY values in the DB table that reside in the Recovery Manager catalog.

```
oracle@octilli:~ > sqlplus rman/rman@rcat

SQL*Plus: Release 9.0.1.0.0 - Production on Sat Oct 6
22:42:08 2001

(c) Copyright 2001 Oracle Corporation.  All rights
reserved.


Connected to:
Oracle9i Enterprise Edition Release 9.0.1.0.0 -
Production
With the Partitioning option
JServer Release 9.0.1.0.0 - Production

SQL> select * from db;

    DB_KEY      DB_ID HIGH_CONF_RECID CURR_DBINC_KEY
---------- ---------- --------------- --------------
       504    3960695               0            505

SQL>
```

2. Then you must run the stored procedure with these values.

```
SQL> execute dbms_
rcvcat.unregisterdatabase(504,3960695);

PL/SQL procedure successfully completed.
```

3. Finally, you can validate that there is no value in the DB table referencing the database.

```
SQL> select * from db;

no rows selected

SQL>
```

Resetting the Recovery Catalog

Resetting the recovery catalog enables RMAN to work with a database that has been opened with the ALTER DATABASE OPEN RESETLOGS command. When you use this command, you cause RMAN to make what is called a new incarnation of the target database. An *incarnation* of the target database is a new reference of the database in the recovery catalog. This incarnation is marked as the current reference for the target database, and all future backups are associated with this incarnation.

Here is an example of how you would connect to the target database and recovery catalog and then reset the database:

```
oracle@octilli:~ > rman target / catalog rman/rman@rcat

Recovery Manager: Release 8.1.5.0.0 - Production

connected to target database:
  TST9 (DBID=2058500149)
connected to recovery catalog database

RMAN> reset database;

compiling command: reset
executing command: reset
```

Real World Scenario

Making Sure a New Incarnation Is Recognized

You have just moved a monthly refresh of the production database to the test server. This is a typical process that a lot of organizations follow so that the developers have fresh data with which to develop new code. The database will be named "test," which is the same name as that of the previous database on the test server.

After the new copy of the test database is operational, you need to make sure that the database is backed up so that none of the developers' work is lost. To do this, you initiate the RMAN backup script for the test database and find that the database cannot be found in the recovery catalog, even though the name and physical structure of the database is the same as it was before you performed the refresh.

The RMAN catalog recognizes that this test database named "test" is a new incarnation and that it is uniquely identified in the recovery catalog. This is because this database was opened with the RESETLOGS option. This database must be reset with the RESET command so that it can be properly recognized as a new incarnation in the recovery catalog. At this point, you can see the difference between the recovery catalog of the old test database and the one of the new test database that was refreshed. As a result, the recovery catalog backup information will not be confused between these databases.

Resynchronizing the Recovery Catalog

Resynchronizing the recovery catalog enables RMAN to compare the control file of the target database to the information stored in the recovery catalog and to update the recovery catalog appropriately. This *resynchronization* can be full or partial. A *partial resynchronization* does not update the recovery catalog with any physical information, such as data files, tablespaces, and redo logs. A *full resynchronization* captures all the previously mentioned physical information plus the changed records. This process also occurs when a backup takes place.

Here is an example of how you would connect to the target database and recovery catalog and then resynchronize the database:

1. Make a physical change to the target database by adding a new data file to the DATA tablespace.

```
oracle@octilli:~ > sqlplus /nolog

SQL*Plus: Release 9.0.1.0.0 - Production on Tue Oct 9
17:52:19 2001

(c) Copyright 2001 Oracle Corporation.  All rights
reserved.

SQL> connect /as sysdba
Connected.
SQL> ALTER TABLESPACE  DATA   ADD
    DATAFILE '/db01/oracle/tst9/data02.dbf' SIZE 20M
```

2. Next, connect to RMAN and resynchronize the catalog to reflect this change.

```
oracle@octilli:~ > rman target / catalog rman/rman@rcat

Recovery Manager: Release 8.1.5.0.0 - Production

connected to target database:
  TST9 (DBID=2058500149)
connected to recovery catalog database

RMAN> resync catalog;

starting full resync of recovery catalog
full resync complete

RMAN>
```

3. Now run a report to view the changes to the TST9 database. Notice the new data file `data02.dbf`, which is the eighth data file in the report.

```
RMAN> report schema;

Report of database schema
File K-bytes    Tablespace           RB segs Datafile Name
---- ---------- -------------------- ------- -------------------
1        204800 SYSTEM               YES     /db01/oracle/tst9/system01.dbf
2         40960 RBS                  YES     /db01/oracle/tst9/rbs01.dbf
3         10240 TEMP                 NO      /db01/oracle/tst9/temp01.dbf
4         10240 USERS                NO      /db01/oracle/tst9/users01.dbf
5          5120 TOOLS                NO      /db01/oracle/tst9/tools01.dbf
6         51200 DATA                 NO      /db01/oracle/tst9/data01.dbf
7         10240 INDX                 NO      /db01/oracle/tst9/indx01.dbf
8         20480 DATA                 NO      /db01/oracle/tst9/data02.dbf

RMAN>
```

Generating Lists and Reports from the Recovery Catalog

RMAN has two types of commands (list and report) that you can use to access the recovery catalog so that you can see the status of what you may need to back up, copy, or restore, as well as general information about your target database. Each of these commands is performed from within the RMAN utility.

Using List Commands

List commands query the recovery catalog or control file to determine which backups or copies are available. These commands provide the most basic information from the recovery catalog. The information generated is mainly what has been done up to this point in time; from this, you can determine what is available or not available.

There are some new features and capabilities that have been added to the list commands in the RMAN version that is compatible with Oracle9*i*. These features improve the output by adding greater information, such as backup sets and the contents of backup sets (backup pieces and files). This new set of features is included in the LIST BACKUP command.

There are also two new list commands in Oracle9*i*. The first is LIST BACKUP BY FILE. This shows the output of the backup sets and copies by file types. The file type listings are grouped by data file, archived log, and control file. The second new command is LIST BACKUP SUMMARY; this causes a summarized version of all RMAN backups to appear.

In each of the three examples below, you must first connect to the target database and recovery catalog using some variation of the LIST command. The first example displays the incarnation of the database. This listing shows when the database was registered in the recovery catalog. Again, you must first connect to the target database and the recovery catalog.

```
oracle@octilli:~ > rman target / catalog rman/rman@rcat

RMAN> list incarnation of database;


List of Database Incarnations
DB Key  Inc Key DB Name  DB ID            CUR Reset SCN  Reset Time
------- ------- -------- ---------------- --- ---------- ----------
1       2       TST9     1268700551       NO  1          03-OCT-01
1       358     TST9     1268700551       YES 66901      05-OCT-01

RMAN>
```

The next example lists the DATA tablespace backups that have occurred in the database. This listing shows when the DATA tablespace was last backed up. Again, you must first connect to the target database and recovery catalog.

```
oracle@octilli:~ >  rman target /catalog rman/rman@rcat

RMAN> list backup of tablespace data;


List of Backup Sets
===================
```

```
BS Key  Type LV Size       Device Type Elapsed Time Completion Time
------- ---- -- ---------- ----------- ------------ ---------------
446     Full    200K       DISK        00:01:42     05-OCT-01
        BP Key: 447   Status: AVAILABLE   Tag:
        Piece Name: /oracle/product/9.0.1/dbs/0ad5rpmm_1_1
  List of Datafiles in backup set 446
  File LV Type Ckp SCN    Ckp Time  Name
  ---- -- ---- ---------- --------- ----
  6       Full 66989      05-OCT-01 /db01/oracle/tst9/data01.dbf

BS Key  Type LV Size       Device Type Elapsed Time Completion Time
------- ---- -- ---------- ----------- ------------ ---------------
488     Full    104K       DISK        00:00:40     05-OCT-01
        BP Key: 490   Status: AVAILABLE   Tag:
        Piece Name: /oracle/product/9.0.1/dbs/0fd5rv49_1_1
  List of Datafiles in backup set 488
  File LV Type Ckp SCN    Ckp Time  Name
  ---- -- ---- ---------- --------- ----
  6       Full 67092      05-OCT-01 /db01/oracle/tst9/data01.dbf

RMAN>
```

Finally, this example lists the full database backups that have occurred in the database. This listing shows when the full database was last backed up. Again, you must first connect to the target database and recovery catalog. This command assumes that you are already connected to the target database and recovery catalog.

```
oracle@octilli:~ > rman target / catalog rman/rman@rcat

RMAN> list backup of database;

List of Backup Sets
===================
```

```
BS Key  Type LV Size       Device Type Elapsed Time Completion Time
------- ---- -- ---------- ----------- ------------ ---------------
261     Full    115M       DISK        00:01:42     04-OCT-01
        BP Key: 262   Status: AVAILABLE   Tag:
        Piece Name: /oracle/product/9.0.1/dbs/02d5p88p_1_1
  List of Datafiles in backup set 261
  File LV Type Ckp SCN    Ckp Time  Name
  ---- -- ---- ---------- --------- ----
  1       Full 66671      04-OCT-01 /db01/oracle/tst9/system01.dbf
  2       Full 66671      04-OCT-01 /db01/oracle/tst9/rbs01.dbf
  3       Full 66671      04-OCT-01 /db01/oracle/tst9/temp01.dbf
  4       Full 66671      04-OCT-01 /db01/oracle/tst9/users01.dbf
  5       Full 66671      04-OCT-01 /db01/oracle/tst9/tools01.dbf
  6       Full 66671      04-OCT-01 /db01/oracle/tst9/data01.dbf
  7       Full 66671      04-OCT-01 /db01/oracle/tst9/indx01.dbf
```

Using Report Commands

Report commands provide more detailed information from the recovery catalog and are used for more sophisticated purposes than list commands are. Reports can provide information about what should be done. Some uses of reports include determining what database files need to be backed up or what database files have been recently backed up. Let's walk through some examples of report queries.

The first example displays all the physical structures that make up the database. This report is used for determining every structure that should be backed up when you are performing a full database backup. Again, you must first connect to the target database and recovery catalog before running any report.

```
RMAN> report schema;

Report of database schema
```

```
File K-bytes    Tablespace     RB segs Datafile Name
---- ---------- -------------- ------- -------------------
1        204800 SYSTEM          YES     /db01/oracle/tst9/system01.dbf
2         40960 RBS             YES     /db01/oracle/tst9/rbs01.dbf
3         10240 TEMP            NO      /db01/oracle/tst9/temp01.dbf
4         10240 USERS           NO      /db01/oracle/tst9/users01.dbf
5          5120 TOOLS           NO      /db01/oracle/tst9/tools01.dbf
6         51200 DATA            NO      /db01/oracle/tst9/data01.dbf
7         10240 INDX            NO      /db01/oracle/tst9/indx01.dbf

RMAN>
```

The second example displays all the backup sets that contain an additional copy or duplicate backups. Again, you must first connect to the target database and recovery catalog before running any report.

```
oracle@octilli:~ > rman target / catalog rman/rman@rcat
RMAN> report obsolete redundancy = 2;

Report of obsolete backups and copies
Type                 Key    Completed Filename/Handle
-------------------- ------ --------- --------------------
Backup Set           261    04-OCT-01
  Backup Piece       262    04-OCT-01 /oracle/product/9.0.1/dbs/02d5p81
Backup Set           283    05-OCT-01
  Backup Piece       284    05-OCT-01 /oracle/product/9.0.1/dbs/03d5pe1
Backup Set           294    05-OCT-01
  Backup Piece       295    05-OCT-01 /oracle/product/9.0.1/dbs/04d5pe1
```

Creating, Storing, and Running RMAN Scripts

RMAN *scripts* can be created to execute a group of RMAN commands. These scripts can be stored within the RMAN catalog. Once they are stored in the recovery catalog, the scripts can then be executed in much the same manner as a stored PL/SQL procedure. Let's walk through an example of creating, storing, and running an RMAN script. In this example, you will back up the complete database:

1. Connect to the recovery catalog.

   ```
   oracle@octilli:~ > rman catalog rman/rman@rcat
   ```

2. While you are in the RMAN utility, create a script called `complete_bac`. This will create, compile, and store the script in the recovery catalog.

   ```
   RMAN> create script complete_bac{
   2> allocate channel c1 type disk;
   3> allocate channel c2 type disk;
   4> backup database;
   5> backup archivelog all;
   6> }

   created script complete_bac

   RMAN>
   ```

3. Once the scripts are created and stored within the recovery catalog, they can be rerun as needed. This assures that the same script and functionality is reproduced for later jobs. Figure 13.2 shows how to create and store scripts with the recovery catalog.

FIGURE 13.2 Create and store RMAN scripts in the recovery catalog

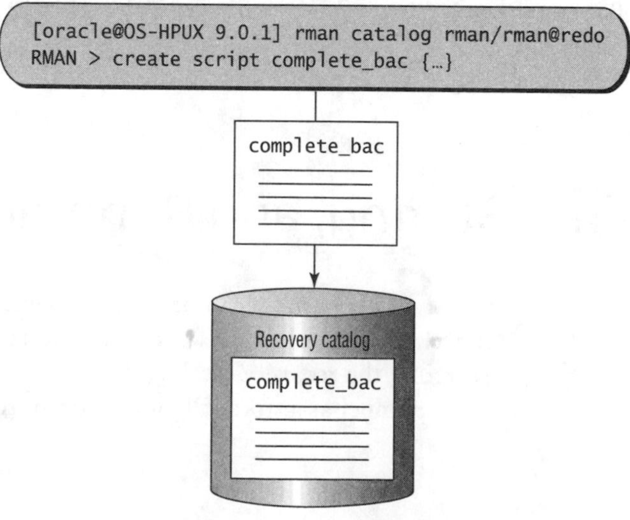

4. Run the stored RMAN script `complete_bac`. Do this by executing the following command when connected to the target database and to the recovery catalog. Note the `ERROR MESSAGE STACK`, which indicates that no archived logs need archiving.

```
RMAN> run { execute script complete_bac; }

executing script: complete_bac

allocated channel: c1
channel c1: sid=11 devtype=DISK

allocated channel: c2
channel c2: sid=8 devtype=DISK

Starting backup at 05-OCT-01
channel c1: starting full datafile backupset
channel c1: specifying datafile(s) in backupset
input datafile fno=00006 name=/db01/oracle/tst9/
data01.dbf
input datafile fno=00002 name=/db01/oracle/tst9/
rbs01.dbf
input datafile fno=00003 name=/db01/oracle/tst9/
temp01.dbf
input datafile fno=00004 name=/db01/oracle/tst9/
users01.dbf
channel c1: starting piece 1 at 05-OCT-01
channel c2: starting full datafile backupset
channel c2: specifying datafile(s) in backupset
including current controlfile in backupset
input datafile fno=00001 name=/db01/oracle/tst9/
system01.dbf
input datafile fno=00007 name=/db01/oracle/tst9/
indx01.dbf
input datafile fno=00005 name=/db01/oracle/tst9/
tools01.dbf
channel c2: starting piece 1 at 05-OCT-01
channel c1: finished piece 1 at 05-OCT-01
```

```
piece handle=/oracle/product/9.0.1/dbs/0fd5rv49_1_1
comment=NONE
channel c1: backup set complete, elapsed time: 00:00:48
channel c2: finished piece 1 at 05-OCT-01
piece handle=/oracle/product/9.0.1/dbs/0gd5rv49_1_1
comment=NONE
channel c2: backup set complete, elapsed time: 00:01:44
Finished backup at 05-OCT-01
RMAN-00571:
==========================================================
====
RMAN-00569: =============== ERROR MESSAGE STACK FOLLOWS
===============
RMAN-00571:
==========================================================
====
RMAN-00579: the following error occurred at 10/05/2001
23:46:58
RMAN-03015: error occurred in stored script complete_
bac
RMAN-03006: non-retryable error occurred during
execution of command: sql
RMAN-12004: unhandled exception during command
execution on channel default
RMAN-20000: abnormal termination of job step
RMAN-11003: failure during parse/execution of SQL
statement: ALTER SYSTEM ARCHIL
RMAN-11001: Oracle Error: ORA-00271: there are no logs
that need archiving
RMAN>
```

Figure 13.3 shows how stored scripts can be run in RMAN.

FIGURE 13.3 RMAN scripts

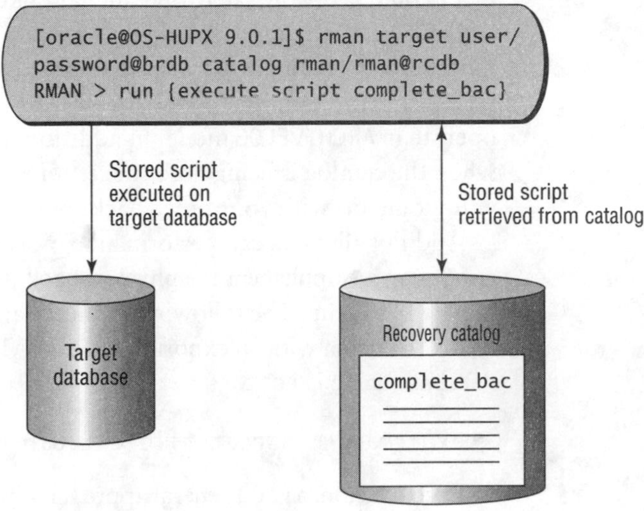

Methods for Backing Up and Recovering the Recovery Catalog

There are a few methods you can use to back up and recover the catalog. Before we address these methods, you need to know one steadfast rule: the catalog database needs to be on a different server than the one on which the target databases are stored. This prevents the catalog database from being impacted by a server-wide failure on a target database server.

If necessary, the catalog database can be backed up by another RMAN catalog or by a user-managed backup. When this kind of backup is conducted, the database can be in ARCHIVELOG mode or NOARCHIVELOG mode depending on the activity.

How you use the catalog determines how complicated you need to make the backup process. For example, let's say the environment you support executes backups only in the evening. These backups are all completed by 6:00 A.M. the following day. In this case, the RMAN catalog backups could go on every day at some time after the backups are complete. This type of environment could probably safely operate in NOARCHIVELOG log mode if desired.

Let's look at a more demanding schedule that would require ARCHIVELOG mode. In this example, backups continue around the clock, so there would be no time to perform a cold backup. This means that the database has to operate in ARCHIVELOG mode. In addition, the catalog backup should occur when the catalog is being used the least in order to avoid contention, just as you would do with your other backups.

Additionally, you can perform an export of the RMAN schema. This is a good way to supplement the physical backup performed by RMAN or a user-managed backup. The following syntax is an example of how to back up the RMAN schema with an export in which RMAN is the schema owner and the database name is rcat.

```
exp rman/rman@rcat file=cat.dmp owner=rman
```

In conclusion, a good general approach is to back up regularly using physical backups: either RMAN or user-managed. These backups should be daily and the database should be in ARCHIVELOG mode to assure complete recovery. For added security, you can add user exports of the RMAN schema. This way you have a fall-back plan in case you have a problem with your physical backup.

Summary

This chapter discussed the considerations you need to take into account when you are using the recovery catalog as well as its major components. You saw many practical examples of how to perform certain tasks in RMAN and the recovery catalog. One such example demonstrated how to create the recovery catalog in a database.

In addition to these examples, this chapter demonstrated various commands and methods you need to use to manage the recovery catalog. Some of these commands are included in the lists and reports groups and are used to query information in the recovery catalog. These commands also help validate backup status and schedule backups.

You also learned how to use scripting capabilities within RMAN to group commands, store them within the catalog, and run stored scripts. These scripts can reduce the number of errors that can occur in scripts or programs not centrally stored in the RMAN schema.

Understanding the recovery catalog is a key to understanding all the features of RMAN. When you choose to implement the recovery catalog, all features of RMAN are allowed. Additional maintenance and administration is involved with recovery catalog database, and this must be considered. Knowing how this information can be stored and utilized in the recovery catalog is key for the test and for getting the most out of RMAN in the workplace.

Exam Essentials

Understand the considerations that you must take into account when you are using the recovery catalog. The recovery catalog considerations consist of the following: you must use a separate and distinct database for the recovery catalog, you must have database administration of the catalog database, you must consider backup strategies for the recovery catalog, and you must use the recovery catalog to provide full functionality of RMAN commands.

Know the components that make up recovery catalog. The components that make up the recovery catalog are as follows: storage of long-term backup and recovery information, storage and reuse of RMAN scripts, and storage of backup information about data files, archived logs, and information about the physical makeup of the target database.

Understand how to create the recovery catalog. To create the recovery catalog, you must create an account with the following privileges: `CONNECT`, `RESOURCE`, and `RECOVERY_CATALOG_OWNER`. Then with RMAN connected to the recovery catalog, the `CREATE CATALOG TABLESPACE` *`<tablespace name>`* command must be executed.

Know the commands you will need to use to maintain the recovery catalog. You will need to be familiar with the following commands that are used to maintain the recovery catalog: `DELETE INPUT`, `KEEP`, `NOKEEP`, `CHANGE`, `DELETE`, `DELETE EXPIRED`, and `CROSSCHECK`.

Know how to register, resynchronize, and reset a database. The register, resynchronize, and reset commands perform initial setup and configuration operations on the recovery catalog. Registering the database creates the initial incarnation of the database in the recovery catalog. Resetting the recovery catalog creates a new incarnation of a database after it has been opened with the RESETLOGS option. Resynchronizing the recovery catalog updates the recovery catalog with changed physical information from the control file of the target database.

Know the different methods you would use to generate reports and lists from the recovery catalog. Be able to use list commands to generate basic information from the recovery catalog in a formatted output, and be able to use reports to provide more complicated outputs that answer more detailed questions.

Know the new Oracle9*i* list commands. You should be aware of the two new list commands that are new to Oracle9*i*: LIST BACKUP SUMMARY and LIST BACKUP BY FILE.

Know how to create, store, and execute RMAN scripts. Make sure that you are familiar with the command syntax that is necessary in order to create and store a RMAN script—CREATE SCRIPT *<script_name>*. You should also know that in order to execute a script, the RUN {EXECUTE SCRIPT *<script_name>* } command must be performed.

Understand the different methods you will need to use to back up and recover the recovery catalog. The recovery catalog can be backed up by using either user-managed or RMAN backups. An export can also be used to back up the RMAN catalog schema.

Key Terms

Before you take the exam, be certain you are familiar with the following terms:

full resynchronization

incarnation

list commands

partial resynchronization

recovery catalog

registering

report commands

resetting

resynchronization

RMAN scripts

unregistering

Review Questions

1. The RMAN utility does not require the use of which of the following?
   - **A.** Recovery catalog
   - **B.** Server sessions
   - **C.** Allocated channel for backup
   - **D.** Allocated channel for restore

2. What are the features supported by the recovery catalog? (Choose all that apply.)
   - **A.** Backup databases, tablespaces, data files, control files, and archived logs
   - **B.** Compressed backups
   - **C.** Scripting capabilities
   - **D.** Tests that determine whether backups can be restored
   - **E.** All of the above

3. Where is the best place to store the database housing the recovery catalog?
   - **A.** On the same server but in a different filesystem than the target database being backed up by the recovery catalog
   - **B.** On the same server and in the same filesystem as the target database that is being backed up by the recovery catalog
   - **C.** On a different server than the target database
   - **D.** None of the above

4. Which privileges are required for the Recovery Manager catalog user account? (Choose all that apply.)
   - **A.** DBA privilege
   - **B.** Connect privilege
   - **C.** Resource privilege
   - **D.** `RECOVERY_CATALOG_OWNER` privilege

5. What command can be performed only once on a target database?

   A. `CHANGE AVAILABILITY OF BACKUPS`

   B. `DELETE BACKUPS`

   C. `REGISTER THE DATABASE`

   D. `RESYNCHRONIZING THE DATABASE`

6. Which of the following statements best describes the target database?

   A. Any database designated for backup by RMAN

   B. The database that stores the recovery catalog

   C. A database not targeted to be backed up by RMAN

   D. A special repository database for the RMAN utility

7. What type of backups can be stored in the recovery catalog of RMAN? (Choose all that apply.)

   A. Non-RMAN backups based on OS commands

   B. Full database backups

   C. Tablespace backups

   D. Control file backups

   E. All of the above

8. Which of the following are instruments used to get information from the recovery catalog? (Choose all that apply.)

   A. `REPORT` command

   B. A query in SQL*Plus

   C. `LIST` command

   D. `RETRIEVAL` command

9. What must you do prior to running the `REPORT` or `LIST` commands?

   A. Determine the log file.

   B. Spool the output.

   C. Connect to the target.

   D. Connect to the target and recovery catalog.

10. What is the main difference between reports and lists?

    A. Lists have more output than reports.

    B. Reports have more output than lists.

    C. Reports provide more detailed information than lists.

    D. Lists provide more detailed information than reports.

11. What command stores scripts in the recovery catalog?

    A. `CREATE SCRIPT` <*SCRIPT_NAME*>

    B. `STORE SCRIPT` <*SCRIPT_NAME*>

    C. `CREATE OR REPLACE` <*SCRIPT_NAME*>

    D. Scripts cannot be stored in the recovery catalog.

12. What are the new Oracle9*i* list commands? (Choose all that apply.)

    A. `LIST BACKUP BY FILE`

    B. `LIST BACKUP SET`

    C. `LIST BACKUP SUMMARY FILE`

    D. `LIST BACKUP SUMMARY`

13. If you add a new data file to a database, what should you do to the incarnation of that database in the recovery catalog?

    A. Execute a reset.

    B. Execute a `resync`.

    C. Execute a register.

    D. Execute a report.

14. The code below is intended to launch a stored RMAN script. Find the line with the incorrect syntax.

```
run {
execute
program
complete_bac; }
```

A. The first line

B. The second line

C. The third line

D. The fourth line

15. The code below is intended to create a script that can be used to copy archived logs. Find the line with the incorrect syntax.

```
Create script
Arch_bac_up {
Allocate channel c1 type disk;
Backup archives all;}
```

A. The first line

B. The second line

C. The third line

D. The fourth line

Answers to Review Questions

1. A. The recovery catalog is optional. The recovery catalog is used to store information about the backup and recovery process, in much the same way as the data dictionary stores information about the database. The other options are all required elements for RMAN to function normally.

2. E. All answers are capabilities of the RMAN utility.

3. C. The recovery catalog database should be on a different server than the target database to eliminate the potential of a failure on one server affecting the backup and restore capabilities of RMAN.

4. B, C, D. The DBA privilege is not required from the recovery catalog user account. This user must be able to connect to the database, create objects within the database, and have the `RECOVERY_CATALOG_OWNER` privilege.

5. C. Registering the database can be performed only once for each database unless the database is unregistered.

6. A. The target database is any database that is targeted for backup by the RMAN utility.

7. E. RMAN can catalog non-RMAN backups based on OS commands as well as full database backups, tablespace backups, and control file backups.

8. A, B, C. The RMAN utility provides the `REPORT` and `LIST` commands to generate outputs from the recovery catalog. SQL*Plus can also be used to manually query the recovery catalog in certain instances.

9. D. Before running any `REPORT` or `LIST` command, you must be connected to the target database and recovery catalog.

10. C. The REPORT command provides more detailed information than the LIST command. The REPORT command is used to answer more "what if" or "what needs to be done" type questions than the LIST command.

11. A. The CREATE SCRIPT *<SCRIPT_NAME>* command stores the associated script in the recovery catalog. This script can then be run at a later date.

12. A, D. The LIST BACKUP OF FILE and LIST BACKUP SUMMARY commands are both new list commands in Oracle9*i*.

13. B. A resync command should be run if the physical components of the target database change.

14. C. The incorrect syntax is program. The correct syntax should be as follows:

```
run {
execute
script
complete_bac; }
```

15. D. The incorrect syntax is BACKUP ARCHIVES ALL;}. This should be BACKUP ARCHIVELOG ALL;}.

Transporting Data between Databases

ORACLE9*i*: DBA FUNDAMENTALS II EXAM OBJECTIVES COVERED IN THIS CHAPTER:

- ✓ **Describe the uses of the Export and Import utilities.**
- ✓ **Describe Export and Import concepts and structures.**
- ✓ **Perform simple Export and Import operations.**
- ✓ **List guidelines for using Export and Import.**

Exam objectives are subject to change at any time without prior notice and at Oracle's sole discretion. Please visit Oracle's Certification website (`http://www.oracle.com/education/certification/`) for the most current exam objectives listing.

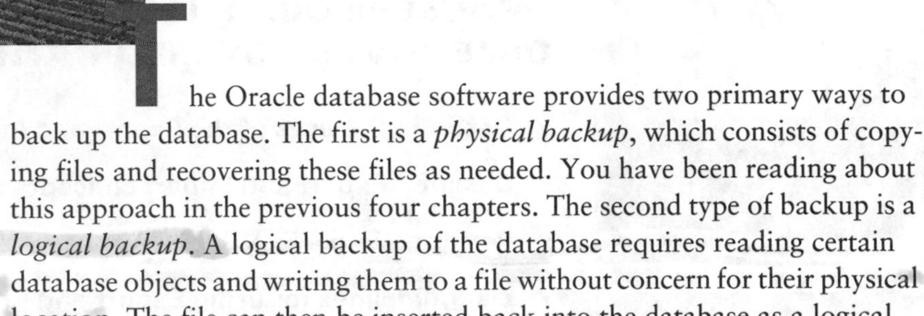

The Oracle database software provides two primary ways to back up the database. The first is a *physical backup*, which consists of copying files and recovering these files as needed. You have been reading about this approach in the previous four chapters. The second type of backup is a *logical backup*. A logical backup of the database requires reading certain database objects and writing them to a file without concern for their physical location. The file can then be inserted back into the database as a logical restore.

Oracle also provides two utilities to handle the backups and recoveries in an Oracle database: the Export utility and the Import utility. The Export utility creates logical backups of the database, and the Import utility performs logical recoveries of the database.

This chapter demonstrates how to back up and recover the database with the Export and Import utilities. It also explains incremental backups and recoveries.

The topics in this chapter are an important part of the test and real-life recovery situations. The Export and Import utilities are a good supplement to a user-managed or RMAN-based backup. These utilities can be used in real-world recovery situations in which developers or end users inadvertently drop tables or delete data.

Using the Export and Import Utilities

The Export and Import utilities primarily perform logical backups and recoveries, but they may be used for such varied operations as the following:

- **Recovering database objects** The primary use of the Export and Import utilities for backup and recovery is to replace an individual object, such as a table or a schema consisting of multiple database objects. Though the entire or full database can be recovered also, this is not common. In some cases, a table may be dropped by a user or a developer, but you may not want to restore the whole database. Though the whole database can be restored, because of the point-in-time nature of exports, the data may be inconsistent.

Recovering using tablespace point-in-time recovery (TSPITR) In Oracle8*i*, the *tablespace point-in-time recovery (TSPITR)* was introduced. The TSPITR was designed to recover large individual objects using a fairly complicated recovery process. As a result, we would recommend that you get help from Oracle Support before you perform a recovery with TSPITR. To successfully perform this type of recovery, you will need to use both physical and logical recovery techniques. In addition, you will need to use a clone database to perform the complete process, and this will require extra resources. With so many drawbacks, you may wonder why anyone would use this. The reason is that TSPITR allows you to recover all the objects in an entire tablespace without recovering the entire database. This is useful in large databases where a complete restore and recovery would take a long time.

There are a couple of specialized parameters you must be familiar with in order to use TSPITR: `TRANSPORT_TABLESPACE` and `DATAFILES`. The `TRANSPORT_TABLESPACE` parameter identifies the tablespace that will be used in the TSPITR process. The `DATAFILES` parameter identifies the data files that support the tablespace to be recovered.

Reorganizing the database to improve performance The Export and Import utilities can also be used to reorganize a database and to restore individual objects. When objects are restored in this manner, the data they contain may be packed or compressed into fewer extents so that it can be retrieved more expeditiously. This is accomplished by using the `COMPRESS=Y` command, which is the default. Below is an example of using this parameter.

```
oracle@octilli:~ > exp userid=test/test compress=Y
file=tst9.dmp
```

Upgrading an object or a database You can also use these utilities to upgrade databases or objects from one version to another. If these utilities are used in this manner, an export is taken of a table or database, and then it is imported into the new database with the upgraded version.

Moving data from one database to another The Export and Import utilities can also be used to move data from one database to another. The binary dump file created by the export process can be sent from one server to another via FTP, and then it can be loaded into a new database.

Real World Scenario

Using Export for Added Protection

Exports provide extra protection above and beyond the normal backup plans, and they are often used to supplement backup protection of individual objects. Under certain circumstances, the export can also serve as a valuable asset for complete recovery.

In this case, a junior DBA inadvertently dropped a tablespace that contained only one table of static data for a small insurance provider. Realizing his error, the junior DBA attempted to recover the database from the previous night's open RMAN backup. To his dismay, there was a problem with the tape hardware, and he was unable to get it working. This hardware issue could not begin to be addressed until the next day at the earliest.

At this point, it was already late in the evening and the DBA knew that the database would begin receiving automated caller information from the east coast early the next morning. As a result, the database was required to be available before the hardware issue could be addressed; if it wasn't, the company's business would be severely impacted.

But the DBA remembered that there was an automated daily export of key tables in the databases, including the one table in the tablespace that was dropped. This export occurred at noon, between the bulk loads.

After careful thought, the DBA re-created this erroneously dropped tablespace. After the DBA finished re-creating the tablespace, he imported the one table that resided within the newly created tablespace. Finally, the DBA finished the process by reloading the few flat files that were necessary so that the table was totally consistent.

By using an export, the DBA completely restored the database and only four hours of service were lost. This situation worked nicely because the data was isolated and fairly static. The primary changes to the table were identified in the flat files.

Export and Import Concepts and Structures

As stated in the introduction to this chapter, the *Export utility* can be used to create logical backups of the Oracle database. The *Import utility* can recover these logical backups. There are two types of exports: the *conventional-path export* and the *direct-path export*.

The conventional-path export is the default mode of the Export utility. This method can be time consuming for large objects or exports. However, it works well for everyday uses.

The direct-path export is enabled by typing **DIRECT=Y** on the command line. This export option is substantially faster than the conventional-path export.

This direct-path option bypasses the SQL evaluation layer as it regenerates the commands to be stored in the binary dump file. This is where the performance improvements are made. Figure 14.1 displays the execution path of each type of export.

FIGURE 14.1 The differences between direct-path and conventional-path exports

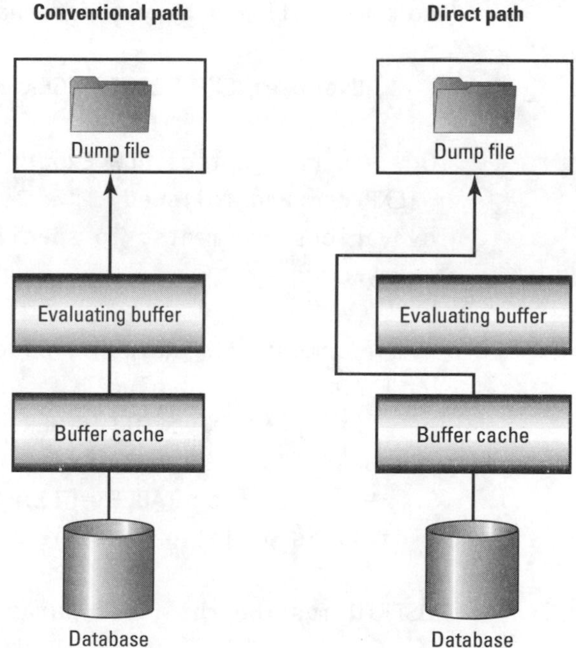

The Export utility performs a full SELECT on a table and then dumps the data into a binary file called a *dump file*. (This file has a .dmp file extension and is named expdat.dmp by default.) The Export utility then creates the tables and indexes by reproducing the Data Definition Language (DDL) of the backup tables. This information can then be played back by the Import utility to rebuild the object and its underlying data.

To display all the export options available, issue the command EXP -HELP from the command line.

```
oracle@octilli:/db01/oracle/tst9 > exp -help

Export: Release 9.0.1.0.0 - Production on Fri Oct 5
23:09:00 2001

(c) Copyright 2001 Oracle Corporation.  All rights
reserved.

You can let Export prompt you for parameters by
  entering the EXP
command followed by your username/password:

     Example: EXP SCOTT/TIGER

Or, you can control how Export runs by entering the
  EXP command followed
by various arguments. To specify parameters, you use
  keywords:

     Format:  EXP KEYWORD=value or
  KEYWORD=(value1,value2,...,valueN)
     Example: EXP SCOTT/TIGER GRANTS=Y
  TABLES=(EMP,DEPT,MGR)
               or TABLES=(T1:P1,T1:P2),
  if T1 is partitioned table

USERID must be the first parameter on the command line.
```

```
Keyword  Description (Default)
------------------------------------------------------
USERID   username/password
BUFFER   size of data buffer
FILE    output files (EXPDAT.DMP)
COMPRESS import into one extent (Y)
GRANTS  export grants (Y)
INDEXES  export indexes (Y)
ROWS     export data rows (Y)
CONSTRAINTS export constraints (Y)
LOG  log file of screen output
DIRECT  direct path (N)
FEEDBACK display progress every x rows (0)
FILESIZE maximum size of each dump file
QUERY    select clause used to export a subset of a table
VOLSIZE  number of bytes to write to each tape volume
FULL         export entire file (N)
OWNER        list of owner usernames
TABLES       list of table names
RECORDLENGTH length of IO record
INCTYPE      incremental export type
RECORD       track incr. export (Y)
PARFILE      parameter filename
CONSISTENT   cross-table consistency
STATISTICS   analyze objects (ESTIMATE)
TRIGGERS     export triggers (Y)

FEEDBACK              display progress every x rows (0)
FILESIZE              maximum size of each dump file
FLASHBACK_SCN         SCN used to set session snapshot back
to
FLASHBACK_TIME        time used to get the SCN closest to
the specified time
QUERY                 select clause used to export a subset
of a table
RESUMABLE             suspend when a space related error is
encountered(N)
```

```
RESUMABLE_NAME       text string used to identify
resumable statement
RESUMABLE_TIMEOUT    wait time for RESUMABLE
TTS_FULL_CHECK       perform full or partial dependency
check for TTS
VOLSIZE             number of bytes to write to each tape
volume
TABLESPACES          list of tablespaces to export
TRANSPORT_TABLESPACE export transportable tablespace
metadata (N)
TEMPLATE template name which invokes iAS mode export

Export terminated successfully without warnings.
oracle@octilli:/db01/oracle/tst9 >
```

There are a few changes in Oracle9*i*'s export features. These are as follows: triggers are no longer exported in the sys schema in full export mode to accommodate the Java virtual machine, and INCREMENTAL/CULMULATIVE/COMPLETE exports are no longer supported as well as the process of creating a 7.*x* export file from an Oracle9*i* database is. Please read your Oracle documentation for complete details on these changes.

Performing Simple Export and Import Operations

Let's look at how a DBA performs a simple export and import. We will use the interactive method of running both the Export and the Import utilities. This means that the user will respond to each of the utilities prompts.

First, we will export a table called t1. Then we will import the same table. Additionally, we will demonstrate how to run an export with a PARFILE so that it doesn't require user interaction. This type of export can be run at the command line, and it can be both scripted and scheduled. The *PARFILE* is a parameter file that has export parameters grouped together in one file so that each parameter does not have to be entered by the DBA on the command line. This process will be demonstrated after the export process that follows. Let's work through each of these examples.

Performing a Simple Export

In this interactive export example, you will perform a full export of the table `t1`, which is owned by the user TEST. Here are the steps used to perform the export:

1. Start the Export utility by executing **exp** on the command line. In Unix, you should first set your `ORACLE_SID` environment variable to point to the database to which you are trying to connect. This can be done by executing `export ORACLE_SID = tst9` at the command line. Alternatively, you could connect via SQL*Net through a `tnsnames.ora` entry that explicitly defines the target database.

```
oracle@octilli:/db01/oracle/tst9 > exp

Export: Release 9.0.1.0.0 - Production on Fri Oct 5
23:18:08 2001

(c) Copyright 2001 Oracle Corporation.  All rights
reserved.


Username: test
Password:

Connected to: Oracle9i Enterprise Edition Release
9.0.1.0.0 - Production
With the Partitioning option
JServer Release 9.0.1.0.0 - Production
```

2. Enter the appropriate buffer size. If you want to keep the default buffer size of 4096KB, press Enter. The buffer size is the buffer used to fetch data. The default size is usually adequate. The maximum size is 64KB.

```
Enter array fetch buffer size: 4096 >
```

3. The next prompt asks for the filename of the dump file. You can enter your own filename or choose the default, `expdat.dmp`.

```
Export file: expdat.dmp > t1.dmp
```

4. The next prompt designates users or tables in the dump file. The USERS choice, (2), exports all objects owned by the user you are using to connect. The TABLE option, (3), exports all designated tables.

```
(2)U(sers), or (3)T(ables): (2)U > 3
```

5. The next prompt asks whether to export the table data.

```
Export table data (yes/no): yes> y
```

6. The next prompt asks whether to compress extents. For example, if a table has 20 1MB extents, and you choose `yes`, the extents will be compressed into one 20MB extent. All extents are compressed into one. If you choose `no`, then the 20 1MB extents will remain. This compression option will reduce fragmentation in the tablespace by compressing the extents or making a bigger initial table extent. This can present problems when the compressed size is large. If the compressed size is large enough, there may not be enough contiguous free space in the tablespace, so the import will fail. This can be remedied by resizing the tablespace.

```
Compress extents (yes/no): yes > y
```

7. The next prompt specifies which tables to export. In this example, you have chosen the `t1` table. When the export is complete, you are prompted for another table or partition. If you are done, hit Enter.

```
Export done in US7ASCII character set and US7ASCII
NCHAR
  character set

About to export specified tables via Conventional Path
...
Table(T) or Partition(T:P) to be exported:
  (RETURN to quit) > t1

. . exporting table                           T1
          3 rows exported
```

```
Table(T) or Partition(T:P) to be exported:
  (RETURN to quit) >

Export terminated successfully without warnings.
oracle@octilli:/db01/oracle/tst9 >
```

This concludes the interactive export of the individual table, `t1`. This same process can be performed without prompts or user interaction by utilizing a parameter file or the command line with specified parameters. Specifying the `PARFILE` at the command line, for example, is one method of performing a non-interactive export. Here is an example of this technique that will export the full database, which includes all users and all objects. This can be done on a table-by-table basis also.

```
oracle@octilli:~ > exp parfile=tst9par.pr
  file=tst9.dmp
oracle@octilli:~ > cat tst9par.pr
USERID=system/manager
DIRECT=Y
FULL=Y
GRANTS=Y
ROWS=Y
CONSTRAINTS=Y
RECORD=Y
```

The following is an example of using the command-line parameter specifications. This technique also does not require user interaction to respond to prompts.

```
oracle@octilli:~ > exp userid=system/manager
  full=y constraints=Y file=tst9.dmp
```

A useful feature of the export is that it can detect block corruption in the database. *Block corruption* occurs when the database block becomes corrupt or unreadable; it will cause an export to fail. Block corruption has to be fixed before a logical backup can be completed.

Performing a Simple Import

The Import utility is used to perform a logical recovery of the Oracle database. This utility reads the dump file generated by the Export utility. As discussed earlier, the Export utility dumps the data in the table and then uses the necessary DDL commands to re-create the table. The Import utility then plays back these commands, re-creates the table, and inserts the data stored in the binary dump file. This section provides a step-by-step outline of how this process works.

The Import utility also has numerous options. To display all the import options available, issue the command `IMP -HELP` from the command line.

```
oracle@octilli:~ > imp -help

Import: Release 9.0.1.0.0 - Production on
Fri Oct 5 23:24:45 2001

(c) Copyright 2001 Oracle Corporation.
All rights reserved.


You can let Import prompt you for parameters by
  entering the IMP
command followed by your username/password:

     Example: IMP SCOTT/TIGER

Or, you can control how Import runs by entering the IMP
   command followed
by various arguments. To specify parameters,
   you use keywords:

     Format:  IMP KEYWORD=value or
  KEYWORD=(value1,value2,...,valueN)
     Example: IMP SCOTT/TIGER IGNORE=Y
   TABLES=(EMP,DEPT) FULL=N
               or TABLES=(T1:P1,T1:P2),
   if T1 is partitioned table
```

```
USERID must be the first parameter on the command line.

Keyword  Description (Default)
-----------------------------------------------------------
USERID  username/password
BUFFER size of data buffer
FILE     input files (EXPDAT.DMP)
SHOW      just list file contents (N)
IGNORE    ignore create errors (N)
GRANTS    import grants (Y)
INDEXES   import indexes (Y)
ROWS      import data rows (Y)
LOG       log file of screen output
DESTROY  overwrite tablespace data file (N)
INDEXFILE write table/index info to specified file
SKIP_UNUSABLE_INDEXES  skip maintenance of
  unusable indexes (N)
FEEDBACK display progress every x rows(0)
TOID_NOVALIDATE  skip validation of specified type ids
FILESIZE maximum size of each dump file
STATISTICS import precomputed statistics (always)
RESUMABLE suspend when a space related error is
encountered(N)
RESUMABLE_NAME text string used to identify resumable
statement
RESUMABLE_TIMEOUT wait time for RESUMABLE
COMPILE compile procedures, packages, and functions (Y)
VOLSIZE number of bytes in file on each volume of a file
on tape)


The following keywords only apply to
   transportable tablespaces
TRANSPORT_TABLESPACE import transportable
   tablespace metadata (N)
TABLESPACES tablespaces to be transported
   into database
```

```
DATAFILES datafiles to be transported into database
TTS_OWNERS users that own data in the transportable
   tablespace set

Import terminated successfully without warnings.
oracle@octilli:~ >
```

The following steps indicate how to perform the recovery of a table with the Import utility. Here the Import utility is in interactive mode.

1. To recover the database, you must validate what should be recovered. In this case, use the export from the `t1.dmp` created in the earlier section entitled "Performing a Simple Export." Here, you are exporting the complete `t1` table, which contains four rows of data.

```
SQL> select * from t1;
C1         C2
---------- ----------------------------------------
         1 This is a test one - before hot backup
         3 This is a test three - after hot backup
         2 This is a test two - after hot backup
         4 This is test four - after complete export
4 rows selected.
SQL>
```

2. Truncate the table to simulate a complete data loss in the table.

```
SQL> truncate table t1;
Statement processed.
SQL>
```

3. From the working directory of the exported dump file, execute the **IMP** command and connect to the user TEST.

```
oracle@octilli:~ > imp

Import: Release 9.0.1.0.0 - Production on
Fri Oct 5 23:31:44 2001

(c) Copyright 2001 Oracle Corporation.
All rights reserved.
```

```
Username: test
Password:

Connected to: Oracle9i Enterprise Edition Release
9.0.1.0.0 - Production
With the Partitioning option
JServer Release 9.0.1.0.0 - Production
```

4. The next prompt is for the filename of the dump file. You can enter the fully qualified filename, or just the filename if you are in the working directory of the dump file.

   ```
   Import file: expdat.dmp > t1.dmp]
   ```

5. The next prompt is for the buffer size of the import data loads. Choose the minimum, which is 8KB.

   ```
   Enter insert buffer size (minimum is 8192) 30720> 8192
   ```

6. The next prompt asks whether to list the contents of the dump file, instead of actually doing the import. The default is `no`; choose that option for this example.

   ```
   Export file created by EXPORT:V09.00.01 via
   conventional path
   import done in US7ASCII character set and
   AL16UTF16 NCHAR character set
   List contents of import file only (yes/no): no > n
   ```

7. The next prompt asks whether to ignore the `CREATE ERROR` if the object exists. For this example, choose `yes`.

   ```
   Ignore create error due to object existence (yes/no):
   no > y
   ```

8. The next prompt asks whether to import the grants related to the object that is being imported. Choose `yes`.

   ```
   Import grants (yes/no): yes > y
   ```

9. The next prompt asks whether to import the data in the table, instead of just the table definition. Choose `yes`.

   ```
   Import table data (yes/no): yes > y
   ```

10. The next prompt asks whether to import the entire export file. In this case, choose `yes` because the import consists only of the table you want to import. If it had multiple objects in the dump file, then you would choose the default, which is `no`.

```
Import entire export file (yes/no): no > y

. . importing TEST's objects into TEST
. . importing table                              "T1"
            4 rows imported
Import terminated successfully without warnings.
oracle@octilli:~ >
```

11. Next, you need to validate that the import successfully restored the table `t1`. Perform a query on the table to validate that there are four rows within the table.

```
SQL> select * from t1;
C1         C2
---------- ---------------------------------------------
         1 This is a test one - before hot backup
         2 This is a test two - after hot backup
         3 This is a test three - after hot backup
         4 This is test four - after complete export
4 rows selected.
SQL>
```

The `IGNORE CREATE ERROR DUE TO OBJECT EXISTENCE` option can be confusing. This option means that if the object exists during the import, then the Import utility ignores the `CREATE` or `REPLACE` errors during the object re-creation. Furthermore, if you specify `IGNORE=Y`, the Import utility continues its work without reporting the error. Even if using the `IGNORE=Y parameter`, the Import utility still does not replace an existing object; instead, it will skip the object.

Guidelines for Using Export and Import

The guidelines for using the Export and Import utilities require that logical backup and recovery of the data is acceptable. Another way to look at this is, "Can the data that is being recovered be from a point in time?"

With exports, there is no way to roll forward as you can with a complete or an incomplete recovery. The data in the export is from the time the export was taken and cannot change. It is like a picture of data at a certain point in time.

That being the case, Export and Import utilities are not the best backup and recovery solutions available to you. These utilities function more like supplements to a good physical backup strategy.

Below is a list of some the guidelines for using the Export and Import utility:

Data should be static. The data that is being exported should be consistent or it should not be in the process of being updated if at all possible. If heavy DML activity is occurring during the export, the dump file will not be useful for recovery purposes.

There should be limited logical references to the tables. The tables should have limited referential integrity constraints. Complex referential integrity presents problems for the Export utility.

The data sets should be small to medium sized (with the exception of TSPITR). The Export and Import utilities are not the best choice for large data sets. These utilities can take long periods of time to export and import data.

Summary

This chapter demonstrated the capabilities of the Oracle logical backup and recovery utilities: Export and Import. During the course of this chapter, you walked through the backup and recovery of a database object that used these tools. You learned how to display all the options available in the Export and Import utilities, and you saw an example of the direct-path export, which is significantly faster than the standard conventional-path export.

In addition, you were introduced to the types of scenarios for which the Export and Import utilities are useful. You also became familiar with the guidelines you would need to follow in order to get the best use out of the Export and Import utilities.

In most environments, the Export and Import utilities do not serve as the primary backup, but rather as a supplement to a physical backup. However, the Export and Import utilities do provide extra protection and eliminate the need for certain physical recoveries.

The topics covered in this chapter will be an important part of the testing and can be equally beneficial in the workplace. The Export and Import utilities are a valuable supplement to any backup and recovery plan. These utilities can prevent a complete recovery and eliminate downtime when user or developer errors occur in databases.

Exam Essentials

Understand the uses of the Export and Import utilities. The Export and Import utilities can be used to recover database objects, reorganize databases for best performance, upgrade a database, or move data from one database to another.

Understand how to perform an export. To perform an export, you must be familiar with the commands involved. You should also know that the two ways to export are through user interaction and by using a `PARFILE`.

Understand how to perform an import. To perform an import, you must be familiar with the commands involved. You should also know that the two ways to import are through user interaction and by using a `PARFILE`.

Identify the guidelines for utilizing Export and Import utilities. When you are using the Export and Import utilities, there are three major guidelines you should follow: your data should be somewhat static, you should limit logical references, and you should make sure your data sets are small to medium sized (with the exception of TSPITR).

Describe the TSPITR concept. Tablespace point-in-time-recovery (TSPITR) is an export of metadata to a cloned database that is conducted while you are using physical recovery attributes to restore individual data files. This is mainly used for large databases where complete recovery would be very time consuming.

Describe the parameters associated with TSPITR. The `TRANSPORT_TABLESPACE` and `DATAFILES` parameters are unique to the use of transportable tablespace features.

Key Terms

Before you take the exam, be certain you are familiar with the following terms:

block corruption	Import utility
conventional-path export	logical backup
direct-path export	`PARFILE`
dump file	physical backup
Export utility	tablespace point-in-time recovery (TSPITR)

Review Questions

1. What type of database utility performs a logical backup?

   A. Export

   B. Import

   C. Cold backup

   D. Hot backup

2. What type of database utility reads the dump file into the database?

   A. Export

   B. Import

   C. SQL*Loader

   D. Forms

3. What is the default dump file named?

   A. `export.dmp`

   B. `expdat.dmp`

   C. `expdata.dmp`

   D. `export_data.dmp`

4. Review the following export command and determine the incorrect syntax.

   ```
   exp
   users=ar/trar2
   conventional=false
   tables=ra_customer_deductions
   ```

   A. The first line is incorrect.

   B. The second line is incorrect.

   C. The third line is incorrect.

   D. The fourth line is incorrect.

5. What types of backup are required to use TSPITR? (Choose all that apply.)

   A. Logical

   B. Physical

   C. Import

   D. Export

6. What is the name of the parameter that reads the parameter file?

   A. `PARAMETER FILE`

   B. `PARFILE`

   C. `PARAFILE`

   D. `PAR-FILE`

7. What is the name of the other database called when you are using TSPITR?

   A. Secondary database

   B. Recovery database

   C. Cloned database

   D. Backup database

8. What is the name of the parameter that is used specifically for TSPITR?

   A. `DATABASE`

   B. `TRANSPORT_TABLESPACE`

   C. `CONTROL`

   D. `COMPRESS`

9. Which export type is the fastest?

   A. Complete

   B. Cumulative

   C. Direct-path

   D. Conventional-path

10. What is the complex recovery method that uses the Export and Import utilities designed for large database objects?

    A. Full Export

    B. Full=Y

    C. TPSTIR

    D. TSPITR

11. What is the export command that can be used in conjunction with database reorganization to improve performance?

    A. `COMPRESS_EXTENT=Y`

    B. `COMPRESS_EXT=Y`

    C. `COMPRESS=Y`

    D. `COMPEXT=Y`

12. Which of the following is a true statement about the Export and Import utilities?

    A. They cannot be used to upgrade a database.

    B. They can be used to upgrade a database.

    C. Only the Export utility can be used to upgrade the database.

    D. Only the Import utility can be used to upgrade the database.

13. Which of the following is a correct statement about how you would use the Export utility on a table without using any export keyword options?

    A. The Export utility loads data into a database.

    B. The Import utility extracts data from a database.

    C. The Export utility performs a full SELECT of a table and then dumps the data into a binary file.

    D. The Export utility performs a full SELECT of a table and then dumps the data into an ASCII file.

14. Which of the following export keyword options selects a subset of a table?

    A. SUBSET

    B. SELECT

    C. WHERE

    D. QUERY

15. Which of the following export keyword options performs a complete database export?

    A. ALL=Y

    B. COMPLETE=Y

    C. TOTAL=Y

    D. FULL=Y

Answers to Review Questions

1. A. The Export utility performs the logical backup of the Oracle database.

2. B. The Import utility is responsible for reading in the dump file.

3. B. The `expdat.dmp` is the default dump filename.

4. C. Conventional path export is the default. The line `conventional=false` is invalid syntax.

5. A, B, D. Both logical and physical database backups are performed with the TSPITR, and exports are logical backups. Import is not a backup; it is a recovery utility in this context.

6. B. The `PARFILE` parameter is the name of the parameter that specifies the parameter file.

7. C. The cloned database is the other database that is recovered when you are using TSPITR.

8. B. The `TRANSPORT_TABLESPACE` parameter is used specifically for TSPITR. It is used to identify the tablespace that needs to be recovered.

9. C. A direct-path export is the fastest. Complete and cumulative exports are data-volume dependent.

10. D. The tablespace point-in-time recovery (TSPITR) is an Export and Import recovery method that is designed for large database objects.

11. C. The `COMPRESS=Y` command can be used to compress extents in a table when a table or database is reorganized for performance reasons.

12. B. When used together, both the Export and Import utilities can be used to upgrade databases to new versions.

13. C. The Export utility performs a full SELECT of a table and then dumps it to the export.dmp file, which is in binary format.

14. D. The QUERY keyword makes the Export utility perform a filtered SELECT of a table so that the complete table is not exported.

15. D. The FULL=Y keyword option causes the export to perform a complete database export including all objects and tablespaces.

Chapter 15

Using SQL*Loader to Load Data

ORACLE9*i*: DBA FUNDAMENTALS II EXAM OBJECTIVES COVERED IN THIS CHAPTER:

✓ Demonstrate usage of direct-load insert operations.

✓ Describe the usage of SQL*Loader.

✓ Perform basic SQL*Loader operations.

✓ List guidelines for using SQL*Loader and direct-load insert.

Exam objectives are subject to change at any time without prior notice and at Oracle's sole discretion. Please visit Oracle's Certification website (`http://www.oracle.com/education/certification/`) for the most current exam objectives listing.

The Oracle SQL*Loader utility is a tool designed to load external data into the Oracle database. This utility loads data from an external file format into tables within an Oracle database.

SQL*Loader has three primary ways it uses to load data: a conventional load, a direct-path load, or an external-path load. Each of these load methods is designed for a different usage.

We will also demonstrate a Data Manipulation Language (DML) statement called direct-path insert. This is not actually part of SQL*Loader, but it is similar to the SQL*Loader direct-path load method.

Finally, we will list some guidelines that explain the best ways to use SQL*Loader. We will outline each topic and then briefly discuss each guideline.

It is important to conquer the topics covered in this chapter as you prepare for the test. In addition, this information has a practical application in the workplace. SQL*Loader can be a valuable utility for multiple uses including moving data from one database to another, making backups of tables, and performing maintenance operations. Familiarity with this tool is a valuable asset to any DBA.

Using Direct-Load Insert Operations

The *direct-load insert* operation is not actually a function of the SQL*Loader utility. Instead, this operation is a DML command, which can be performed within the database using SQL*Plus. The direct-load insert has similarities to the SQL*Loader direct-path load, which we will discuss in more detail in the next section, "Using SQL*Loader." Both the direct-load insert and SQL*Loader direct-path load will bypass the buffer cache and write directly to blocks within the tables you are loading. This functionality allows both of these operations to be extremely fast.

Direct-load insert comes in two flavors: serial direct-load insert and parallel direct-load insert. *Serial direct-load insert* is the normal operation that uses one server process to insert data beyond the high-water mark. Serial direct-load insert can be used on unpartitioned, partitioned, and subpartitioned tables. Below is an example of serial direct-load insert.

```
SQL> INSERT /*+ APPEND / INTO T1_NEW
1> NOLOGGING
2> SELECT * FORM T1
3> COMMIT;
```

The second type of direct-load insert is called parallel direct-load insert. *Parallel direct-load insert* is the same DML insert operation as serial direct-load insert, but in this case, the statement or table is put into parallel mode. This description implies that the database must be configured for parallel operations, which means that you must have parallel query slaves configured in your initialization parameters. (This topic is covered in more detail in *OCP: Oracle9i Performance Tuning Study Guide,* by Joseph C. Johnson [Sybex, 2002].)

Furthermore, you must enable parallel DML for the session in which you will be performing the parallel direct-load insert. You will do this with the `ALTER SESSION ENABLE PARALLEL DML` command. After you have used this command, you must enable a hint or place the table to be inserted into parallel mode. A hint is created with a multiple line comment with a plus symbol, such as `/*+ PARALLEL (TEST.T1_NEW, 4) */`. A *hint* is a mechanism that influences the explain path of a query so that the query performs in a certain way. Alternatively, you can alter the table `T1_NEW` to be in degree of parallel 4 with the following command: `ALTER TABLE T1_NEW PARALLEL (DEGREE 4)`.

The parallel direct-load insert causes multiple parallel server processes to break up the insert function into multiple temporary segments, and it also causes the parallel coordinator to merge the temporary segments into the table. Below is an example of parallel direct-load insert statement.

```
SQL> ALTER SESSION ENABLE PARALLEL DML;
SQL> INSERT /*+PARALLEL (TEST.T1_NEW, 4) / INTO T1_NEW
1> NOLOGGING
2> SELECT * FORM T1
3> COMMIT;
```

Using SQL*Loader

*SQL*Loader* is an Oracle utility that was designed to load or transport external data from one database to another. SQL*Loader is often used in nightly extracts from other non-Oracle-based systems with which your database may interface. It has become the tool of choice for loading data into the Oracle database in order to build or refresh Data Warehouse or Data Marts. This new-found popularity results from its speed and versatility on large data sets for both Oracle and non-Oracle sources.

Because of SQL*Loader's parsing capabilities, the external files it works with can be in various formats. As a result of this versatility, you can use SQL*Loader to do the following:

- Load data from multiple data files or input files during the same load session.
- Load data into multiple tables during the same load session.
- Combine multiple input records into a logical record for loading.
- Specify the character set of the data.
- Accept input fields of fixed or variable length.
- Selectively load data (you can load records based on the records' values).
- Manipulate the data before loading it using SQL functions.
- Generate unique, sequential key values in specified columns.
- Use the operating system's filesystem to access the data files.
- Load data from disk, tape, or named pipe.
- Append data to and replace existing data in the tables.
- Load data directly into data blocks by passing the buffer cache.
- Use secondary data files for loading large binary objects (LOBs) and collections.

There are three main file structures that you will need to be familiar with when you are using SQL*Loader: the control file; log files, which include bad logs, discard logs, and general logs; and input data, or data files. These file structures will be discussed in detail in this section.

SQL*Loader also uses three methods to load data into the database—the conventional load, the direct-path load, and the external-path load—and three other methods in parallel mode to further improve performance—parallel conventional load, intersegment concurrency with direct-path load, and intrasegment concurrency with direct-path load. Both sets of these methods are also discussed in the following pages.

Control Files, Log Files, and Input Data or Data Files

SQL*Loader's three main components are the control file, the log files, and the input data, or data files. The *control file* is the logic behind the data load that determines how and what data will be loaded. The *log files* include the bad, the discard, and the general log files. The *bad log* documents records that were rejected by the Oracle database or SQL*Loader because they have an invalid format or unique key violations, or because they have a required field that is null. The *discard log* contains records that were discarded in the load process or didn't meet the control file load criteria. The *general log* file contains a detailed summary of the load process. The *data file*, or input data, is the raw data that will be loaded. Figure 15.1 displays this SQL*Loader process utilizing the logs, the data files, and the control file.

FIGURE 15.1 SQL*Load input and output files

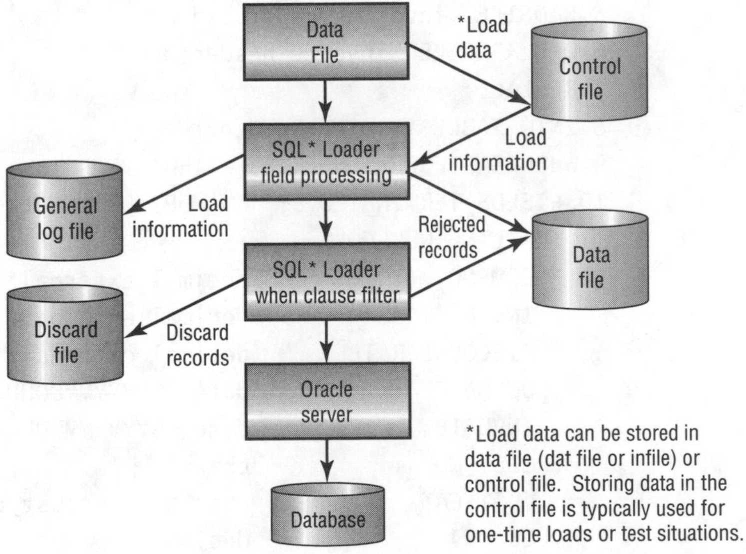

Control Files

The control file is a fairly detailed component of SQL*Loader that is responsible for most of the functionality in the load process. The control file does just what its name implies; it controls the SQL*Loader process. The control performs the following functions in the SQL*Loader process:

- Shows you where to find the data
- Supplies the data format
- Houses configuration and setup information
- Tells you how to manipulate data

Actual load data can be kept in the file, but this should only be performed for sample or test loads. The example below shows a control file that contains no input data; an external file (`invoice_header.dat`), which is designated with the `INFILE` parameter, is used to reference this input data. The line numbers to the left are used to identify the lines we will be discussing in more detail.

```
1 -- Invoice Header Sample Control File
2 -- Created 10-19-01
3 LOAD DATA
4 INFILE 'invoice_header.dat'
5 BADFILE 'invoice_header.bad'
6 DISCARDFILE 'invoice_header.dsc'
7 REPLACE
8 INTO TABLE invoice_header
9 WHEN SALSESPERSON (100) = 'EDI'
10 FIELDS TERMINATED BY  ',' OPTIONALLY ENCLOSED BY '"'
11 TRAILING NULLCOLS
12 ( COMPNO              decimal external
   , INV_NO              decimal external
   , DISCOUNT_RATE       decimal external ":discount_rate * .90"
   , DUEDATE             date "SYYYYMMDDHH24MISS"
   , INVDATE             date "SYYYYMMDDHH24MISS"
   , CUST_NO             char
   , CUST_CAT            char NULLIF cust_cat=BLANKS
   , CO_OBJ              decimal
```

```
, SALESMAN            char "UPPER(:salesman)"
, CUSTREF             char
)
```

Control files have many options that need to be addressed; the above example demonstrates many of these features. Let's walk through each of these features and capabilities identified by the line numbers in this example.

Lines 1, 2 These line numbers identify a comment section in the control file; such a section is designated with double hyphens (`--`).

Line 3 The `LOAD DATA` statement in this line tells SQL*Loader that this is the beginning of a data load. If you are continuing from an aborted process, you could use the `CONTINUE LOAD DATA` statement here instead.

Line 4 The `INFILE` keyword specifies the data that should be read from an input file; in this example, the input file is `invoice_header.dat`.

Line 5 The `BADFILE` keyword specifies the name of the file that will store the rejected records.

Line 6 The `DISCARDFILE` keyword specifies the name of the file that will store the discarded files.

Line 7 The `REPLACE` keyword is one of the options you can use when you want to replace the existing data in a table with the data that you are loading into it. In this case, the existing data is deleted before the new data is copied in. Alternative keywords to use in similar situations are `APPEND`, for a table that is not empty but one in which you want to retain the data that is present, and `INSERT`, for a table that is empty.

Line 8 The `INTO TABLE` keyword allows you to identify the table—`invoice_header` in this example—fields, and their data types.

Line 9 The `WHEN` clause evaluates one or more field conditions to `TRUE` or `FALSE`. If the conditions are evaluated to `TRUE`, then the record is loaded, otherwise, the record is not loaded.

Line 10 The `FIELDS TERMINATED BY` clause is the field delimiter or the character that separates the fields within the `INFILE` file `invoice_header.dat`. The `OPTIONALLY ENCLOSED BY` clause says that fields can also be enclosed by double quotes (`" "`).

Line 11 The `TRAILING NULLCOLS` clause tells SQL*Loader to handle any other columns that are not present in the record as null columns.

Line 12 The remainder of the lines between parentheses () contain the field list that provides details about column formats in the table being loaded.

Log Files

The SQL*Loader log files consist of the bad files, the discard files, and the general log files. Each of these log files records information from the SQL*Loader activities at different parts of the load process. The bad and discard files have the information stored in a load data format. These files could actually be loaded again if desired. The general log is an actual log file that contains information about the overall SQL*Loader process. The input or data file is actual data that will be loaded into the table. We will discuss each of the files in more detail in the upcoming sections.

The Bad Files

Bad files are the first of the three log files generated by the SQL*Loader utility. These files contain the records that were rejected by the Oracle database or did not meet the format criteria in the control file. These logs are created so that they can be used in the reload process if needed. The type of situation in which this type of file could be useful would be one in which you had large input files. Bad log files can be much smaller, and therefore, problems that occurred in the load process would be much easier to identify in these smaller files.

Discard Files

Discard files are created by SQL*Loader if you have designated that they should be created; this process is optional. These log files contain the records that did not match any of the record selection criteria. Hence, these records were excluded from the load. This wasn't because they were unacceptable to the load as was the case with the data in the bad file, but instead it was because these records got filtered out properly according to the way the control file had been set up.

General Log Files

These files store information about the load process in general. This information is used to determine when the SQL*Loader process was performed and how it went. Below is a list of the information that is covered in the general log file.

- Date of the load
- Version information

- Input files
- Output files
- Command line arguments
- Table name
- WHEN clause criteria
- INSERT, APPEND, and REPLACE specifications
- DEFAULTIF or NULLIF keyword usage specifications (optional)
- RECNUM, SEQUENCE, CONSTANT, or EXPRESSION keyword usage specifications (optional)
- DATETIME or INTERVAL specifications (optional) followed by the designated masking
- Data record errors
- Discarded records
- Record load count
- Rejected record count
- Null field record count
- Bind size
- Records loaded per partition

Input Data or Data Files

Input data, a data file, or an input file all describe the same file; one that contains the data that will be loaded into the database table or external table. This file can be in various formats. A common format that is easy to work with is called comma delimited. A comma-delimited data file has commas that separate the fields within the file. When the data file is loaded into the database, the data between each comma is loaded into a column in the table. Whatever the format of the data file, SQL*Loader has robust parsing capabilities and is capable of loading most formats.

Conventional Load, Direct-Path Load, and External-Path Load

There are three methods to load data with SQL*Loader. These methods are conventional load, direct-path load, and external-path load. The conventional load is the default and will load data in much the same way as insert statements are performed in SQL*Plus. The direct-path load is designed to improve the performance of the conventional load by providing similar functionality. Lastly, the external-path load is a specialized load designed so that SQL*Loader will work with external tables.

Conventional Load

Conventional load is the first of three methods you can use to load data with SQL*Loader. A conventional load is much slower than a direct-path load. The conventional load builds a bind array, and when this bind array is full, a SQL insert statement is executed. This method is comparable to the one that Oracle uses to process normal DML statements such as inserts. Conventional load is the default method that SQL*Loader uses.

Direct-Path Load

The *direct-path load* is initiated by using the `DIRECT=TRUE` keyword on the command line. This method is much faster than conventional load. The direct-path load does not use a bind array; instead it uses the direct-path API to load data more directly into the database without the overhead of standard SQL command processing. Because the data actually bypasses the normal SQL processing layers, Oracle must load this data into blocks that are unused or are above the high-water mark of the table. The *high-water mark* is the last used block in the table whether there is data in the block or not. Table 15.1 compares conventional loads and direct-path loads, and Figure 15.2 displays the functional differences between these two methods.

TABLE 15.1 Conventional Load versus Direct-Path Load

Conventional Load	Direct-Path Load
Uses standard commits to save data	Uses data saves
Always generates redo information	Generates redo information when certain conditions are met
Fires insert triggers	Does not fire insert triggers
Can load into clustered tables	Cannot load into a clustered table
Enforces constraints	Does not enforce constraints

TABLE 15.1 Conventional Load versus Direct-Path Load *(continued)*

Conventional Load	Direct-Path Load
Allows users to modify the table data during load process or have active transactions	Locks users out so that they cannot make changes or have active transactions
Allows SQL functions to be used in the control file	Does not allow SQL functions to be used in the control file

The direct-path load functions in a similar manner to the way the direct-path insert does. Each control file and input data file is loaded into a temporary segment and then it is merged into the table above the high-water mark. See Figure 15.2, which shows SQL*Loader parallel direct-path load in comparison to conventional load.

FIGURE 15.2 SQL*Loader overview of direct-path load versus conventional load

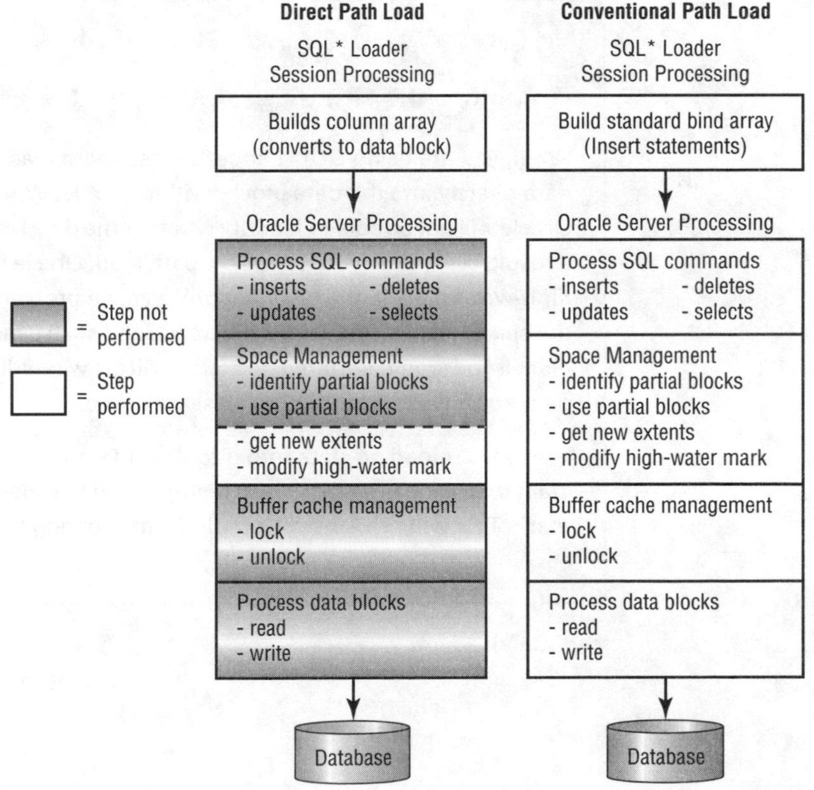

External-Path Load

This *external-path load* is specialized to allow the SQL*Loader utility to be used on external tables. By default, the external-path load is attempted in parallel if the table is made up of multiple data files. *External tables* are tables that are stored outside the database and have special restrictions (such as they are read-only). External tables are used primarily as temporary storage tables that can be loaded into normal database tables at some point.

Let's go through a brief overview of the necessary components for creating the external table. The command used to create external tables is very similar to a standard table creation command; it is `CREATE TABLE <table name> ORGANIZATION EXTERNAL`. In addition, a logical directory that designates the files that will make up the external table will need to be created. This command is `CREATE DIRECTORY EXTERNAL_TAB_DIR as '/u01/ora9i/ext_files'`. Once these steps have been completed, the schema that will create the table will need read and/or write privilege granted to the external directory, which in our case is `EXTERNAL_TAB_DIR`.

Real World Scenario

Adjusting the High-Water Mark with Direct-Path Load

When you are using SQL*Loader's direct-path load method, you can insert data directly into the data blocks within a table. When you do this, however, Oracle will not be able to identify whether the data blocks have data or not. As a result, every time you use direct-path load, Oracle must put data in past the high-water mark in the table. But this is not a problem if you are prepared for the space usage in the table to increase and such usage is part of your growth plan. If you aren't prepared, the table will grow rapidly each time you load the data and it will consume unnecessary space.

If you are reloading data into a table and replacing the old data, you may want to truncate the table before you do so in order to reset the high-water mark. This will prevent your table from growing the size of the data load each time the table is loaded.

SQL*Loader Parallel Load Methods

SQL*Loader can be run in parallel to further improve performance of large data loads. There are three main variations of parallel loads: parallel conventional load, intersegment concurrency with direct-path load, and intrasegment concurrency with direct-path load. Here we explore each of these load methods.

Parallel conventional load *Parallel conventional load* is performed by issuing multiple SQL*Loader commands, each with their own control file and input data file, all to the same table. The input data file is logically split on the record boundaries in the table. For example, records 1 through 100 are loaded using the `inv.dat` input file, and records 101 through 200 are loaded using the `inv2.dat` input file.

```
oracle@octilli:> sqlldr test/test control=inv.ctl
load=inv.dat
oracle@octilli:> sqlldr test/test control=inv2.ctl
load=inv2.dat
```

Intersegment concurrency with direct-path load *Intersegment concurrency with direct-path load* is performed by using direct-path load to load into multiple tables or partitions within a table at the same time. This method is performed in the same way that parallel conventional load is, but it adds the `DIRECT=TRUE` keyword and uses different tables. Notice that the first load is going into the `inv.dat` table and the second is going into the `orders.dat` table as designated by the control file and input file name.

```
oracle@octilli:> sqlldr test/test control=inv.ctl
load=inv.dat direct=true
oracle@octilli:> sqlldr test/test control=orders.ctl
load=orders.dat direct=true
```

Intrasegment concurrency with direct-path load *Intrasegment concurrency with direct-path load* is performed by using direct-path load to load data into a single table or partition. This can be performed by placing the `DIRECT=TRUE` and `PARALLEL=TRUE` option on the command line. In this parallel server, processes load the data into temporary segments and then merge them into the individual segments.

```
oracle@octilli:> sqlldr test/test control=inv.ctl
load=inv.dat direct=true parallel=true
```

Performing Basic SQL*Loader Operations

The basic SQL*Loader functions are initiated by executing the `sqlldr` command at the OS command prompt. Here is an example in Unix that shows you all of the other commands and options available to the SQL*Loader utility.

```
oracle@octilli:/oracle/admin/tst9/adhoc > sqlldr

SQL*Loader: Release 9.0.1.0.0 - Production on Tue Oct 16
21:11:51 2001

(c) Copyright 2001 Oracle Corporation.  All rights
reserved.


Usage: SQLLOAD keyword=value [,keyword=value,...]

Valid Keywords:

    userid -- ORACLE username/password
   control -- Control file name
       log -- Log file name
       bad -- Bad file name
      data -- Data file name
   discard -- Discard file name
discardmax -- Number of discards to allow
(Default all)
      skip -- Number of logical records to skip
(Default 0)
      load -- Number of logical records to load
(Default all)
    errors -- Number of errors to allow
(Default 50)
      rows -- Number of rows in conventional path bind
array or between directs
             (Default: Conventional path 64, Direct path
all)
```

```
  bindsize -- Size of conventional path bind array in
bytes  (Default 256000)
    silent -- Suppress messages during run
(header,feedback,errors,discards,par)
    direct -- use direct path
(Default FALSE)
   parfile -- parameter file: name of file that contains
parameter specifications
  parallel -- do parallel load
(Default FALSE)
      file -- File to allocate extents from
skip_unusable_indexes -- disallow/allow unusable indexes
or index partitions  ()
skip_index_maintenance -- do not maintain indexes, mark
affected indexes as unu)
commit_discontinued -- commit loaded rows when load is
discontinued  (Default F)
  readsize -- Size of Read buffer
(Default 1048576)
external_table -- use external table for load; NOT_USED,
GENERATE_ONLY, EXECUTE)
columnarrayrows -- Number of rows for direct path column
array  (Default 5000)
streamsize -- Size of direct path stream buffer in bytes
(Default 256000)
multithreading -- use multithreading in direct path
 resumable -- enable or disable resumable for current
session  (Default FALSE)
resumable_name -- text string to help identify resumable
statement
resumable_timeout -- wait time (in seconds) for RESUMABLE
(Default 7200)

PLEASE NOTE: Command-line parameters may be specified
either by
position or by keywords. An example of the former case is
'sqlldr
scott/tiger foo'; an example of the latter is 'sqlldr
control=foo
userid=scott/tiger'. One may specify parameters by
position before
```

```
but not after parameters specified by keywords. For
example,
'sqlldr scott/tiger control=foo logfile=log' is allowed,
but
'sqlldr scott/tiger control=foo log' is not, even though
the
position of the parameter 'log' is correct.
oracle@octilli:/oracle/admin/tst9/adhoc >
```

SQL*Loader can be run by using the command line and the parameters can be used within the line. There are many variations that can be performed, but we will demonstrate some common examples to illustrate the basic uses. This first example uses 10 records that are contained in the `invoice_header.dat` input file and in the `invoice_header.ctl` control file. Below are examples that show the control file first, then show the input file containing the load data, and finally show the actual `sqlldr` command.

```
load data
infile invoice_header.dat
into table invoice_header
fields terminated by ',' optionally enclosed by '"'
trailing nullcols
( COMP_NO                          decimal external
, INV_NO                          decimal external
, CUST_NO                          decimal external
, DUE_DATE                         date "SYYYYMMDDHH24MISS"
, INV_DATE                         date "SYYYYMMDDHH24MISS"
, CUST_NAME                        char
, CUST_CAT                        char
, CUST_OBJ                         decimal external
, SALESMAN                        char
, CUST_REF                         char
)

20,141596,1154427,20000925000000,20000827000000,CUSTONE,20,,
EDI,09020
20,141597,1153954,20000925000000,20000827000000,SUPERSTOR,20
,,EDI,09020
```

```
20,141598,1154365,20000925000000,20000827000000,MINIMART,20,
,EDI,09020
20,141599,1154422,20000926000000,20000827000000,PRICEBUST,20
,,EDI,09020
20,141600,1154419,20000926000000,20000827000000,BIGSTORE,20,
,EDI,15010
20,141601,1154481,20000926000000,20000827000000,MAPAPS,20,,E
DI,09020
20,141602,1154477,20000927000000,20000827000000,HOLEWALL,20,
,EDI,15010
20,141603,1153487,20000927000000,20000827000000,CUSTTWO,20,,
EDI,09020
20,141604,1153417,20000927000000,20000827000000,LITTSTORE,20
,,EDI,07020
20,141605,1153327,20000927000000,20000827000000,MEDSTORE,20,
,EDI,07020

oracle@octilli: > sqlldr test/test control=invoice_
header.ctl
SQL*Loader: Release 9.0.1.0.0 - Production on Tue Oct 16
21:11:51 2001

(c) Copyright 2001 Oracle Corporation.  All rights reserved.

Commit point reached - logical record count 9
Commit point reached - logical record count 10
oracle@octilli: >
```

Next, we will demonstrate an example of how to use the direct-path load method to load the same data. We will use the same control file and the same table as in the previous example.

```
oracle@octilli: > sqlldr test/test control=invoice_
header.ctl direct=true

SQL*Loader: Release 9.0.1.0.0 - Production on Tue Oct 16
21:11:51 2001

(c) Copyright 2001 Oracle Corporation.  All rights
reserved.
```

```
Load completed - logical record count 10.

oracle@octilli: >
```

Guidelines for Using SQL*Loader and Direct-Load Insert

In order to use SQL*Loader effectively, you need to consider the following guidelines:

Use the parameter file to specify and simplify the use of commonly used command line options. This is a good choice for repeatable loads that can be scheduled. The parameter is similar to the parameter file used in the export and import utility. With the commands in a parameter file, the DBA will not need to interactively reply to prompts when the utility is executed.

For a small, one-time load, you should place only small data sets in the control file. This approach restricts the use of the control file for new data sets. This method is primarily used to load sample or test data because the control file information is combined with the raw data. The raw data would need to be combined or concatenated to the control file each time it was loaded. This is more cumbersome than keeping the data separate in a data file.

Optimize performance by allocating sufficient initial space. When you optimize in this manner, you prevent dynamic extent allocation, which slows the load process.

Optimize performance by presorting data on the big indexes. Optimizing in this manner helps to alleviate the work that must be performed in the temporary segments in order for indexes to be rebuilt.

Optimize performance by using different files for temporary segments in order to perform parallel loads. You should use different data files to represent the location of your temporary segments for each parallel `sqlldr` command line execution. This is done by using the `FILE` option in the control file to designate the data file where the temporary segments are created during the parallel load operation.

Summary

The Oracle SQL*Loader utility is a tool designed to load external data into the Oracle database. There are three methods of loading data when you are using the SQL*Loader: the conventional load, the direct-path load, and the external-path load.

The direct-path insert DML statement that is run in SQL*Plus is similar to the direct-path load in SQL*Loader. This method has both serial and parallel load options.

There are some basic SQL*Loader activities that can help you to become familiar with some of the uses of the SQL*Loader tool, and there are several commands, formats, and methods that you can use to run SQL*Loader. In addition, there are several usage guidelines for SQL*Loader.

The topics covered in this chapter will be covered on the test and are valuable in real-world situations. SQL*Loader and direct-load insert can be used for a variety of purposes. SQL*Loader is very useful to bulk load data from one database to another. The direct-load insert operation is useful when you are making table backups within the database or you are moving data from one table to another. Both of these tools can be valuable assets for the DBA.

Exam Essentials

Understand direct-load insert operations. Know that direct-load insert is a DML statement that passes data from one table to another within the Oracle database. When you use this DML statement, you can bypass the SQL buffer cache and direct loads into the data blocks within the targeted tables.

Know the files used with SQL*Loader. Be able to list the files used with SQL*Loader—the control file, the bad log, the discard log, the general log, and the input data, or data file—and make sure you understand the purpose of each of these files.

Know the methods SQL*Loader uses to load data. SQL*Loader uses the conventional load, the direct-path load, and the external-path load to load data. The direct-path load is used to improve performance, the conventional load is used for normal operations, and the external-path load is a specialized load option used only for external tables.

Identify the parallel SQL*Loader methods for loading data. Be able to pick out the differences between a parallel conventional load, an intrasegment concurrency with direct-path load, and an intersegment concurrency with direct-path load.

Understand how to use SQL*Loader. Be sure you are familiar with the command line references you will need in order to execute SQL*Loader. Be able to use a command such as `sqlldr username/password control=control.ctl` at the OS prompt.

Understand the guidelines for efficiently using SQL*Loader. Be familiar with the guidelines that must be followed to efficiently use SQL*Loader: using parameter files for common commands, refraining from keeping data in the control file, avoiding dynamic space allocation, alleviating sorting in the index process, and distributing the temporary segments on different data files with SQL*Loader `FILE` keyword.

Key Terms

Before you take the exam, be certain you are familiar with the following terms:

bad log	high-water mark
control file	hint
conventional load	intersegment concurrency with direct-path load
data file	intrasegment concurrency with direct-path load
direct-load insert	log files
direct-path load	parallel conventional load
discard log	parallel direct-load insert
external tables	serial direct-load insert
external-path load	SQL*Loader
general log	

Review Questions

1. What insert statement will bypass the SQL buffer cache so that data may be loaded?

   A. SQL*Loader direct-path load

   B. SQL*Loader conventional load

   C. Direct-load insert

   D. SQL*Loader external table

2. Which of the following methods causes the target table to be in parallel mode when it is using the direct-path insert statement? (Choose all that apply.)

   A. Using the ALTER TABLE command

   B. Using multiple direct-path load SQL*Loader statements

   C. Using hints with the PARALLEL clause

   D. Using one SQL*Loader direct-path load statement

3. Which of the following is the SQL*Loader file structure that is responsible for formatting the data to be loaded?

   A. Bad file

   B. Format file

   C. Control file

   D. Discard file

4. Which log file contains cumulative information about the number of records loaded in a SQL*Loader run?

   A. Bad log

   B. General log

   C. Discard log

   D. Control file

5. What log file contains records that were rejected by the database?

   A. Bad log

   B. General log

   C. Discard log

   D. Control file

6. What log file contains records that were filtered out of the load due to clauses in the control file?

   A. Bad log

   B. General log

   C. Discard log

   D. Control file

7. Which file contains the data that gets loaded in the SQL*Loader run? (Choose all that apply.)

   A. Input file

   B. Control file

   C. Data file

   D. Log file

8. Which SQL*Loader load keyword deletes data in table before loading?

   A. `APPEND`

   B. `DELETE`

   C. `REPLACE`

   D. `INSERT`

9. What SQL*Loader technique allows parallel processing?

   A. Running multiple `sqlldr` command lines on the same table with different input files

   B. Using the `PARALLEL` hint

   C. Using the `ALTER TABLE` command on the target table

   D. Using the `PARALLEL` command on the `sqlldr` command line

10. What SQL*Loader method cannot load into clustered tables?

    A. Conventional load

    B. Direct-path load

    C. Using the `ALTER TABLE` command on the target table

    D. Parallel load hints

11. Which SQL*Loader method uses bind arrays?

    A. Direct-path load

    B. Conventional load

    C. Direct-path insert

    D. Parallel load hints

12. Which SQL*Loader method cannot have active transactions during the load process?

    A. Conventional load

    B. Direct-path load

    C. Data stored in the input file only

    D. Data stored in the control file only

13. What must you do to enable direct-path insert? (Choose all that apply.)

    A. Use the `ALTER SESSION ENABLE PARALLEL DML;` command.

    B. Use an `INDEX` hint.

    C. Use a `PARALLEL` hint.

    D. Run multiple direct-path inserts at the same time.

14. Which of the following is a true statement regarding SQL functions and SQL*Loader?

    A. SQL functions cannot be used in a conventional load.

    B. SQL functions can be used in a direct-path load.

    C. SQL functions cannot be used in a direct-path load.

    D. SQL functions can be used in both conventional and direct-path loads.

15. Which of the following is a true statement regarding active transactions or changes when you are using SQL*Loader?

    A. No active transactions or changes can be performed on a conventionally loaded table.

    B. No active transactions or changes can be performed on a direct-path loaded table.

    C. Active transactions or changes can be performed on a direct-path loaded table.

    D. Active transactions or changes cannot be performed on a direct-path loaded or a conventionally loaded table.

Answers to Review Questions

1. C. The direct-load insert statement will bypass the buffer cache while it performs an insert. SQL*Loader direct-path load will also bypass the buffer cache, but it is not an insert statement.

2. A, C. Both the `ALTER TABLE` command and hints used with the `PARALLEL` clause will allow the table to be placed in parallel.

3. C. The control file is responsible for formatting the data to be loaded.

4. B. The general log contains cumulative information about the number of records that were loaded.

5. A. The bad log contains records that were rejected by the database.

6. C. The discard log contains data that was filtered out of the load as designed in the control file.

7. A, B, C. The input file, or data file, and the control file can contain data that is loaded in the SQL*Loader run.

8. C. The `REPLACE` command deletes the current data in a table first before it inserts new data.

9. A. Running multiple `sqlldr` command line entries with multiple data files will cause parallel loads.

10. B. The direct-path load cannot load data into a clustered table.

11. B. The conventional load uses bind arrays to temporarily store the data before inserting into the database.

12. B. Direct-path load cannot have active transactions taking place on the table you are loading. This is because there is a lock placed on the table and the data is directly loaded into blocks.

13. A, C. To enable direct-path insert, the session you are performing parallel DML on must have PARALLEL DML enabled. Secondly, you must either use a PARALLEL hint or place the table being inserted into parallel.

14. C. No SQL functions can be used in the control file when you are using a direct-path load. This is because a direct-path load bypasses standard SQL statement processing for performance reasons.

15. B. Active transactions or changes cannot be performed on a direct-path loaded table. Users are prevented from making changes.

Glossary

A

Application layer A layer of the Oracle Net stack that interacts with the user. This layer accepts commands and returns data.

archived logs Also known as offline redo logs. Logs that are copies of the online redo logs and are saved to another location before the online copies are reused.

ARCHIVELOG mode A mode of database operation. When the Oracle database is run in ARCHIVELOG mode, the online redo log files are copied to another location before they are overwritten. These archived log files can be used for point-in-time recovery of the database. They can also be used for analysis.

archiver process (ARC*n*) Performs the copying of the online redo log files to archived log files.

ARC*n* See *archiver process (ARCn)*.

ATL See *automated tape library (ATL)*.

automated tape library (ATL) A tape device that can interface with RMAN and can automatically store and retrieve tapes via tape media software.

automatic archiving The automatic creation of archived logs after the appropriate redo logs have been switched. The LOG_ARCHIVE_START parameter must be set to TRUE in the `init.ora` file for automatic archiving to take place.

automatic channel allocation This type of channel allocation is performed by setting the RMAN configuration at the RMAN command prompt. This is done by using the CONFIGURE DEFAULT DEVICE or CONFIGURE DEVICE command.

AVAILABLE The RMAN command used to make a backup set available or accessible in the RMAN repository.

B

BACKUP The RMAN command is used to perform a backup that creates a backup set.

backup and recovery strategy The backup and recovery plan for an organization's databases, applications, and systems that is formalized and agreed upon by the required groups in the organization.

BACKUP CONTROLFILE TO TRACE A create control file command, which makes an ASCII backup of the binary control file, which can then be executed to re-create the binary control file. The BACKUP CONTROLFILE is dumped as a user trace file. This file can be viewed, edited, and run as a script after you edit the comments and miscellaneous trace information.

backup piece A physical object that stores data files, control files, or archived logs and resides within a backup set.

backup script A script written in different OS scripting languages, such as Korn shell or C shell in the Unix environments.

backup set A logical object that stores one or more physical backup pieces containing either data files, control files, or archived logs. Backup sets must be processed with the RESTORE command before these files are usable.

bad log A SQL*Loader log which documents records that where rejected by the Oracle database or SQL*Loader because they had an invalid format or unique key violations, or because they has a required field that was null.

bequeath connection A connection type in which control is passed directly to a dedicated spawned process or a dispatched process. No redirection is required.

block The smallest unit of storage in an Oracle database. Data is stored in the database in blocks. The block size is defined at the time of database creation and is a multiple of the operating system block size.

block corruption A block within the database that is corrupt.

bounded time recovery Instance recovery that the DBA controls or puts bounds on the time that it takes for an instance to recover after instance failure.

C

cancel-based recovery A type of incomplete recovery that is stopped when the DBA executes a CANCEL command during a manual recovery operation.

cataloging Storing information in the Recovery Manager catalog. This is done by issuing the RMAN CATALOG command.

CHANGE The RMAN command used to change the status of a backup set to either AVAILABLE or UNAVAILABLE.

change-based recovery A type of incomplete recovery that is stopped by a change number designated when the recovery is initiated.

change vector See *redo log entry*.

channel allocation Allocating a physical device to be associated with the server session.

checkpoint The process of updating the SCN in all the data files and control files in the database in conjunction with all necessary data blocks in the data buffers being written to disk. This is done for the purposes of ensuring database consistency and synchronization.

checkpointing See *checkpoint*.

checkpoint process (CKPT) The checkpoint process updates the headers of data files and control files; the actual blocks are written to the file by the DBW*n* process.

CKPT See *checkpoint process (CKPT)*.

closed backup A backup that occurs when the target database is closed or shut down. This means that the target database is not available for use during this type of backup. This is also referred to as an offline or cold backup.

cold backup See *closed backup*.

commit To save or permanently store the results of a transaction to the database.

complete recovery A recovery situation in which no data is lost.

CONFIGURATION parameters The parameters that determine the RMAN settings.

consistent backup A backup of a target database that is mounted but not opened and was shut down with either a SHUTDOWN IMMEDIATE or SHUTDOWN NORMAL option, but not with SHUTDOWN ABORT. The database files are stamped with the same SCN at the same point in time. This occurs during a cold backup of the database and no recovery is needed.

control file (database) The file that stores the RMAN repository information and records the physical information about the database. The control file contains the database name and timestamp of database creation, along with the name and location of every data file and redo log file.

control file (SQL*Loader) The logic behind the data load that determines how and what data will be loaded. This is the SQL*Loader control file, not to be confused with the database control file.

conventional-path export The standard export that goes through the SQL-evaluation layer.

conventional load The conventional load is the default load process for SQL*Loader. The conventional load builds a bind array, and when this bind array is full, a SQL insert statement is executed.

COPY The RMAN command that performs an image copy.

CROSSCHECK TheRMANcommandusedtocomparetheRMANrepository to the stored media backups.

cross checking The process of comparing the RMAN repository with the media backups that are stored using the CROSSCHECK command.

cumulative incremental backup Backs up only the data blocks that have changed since the most recent backup of the next lowest level—*n* – 1 or lower (with *n* being the existing level of backup).

current online redo logs Logs that are actively being written to by the LGWR process.

D

database The physical structure that stores the actual data. The Oracle server consists of the database and the instance.

database buffer cache The area of memory that caches the database data. It holds the recent blocks that are read from the database data files.

database buffers See *data block buffers.*

database writer process (DBW*n*) The DBW*n* process is responsible for writing the changed database blocks from the SGA to the data file. There can be up to 10 database writer processes (DBW0 through DBW9).

data block See *block.*

data block buffers Memory buffers containing data blocks that get flushed to disk if modified and committed.

data dictionary A collection of database tables and views that contain metadata about the database, its structures, its privileges, and its users. Oracle accesses the data dictionary frequently during the parsing of SQL statements.

data file (database) The data files or data files in a database contain all the database data. A data file can belong to only one database and tablespace.

data file (SQL*Loader) The data file, input data, or infile all describe the same file, one that contains the raw data that is loaded in SQL*Loader.

DBVERIFY utility An Oracle utility used to determine whether data files have corrupt blocks.

DBW*n* See *database writer process (DB*Wn*).*

dedicated server Type of connection in which every client connection has an associated dedicated server process on the machine where the Oracle server exists.

degree of parallelism The number of parallel processes you choose to enable for a particular parallel activity such as recovery.

differential incremental backup A type of backup that backs up only data blocks modified since the most recent backup at the same level or lower.

direct-load insert A faster method to add rows to a table from existing tables by using the `INSERT INTO ... SELECT ...` statement. Direct-load insert bypasses the buffer cache and writes the data blocks directly to the data files.

direct-path export The type of export that bypasses the SQL-evaluation layer, creating significant performance gains.

direct-path load The type of SQL*Loader load that is initiated by using the `DIRECT=TRUE` keyword. This load process loads in the data blocks directly above the high-water mark and designs for performance capabilities.

dirty buffers The blocks in the database buffer cache that are changed but are not yet written to the disk.

disaster recovery Recovery of a database that has been entirely destroyed due to fire, earthquake, flood, or some other disastrous situation.

discard log The log that stores the records that are discarded in the SQL*Loader because the control file load criteria was not met.

disk failure See *media (disk) failure.*

dispatchers Process in an Oracle Shared Server environment that is responsible for managing requests from one or more client connections.

distributed transactions Transactions that occur in remote databases.

dump file The file where the logical backup is stored. This file is created by the Export utility and read by the Import utilities.

dynamic service registration The ability of an Oracle instance to automatically register its existence with a listener.

E

Export (exp) utility A utility that Oracle uses to unload (export) data to external files in a binary format. The Export utility can export the definitions of all objects in the database. It also makes logical backups of the database.

external-path load The specialty SQL*Loader process designed to load external tables.

external table A table that resides in a file outside of the Oracle database but is accessible through the database via SQL.

extproc The default name of the callout process that is used when executing external procedures from Oracle.

F

firewall Generally, a combination of hardware and software that is used to control network traffic and prevent intruders from compromising corporate network security.

full backup A type of backup that backs up all the data blocks in the data files, modified or not.

full resynchronization All physical changes to the database, including control files, data files, and redo logs. In addition, changed records are updated in the RMAN repository during this process.

G

general log The log file that contains a detailed summary of all aspects of the load process.

Generic Connectivity One of the Heterogeneous Services offered by Oracle that allows for connectivity solutions based on third-party connection options such as OLEDB and ODBC.

H

header block The first block in a data file; it contains information about the data file, such as size information, transactional usage, and checkpoint information.

Heterogeneous Services Facilitythatprovidestheabilitytocommunicate with non-Oracle databases and services.

high-water mark (HWM) The maximum number of blocks used by the table. The high-water mark is not reset when you delete rows.

hint A multiline comment with a plus symbol within an SQL statement. The mechanism influences the explain plan of a query.

host The name of the physical machine on which the Oracle server is located. This can be an Internet Protocol (IP) address or a real name that is resolved via some external naming solution, such as DNS.

hostnaming method A names resolution method for small networks that minimizes the amount of configuration work the DBA must perform.

hot backup Also called an opened, or online, backup. Occurs when the database is open and a physical file copy of the data files associated with each tablespace is made (placed into backup mode with the `ALTER TABLESPACE [BEGIN/END] BACKUP` commands).

I

image copies Copies of data files, control files, or archived logs, either individually or as a whole database. These copies are not stored in an RMAN format. These are stored in a standard file format much like a file that must be stored in disk.

Import utility An Oracle utility used to read and import data from the file created by the Export utility. A selective import can be performed using the appropriate parameters. The Import utility reads the logical backups generated by the export.

incarnation A reference of a target database in the recovery catalog.

incomplete recovery A form of recovery that doesn't completely recover the database to the point of failure. The three types of incomplete recovery arecancel-based,time-based,andchange-based.Incompleterecoveryrequires a `RESETLOGS`.

inconsistent backup A backup of the target database that is conducted when it is opened but has crashed prior to mounting, or when it was shut down with the `SHUTDOWN ABORT` option prior to mounting. In this type of backup, the database files are stamped with different SCNs, which occurs during a hot backup of the database. Recovery is needed.

incremental backup A type of backup that backs up only the data blocks in the data files that were modified since the last incremental backup. There are two types of incremental backups: differential and cumulative.

`init<ORACLE_SID>.ora` The parameter file that contains the parameters required for instance startup.

instance The memory structures and background processes of the Oracle server.

instance failure An abnormal shutdown of the Oracle database that then requires that the latest online redo log be applied to the database when it restarts to assure database consistency.

instance recovery The automatic recovery of an Oracle database instance that results from an instance failure or an abrupt shutdown of the database.

interactive export An export in which the user responds to prompts from the Export utility to perform various actions.

intersegment concurrency with direct-path load A type of parallel direct-path load performed by using direct-path load to load into multiple tables or partitions within a table at the same time.

intrasegment concurrency with direct-path load A type of parallel direct-path load performed by using direct-path load to load data into a single table or partition.

IP-filtering firewall Type of firewall that monitors the network packet traffic on IP networks and filters out packets that either originated or did not originate from specific groups of machines.

J

Java Database Connectivity Connectivity solution used to connect Java-based applications to a database server.

L

Large Pool An optional area in the SGA used for specific database operations, such as backup, recovery, or the User Global Area (UGA) space, when using an MTS configuration.

LGWR See *log writer process (LGWR)*.

List commands RMAN commands that perform simple queries of the catalog to tell what has been done to date.

listener Server-side process that is responsible for listening and establishing connections to an Oracle server based on a client connection request.

`listener.ora` Configuration file for the Oracle listener located on the Oracle server.

load balancing Ability of the Oracle listener to balance the number of connections between a group of dispatcher processes in an Oracle Shared Server environment.

locally managed tablespace A tablespace that manages the extent allocation and de-allocation information through bitmaps in its associated datafiles.

localnaming method Names resolution method that relies on resolving an Oracle Net service name via a physical file, the `tnsnames.ora` file.

LOG_ARCHIVE_DEST An `init.ora` parameter that determines the destination of the archived logs. Cannot be used in conjunction with LOG_ARCHIVE_DEST_*n*.

LOG_ARCHIVE_DEST_*N* An `init.ora` parameter that determines the other destinations of the archived logs, remote or local. This parameter supports up to five locations, *N* being a number 1 through 10. Only one of these destinations can be remote. Cannot be used with LOG_ARCHIVE_DEST or LOG_ARCHIVE_DUPLEX_DEST.

LOG_ARCHIVE_DUPLEX_DEST An `init.ora` parameter that determines the duplexed, or second, destination of archived logs in a two-location archived log configuration. Cannot be used in conjunction with LOG_ARCHIVE_DEST_*n*.

LOG_ARCHIVE_START An `init.ora` parameter that enables automatic archiving.

log buffers Memory buffers that contain the entries that get written to the log files.

log file A file to which the status of the operation is written when utilities such as SQL*Loader or Export or Import are being used.

logging The recording of DML statements, creation of new objects, and other changes in the redo logs. This process also records significant events, such as starting and stopping the listener, along with certain kinds of network errors.

logical backup Reads data in the database and stores it in an Export file to create a snapshot of all data in the database. Cannot be used in conjunction with incomplete recovery.

logical objects Objects that do not exist outside of the database, such as tables, indexes, sequences, and views.

logical structures The database structures that are seen by the user. Tablespaces, segments, extents, blocks, tables, and indexes are all examples of logical structures.

LogMiner A utility that can be used to analyze the redo log files. It can provide a fix for logical corruption by building redo and undo SQL statements from the contents of the redo logs. LogMiner is a set of PL/SQL packages and dynamic performance views.

log sequence number A sequence number assigned to each redo log file.

log writer process (LGWR) Responsible for writing the redo log buffer entries (change vectors) to the online redo log files.

lsnrctl Command line utility used to control and monitor the Oracle listener process.

lsnrctl services Command used to view information about what services a particular Oracle listener is listening for.

`lsnrctl stop` Command to stop the default or currently selected Oracle listener.

M

manual archiving The execution of commands to create archived logs. Archived logs are not automatically created after redo log switching.

manual channel allocation This type of channel allocation is performed any time you issue the command `ALLOCATE CHANNEL`. A manual command for allocating a channel is `ALLOCATE CHANNEL` *`<channel name>`* `TYPE DISK`.

mean time to recovery (MTTR) The mean (average) time needed to recover a database from a certain type of failure.

media (disk) failure A physical disk failure, or one that occurs when the database files cannot be accessed by the instance.

media management library (MML) or Media Management Layer A tape media library that allows RMAN to interface with a tape hardware vendor's tape backup device. Also referred to as Media Management Layer.

media recovery Recovery operation that results from a media (disk) failure.

middleware Software and hardware that sits between a client and the Oracle server. Middleware can serve a variety of functions such as load balancing, security, and application-specific business logic processing.

MML See *media management library (MML)*.

MTTR See *mean time to recovery (MTTR)*.

multiplexing Oracle's mechanism for writing to more than one copy of the redo log file or control file. This process involves mirroring, or making duplicate copies. Multiplexing ensures that even if you lose one member of the redo log group or one control file, you can recover using the other one. It intersperses blocks from Oracle data files within a backup set.

N

`NAMES.DIRECTORY_PATH` An entry found in the `sqlnet.ora` file that defines the net service name search method hierarchy for a client.

National Language Support (NLS) Enables Oracle to store and retrieve information in a format and language that can be understood by users anywhere in the world. The database character set and various other parameters are used to enhance this capability.

net service name The name of an Oracle service on a network. This is the name the user enters when they are referring to an Oracle service.

Network Program Interface (NPI) A layer in the Oracle Net stack found on the Oracle server that is responsible for server-to-server communications.

NLS See *National Language Support (NLS).*

NOARCHIVELOG mode A mode of database operation, whereby the redo log files are not preserved for recovery or analysis purposes.

nologging In this process, recording DML statements, creating new objects, and other changes in the redo logs do not occur—therefore changes are unrecoverable until the next physical backup.

non-current online redo logs Online redo logs that are not in the current or active group being written to.

non-media failures Failures that occur for reasons other than disk failure. The types of failure that make up this group are the statement failure, the process failure, the instance failure, and user error.

NPI See *Network Program Interface(NPI).*

***n*-tier architecture** A network architecture involving at least 3 computers, typically a client computer, a middle-tier computer, and a database server.

O

OEM See *Oracle Enterprise Management (OEM).*

OFA See *Optimal Flexible Architecture (OFA).*

offline backup See *closed backup.*

offline redo log See *archived logs.*

online backup See *hot backup.*

online redo logs Redo logs that are being written to by the LGWR process at some point in time and have not been archived.

OPA See *Open Protocol Adapters (OPA) layer.*

opened backup See *hot backup.*

Open Systems Interconnection (OSI) A widely accepted model that defines how data communications are carried out across a network.

OPI See *Oracle Protocol Interface (OPI) layer.*

Optimal Flexible Architecture (OFA) A standard of presenting the optimal way to set up an Oracle database. It includes guidelines for creating database file locations for better performance and management.

Oracle Advanced Security An optional package offered by Oracle that enhances and extends the security capabilities of the standard Oracle server configuration.

Oracle Call Interface (OCI) layer A layer of the Oracle Net stack that is responsible for all of the SQL processing that occurs between a client and the Oracle server.

Oracle Connection Manager An optional middleware feature from Oracle that provides multiplexing, Network Access Control, and Cross Connectivity–Protocol Connectivity.

Oracle Enterprise Manager (OEM) A DBA system management tool that performs a wide variety of DBA tasks, including running the RMAN utility in GUI mode, managing different components of Oracle, and administering the databases at one location.

ORACLE_HOME The environment variable that defines the location where the Oracle software is installed.

Oracle Net Foundation layer A layer of the Oracle Net Stack that shields both the client and server from the complexities of network communications and is based on the Transparent Network Substrate (TNS).

Oracle Program Interface (OPI) layer A layer of the Oracle Net Stack residing on the server. For every request made from the client, the Oracle Program Interface is responsible for sending the appropriate response back to the client.

Oracle Protocol Adapters (OPA) layer A layer of the Oracle Net Stack that maps the Oracle Net Foundation layer functions to the analogous functions in the underlying protocol.

Oracle Recovery Manager (RMAN) The Recovery Manager utility, which is automated and is responsible for the backup and recovery of Oracle databases.

Oracle Shared Server A connection configuration that enhances the scalability of the Oracle server. Shared Server is an optional configuration of the Oracle server that allows the server to support a larger number of concurrent connections without increasing physical resource requirements.

ORACLE_SID The environment variable that defines the database instance name. If you are not using Net8, connections are made to this database instance by default.

OSI See *Open Systems Interconnection (OSI)*.

Oracle Transparent Gateway A connectivity solution that seamlessly extends the reach of Oracle to non-Oracle data stores, which allows you to treat non-Oracle data sources as if they were part of the Oracle environment.

P

parallel conventional load This type of conventional load is performed by issuing multiple SQL*Loader commands, each with their own control file and input data file, all to the same table.

parallel direct-load insert This type of direct load is the same DML insert operation as serial direct-load insert, but in this case, the statement or table is put into parallel mode.

PARALLEL_MAX_SERVERS An `init.ora` parameter that determines the maximum number of parallel query processes at any given time.

parallel query processes Oracle background processes that process a portion of a query. Each parallel query process runs on a separate CPU.

parameter file (Export, Import, SQL*Loader) Text file with command-line parameters for the utility, one per line.

parameter file (`init.ora`) A file with parameters used to configure memory, database file locations, and limits for the database. This file is read when the database is started.

`PARFILE` The parameter file that stores options for Export, Import, or SQL*Loader.

partial resynchronization In a partial resynchronization, RMAN reads the current control file to update modified information, but it does not resynchronize the metadata about the database physical schema, such as data files, tablespaces, redo threads, rollback segments produced when the database is open, and online redo logs.

PGA See *Program Global Area (PGA)*.

physical backup A copy of all the Oracle database files, including the data files, control files, redo logs, and `init.ora` files.

physical structure The database structure used to store the actual data and operation of the database. Data files, control files, and redo log files constitute the physical structure of the database.

ping A TCP/IP utility that is used to check basic network connectivity between two computers.

PMON See *process monitor process (PMON)*.

port A listening location used by TCP/IP. Ports are used to name the ends of logical connections, which carry conversations between two computers in a TCP/IP network.

process A daemon, or background program, that performs certain tasks.

process failure The abnormal termination of an Oracle process.

process monitor process (PMON) Performs recovery of failed user processes. This is a mandatory process and is started by default when the database is started. It frees up all the resources held by the failed processes.

Program Global Area (PGA) An area of memory in which information about each client session is maintained. This information includes bind variables, cursor information, and the client's sort area.

proxy-based firewall A firewall that prevents information from outside the firewall from flowing directly into the corporate network. The firewall acts as a gatekeeper, inspecting packets and sending only the appropriate information through to the corporate network.

R

RAID See *Redundant Array of Inexpensive Disks (RAID).*

read-only tablespace A tablespace that allows only read activity, such as SELECT statements, and is available only for querying. The data is static and doesn't change. No write activity (for example, INSERT, UPDATE, and DELETE statements) is allowed. Read-only tablespaces need to be backed up only once.

read-write tablespace A tablespace that allows both read and write activity, including SELECT, INSERT, UPDATE, and DELETE statements. This is the default tablespace mode.

RECOVER DATABASE This RMAN command is used to determine the necessary archived logs to be applied to the database during the recovery process.

recovery The process that consists of starting the database and making it consistent using a complete or partial backup copy of some of the physical structures of the database.

recovery catalog Information stored in a database used by the RMAN utility to back up and restore databases.

Recovery Manager (RMAN) See *Oracle Recovery Manager (RMAN).*

redirect connection A connection that requires the Oracle listener to send information back to a client about the location of the appropriate port to which to connect.

redo buffers See *log buffers.*

redo log buffer The area in the SGA that records all changes to the database. The changes are known as redo log entries, or change vectors, and are used to reapply the changes to the database in case of a failure.

redo log entry See *redo record.*

redo log file See *redo logs*.

redo logs The redo log buffers from the SGA are periodically copied to the redo logs. Redo logs are critical to database recovery. They record all changes to the database, whether the transactions are committed or rolled back. Redo logs are classified as online redo logs or offline redo logs (also called archived logs), which are simply copies of online redo logs. There are also current redo logs that are being actively written to, and non-current redo logs that are not actively being written to.

redo record A group of change vectors. Redo entries record data that you can use to reconstruct all changes made to the database, including the rollback segments.

Redundant Array of Inexpensive Disks (RAID) The storage of data on multiple disks for fault tolerance, and to protect against individual disk crashes. If one disk fails, then that disk can be rebuilt from the other disks. RAID has many variations to redundantly store the data on separate disks, the most popular of which are termed RAID 0 through 5.

refuse packet A packet sent via TCP/IP that acknowledges the refusal of some network request.

registering The process of using the `REGISTER` command, which is required so that RMAN can store information about the target database in the recovery catalog.

Report commands These RMAN commands provide queries of the catalog that are more detailed than lists and that tell you what may need to be done.

request queue A location in the SGA in an Oracle Shared Server environment in which the dispatcher process places client requests. The shared server processes then process these requests.

`RESETLOGS` The process that resets the redo log files' sequence number.

resetting Updating the recovery catalog for a target database that has been opened with the `ALTER DATABASE OPEN RESETLOGS` command.

response queue The location in the SGA in an Oracle Shared Server environment where a shared server places a completed client request. The dispatcher process then picks up the completed request and sends it back to the client.

restore To copy backup files to disk from the backup location.

RESTORE DATABASE The RMAN command that is responsible for retrieving the database backup and converting it from the RMAN format back to the OS-specific file format on disk.

resynchronization The process of updating the recovery catalog with either physical or logical information (or both) about the target database.

reusable section The information stored within the target database's control file that is used to backup and recover the target database.

RMAN See *Oracle Recovery Manager (RMAN)*.

RMAN-based backup Performed by the Oracle Recover Manager utility, which is part of the Oracle software.

RMAN repository The information necessary for RMAN to function in the recovery catalog, or the control files if the recovery catalog is not used, is called the *RMAN repository*.

RMAN scripts Scripts that use RMAN commands that can be stored on the filesystem or within the recovery catalog.

roll back To undo a transaction from the database.

roll forward and roll backward process Applying all the transactions, committed or not committed, to the database and then undoing all uncommitted transactions.

row chaining Storing a row in multiple blocks because the entire row cannot fit in one block. Usually this happens when the table has LONG or LOB columns. Oracle recommends using CLOB instead of LONG because the LONG data type is being phased out.

row migration Moving a row from one block to another during update operation because there is not enough free space available to accommodate the updated row.

S

SAN See *System Area Network (SAN)*.

SCN See *system change number (SCN)*.

serial direct-load insert The direct-load insert operation that uses one server process to insert data beyond the high-water mark. This is the default for direct-load insert.

server process A background process that takes requests from the user process and applies them to the Oracle database.

session A job or a task that Oracle manages. When you log in to the database by using SQL*Plus or any tool, you start a session.

`SET UNTIL [TIME/CHANGE/CANCEL]` The clause in RMAN that is necessary to perform an incomplete recovery by causing the recovery process to terminate on a timestamp or SCN, or to be manually cancelled.

SGA See *System Global Area*.

Shared Global Area See *System Global Area*.

shared server processes Processes in an Oracle Shared Server configuration that are responsible for actually executing the client requests.

single point of failure A point of failure that can bring down the whole database.

single-tier architecture A network architecture in which a client is directly connected to a server via some type of hard wire link, such as a serial line.

SMON See *system monitor process (SMON)*.

`spfile<ORACLE_SID>.ora` The server parameter file that stores persistent parameters that are required for instance startup and those that are modified when the database is started.

SQL*Loader A utility used to load data into Oracle tables from text files.

statement failure Syntactic errors in the construction of a SQL statement.

static service registration The inputting of service name information directly into the `listener.ora` file via Oracle Net Manager.

structure Either a physical or logical object that is part of the database, such as a file or a database object.

System Area Network (SAN) Two or more computers that communicate over a short distance via a high-speed connection. An example would be a configuration of web servers with high-speed connections to database servers.

system change number (SCN) A unique number generated at the time of a `COMMIT`, acting as an internal counter to the Oracle database, and used for recovery and read consistency.

System Global Area (SGA) A memory area in the Oracle instance that is shared by all users.

system monitor process (SMON) Performs instance recovery at database startup by using the online redo log files. SMON is also responsible for cleaning up temporary segments in the tablespaces that are no longer used and for coalescing the contiguous free space in the tablespaces.

T

tablespace A logical storage structure at the highest level. A tablespace can have many segments that may be used for data, index, sorting (temporary), or rollback information. The data files are directly related to tablespaces. A segment can belong to only one tablespace.

tablespace point-in-time recovery (TSPITR) A type of recovery whereby logical and physical backups are combined to recover a tablespace to a different point in time from the rest of the database.

TAG This command is used to assign a meaningful logical name to backups or image copies.

target database The database that will be backed up.

third mirror A method of performing a copy of a mirrored disk at the hardware level.

time-based recovery A type of incomplete recovery that is stopped by a point in time designated when the recovery is initiated.

TNS_ADMIN An environmental variable in Unix and a Registry setting in Windows NT that defines the directory path of the Oracle Net files.

tnsnames.ora The name of the physical file that is used to resolve an Oracle Net Service name when you are using the localnaming resolution method.

tnsping An Oracle-supplied utility used to test basic connectivity from an Oracle client to an Oracle listener.

tracing Process that records all events that occur on a network, even when an error does not happen. This facility can be enabled at the client, the middle-tier, or the server location.

transaction Any change, addition, or deletion of data.

transportable tablespace A feature that was introduced in Oracle8*i* whereby a tablespace belonging to one database can be copied to another database.

TSPITR See *tablespace point-in-time recovery (TSPITR).*

Two-Task Common (TTC) layer A layer in the Oracle Net stack that is responsible for negotiating any datatype or character set differences between the client and the server.

two-tier architecture A network architecture that is characterized by a client computer and a back-end server that communicate using some type of network protocol, such as TCP/IP.

U

UNAVAILABLE The RMAN command used to make a backup set unavailable or not accessible in the RMAN repository.

unregistering Removes the information necessary to back up the database. This task is not performed in the RMAN utility; instead, it is performed by executing a stored procedure as the recovery catalog's schema owner.

UNTIL CANCEL The clause in the RECOVER command that designates cancel-based recovery.

UNTIL CHANGE The clause in the RECOVER command that designates change-based recovery.

UNTIL TIME The clause in the RECOVER command that designates time-based recovery.

user error An unintentional, harmful action on a database—such as deletion of data or dropping of tables—by a user.

User Global Area (UGA) An area in the System Global Area (SGA) used to keep track of session-specific information in an Oracle Shared Server environment.

user-managed backup A backup that consists of any custom backup; such a backup is usually performed in an OS script such as a Unix shell script or the DOS-based batch script.

V

virtual circuit The shared memory segment utilized by the dispatcher to manage communications between the client and the Oracle server. The shared server processes use the virtual circuits to send and receive information to the appropriate dispatcher process.

Virtual Interface (VI) protocol A lightweight network communication protocol that places the messaging burden on high-speed network hardware and removes it from the sending and receiving computer hardware.

W

whole database backup A backup that gets the complete physical image of an Oracle database, such as the data files, control files, redo logs, and `init.ora` files.

Index

Note to the Reader: Throughout this index **boldfaced** page numbers indicate primary discussions of a topic. *Italicized* page numbers indicate illustrations.

A

B

C

D

E

F

G

H

M

N

O

P

R

S

T

U

V

W

TELL US WHAT YOU THINK!

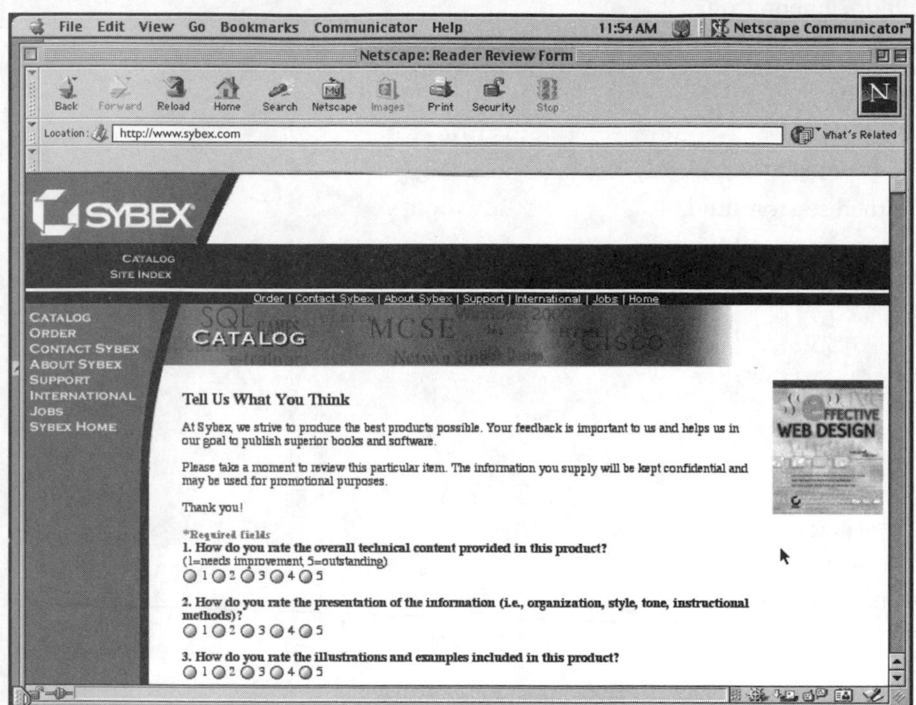

Your feedback is critical to our efforts to provide you with the best books and software on the market. Tell us what you think about the products you've purchased. It's simple:

1. Visit the Sybex website
2. Go to the product page
3. Click on **Submit a Review**
4. Fill out the questionnaire and comments
5. Click **Submit**

With your feedback, we can continue to publish the highest quality computer books and software products that today's busy IT professionals deserve.

www.sybex.com

SYBEX Inc. • 1151 Marina Village Parkway, Alameda, CA 94501 • 510-523-8233

SYBEX®